THE ECONOMIC DEVELOPMENT OF *Kenya*

Report of a Mission Organized by the
International Bank for Reconstruction and Development
at the Request of
the Governments of Kenya
and the United Kingdom

THE ECONOMIC DEVELOPMENT

OF KENYA

PUBLISHED FOR

The International Bank for Reconstruction and Development
BY The Johns Hopkins Press, Baltimore

THE MISSION

Edmond H. Leavey,   Chief of Mission

C. H. Thompson,   Chief Economist
C. Arnold Anderson,   Adviser on Education
Michael Jordan,   Economist
Marc E. A. Langevin,   Adviser on Transport and Communications
Paul A. Morawetz,   Adviser on Industry
Theodore Morgan,   Adviser on Fiscal Matters
E. Paul Orcutt,   Adviser on Livestock
Sir Herbert Stewart,   Adviser on Agricultural Production
Thomas H. Strong,   Agricultural Economist

This is the report of an economic survey mission to Kenya which was organized by the International Bank for Reconstruction and Development at the request of the Governments of Kenya and the United Kingdom. The task of the mission, as prescribed by its terms of reference, was to undertake a general review of the economic potential of Kenya and to make recommendations designed to assist the Government in development planning for the period to 1967, and in formulating policies which would further expand and stimulate the economy and so raise the standard of living of the people.

The mission consisted of ten members representing four nationalities, and included in its membership two representatives of the permanent staff of the Bank. The mission assembled in Washington in September 1961, was in Kenya from mid-September to mid-December of that year, and commenced the preparation of its report at the headquarters of the Bank in Washington at the beginning of 1962. In August 1962 the Mission Chief and Chief Economist returned to Kenya for further consultations.

During the preparation of the report, the mission was requested informally to submit its views on problems concerning Kenya's recurrent budget and did so in March of 1962. At the same time, a member of the mission visited London for discussion concerning the results of the Kenya Constitutional Conference held there during the early months of the year.

This report, as is evident from the dates quoted, was prepared at a time of important political changes accompanying Kenya's move toward independence. These changes were still continuing as this report was being written. The Constitutional Conference, held in London in February–April 1962, produced the framework of a new constitution for Kenya but much still depended on how the framework would be filled and on the subsequent decisions reached on material points.

Future relationships between the three principal East African countries, now joined in a Common Services Organization and customs union arrangement, were also yet to be decided. Throughout this report we have endeavored to refrain from making any recommendations which, if adopted, would impede the governments of the East African countries from making such changes in their political relationships as they might consider desirable.

The mission wishes to acknowledge with sincere appreciation the complete cooperation it received from the Governments of Kenya and the United Kingdom, and from the East Africa High Commission (now the East Africa Common Services Organization). A special word of appreciation is, however, due the Minister of Finance, Mr. K. W. S. Mac-Kenzie and later Mr. J. S. Gichuru, for the assistance rendered by that Ministry in coordinating the mission's activities in Kenya. Representatives of the various statutory Boards and Commissions, and officials of all the local governmental organizations visited by members of the mission, were likewise most helpful. The mission also acknowledges with grateful thanks the generous assistance given it by a large number of persons in Kenya engaged in all segments of private business, professional occupations and civic activities.

In transmitting the report to the Governments of Kenya and of the United Kingdom, the President of the Bank noted that, since the Executive Directors and the management customarily do not review the recommendations of missions in detail, the report as transmitted represented the views of the mission rather than positive recommendations of the Bank. The letter of transmittal added, however, that the Bank believed that the findings of the report deserved the most careful consideration and discussion. Similarly, while other international agencies were given an opportunity to comment on the portions of the report of particular interest to them, responsibility for the recommendations of the report is to be regarded as that of the mission alone.

CONTENTS

The Mission v
Preface vii

THE REPORT

1. THE PROBLEMS OF TRANSITION 1

2. THE COUNTRY AND ECONOMY 4

    Principal Geographic Features 4
    Political History 7
    Administration 11
    The Structure and Growth of the Economy 15
    External Economic Relations 23
    East African Relationships 29

  Problems of Economic Development 33

3. PROGRAM FOR ECONOMIC DEVELOPMENT .... 41 ✓

    Measures to Promote Economic Growth
      During the Next Few Years 41
    Development Planning in Kenya 45
    Resources and Priorities 47
    Suggested Development Program 1963/64–1966/67 51
    Financing the Program 55
    East African Common Services Organization 59
    Concluding Remarks 61

4. AGRICULTURE 63

  Pattern of Agriculture 63
    The Role of Agriculture in Kenya's Economy 63
    Land Use 64
    Land Tenure 65
    Availability of Land 67

  Development of Farming 69
    The Nonscheduled Areas 70
    Development of the High-Potential Land 72
    Land Consolidation and Enclosure 73
    Farm Development 73

Development of Lands of Medium and
Low Potential 75
Land Settlement 76
Irrigation 77
The Tana River Catchment 78
Kenya Nile Basin 80

The Scheduled Areas 81
Land Settlement 82
African Settlement in the Scheduled Areas 83

Government Assistance to Farming 86
Agricultural Extension 87
Agricultural Education 89

Crop and Livestock Improvement 92
A Policy for Mineral Fertilizer 92
Crop Research 95
Livestock Performance 97
Other Animals 102

Production and Marketing Policies 104
East African Relations 106
Work on Economic Matters in the Ministry 107
Organization 108

Prospects for Individual Commodities 116
Coffee 116
Tea 121
Sisal 123
Pyrethrum 125
Dairying 126
The Meat Industry 128
The Wool Industry 129
Sugar 130
Maize 132
The Other Grains 134
Cotton 137
Oil Crops 138
Wattle 139
Horticultural Crops 139

Forests and Fisheries 140
Forests 140
Fisheries 141

Summary of Proposed Expenditures 142

5. MINING AND MANUFACTURING 146

Mining 146
Oil Exploration 147
Other Minerals 149

Manufacturing 150

   The Structure of Industry 151

   Factors Affecting the Growth of Manufacturing 153

   Principal Manufacturing Industries 154
      The Food Industry 154
      Beverages and Tobacco 155
      Textiles 156
      Shoes 157
      Sawmilling, Woodwork and Matches 157
      Paper, Printing and Packaging 157
      Soap and Chemicals 158
      Clay, Cement and Concrete Products 158
      Metal Products, Machinery and Engineering 158

   Government Policy 159
      Customs and Excise Tariff 159
      Industrial Licensing 164
      Industrial Research 166
      Industrial Land 166
      Financial Assistance for Industrial
        Development 167

   Concluding Remarks 168

6. TOURISM AND WILDLIFE 170

   Tourism 170
   Wildlife 172
   Public Expenditures on Tourism and Wildlife 174

7. BASIC SERVICES 176

   Power 176

   Transport and Communications 179

   Roads 181
      Capital Programs 182
      Maintenance 185
      Staffing and Training 187

   East African Railways and Harbors 188
      General 188
      Railways 189
      Harbors and Shipping 193

   Civil Aviation 196
      Civil Airlines 197
      Airports 198
      Operational Control of Civil Aviation 200
      Meteorological Services 201

   East African Posts and Telecommunications 203
      Services Provided 203

Finance and Development 204
Personnel and Training 206

Radio and Television 206

Concluding Remarks 208

8. SOCIAL SERVICES AND MANPOWER 210

Manpower 210
Localization 212
Unemployment 215
Wages and Industrial Relations 217

Education 221

Primary Education 224
The Grant System for Primary Education 225
Primary Expansion Policy 226
The Primary Teacher Supply 228
Teacher Support and Curriculum in
    Primary Schools 229

Post-Primary Education 230
Secondary Education 230
The Secondary Teacher Situation 233
Science-Technical Streams 233
Trade Schools and Vocational Training 234
Post-Primary Bursaries and Fees 235

Higher Education 236

Summary of Proposed Expenditures 237

Health 238
Present Health Conditions 238
Medical and Health Services 240
Preventive Health Services 243
Staff 244
Finance 247

Housing 251

9. MONEY AND BANKING 257

The Currency System 257
The Role of Commercial Banks 261
Agricultural Credit 264
Post Office Savings Bank 268
Other Financial Institutions 269
Concluding Remarks 271

10. PUBLIC FINANCE 273

East African Common Services Organization 273
Kenya Government 274

The Burden of Total Taxes by Income Levels 278

The Budgetary Problem 279

Measures to Meet the Budgetary Problem 283
    Direct Taxes on Individuals 285
    Taxes on Company Profits 288
    Depreciation Allowances 289
    Tax Relief for Pioneer Industries 289
    Customs and Excise Duties 290
    Other Taxes 291
    Concluding Remarks 293

Local Government 294
    Income and Expenditure of Local Authorities 294
    Financial Assistance from the Kenya Government 296
    Financial Relationships Between Central
        and Local Governments 297

SUMMARY OF MAIN CONCLUSIONS AND
RECOMMENDATIONS BY SECTORS 301

    Basic Agricultural Policy 301
    Water for Agriculture 302
    Policies for Agricultural Production
        and Marketing 302
    Organization for Agricultural Development 304
    Agricultural Staff 305
    Research in Agriculture 305
    Animal Husbandry 305
    Mining and Manufacturing 306
    Tourism and Wildlife 307
    Power 307
    Roads 307
    Railways and Harbors 307
    Posts and Telecommunications 308
    Manpower 308
    Education 309
    Health 309
    Housing 310
    Money and Banking 310
    Public Finance 311

ANNEXES

A. PLANNING ARRANGEMENTS 315
B. AGRICULTURAL CENSUS TAKING 318
C. AGRICULTURAL BOARDS AND COMMITTEES, KENYA 321
D. THE NAIROBI-MOMBASA ROAD 331
E. THE CAPACITY OF THE MOMBASA-NAIROBI-NAKURU
   RAILWAY LINES 334

STATISTICAL APPENDIX

S.1   Civil Population Estimates 339
S.2   Migration 339
S.3   Total Reported Employment 340
S.4   Reported Unemployment 341
S.5   Gross Domestic Product by Industrial Origin 341
S.6   Gross Domestic Product by Industrial Origin 342
S.7   Composition of Gross Domestic Product by Type
        of Factor Income 342
S.8   Gross Capital Formation 343
S.9   Land Areas as at December 31, 1961 344
S.10 Production of Major Crops for Sale 345
S.11 Estimated Acreages of Principal Crops in the
        Nonscheduled Areas, 1960/61 345
S.12 Prices to Producers for Selected Agricultural
        Products 346
S.13 Prices to Producers for Agricultural Products 346
S.14 Mineral and Industrial Production—Numbers
        of Establishments 347
S.15 Mineral and Industrial Production—Numbers
        Employed 348
S.16 Mineral and Industrial Gross Production 349
S.17 Electricity Generation and Distribution 350
S.18 Posts and Telecommunications Operating Statistics 351
S.19 Motor Vehicles—Licensed and Newly Registered 351
S.20 Public Health—Number of Beds and Patients 352
S.21 Nairobi City Water Sales 352
S.22 Currency in Circulation—Coins and Total Currency 353
S.23 Liquidity of Commercial Banks 353
S.24 Post Office Savings Bank 354
S.25 Kenya Government Public Debt 354
S.26 Kenya Government Revenue 355
S.27 Kenya Government Expenditures 356
S.28 Total Reported Annual Wage Bill 357
S.29 Statutory Minimum Wages 358
S.30 Cost of Living and Consumer's Price Indices 359
S.31 External and Interterritorial Trade 360
S.32 Domestic Exports—Main Commodities by Value 361
S.33 Quantity of Domestic Exports 362
S.34 Classification by Stage of Production and Use of
        Retained Imports 363
S.35 Imports by Country of Origin 364
S.36 Destination of Domestic Exports by Country 365
S.37 Kenya's Exports to Tanganyika and Uganda 366
S.38 Kenya's Imports from Tanganyika and Uganda 367
S.39 External Trade Indices 368
S.40 Reported Completion of New Private
        Buildings—Main Towns 368

LIST OF MAPS

Kenya General .... facing page xvi
Main Cash Crops and Forests .... "   "   62
Mean Annual Rainfall .... "   "   63
National Parks and Game Reserves .... "   " 174
Transport .... "   " 178

NOTE: The maps contained in this report are for illustrative purposes only and do not imply any legal endorsement on the part of the mission or the International Bank.

LIST OF CHARTS

1. Composition of Gross Domestic Product by Sectors 17
2. Exports to Countries Outside East Africa 24
3. Value of Major Agricultural Products Marketed 115
4. Wages and Prices 220
5. Educational Pyramids of Primary and Secondary
   School Pupils, 1962 222

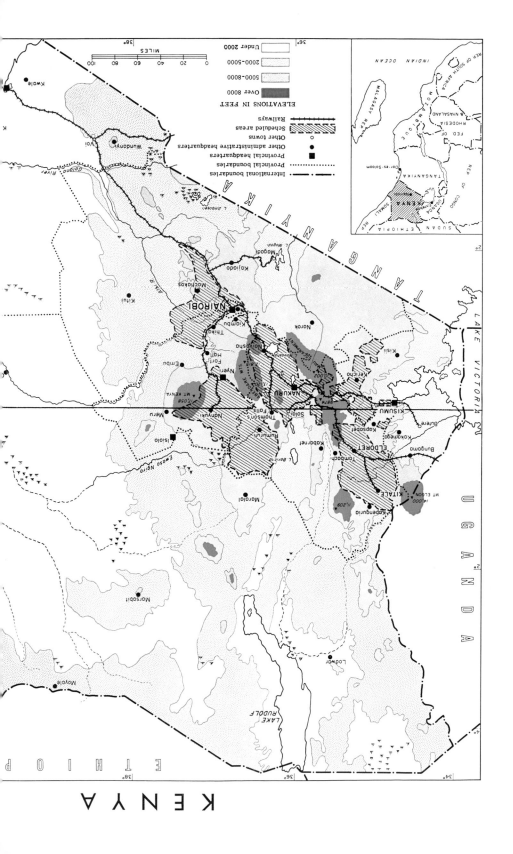

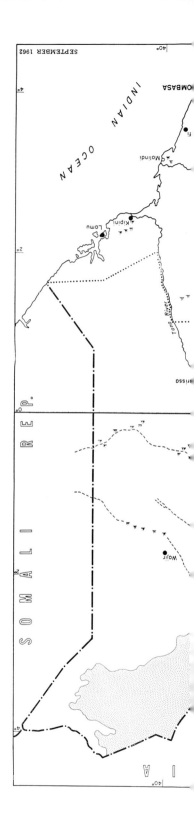

THE REPORT

CHAPTER 1 *THE PROBLEMS OF TRANSITION*

The coming of independence to Kenya will place the responsibility for the country's future squarely upon the shoulders of the people of Kenya themselves. Independence will make more urgent the need for economic development, which itself provides the opportunities to attain many of the political and social objectives which will be sought. Although there is certainly a great potential for development, immediate economic prospects are clouded by the uncertainty and difficulty associated with rapid political change.

The move from a unitary to a regional system of government will have an impact on the economy still difficult to assess. The division of functions between the central and the regional authorities has not yet been fully defined, nor has the division of revenues. Furthermore, internal self-government, and subsequently independence, will entail far-reaching consequences in the field of public administration. While progress has already been made in recruiting public officials locally, the supply of individuals with adequate training and experience is still limited. Kenya therefore presently depends heavily on the services of expatriate civil servants who constitute most of the senior administrative and professional staff available. Much of the economic development of the country during the years of transition will depend on having their services or the services of others like them.

Outside the public sector, non-African residents of Kenya—Asian and European—have so far had a preponderant role in building up the money economy, by supplying both the necessary skills and capital. European farms still provide about three-quarters of Kenya's exports. Africans in increasing numbers are acquiring advanced skills and entering the money economy—and indeed a speeding-up of this process should figure largely in future public policy. But Kenya remains a low-income country, and economic growth will depend for some time to come on funds from abroad to supplement local savings much of which, in any event, is made by Asian and European residents. If Kenya's resources are used wisely, thus providing hope of soundly based advance, there is every likelihood that external assistance—both in the form of finance and of expertise—will continue to be forthcoming.

1

Economic growth is not automatic and, if the living standards of the people are to be raised, Kenya must adopt a program for development in the public sector to give emphasis to activities with the highest potential returns, and measures to stimulate and encourage expansion of production in the private sector. But such measures will come to nought unless steps are first taken to restore confidence, to remove as soon as possible the present uncertainties as to political and social conditions, and so arrest the declining trend in investment.

In developing suitable programs and policies for economic development, it should be recognized that Kenya's is essentially an agricultural economy and that it is through development in this sphere that further advances in other sectors of the economy will be made possible. Thus, while there is already some scope for manufacturing, and there will undoubtedly be more as incomes throughout East Africa rise, Kenya will need to give most attention to its agricultural sector and its related services in the next few years.

Efforts should first be directed toward replacing subsistence farming with modern methods of production and developing those farms already producing for the market. The transformation of African agriculture that has already been achieved since the introduction of the Swynnerton Plan in the mid–1950's has been remarkable. The pattern for development has been established. The task of the next few years will be to continue the progress which has already been made. Changing factors will, however, create a need to reconsider the crop pattern. The world market outlook for some of Kenya's agricultural exports is not favorable, but there should be opportunities for others.

To promote growth, human resources will need to be well utilized. This means assuring a place in the economy to Kenyans of Asian and European origin, as well as developing the potential of the Kenyans of African origin. Heavy stress must be placed on education and training for participation in a modernizing economy. One of the factors that affords high hopes for the long-term outlook for economic and social advance is the enthusiasm of the African people for education. There is no doubt that they wish to participate in the development ahead and the object of public policy should be to make this possible.

Fundamentally, much of Kenya is well endowed by nature for the expansion of agricultural production, and much has been done toward that end. With sound economic policies, the prospects for revival and continuation of growth are favorable. But economic progress will depend very much on the uses to which Kenya's limited available resources, both human and financial, are applied. Unlike some countries, Kenya will become independent in a situation of financial difficulty and without possessing any appreciable reserves. The next few years will, therefore, call for restraint in spending and serious concentration of funds and selected manpower on those projects and activities needed to form the foundation for future economic progress.

CHAPTER **2** *THE COUNTRY*
AND ECONOMY

Principal Geographic Features

Kenya lies at the edge of the old, stable land mass of southern Africa. There, the vast expanses of gently undulating plateau lands—so characteristic of the African landscape—are abruptly interrupted. The spectacular fracture of the Rift Valley runs the entire length of the country, housing a string of lakes from Rudolf in the north to Magadi in the south. Extinct volcanoes—the 17,000-foot peak of Mount Kenya, astride the equator yet permanently capped by snow—tower over the countryside before the land falls away to the Indian Ocean and the deserts of the Horn of Africa. Such a location has endowed Kenya with a wide range of physical characteristics, affording a remarkable variety of natural vegetation and changing limitations on land use within a comparatively small area. Its area of 225,000 square miles, extending four degrees each side of the equator, is comparable to that of France. A narrow, mainly fertile belt, tropical in vegetation, borders the 250 miles of Kenya's coast line along the Indian Ocean. More than half the country is an arid lowland, gradually passing from the poor scrub land of the coastal hinterland to the barren desert of the remoter areas of the Northern Province toward the frontiers of the Somali Republic to the northeast, Ethiopia to the north, and the Sudan to the northwest. As the land rises inland, the vegetation and the prospects for cultivation improve, and the climate moderates to subtropical and temperate. In the middle altitudes, the rising grasslands provide a home for game and herds of domestic cattle. The plateau and upland areas lying between 5,000 and 9,000 feet, which cover roughly the southwestern quarter of Kenya, comprise some of the best land for settlement and agriculture in Africa. Eventually, the land drops away to the basin of Lake Victoria, housing the rich lands of Nyanza on the lake's northeastern shore.

Lying in equatorial latitudes, Kenya experiences differences in climatic conditions caused mainly by variations in altitude. Seasonal changes in temperature are only slight, but while the mean temperature at the coast is over 80 degrees, at 9,000 feet it is about 55 degrees. Altitude has an even more dramatic effect on rainfall, which varies from over 100 inches a year around Mount Kenya to less than 10 inches in the north toward the northern frontiers. Over the greater part of the coun-

4

try the rain falls in distinct seasons, although different climatic regimes are active. The wet season at the coast occurs between April and July—over half of Mombasa's 40-inch precipitation falls in these four months. Although the rain fails to penetrate far into the low-lying hinterland, the moisture-laden winds also bring rain to the central upland areas during March to May, where a second rainy season extends from October to December. Annual rainfall there is usually in the range of 45–75 inches. West of the Rift Valley the climate is characterized by a marked wet season from March to September, the volume of rainfall diminishing toward the north to less than 20 inches in Turkana. In the region bordering on Lake Victoria rainfall is spread more evenly through the year. Kisumu on the shore of the lake receives a mean total of roughly 40 inches.

The droughts and floods of 1960 and 1961 have been awesome witnesses to the effects of the variations in amount and lack of reliability of rainfall on the economy of Kenya. Clearly the influence of this factor is felt most keenly by agriculture. The area capable of intensive cropping or grazing without irrigation is limited to a narrow strip of land along the coast and to the higher elevations, which have a good probability of receiving 35 inches or more rain. The greater part of the land area of Kenya, therefore, can support only extensive grazing. The potentiality for increasing the cultivated area by irrigation is also limited by the availability of water. There are few perennial rivers in Kenya. Only two reach the ocean throughout the year—the Tana and the Galana; others succeed in reaching it, or Lake Rudolf, for a few months but then dry up, submerge or turn into swamps. The rivers of Nyanza form part of a different drainage system flowing into Lake Victoria and eventually to the Nile.

The peoples of Kenya, apart from the recent immigrants, belong to four of the linguistically defined racial groups of Africa; though even these are not always easy to isolate, nor confined to distinct geographic regions. The Bantu are most numerous, comprising almost two-thirds of the people of Kenya, and—though speaking many dialects—are mutually intelligible. They include the Kikuyu and kindred tribes of the plateau, the Baluhya and Kisii in Nyanza, and a number of coastal tribes, some of which have intermarried with Arabs. The traditional economy of these tribes is based on a system of shifting crop cultivation which, particularly in the highland areas, often attained a high subsistence level, although they also keep cattle. The second group is more homogeneous: the Nilotic Juluo of the Lake Victoria shore, comprising many tribal units that are bound together by very close kinship affiliations. The Nilo-Hamitic group is more difficult to define. These peoples are spread throughout the country: the Masai in the south, the Nandi and Kipsigis in the highlands above Lake Victoria, and the Turkana in the northwest. All traditionally pastoral, they have no common language and differ in their adaptability to sedentary agriculture. The remaining group is composed of the nomadic Hamitic tribes of the Northern Province, distinctive from the other African peoples of Kenya in being Caucasian in origin and Muslim in religion. Swahili is a common, second language among many of the peoples of Kenya. Communication among different tribes, however, is often difficult. Illiteracy is high especially among older people, and the use of the many vernaculars is still common.

Foreign traders had held a footing along the coast of Kenya for many centuries, but the immigrant communities approached their present size only when permanent settlements were established there after the country had opened up at the end of the nineteenth century. The largest of these communities consists of about 175,000 "Asian" peoples who are, however, heterogeneous in origin and religion. They are mainly engaged in commerce in the larger towns and trading places of Kenya, though many others are employed in the civil service and as artisans. There are also about 70,000 people of European origin in Kenya. Initially, this community was composed of administrators and farmers, but more recently, and particularly with the growth of the larger towns, an appreciable proportion is occupied in private commerce and industry. About 35,000 Arabs live in Kenya, almost all landowners and traders along the coast.

In such sharply contrasting natural conditions, Kenya's population is concentrated in the more favored areas—along the coast, around Lake Victoria, and in the plateau lands. The first census of population in Kenya was taken in 1948. It is believed, though this is conjecture, that the African population has had a rate of natural increase of 2.25 percent a year since then and that there were about 7.3 million people in Kenya in 1961.[1] Less than 5 percent of these lived in the expanses of the Northern Province, which cover more than half the land area of the country, but over 60 percent were settled in the Nairobi-Nyeri region of Central Province and in Nyanza, comprising about one-eighth of the total area. In some districts there are more than 1,000 people to the square mile, forming what are among the most densely peopled parts of Africa. But the capacity of the land to yield a livelihood does not always match such a pattern of distribution. Not only in the most thickly populated areas

[1] Another census was taken in 1962, but until the results of this are known there is no direct information on the rate of natural increase of the population. There are no reliable estimates of fertility or mortality. The present estimates are a revised extrapolation of the 1948 figures, based on the findings of more recent counts in Tanganyika and Uganda.

of Nyanza, but in other regions as well, the reluctance of people to leave the security of their established homes to settle in new areas, and the division of land on a tribal reserve system have prevented people moving from areas where production under present techniques is reaching its limit to others which could support them better. This situation lends urgency to the problems of developing agriculture both by means of raising the productivity of existing landholdings, and by settling farmers on underdeveloped land.

Kenya remains a predominantly rural country. There are few large towns; probably less than ten have over 10,000 inhabitants. The most important are Nairobi, the seat of Government with a population of about 300,000, Mombasa, the port (population 190,000), and Nakuru and Kisumu, provincial and communications centers. These permanent settlements were established by the newly arrived immigrants. Africans have been attracted to the towns by the prospect of an increased money income to meet the new wants of a cash economy, which a small, fragmented landholding in one of the more overcrowded African land units could not provide. The towns undoubtedly have other attractions also; the prospect of amenities and an atmosphere of sophistication for those educated to an extent that they feel superior to agricultural work and society, and a release from traditional communal restraints. African urban society faces many social problems; the population is largely transitory, men far outnumber women, and the standards of living are often poor. Yet a class of permanently settled African town dwellers is undoubtedly growing up, including those employed in the civil service and industry. It has been estimated that 50 percent of the African male population of Nairobi have been resident there for more than three years.

The basic unit of traditional society in Kenya was the homestead. Although a few homesteads might be clustered together, perhaps at a market place, the pattern of settlement was dispersed. In recent years larger villages have grown up in the countryside. This trend has occurred chiefly as a result of the security measures taken during the Mau Mau emergency and under the impact of the consolidation of landholdings, both requiring the concentration of a scattered population, and it has advanced furthest in the Central Province. These villages have created a new social environment in the rural areas, introducing problems of living in aggregated units, which are likely to be significant in the future economic development of Kenya.

Political History

The traditional political systems of the indigenous peoples of Kenya differed so much as to make it difficult to generalize about them, but they had the common characteristic of being based on a loose affiliation of extended family units in tribal groups. Obligations and activities were tightly binding and were derived from territorial units, from kinship groups or from age classes, depending on the tribe. Authority was usually exercised through councils of elders rather than through individual chiefs. Occasionally a strong leader might exert himself and exercise an extraordinary personal power, but this seldom survived him.

Though in general these indigenous societies remained isolated from the outside world, other civilizations had discovered the coast and established limited colonial authority there. There is a history of foreign contacts stretching back to the ancient Greeks. Following Vasco da Gama's landing at Malindi in 1498 on his way to India, the Portuguese succeeded in establishing control over the coastline and its trade. They were expelled by the Omani Arabs at the beginning of the eighteenth century, but subsequent conflicts among local rulers were only resolved when the Sultan of Zanzibar enforced his authority over the littoral and claimed a loose sovereignty over the interior, which had by then been penetrated in the search for ivory and slaves. In the course of the nineteenth century, European influence was extended and concessions obtained beyond the coastal area from native chiefs by various private interests—missionaries, explorers and commercial enterprises. These disconnected activities were quickly brought within the framework of national "spheres of interest" during the last years of the century. As competition among rival European nations in East Africa intensified, the Governments of the United Kingdom, Germany and Italy reached a series of agreements to delimit the area of their claims to influence. Britain's sphere was defined by the Umba and Juba Rivers and so extended over the area of what is now Kenya. The Imperial British East Africa Company, which had been operating in the area, found it impossible to continue operations and the British Government took over the Company's rights and obligations and declared a Protectorate in 1895.

British interests in Kenya at this time had grown primarily as a result of the access it provided for missionaries and traders to Uganda, but were stimulated by the construction of the railway from Mombasa to Lake Victoria, begun in 1896. As this project went forward, the potentialities of the upland regions of Kenya for farming came to be appreciated and the British Government adopted a policy of encouraging settlement by Europeans. The lines of a land policy were laid down in a series of measures beginning with the Crown Land Ordinance of 1902 which established the conditions under which land might be alienated, and reserved an area of the "highlands" for European settlers and prescribed specific other areas as tribal reserves. The construction of the railway had required foreign skilled laborers, most of whom came from India, many remaining in Kenya after this work had been finished. In 1905, authority over the Protectorate was transferred from the British Foreign Office to the Colonial Office, and in the following year an Order-in-Council outlined the form of government for Kenya, on the basis of which were appointed a Governor, an Executive Council and a Legislative Council, the latter containing representatives of the European settlers.

After World War I, during which the conflict between the belligerents was introduced directly into East Africa, several significant developments took place. A new wave of settlers and immigrant enterprises established themselves in Kenya. The Devonshire White Paper of 1923 provided for the representation of the interests of all of the major ethnic groups in the Legislative Council, and so formed a basis from which subsequent re-alignment of membership might take place. It also enunciated the principle that African interests were primary in Kenya, although largely as an expression of how the responsibility of the Colonial Government's trusteeship should be exercised. Africans were already being brought into participation in local government through the formation of native councils, headmen being responsible for a number of local functions. Steps were taken that were to lead to a common East African trading area and to a joint institutional approach to providing a range of economic and other services. Barriers to trade between Kenya and Uganda were removed, and their customs organizations combined in 1917. A uniform external tariff with Tanganyika was adopted in 1922. Subsequently the Governor's Conference, an embryo form of East African organization, began to meet and to coordinate various economic functions among the territories, which were later formalized in the East Africa High Commission.

The progress in Kenya's constitutional arrangements since World War II has culminated in the rapid advances made in recent years. This progress has been manifested in the changing composition of the Legislative Council, which has been adjusted to allow a more uniform basis for representation of the different ethnic communities, and membership by election rather than by nomination. As a result of modifications to the constitution in 1960 a majority of nonofficial African members took their places in the Legislative Council, only a minority of seats being reserved for the other communities. In addition, a system of responsible government has been extended by making the Council of Ministers the principal instrument of the executive and by gradually changing the balance of its composition from official to nonofficial members.

Political change toward what had become by 1950 the acknowledged objective of self-government, and an African majority in the organs of government, has not been achieved without serious conflicts. The Mau Mau rebellion which broke out in Central Province in 1952 led to the declaration of an Emergency in Kenya lasting until 1960. The first African members elected directly to the Legislative Council in 1957 refused to accept ministerial responsibility until the racial limitations on the exercise of political responsibility were removed. However, successive constitutional developments have now brought Kenya to the threshold of independence.

A number of political issues, which have very important economic consequences, remain unresolved. The political atmosphere as well as specific decisions will influence the general setting within which the potentialities for economic growth and higher standards of living may be realized. This atmosphere will largely determine the existence of incentives to invest, the capacity to tax and to execute development policies, and the readiness of experienced technicians and administrators to remain and assist the task of growth. But more specific, urgent questions exist. The prospect for increasing productivity in the agricultural sector of Kenya depends crucially on sound land policy. Security of tenure, whether for African or non-African, careful concern for an economic size of farm units, and the provision of adequate supervision of settlement programs are essential if a pattern of land use to promote satisfactory expansion of output, upon which development in other sectors so much depends, is to be achieved.

A conference to discuss the future constitution of Kenya was held at Lancaster House in London from February 14 to April 6, 1962. A framework for a new constitution was agreed upon, providing for a central government responsible for a wide range of activities together with regional authorities drawing their powers from the constitution.[2] From the economic standpoint, it is important that relationships between the branches of government should produce an adequate balance between the needs to coordinate development policies at the center and to elicit the valuable contribution which active local participation can make to the mobilization of resources for growth.

The diversity of the peoples of Kenya within boundaries arbitrarily determined by the arrangements of colonial administrations poses difficulties in creating a unified, independent Kenya. The Somalis in the north, removed both in distance and antecedents from the populous centers of Kenya, related rather to other tribes across the long common desert frontier in Somalia, have already presented a demand to secede

[2] *Report of the Kenya Constitutional Conference, 1962,* London HMSO, Cmd. 1700.

from the country. The peoples of the coast are not so distinct and separate a group, but also claim a special autonomy based on an historical allegiance to the Sultan of Zanzibar, and constitutional status as a Protectorate of the British Government. A commissioner appointed by the Sultan and Secretary of State in 1961 to consider the problem of the Coastal Strip recommended that it should be integrated administratively with Kenya before independence.[3]

The future political significance of the present geographic unit of Kenya may also be changed by some federation of independent East African states, which it is hoped would resolve many of the internal conflicts. Kenya is at present associated with Tanganyika and Uganda in a currency board, a customs union and in the joint institutions of the Common Services Organization, and all Kenya's political leaders are believed to approve at least of the general principle of a political federation of the area.

Administration

Following the pattern in British Colonial areas at an advanced stage preparatory to self-government, constitutional authority for the Government of Kenya is still vested in a Governor, who acts on behalf of the Colonial Office of the United Kingdom Government. In practice, however, policy is formulated and executed by the Council of Ministers, whose advice the Governor must seek on a wide range of subjects. The Ministers are responsible to the Governor who appoints them, but also to the Legislative Council for their particular departmental functions.

Outside the center, the machinery of government consists of the characteristic system of British Colonial provincial administration, together with an individual development of local authorities. The Commissioners of the six provinces (and the officer of the Nairobi Extra-Provincial District), and of the 39 districts are responsible for executing government policy, maintaining law and order and supervising African local government and courts in their areas. They coordinate the activities of a parallel hierarchy of specialized officials—such as agriculture, education, health—who also act as representatives of the central government within their technical fields, and play an important role in implementing policy. At lower levels of the administration a variety of minor tribal authorities, chiefs and headmen act as agents in the smaller local units of government, normally known as locations.

Traditional tribal organization in Kenya was not generally highly

[3] *The Kenya Coastal Strip,* Report of the Commissioner, December 1961, London, HMSO, Cmd. 1585.

centralized and so did not provide a structure that might be readily adapted to assume the rights and obligations of responsible local authorities. New councils were appointed to take on local government functions, which have since developed into the system of 33 African District Councils (ADC). The ADC's have wide powers to operate, particularly in the fields of education and public health. With the help of extensive government grants, and the guidance of selected government officials, the Councils have enlarged the scope of their operations to a point where the larger among them operate annual budgets of half a million pounds. They may raise revenue by levying poll taxes and may borrow. Some functions have been delegated in turn to the Location Councils. As their role has extended, the ADC's have been transformed into more representative and responsible institutions. District Commissioners, who in the past supervised their activities, sitting as Chairmen, have been handing over their authority to the Councils and to local Chairmen.

The presence of the immigrant settler communities in Kenya, and particularly their concentration in the areas originally reserved for them, has resulted in the development of separate local government institutions there. The organization is headed by seven County Councils and below them 26 Urban and Rural District Councils. These Councils have more flexible powers of taxation than the ADC's—though they depend mainly on central government grants supplemented by a land tax for the bulk of their revenue—and are empowered to provide a variety of public and welfare services.

Perhaps most rapid progress in local government in Kenya has been made in the urban areas. Towns grew up quickly along the railway as the line was built and the country opened up. Nairobi was founded as a railway works center in 1899, and was first to establish itself independent of government control. It became a self-accounting authority in the 1920's, relying to a considerable extent on its own resources. On this model a sequence of increasing local autonomy for towns as they developed was set up. The City Council of Nairobi, the Municipal Councils, Municipal Boards, and a variety of smaller townships and trading centers, possess different degrees of responsibility for their own affairs, and of representation for their populations. Many of the circumstances on which the separate evolution of local government bodies was based have now been altered. We understand that legislation is being prepared to unify the institutional structure of local government, bringing together the ADC's and County Councils into a common system.

The civil service has been open to all races since 1955, but the higher ranks are still largely filled by expatriate officials of the British Overseas

Civil Service, and there is a disproportionate number of Europeans and Asians in the administration as a whole. In 1960, more than 90 percent of the officers in the administrative and professional grades of the Kenya Civil Service were Europeans. The total composition of the Service was 10 percent European, 8 percent Asian and Arab, and 82 percent African. As independence approaches, a policy of "localization" has been introduced to develop as rapidly as efficient standards permit a local civil service which reflects more closely the composition of the country. But there are not enough Africans with sufficient educational qualifications and experience to replace the colonial civil servants immediately. It will take a number of years to achieve this objective and during the transitional period a decline in the efficiency of the civil service is to be expected, and expatriate personnel will be needed if government services are to be maintained at acceptable standards. However, the changing conditions of service which are reflected in the policy of "localization," and the uncertainties of political development have bred a sense of insecurity among expatriate officials as well as among other immigrants that may cause them to leave Kenya rather than stay. This problem is recognized, and an attempt has been made to overcome it by a plan under the United Kingdom Overseas Aid Scheme to compensate expatriate officials whose position and livelihood are threatened by constitutional developments. It is intended that the arrangements should provide conditions of service that will encourage officials to stay as long as they are required, while assisting those who retire. The system is also to be financed partly by the United Kingdom so as to relieve the independent government of the additional costs that are incurred by employing expatriate officials.

The scope of governmental activities was greatly enlarged after World War II. This is illustrated by the growth of central government expenditures which trebled in money terms between 1946 and 1953, even before the Emergency added substantially to the costs of the usual functions of law enforcement and security. Social services have been provided on an increasing scale. The schools and medical facilities which had been pioneered by the religious missions have been supplemented and brought under the general supervision of the Government. Primary education has become virtually universal for European and Asian children, and now nearly three-fourths of all Africans enter schools—more than nine-tenths of the boys and about half the girls. This proportion is larger than in most countries at a comparable stage of development. Although the rate of attrition among students is high, at the same time, the educational system has extended to higher levels—the University of East Africa having constituent colleges in Kampala and Dar es Salaam as well as Nairobi, and covering education in both liberal subjects and technical fields. The provision of medical services has proceeded with the expansion of a medical department responsible for state hospital facilities, for epidemiology and research. A decentralized system of health centers has been instituted to provide a widespread coverage for both curative medicine and preventive hygiene throughout the local areas. To meet the social and welfare problems accompanying the process of urbanization, the Government has promoted the building of houses for lower income groups, by making loans to local authorities and assisting them in carrying out projects.

Government services have been expanded in the economic as well as the social field. Before World War II, the official approach to problems of development was essentially piecemeal, and limited almost entirely to the agricultural sector. Agricultural schools for Africans were opened, for instance, and veterinary services were developed. Toward the end of the war period an approach to development planning was made on the initiative of the Colonial Office, which was seeking to integrate local resources and the need for finance from Britain in the dependent territories. This approach was, and has remained, primarily directed toward budgeting for public sector expenditures on projects and services designed to assist development. Financial planning was set down in a series of programs, initially for a ten-year postwar period, but later covering the three-year periods 1954–57, 1957–60, and 1960–63. Machinery was established for formulating development policy and keeping the programs under review. At first, a separate planning organization was set up, but as a system of ministerial responsibilities evolved, policy-making authority was transferred to a Development Committee, under the Council of Ministers, and executive power was concentrated in the Treasury.

The most spectacular of the Government's planning efforts have been directed toward transforming the economy of the land in African areas through the Swynnerton Plan.[4] Primary emphasis in the 1946–55 Ten-Year Program had been placed upon expanding production rapidly, particularly in the agricultural field, but the Swynnerton Plan embodied and extended role for the Government in planning.[5] It sought, by consolidating and enclosing landholdings and establishing individual title to land, by providing capital and supervisory services, and by en-

---

[4] *A Plan to Intensify the Development of African Agriculture in Kenya*, compiled by R. J. M. Swynnerton, Colony and Protectorate of Kenya, Nairobi, 1954. At that time, as we mention above, land in Kenya was administered under ordinances recognizing various African and non-African settlement areas. Since then racial restrictions to landholding have been abolished, although a distinction between the "scheduled" and "nonscheduled" areas still remains in legislation.

[5] *The Development Program 1954–57*, Sessional Paper No. 51 of 1955, Nairobi, p. 4.

couraging the extended production of cash crops and improved livestock, to enable farmers to derive an appreciable money income beyond
the needs of subsistence. These objectives led to some significant new
planning procedures. The Plan both encouraged and depended upon
the cooperative effort of farmers in adopting new patterns of land tenure, in the planning of their farms, and in undertaking intensive methods of farming. It set targets for farm incomes. And in pursuit of these
targets it sought to coordinate assistance to each stage of farm development: the preparatory work in education and farm layout, the provision
of water and credit for production, facilities for marketing output and
to safeguard the long-term needs of soil conservation. The program concentrated on raising the productivity of existing farms in those areas
where the pressure of people on the land limited potentialities for a
higher level of agriculture, but farmers were also to be resettled in underdeveloped parts of the country. A more thorough appraisal of the
Swynnerton Plan, and of its objectives in relation to the future development of agriculture in Kenya will be given in Chapter 4.

The administration of a number of services, operated jointly by the
East African countries, is carried out through separate, interterritorial
institutions. These services occupy a significant position in the economy
of Kenya and will be dealt with in a subsequent section of this chapter.

The Structure and Growth of the Economy

The subsistence economies of the indigenous tribal communities of
Kenya were concerned with the constant pressing problems of survival,
rather than with the prospects for growth. Tribes followed varied patterns of agriculture, but apparently both cultivators and pastoralists
lived close to starvation and under the threat of attack and disease. Fam-
ines were frequent, and contributed to what observers at the turn of the
century believed to be a decline of the African population.[6] In traditional society, customary practices of land tenure, rights of usage and
inheritance laws led to fragmented, scattered holdings. The menfolk fulfilled the functions of protection and hospitality, while most of the cultivation of land was done by women using simple techniques. Under
these conditions the yields of production were uncertain and the capacity for improvements and diversification limited. The horizons of consumer wants were correspondingly narrow, and could generally be satisfied through the network of mutual kinship obligations.

[6] J. E. Goldthorpe, "The African Population of East Africa: A Summary of its Past
and Present Trends," Appendix VII, *East Africa Royal Commission 1953–55 Report,*
London, HMSO, Cmd. 9475, pp. 462, 473.

After British administration was set up, and immigrant communities arrived in Kenya, this static, indigenous economy began to be transformed. New wants were evoked, new capacities developed as a cash economy was introduced and the first steps toward economic development taken. The use of money and the exchange of goods were extended among the indigenous population by the Government's levying of taxes, by the trader's display of new products, and by the expanded market for surplus production of food crops provided by the improved communications system. The establishment of law and order curtailed tribal warfare, and the development of medical services limited endemic diseases (smallpox, sleeping sickness and malaria) so that the population grew, and more men were available for peaceful tasks.

Meanwhile, European and Asian enterprise developed rapidly—though not all were successful—and to some extent independently of the slower process of modernization of the African sector. A new range of crops for export—tea, coffee, sisal—was produced, and trading and service industries expanded primarily in response to the demands of the immigrant peoples. These activities, however, provided a further indirect stimulus to the indigenous economy. The plantations and farms of the settlers offered employment for African labor, supplementing subsistence incomes. African farmers were introduced to cash crops, to improved methods of farming, and provided with a greater range of implements. The growth of the economy before World War II was still hesitant and experimental. There were many failures among settlers as they established a modern farming industry in Kenyan conditions. Indigenous farmers did not always respond to opportunities for growing for the market, nor to efforts to change customary systems of land tenure and land usage.

The economy of Kenya now has a dual character, in which the two patterns of production exist side by side. The bulk of the population are still peasants devoting a considerable part of their resources to growing staple food crops for the immediate subsistence needs. But the modern monetary sector, based on specialized production of goods for cash, is estimated to contribute more than three-quarters of the value of total production. Indeed, the two sectors are no longer altogether distinct. African farmers are expanding their production of goods for the market rapidly. They received £6 million from the sale of their crops and livestock products in 1956, and by 1960 had expanded this income to £10 million. Other Africans have left the land and entered completely into the money economy as wage and salary earners or as entrepreneurs. Nevertheless, it is true that there is still a wide gap between the economy of the small holding and that of the plantation, the factory and the office.

CHART I

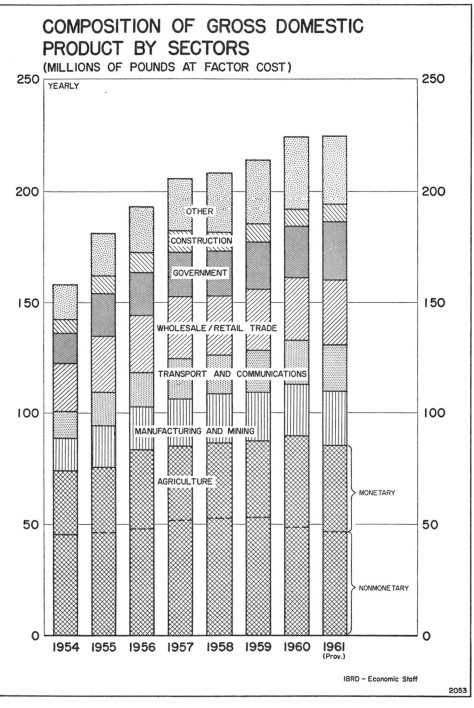

COMPOSITION OF GROSS DOMESTIC
PRODUCT BY SECTORS
(MILLIONS OF POUNDS AT FACTOR COST)

YEARLY

OTHER

CONSTRUCTION

GOVERNMENT

WHOLESALE / RETAIL TRADE

TRANSPORT AND COMMUNICATIONS

MANUFACTURING AND MINING

AGRICULTURE

MONETARY

NONMONETARY

1954   1955   1956   1957   1958   1959   1960   1961
(Prov.)

IBRD – Economic Staff

2053

The greater part of the value of marketed agricultural output is derived from non-African farms and plantations, £36 million of a total of £46 million in 1961. The process of economic growth—the attainment of a high rate of capital formation, of increased productivity and higher levels of income—is going to require a more extensive transformation of the attitudes and practices of the traditional sector.

The existence of such a dual economy complicates description of the stage of economic development reached by Kenya. The per capita gross domestic product was estimated at about £30 in 1961. But the disproportionate role of the immigrant communities in total production indicates that few Africans reach such an average level, and makes the comparison of incomes with other African territories where the population is more homogeneous rather artificial. There does not appear to be much endemic poverty in Kenya, but the famine of 1960/61—resulting from exceptional climatic conditions—demonstrates how close to subsistence many Africans live, not only pastoralists like the Masai, but also cultivators like the Kamba.

The composition of production, however, illustrates the structure of the economy. Probably more than 85 percent of the African population and about 35 percent of the Europeans are engaged on the land, so that the economy is highly dependent on the primary sector. The contribution from this sector has amounted to £85–90 million per annum in the last few years, or about 40 percent of Gross Domestic Product (GDP). Agriculture and livestock provide over 85 percent of export earnings. Cash crops for export form by far the most valuable part of marketed production of agriculture. Coffee, tea, sisal and pyrethrum have played a continuously important role as export crops. The coffee is a mild arabica type, which requires exacting physical conditions of cultivation such as exist in the middle altitudes in the highlands. Tea grows at higher levels and is generally of a medium quality standard. Sisal is found in the drier, semi-intensive farming areas. Rearing of livestock is the main pursuit in the areas of low rainfall which cover most of the country. Since World War II, agricultural plans have placed emphasis on the development of mixed farming in the high potential areas and on modern ranching based on improved breeds, with the result that livestock has made an increasingly significant contribution to farm incomes and export earning. Kenyan agriculture also produces a significant volume of other crops, especially grains, among them maize and rice, wheat and barley, mainly for consumption within East Africa.

Economic activity in Kenya is quite widely diversified for a country with an average product per head of only about £30. The share of the primary sector in GDP is often taken as a measure of underdevelopment, but in this respect Kenya compares favorably with Tanganyika and Uganda, where the share is about 60 percent. Wholesale and retail trade, manufacturing, and transport and communications[7] each contribute roughly 10 percent of Kenya's total production. The importance of the distributive trades reflects partly the volume of external and interterritorial commerce, which is discussed in a later section of this chapter. The development of manufacturing industry has been based largely on the processing of agricultural raw materials; the gross value of these products amounting to £33 million in 1957, or 58 percent of the total of all manufacturing. Industrial concerns are predominantly smallscale, nearly 60 percent of them employing less than 20 people. Nevertheless, a broadening of the industrial structure has taken place to a significantly further degree than elsewhere in East Africa.

Kenya is well provided with basic economic services. The railway has been the backbone of freight transportation since the time of its construction, keeping pace with an increase of traffic of more than 25 percent during the 1950's. It is operated by the East African Railways and Harbours Administration as a joint East African venture. In addition to the main line, extending 1,081 miles from the coast to Kampala in Uganda and beyond, several branch lines reach other important areas of the country such as Kisumu, the main port on Lake Victoria; and Nanyuki through the rich farming area of Central Province. In 1962 only 925 miles of the road network were bituminized, but there are good gravel roads and programs to improve trunk and feeder road communications are being undertaken. Mombasa, with its fine deep water harbor, is the chief port of East Africa and handles almost all overseas traffic of Kenya and Uganda, and part of that from northern Tanganyika. International airlines serve Nairobi. An increasing demand for electric power has been fulfilled by the expansion of local generation and through bulk supplies from the Owen Falls hydroelectric station in Uganda.

The focal position which Nairobi has come to occupy in the economy not only of Kenya, but of East Africa as a whole, has contributed to the changing character of activity in the country. It is the largest city in the region, and many commercial and financial and industrial enterprises have been attracted there by virtue of its geographic location, particularly its direct communications link with the coast, and partly by virtue

[7] Kenya's production of these services is somewhat understated in the statistics; for national accounting purposes, an arbitrary allocation of the operating surpluses of the East African services is made between Kenya, Tanganyika and Uganda, one-third to each.

of the early establishment of ancillary services. The East African Common Services Organization, the commercial banks and other private businesses now have their headquarters in Nairobi.

Tourism has become a significant industry in Kenya, and adds to the diversity of economic activity. The country's wildlife, its climate and range of scenery have attracted foreigners since its discovery, and these natural assets have been enhanced by the development of modern hotels and ancillary services.

Since World War II, it appears that Kenya has enjoyed a period of considerable economic expansion despite the effects of the Mau Mau Emergency and the changing prospects for its main export commodities in world markets. A variety of statistical indicators has become available from which a more complete picture of economic activity can be built up. A discontinued series of national accounts suggests that the value of production in money terms in Kenya grew from £53 million to £127 million, or at a rate of over 13 percent a year, between 1947 and 1954. Part of this increase—perhaps more than 4 percent a year—was attributable to inflation.[8] The figures probably understate the importance of the relatively slow-growing subsistence sector and therefore exaggerate to some extent the growth of total production. However, other measures indicate the real development which took place both in agriculture and in the expansion of secondary industry. There were large increases in the volume of output from European farms and plantations. Wheat production rose from 73,000 tons in 1946 to 133,000 tons in 1954, milk from 5.5 million gallons to 12.8 million gallons. The growth of industry is indicated by the use of cement and electricity: consumption of cement in Kenya increased from 22,000 tons in 1946 to 137,000 tons in 1954; sales of electricity rose over the same period from 34 million kwh to 162 million kwh.

For more recent years, an improved series of domestic income statistics has been compiled. Output increased from £158 million to £224 million between 1954 and 1960 in terms of current prices or by about 6 percent a year (see Statistical Appendix, Table 5). A number of attempts have been made to calculate the rate at which real production expanded over this period by correcting the statistics for the effect of price changes.[9] These adjustments for the extent of inflation are based on rather bold assumptions of the applicability of the limited price indices available

[8] Cf. Sessional Paper No. 51 of 1955, p. 40.

[9] W. T. Newlyn, " 'Take-Off' Considered in an African Setting," *Yorkshire Bulletin of Economic and Social Research*, May 1961. C. P. Haddon-Cave, "Real Growth of the East African Territories, 1954–60," *East African Economics Review*, June 1961.

(such as the Nairobi Cost-of-Living Index), and they should be taken as only an indication of the order of magnitude of the rate at which production in constant prices expanded. The results suggest that the real growth of the monetary economy (excluding subsistence) attained an average annual rate of about 6 percent up to 1958, and of the total economy between 4 percent and 5 percent from 1954–60. However, since the terms of trade shifted against Kenya by 15–20 percent during the 1950's, particularly after 1954 when the prices of some exports—coffee, sisal—began to fall markedly, real income grew somewhat slower than output (see Statistical Appendix, Table 39). If population increased in this period by 2 percent a year, which now appears to be a conservative assumption, per capita product rose by over 2 percent a year.

Growth in total production in the money economy since 1954 has been derived from an expansion of all major sectors at roughly similar rates. As prices in the industrial and services sectors probably rose more than those in agriculture, the increase in real output by primary producers was proportionately greater than in secondary and tertiary industries. There was a growth in production of a range of agricultural commodities—coffee and tea being among the most striking. This was derived from both African and non-African farms: African farming was stimulated by an expansion of official programs for development, non-African farming by a new wave of European settlement. The country still has advantages in exporting increasing quantities of agricultural products while the restricted East African market for industrial goods limits the scope of cost-reducing investments in manufacturing and other secondary sectors.

Kenya, in common with the other East African countries, has achieved a quite considerable level of investment for a country with such a low per capita income during the period of substantial growth. Total expenditure on fixed assets was estimated to have reached over £45 million in 1956 and 1957, or about 25 percent of GDP, and although this fell to about £41 million in 1960 it was still equivalent to roughly 18 percent of GDP. Investment undoubtedly plays a major strategic role in economic development, but this ratio is suspect as an indicator of the processes of growth. The presence of the immigrant communities in Kenya reduces the significance of the concept of an average per capita income, and of judging performance by this standard. The subsistence sector satisfies the need of a large part of the population for food, so that consumption imposes less of a claim on total monetary income than in an economy where more of these requirements have to be met through marketed produce. Even so, the calculations of investment exclude African agriculture, and thus the contribution that indigenous farmers make to the country's store of assets by farm improvements or house building is not taken into consideration.

The composition of capital formation in the monetary sector is nevertheless instructive. Investment by the public sector—largely in construction—has averaged about £15.5 million a year since 1954. It has varied from year to year between about one-half to one-third of total investment. Private investment in agriculture, buildings and transport has accounted for a further 40 percent of all capital formation.[10] Only a small part of capital expenditure has gone into manufacturing industry (i.e., industrial machinery), and this fact helps to explain the limited progress of industrialization in the economy as a whole. Expansion of secondary industry has been concentrated in final stage manufacturing, processing or in consumer goods production and, while the scale of operation may have reflected accurately the size of the potential market, it did not provide those external economies that might have eased the costs of further industrial investments.

In the last few years the pace of development has been interrupted, as Kenya has entered the period of uncertainty that forms the background to the mission's study. Kenya's economic expansion in earlier years had not been free from interruptions and in 1958, under the impact of a shortage of capital and a decline in export prices, the GDP rose by less than 1 percent over the previous year even in terms of current prices. Production increased by about 3 percent in 1959 and 5 percent in 1960, based largely on the expansion of agricultural exports, but this did not amount to a recovery to previous rates of growth and was partly attributable to rising prices.

Even this modest achievement was not maintained in 1961. Constitutional decisions in 1960, which established that power would be transferred progressively to the local African people, led to an attitude of uncertainty about the future among the immigrant communities concerning political developments which has seriously affected economic prospects. Perhaps the most ominous for future development is a decline in investment activity, which, if not offset, must sooner or later make itself felt on output. Total investment expenditures have not materially increased over the level in the 1958 slump year, and are well below that of 1956. In a number of fields capital formation has declined, as is strik-

[10] The data include expenditure on private motor cars on the grounds that most cars in Kenya are used in part for business purposes, which also inflates the rate of investment in comparison with other countries which frequently classify cars as consumer durable goods. Cf. *Capital Formation in Kenya 1954–60*, East African Statistical Department, July 1961.

ingly illustrated by the value of agricultural machinery imports and plans for construction. The capital formation fell by nearly £7 million to £34.4 million in 1961 despite increased outlays on public works projects and other government capital goods. The slowing down of economic growth has brought a fall of 32,500, or more than 5 percent, in the number of persons employed between 1960 and 1961, which has aggravated the problem of utilizing the country's human resources more fully, and added to the difficulties of social adjustment to a modern economy.

Funds that might have been invested in Kenya have been leaving the country. The withdrawal of almost 20 percent of the deposits of the commercial banks led them to restrict their credit policies in 1960; and there are no immediate prospects that these restrictions will be removed. The outflow of capital has been accompanied by a net emigration of non-Africans, whose skills have contributed so much to Kenya's development. Immigration of Asians as well as Europeans is now being more than offset by departures.[11] The experience of other territories as they approached independence suggests that many expatriate officials will leave Kenya when offered compensated terms of retirement. Hence an outflow of civil servants will add to the exodus from the private sector. The mission therefore addresses itself to the problems of development in Kenya under difficult immediate conditions, which must inevitably seriously limit the scope and content of its recommendations.

External Economic Relations

External trade plays a significant role in the economy of Kenya as it does in the economies of many other underdeveloped countries. The value of goods traded with other countries (including Tanganyika and Uganda) amounted to £132 million in 1961. Exports totaled £56 million, or the equivalent of about 25 percent of GDP. The ratio of trade to total production has not varied greatly since 1954. Imports were valued at £69 million in 1961, or about 31 percent of total expenditures. The magnitude of the movements of goods in and out of Kenya reflects the dependence of the economy on foreign sources of supply for many types of capital and consumer goods, and the productive advantages the country possesses in several important, internationally traded commodities. At present levels of income, the domestic market is insufficient to absorb a rapid, material expansion of production, or to support a substantial diversification of the industrial structure of the economy, and

---

[11] Migration statistics are likely to understate emigration in that they do not account for temporary emigrants who become permanent emigrants.

CHART 2

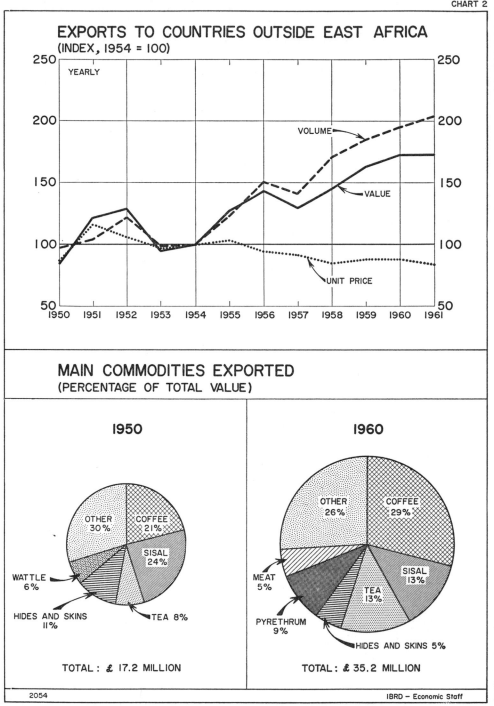

EXPORTS TO COUNTRIES OUTSIDE EAST AFRICA
(INDEX, 1954 = 100)

YEARLY

VOLUME

VALUE

UNIT PRICE

MAIN COMMODITIES EXPORTED
(PERCENTAGE OF TOTAL VALUE)

1950

OTHER 30%
COFFEE 21%
SISAL 24%
WATTLE 6%
HIDES AND SKINS 11%
TEA 8%

TOTAL : £ 17.2 MILLION

1960

OTHER 26%
COFFEE 29%
SISAL 13%
MEAT 5%
TEA 13%
PYRETHRUM 9%
HIDES AND SKINS 5%

TOTAL : £ 35.2 MILLION

2054

IBRD – Economic Staff

growth has been achieved largely through improvements in the agricultural sector and the sale of its output abroad.

Although the significance and basic pattern of Kenya's external trade have not changed in recent years, divergent trends have appeared. It is convenient to separate Kenya's trade with the rest of East Africa, which has developed within a common economic framework, from its trade with the rest of the world. The value of Kenya's imports and exports are summarized in Statistical Appendix, Table 31.

Imports of goods from outside East Africa into Kenya increased very rapidly between 1950 and 1955—from £34 million to £72 million—but after that they fluctuated in value at a level somewhat below the peak. The composition of imports did not drastically alter over the period from 1950 to 1961, although quite sharp changes were registered from year to year. Kenya imports large quantities of producers' goods—industrial, transportation and agricultural machinery and materials and the proportion of these in total imports has changed little since 1950 (see Statistical Appendix, Table 34).[12] The scale of production needed to manufacture these lines has remained beyond the scope of the domestic economy. Consumer goods—private motor cars, appliances, clothing and textiles—average about 25 percent of the total. Since prices Kenya paid for imports increased only slightly during the 1950's, changes in their total value reflect largely the volume of goods imported.[13]

Exports grew steadily over the decade and by 1960 had doubled their value of 1950. They rose from £17 million to £35 million or at an average rate of more than 7 percent a year. The variety of conditions for cultivation in Kenya is reflected in the considerable range of agricultural products it exports and has reduced the vulnerability of the country's export earnings to sudden changes in the market for any particular commodity. Increases in the value of exports have been spread over several commodities. This range of agricultural exports also has compensated partly for the paucity of known mineral resources in Kenya. With the exception of a period from the later 1930's to the late 1940's, when a gold deposit in Nyanza Province was being exploited, minerals have contributed less than 10 percent of all exports.

Coffee remains Kenya's predominant commodity export, earning £10.6 million or about 30 percent to total exports in 1961. Although Kenyan coffee sells at a premium even in depressed world markets, ex-

[12] The statistics overstate the imports of capital goods into Kenya, as imports of these goods by the East African Services are attributed entirely to Kenya, although financed by all three countries.

[13] The Kenya import unit value index for 1960 was 110 (1954 = 100). Average values rose by 8 percent between 1950–54 according to the old 1950–based index of EAQESB.

ports have fallen from their peak value of £13.7 million attained in 1956, when they amounted to 47 percent of aggregate export earnings. Physical output has surpassed the crop of that year, but prices have fallen by almost 30 percent. Sisal exports provided £4.2 million, or about a further 12 percent of the total in 1961. This represents a recovery of earnings from this commodity to the level of the early 1950's, now that output has increased sufficiently (i.e., by 60 percent over 1950) to offset substantially lower prices. Exports of several other cash crops have increased in value, notably tea and pyrethrum, which together accounted for £7.1 million or 20 percent of export earnings in 1961. There has been a sharp rise in exports of meat and meat preparations in recent years. A variety of minor products—cotton, hides and skins, wattle bark and extract and sodium carbonate—have fluctuated in value, although only cotton among these has maintained its share of total export earnings.

Despite unfavorable price movements in the latter half of the decade, the value of Kenya's exports rose because of increases in the physical volume of output for the world market, which doubled between 1954 and 1961 (see Statistical Appendix, Table 33). The export price index in 1961 was at about the same level as 1950 (84 on the revised 1954-based index). This price experience compares well with that of Tanganyika and Uganda, whose export prices over the period fell: for the former from 97 to 86, the latter from 82 to 64 (1954 = 100). In the changing conditions for Kenya's imports and exports, the terms of trade—the measure of the volume of exports required to finance a given volume of imports—have deteriorated by 15–20 percent between 1950 and 1961. While this movement limits the extent to which increases in production for export are transferred into rising levels of income, by virtue particularly of the composition of its trade, Kenya has until now fared well by comparison with other developing countries.

This pattern of commodity trade has been accompanied by some marked shifts in markets for exports and sources of imports (see Statistical Appendix, Tables 35 and 36). The fall in the proportion of trade between Kenya and British Commonwealth countries, particularly the United Kingdom, has been the most striking development, although these countries remain Kenya's major trading partners. Commonwealth preferential tariff rates apply to a number of the agricultural products exported by Kenya, for example coffee and tea, but generally these are not large.[14] The East African tariff provides no preferential treatment,

[14] The U.K. tariff on coffee is the equivalent of 13 percent for Commonwealth countries vis-a-vis 20 percent for other GATT members, and on tea zero vis-a-vis 6 percent.

being bound by the terms of the Congo Basin Treaty. In 1950, sterling area countries took 55 percent of Kenya's exports; in 1961 only 41 percent. Most of this decline is accounted for by trade with the United Kingdom, whose share was reduced from 35 percent of all exports to 24 percent. The importance of Commonwealth countries as suppliers of imports has also diminished. The analysis of import statistics by country of origin has changed. Since 1956, statistics have measured direct imports (i.e., goods imported from outside East Africa, for consumption and warehousing in Kenya, including those subsequently transferred to Tanganyika and Uganda) rather than the total net of transfers to the other East African countries, as they had done in earlier years. The proportion of total imports supplied by Commonwealth countries has declined since the early 1950's, from 77 percent in 1956 to 55 percent in 1961.[15] As with exports this change reflects primarily the position of United Kingdom trade with Kenya. Imports from the United Kingdom fell from 58 percent to 36 percent over the same years.

Conversely, trade in other directions increased in importance. This was particularly true of trade with the countries of the European Economic Community (EEC), with other underdeveloped countries, and with Japan. The EEC countries provided an expanding market for Kenyan exports in the early 1950's, increasing their share of the total from less than 20 percent in 1950 to 30 percent in 1955, after which the figure has fluctuated. The most significant element of this trade is the role of West Germany as the leading customer for Kenya's coffee. This country took 10 percent of Kenya's exports in 1950; 17 percent in 1961. More than four-fifths of its purchases were of coffee. The EEC area in general, and West Germany in particular, also grew in relative importance as suppliers to Kenya, from less than 10 percent and about 1 percent respectively in 1950 to 15 percent and 5 percent in 1961. Trade with Japan grew steadily over the decade as restrictions on it were relaxed; this country accounted for only about 1 percent of both exports and imports in 1950, but took 4 percent of exports and supplied 10 percent of imports, predominantly textiles, by 1961. Imports of petroleum have increased the share of Iran in imports from negligible in the early 1950's to 7 percent in 1961. Trade with dollar countries has shown no consistent change in importance over the decade, involving an average 15 percent of exports and 5 percent of imports.

Trade with Tanganyika and Uganda within the East African customs union area has become of increasing importance for Kenya. During the 1950's East African trade has grown rapidly both in value and in rela-

[15] Excluding parcel post, which is not allocated by country of origin in the trade statistics since 1952.

tion to total trade. In 1950, Kenya exported £3.6 million and imported £3.4 million locally produced goods; by 1961 exports had reached £15.9 million and imports £7.0 million or, taken together, the equivalent of about one-fifth of all Kenya's trade.[16] The development of the East African market for a significant range of locally produced goods has acted as a stimulus toward the diversification of production within the three countries of the customs union. Trade among them is carried on in a variety of processed agricultural goods and light manufactures, in which production has reached a degree of territorial specialization. The major commodities exported by Kenya to Tanganyika and Uganda in 1961 were cigarettes (£1.7 million), clothing (£0.9 million), cement (£0.7 million), and flour (£0.7 million). Sugar (£1.6 million), cotton seed oil (£0.8 million), cotton textiles (£0.8 million) and tobacco (£0.6 million) were the main items imported. The pattern of trading relationships within East Africa has offered the possibility for both a more rapid and a more diversified expansion of production than a complete reliance on the international markets for primary commodities.

Kenya's growing volume of trade with Tanganyika and Uganda is also significant in that an increasing surplus has helped to meet the considerable deficit it has persistently incurred from international trade. In 1961 Kenya had an adverse balance of trade of £27 million with countries outside East Africa and in recent years the size of this annual deficit has ranged between £23 million and £44 million. The extent of these deficits is somewhat misrepresented in the trade accounts, which include imports by the common services organizations—as for example the inclusion of Comet aircraft for the East African Airways Corporation in Kenya figures for 1961. This qualification, however, hardly alters the general picture. Kenya has partially offset the deficits on external trade by selling more to the other countries of East Africa than it has purchased from them. In 1961, Kenya had a surplus of £9.0 million from East African trade, with the result that the balance of all visible trade showed payments exceeding earnings by £18 million.

The difficulties of measuring economic transactions within East Africa have prevented comprehensive balance of payments accounts for the individual countries from being drawn up. Transactions among the countries are not controlled, are conducted in a common currency and often take place within enterprises that operate branches throughout East Africa. An outline picture in recent years may still be suggested. The

---

[16] The aggregates for the two years are not strictly comparable as before 1958 goods traded were valued inclusive of excise duties, or customs duties on imported raw materials used in locally manufactured goods. This discrepancy, however, tends to understate the growth in the value of trade over the period.

deficit on account of visible trade against Kenya is financed from earnings on current invisibles, from capital imports and by movements of sterling balances. The position of Nairobi as the main commercial center of East Africa and other factors give rise to invisible earnings of considerable importance for Kenya. Since East Africa as a whole has made substantial net payments abroad on account of invisibles, however, it seems likely that significant capital movements have been required to meet the remaining deficit which was probably of the same order of magnitude as the over-all imbalance on visible trade. As a result of shrinking confidence in the prospects for investment in Kenya, the form of these transactions has changed in the last few years, but the inflow of funds both from Tanganyika and Uganda, and from outside East Africa, appears to have played a considerable role in Kenya's external economic relations. The residual balancing item which covers any final excess of payments over receipts is the drawing down of the foreign-held assets of the commercial banks, and these have declined sharply in recent years. Looking to the future, Kenya may find difficulty in financing. a deficit on its current balance of payments of recent magnitudes without the inflow of private capital as in the past. The improvement of the country's trading position to anticipate this danger, both by expanding export earnings and by import saving, may become a matter of urgency for economic policy.

East African Relationships

Kenya, Tanganyika and Uganda have for many years cooperated in a range of economic activities. Cooperation developed while each of them was under British administration, and the territories became associated in a pattern of interterritorial relationships. The administrative arrangements have been modified to meet changing conditions. In 1948 the East African High Commission was established as a separate governmental institution. The High Commission was composed of the Governors of the three territories, with a permanent executive and advisory staff, and a Central Legislative Assembly empowered to legislate on certain defined matters of common interest. The Assembly consisted of *ex officio* members from the administrative staff and members from each territory, some appointed by the Governor, others elected by the territorial legislature.

During the late 1950's increasing criticism of the existing arrangements was heard, particularly from Tanganyika and Uganda concerning the operations and effects of the customs union. The East African Economic and Fiscal Commission was appointed in 1960 to consider various aspects of economic coordination between the territories, and subsequently recommended adjustments to the present system.[17] The changes in the constitutional status of the separate territories as they move toward independence have also required modification of the organization of the common services. A conference in June 1961 agreed that these services should continue to be provided on an East African basis "whatever constitutional changes might take place in the future in East Africa," but that they should be administered by an East African Common Services Organization, constituted differently than the East African High Commission.[18] Responsibility for general policy rests with the East African Common Services Authority, consisting of the principal elected minister in each of the countries. Additional groups of relevant ministers are responsible for formulating policy in the fields of communications, finance, commerce and industry, and social and research services. A new Central Legislative Assembly with specific legislative powers consists of the ministers composing the triumvirates, nine members elected by the legislatures of each country, the Secretary-General and Legal Secretary of the Organization. This new Organization came into existence on December 11, 1961. It seems clear, however, that this arrangement may not remain undisturbed by future political developments; it can be terminated by any one of the countries, and federation is a live issue of current discussion in East Africa. If this objective is realized, it will permit a far greater integration of economic policies than now exists; but if it is not, separatist political tendencies might threaten the extent of economic cooperation that has been achieved and the economic case for continuing it, which is partly, at least, independent of political considerations. To illustrate the nature of this economic case, the East African relationships in different economic fields will be described separately.

The present customs union grew up in stages, after free trade between Kenya and Uganda was established in 1917. Barriers to interterritorial movements of goods and factors of production have been substantially reduced since then, although fiscal policy—including the power to set rates of customs and excise duties—is still the responsibility of the individual countries, and the almost complete uniformity of rates has been based on negotiations among them. It has been generally presumed that the customs union confers economic benefits on East Africa as a whole, derived from the expanded possibilities it offers for production to be

---

[17] *East Africa, Report of the Economic and Fiscal Commission, February 1961,* London, HMSO, Cmd. 1279. (Usually known as the Raisman Commission.)

[18] *The Future of the East Africa High Commission Services,* Report of the London Discussions, June 1961, London, HMSO, Cmd. 1433.

diversified accordingly to the comparative advantages of the different regions, and to operate in units enjoying greater economies of scale.[19] There are in addition administrative advantages in not having to maintain customs barriers along the long boundaries between the countries and separate customs organizations. Now, for example, the documentation of goods intended for Uganda and Tanganyika and passing through Mombasa can be processed at the port, without separate road or rail checks at the land frontiers.

The most serious criticism of the customs union has indeed not been directed against its over-all effects, but rather against certain policies that are said to have tended to restrict its benefits, or that the benefits have been distributed so unevenly among the countries that the interests of a particular country are being sacrificed. The first of these criticisms has primarily concerned the policies of the statutory marketing boards for agricultural products, particularly in Kenya, which limit the free market for these commodities, and the system of industrial licensing, which attempted to control and encourage the establishment of new industries by granting them special privileges. The Raisman Commission recommended measures designed to relieve dissatisfaction from these sources, and these problems will be discussed in subsequent chapters of the report.

It has also been argued that most of the benefits of the customs union have accrued to Kenya. A description of unequal growth rates between the territories was given by the Raisman Report,[20] which characterizes the expansion of output during the 1950's as very rapid in Kenya but as a bare improvement in Uganda. However, the national accounts estimates supporting this description contains uncertain elements, particularly the volume of agricultural output, and there are considerable difficulties in correcting the statistics for price changes. Elsewhere, it has been suggested that real production increased by 6 percent a year in Uganda, 5 percent in Kenya and 4 percent in Tanganyika, although as a result of shifts in the terms of trade, income in the three countries did not grow in the same proportions.[21] It is not at all clear from such an exercise that Kenya enjoyed a substantially faster rate of growth than its East African neighbors. Nor would such a finding necessarily prove that any disparities in rates of growth had occurred *as a result* of the customs union. The mission does not intend to suggest that economic growth within a customs union area may not concentrate in areas where conditions for production are particularly favorable. But the evidence

[19] Raisman, *op. cit.*, paras. 46–48.
[20] *Ibid.*
[21] Haddon-Cave, *op. cit.*

of the economic indicators does not indicate that this tendency has advanced in East Africa to the point where it has promoted growth in one country at the expense of stagnation in another.

A system of transfer payments between Kenya, Tanganyika and Uganda, based on the recommendations of the Raisman Commission, has been introduced, in part to compensate for an uneven distribution of the benefits of the customs union. A Distributable Pool has been established, the receipts of which are derived from 40 percent of the income tax paid by companies engaged in manufacturing and finance, and from 6 percent of customs and excise revenue of all the countries. After deduction of the costs of collecting those taxes, half the proceeds of the Pool are distributed equally among the three countries.

A variety of services which have come to be operated on an East African basis are administered under the East African Common Services Organization. The largest group of these are transportation and communications services—railways and harbors, posts and telecommunications and airways—which are "self-contained," in that they intend to cover at least their current costs from their own charges. There are in addition a variety of other "non-self-contained" services, which include the revenue collecting services for customs and excise, the income tax, economic and statistical units, and a range of research activities and services. The mode of financing the "non-self-contained" services has been changed with the replacement of the High Commission by the Common Services Organization. They are now to be supported from the other half of the proceeds of the Distributable Pool. This method gives the Common Services Organization an independent source of revenue, and it no longer depends on amounts voted specifically for each of the services by each of legislatures. It can be seen from the extent of these services that they play an important role in the economic life of the three countries. The Railways and Harbours, and Posts and Telecommunications, contributed £27 million or over 11 percent of total capital formation in Kenya during the years 1954–60. The benefits derived from these operations vary with the particular service, some of which may be of marginal significance for immediate economic developments. In general, however, assuming that the functions performed by the Common Services Organization are desirable in themselves and of sufficiently uniform interest, the system of joint administration is more economical of cost and personnel than separate units would be. The costs may not be shared among the countries in proportion to the benefits received, and an element of subsidy may well exist providing a uniform level of service throughout the three countries.

Perhaps a more serious problem may arise from the difficulties of coordinating the fiscal and investment policies for which the Common Services Organization are responsible, but which depend upon the unanimous agreement of the separate governments. The maintenance of the customs union requires an approximate uniformity of rates of taxation in the three countries, whatever their *separate* budgetary or development needs. Divergencies in the investment effort, or the relative priority of different sectors between the countries may hinder the formulation of an agreed plan for the individual common services. The new machinery of the Common Services Organization concentrates responsibility for formulating policy in a series of ministerial committees. How effective an instrument of coordination this machinery will become remains to be seen.

A final aspect of Kenya's formal economic relationships with the other East African countries is concerned with the region's common currency. The East African shilling is the unit of currency not only for Kenya, but also for Tanganyika, Uganda, Zanzibar and Aden. The East African shilling is issued by the East African Currency Board against deposits of sterling, and is freely convertible into sterling at par (plus or minus a small commission). This currency board system at first required that the currency in circulation be backed 100 percent by sterling assets, and any change in one brought about a corresponding change in the other. Since 1955, the Currency Board has been authorized to issue up to the equivalent of a certain sum, now £20 million, against securities of the local governments. The power of fiduciary issue allows a degree of management in credit creation without the full machinery and responsibilities of a central bank. The Board's sterling assets constitute the bulk of East Africa's foreign exchange reserves, and thus it is important that monetary developments be accompanied by the fullest collaboration among the members. (For a further discussion of the Currency Board, see Chapter 9.)

PROBLEMS OF ECONOMIC DEVELOPMENT

The approach of independence has added a new urgency to some of the salient problems confronting future economic development in Kenya. Although the long-run capacity for growth of the economy may be enhanced by this sense of urgency and by a heightened determination of a self-governing people, the short-run outlook has been clouded by uncertainties associated with rapid change. Kenya has enjoyed years of increasing wealth since World War II, but remains a poor country.

There are in the first place a number of general physical limitations to achieving substantial rates of growth in output in Kenya. Perhaps the most crucial of these are the impediments to raising the productivity of agriculture. The mission believes that increased output of primary products will have to provide the basis for an expansion of the economy as a whole. The prospects for increasing agricultural production depend in part on the availability of land. Only a small part of Kenya comprises agriculturally useful land. Two-thirds of the country, receiving 20 inches or less rainfall a year, is uncultivated and of very limited capacity for grazing. Although there is no over-all scarcity of land in relation to population at present, the restriction of land to individual tribes has led to the underutilization of land in some areas of high-potential farming country at the same time as other areas, some of them less well endowed, are overcrowded and overfarmed. Problems also exist concerning the use of presently available land, deriving from customary systems of landholding and traditional methods of cultivation. The fragmentation of farm units, and the preponderance of communal over individual rights to the ownership of land are not new difficulties to improved agriculture in Kenya and substantial progress toward consolidation and the establishment of individual title to land has been made in some areas. Experience has shown, nevertheless, that the techniques for overcoming resistance to changes in patterns of landholding cannot be easily transferred from one region to another, and unless there is economic pressure on the farmer, government programs may prove costly and ineffective. Subsistence cultivation also lessens the incentives of farmers to raise their productivity by adopting new methods, or by switching to alternative crops. Peasant cultivators who shift to growing for the cash market encounter new risks: they must face the uncertainties of variable prices as well as the old uncertainties of the yield of their crops.

Kenya is fortunate in possessing an agricultural sector which is, at least in part, intensively developed. By far the greatest proportion of marketed output comes from some 3,600 European and Asian farms and plantations. Production from these farms composes more than three-quarters of Kenya's agricultural exports. Africans are no longer debarred from owning land in the areas formerly reserved for members of the other racial communities, and various schemes have been introduced, and are now being expanded, to settle Africans in those areas. The mission urges that these schemes should be implemented in such a way as to avoid prejudicing the production of these areas upon which the economy so much depends for maintaining export earnings. The productivity of newly settled African farms also requires careful technical attention and expensive ancillary services.

The existence of opportunities for industrial investment is commonly identified as a major condition for economic growth. The limitations on rapid growth of the industrial sector are largely associated with the restricted scope for expansion offered by the local market at present levels of income. Judging from the composition of commodity imports into East Africa, opportunities for the growth of certain lines of industry exist. In basic industries, however, a reasonable return on investment would require a scale of operation that East Africa cannot support, and a supply of capital that it does not command. Under such conditions development that might provide important external economies for future industrial expansion is unlikely. The known mineral resources of Kenya are sparse, and do not provide a cheap source of materials for developing industry. But the mission does not believe the present limited scope for industrialization should be regarded as seriously prejudicing the immediate prospects for increasing the total output of the economy.

Kenya will depend, like so many other underdeveloped countries, largely upon production for export to achieve a satisfactory rate of income growth. The prospects for this will be significantly determined by world market conditions for its major export crops. Although Kenya's exports are quite well diversified, none of the chief commodities command an assured market for substantially increased sales on which hopes for enlarged export earnings can be pinned. The conditions of world trade, affected by regional trading arrangements and domestic price support programs, the possible competition of synthetic substitutes, the rate of growth in industrial countries—and the small proportional increases in requirements of primary commodities to which it gives rise—do not promise a rapidly growing demand for products during the 1960's.[22] Fluctuations in commodity prices, which occur without reference to supply conditions in Kenya for almost all the export crops, may rapidly shift the relative returns to be gained from them and largely determine the extent to which increases in the volume of production are translated into increases in income. The prospects for coffee, in particular, are narrowly circumscribed by the world market situation and international agreement to limit exports from producing countries, despite the advantages of cost and quality which Kenyan coffee possesses.

A second group of limitations to development in Kenya are human ones. In a subsistence economy, the capacity for growth is restricted by a limited range of skills sufficient to satisfy only a narrow horizon of wants, and by the sanctions society operates to ensure that efforts are directed toward meeting immediate needs. In order to improve living standards, both the desire for a growing output of goods and services

[22] FAO, *Agricultural Commodities—Projections for 1970*, Rome, 1962.

and a willingness by individuals to exert greater efforts to acquire them are necessary. The extent to which changes in traditional attitudes have already occurred in Kenya has varied a great deal from place to place. The mission believes, however, that one of the prime tasks of an independent government in the economic field is to stress that development can only be achieved through the efforts of people generally out on the farms and in the villages and towns, and to stimulate them to that effort. It is important, in particular, to devise widespread incentives to increase production throughout the economy. The responsibility for this falls particularly on the various agricultural marketing organizations. Likewise, as the economy diversifies, a readiness to undertake risk and a growing realization of the importance of responsible standards of business conduct should also be cultivated.

The spread of education is an essential feature of the introduction of a modern economy. As economic activity increases in complexity, it makes continuous demands on the range and level of human skills. The educational system must, therefore, be appropriate to meet these demands. It is difficult to measure the returns to be gained from investing in education. Clearly, there are heavy costs associated with a failure to provide the trained manpower needed to extend the use of technological improvements and so raise productivity. The most immediate benefits to the economy are likely to be gained by assuring the supply of directly productive skills, particularly in agricultural extension, which in turn depend upon an expansion of secondary education.

As a corollary to the appropriateness of the country's educational system for meeting the manpower requirements of development, there is the danger of creating a large group of young people dissatisfied with traditional society and its standards, but not equipped with adequate training for the jobs to which they aspire. It seems clear that such a discontinuity between skills and aspirations has made a major contribution to the existence of a serious level of unemployment in Kenya.[23] The population is believed to be growing at a substantial rate, and the traditional sector possesses only limited capacity for supporting wage employment. Secondary industries have not developed to the point where a steadily expanding work force has been established. About 28 percent of the able-bodied males in Kenya were in paid employment in 1960, most of them in non-African owned agricultural enterprises, and this proportion had not increased significantly during the 1950's.[24] Under these conditions, an unfortunate combination of high labor costs to-

[23] A. G. Dalgleish, *A Survey of Unemployment,* Government Printer, Nairobi, 1960.
[24] East African Statistical Department, Kenya Unit, *Reported Employment and Wages in Kenya 1948–1960,* August 1961.

gether with a considerable pool of unemployed labor may exist. People are not trained for the kinds of jobs for which there is demand. The problem of unemployment has been aggravated recently by the slowing down of economic activity: between 1960 and 1961, the numbers employed fell more than 5 percent. Unemployment is concentrated partly in urban areas, where overcrowding, lack of adequate sanitation, instability of the work force, and the moral dilemmas of a new environment place an added burden on social services that the country can ill afford.

The availability of an adequate supply of human skills in Kenya will depend at least for a number of years not only on education, but also on the presence of non-Africans, both in the civil service and in private activity. Most of the technical and professional services—accounting and engineering are obvious examples, but there are many others—are now provided almost exclusively by them. They are the main source of experience for the management of organized industry and the government services. For the expansion of education, reliance must be placed primarily on non-Africans for some years to come. Africans have demonstrated their capacity in both private and public affairs, but the demands of an expanding economy for technical, administrative and managerial skills will outrun the speed at which talents can be developed and experience accumulated. Under such conditions, expatriate manpower now in Kenya represents a valuable asset, but one in danger of being lost. If these skilled people should leave Kenya in large numbers during the next few years, it would be difficult, if not impossible, to maintain many of the economic activities on which the present level of output rests. Even if replacements from abroad could be found to man the essential services needed to avoid drastic dislocation of the economy, to do so would almost certainly inflate the costs of the services and lose the benefit of an extensive knowledge of local conditions. The requirements for retaining the supply of human resources in the non-African communities are, however, not so much economic as political and social. The ability of the Government to plan and the country to achieve economic development at the same time as political independence depends upon a continued supply of qualified personnel no matter what their origin.

The localization of the civil service in Kenya poses a difficult question of determining the appropriate level of salaries for government personnel in the future. Expatriates have received an added "inducement" allowance—paid by the United Kingdom Government—to encourage them to serve overseas rather than accept other jobs at home. But even the basic salary scales for civil servants are out of proportion to incomes received in other occupations in Kenya. The size of the civil service is related to past rather than current and future conditions, and the mission believes it should be reviewed. We also consider that the grading of posts should be adjusted to reflect the employment of less experienced officers as a consequence of localization.

The supply of capital is another of the major determinants of growth. In the past, Kenya has apparently been able to finance an appreciable part of its capital formation, particularly in the private sector, from domestic East African sources. Local financial institutions—the commercial banks, insurance companies—grew into important sources of investible funds. As a result of the current crisis of confidence, private capital has become increasingly scarce and is unlikely to be available again until conditions in East Africa warrant a favorable reappraisal of the risks of investing there, and may already have found and been developing more attractive prospects elsewhere. Increases in the number of savings deposits by Africans indicate that many of them have a surplus of disposable income over their consumption needs, but these deposits have not so far provided a substantial source of funds for investment purposes. At present, the prospects for financing capital formation out of domestic private savings are extremely limited.

Nor does the public sector offer a more promising picture. Since the early years of the Emergency, Kenya's government finances have relied on some external assistance to cover even current expenditures. The mission makes some recommendations (see Chapter 10) with the aim of changing this pattern, but a period of adjustment will be required. A curtailment of government expenditures as well as an expansion of receipts will be needed, and, in June 1962, an Economy Commission was appointed to advise the Government on measures to reduce expenditure with a view to bringing the recurrent budget into early balance. Taxation in Kenya was the equivalent of 18 percent of the GDP of the monetary economy in 1960 and the capacity of the Government to mobilize savings through taxation is limited. The mission has, therefore, drawn up its program of development expenditures taking into account the scarcity of available capital (see Chapter 3). We also believe that a revival of economic activity must in the first place depend on a return of private confidence rather than on public expenditure programs.

There remains the possibility of augmenting the supply of development funds from external sources. A large proportion of investment in large-scale industries in Kenya in the past has been financed by an inflow of funds from abroad, which has also brought more advanced techniques into the country. It is clearly to the benefit of Kenya that foreign investment should be encouraged in the future, and the mission considers that demonstration of a favorable attitude on the part of the independent Government of Kenya toward overseas capital would be an appropriate and necessary measure to attract funds. A more detailed consideration of this subject will be given in Chapter 3, but the use of foreign capital involves a number of general problems. Capital commands a price, and regard should be paid to the capacity of the country to service its foreign debt. This capacity is dependent upon the country's foreign exchange earnings and on the ability of the Government to mobilize these earnings for development purposes. At present, existing external liabilities are the equivalent of about 12 percent of current export earnings, or 14 percent of the revenues of the Kenya Government, and this burden can be expected to increase in the next few years.[25] Kenya does not possess large foreign exchange reserves, which might be drawn on to escape the limitations imposed on further borrowing by this already considerable debt burden. These reserves are mainly sterling assets held by the Government, local authorities, statutory boards, the commercial banks, the Post Office Savings Bank and the East African Currency Board. The latter are by far the most substantial, totaling £56 million in 1961, but are creditable to all members of the Currency Board. The reserves cover about four to five months' imports by the East African countries. It is important for economies such as these, in which external trading transactions loom so large, to be prepared to face fluctuations in receipts and payments with adequate reserves in hand. Also, under the currency board system now operating, a drawing down of reserves would also have a serious deflationary impact upon the domestic money supply unless it were offset by an increase in the fiduciary issue or by the readiness of the commercial banks to extend credit facilities.

The Government may have to face other questions before undertaking further foreign borrowing. Limitations are frequently imposed on the use of funds provided by bilateral agencies, which sometimes conflict with the needs of the recipient. Loans may be "tied" to the purchase of goods from the creditor country, or available only for certain kinds of projects. This may tend to divert attention from the highest priority areas of investment, and the desirability of a loan should be judged in terms of the costs and benefits accruing from it rather than simply by the ease with which finance is granted. Secondly, the project which is to be

[25] Kenya's external debt, largely denominated in sterling, amounted to about £47.5 million equivalent at the end of 1961, the annual service payments on which will increase from £2.7 million equivalent to about £4.3 million equivalent by 1970; and other obligations payable in sterling in the form of pension payments at present amount to £1.7 million a year, but which will increase considerably in the next few years as expatriate officials take accelerated retirement. In addition, Kenya bears contingent liability with Tanganyika and Uganda for the external debt of certain of the Common Services—£60 million equivalent in 1961—recourse to which would be shared equally among the three territories. Kenya's share of the servicing burden of this debt would equal roughly an additional 3 percent of the present value of exports.

financed may make extensive demands on local funds and personnel for recurrent purposes associated with the capital investment, and there may be the danger of diverting these from other more valuable programs. Considerations such as these may militate against proceeding with a particular project, or financing it from a particular source. In agricultural countries such considerations are especially important, for in agriculture working capital and supervisory requirements are heavy in relation to fixed capital outlays.

The task of development in Kenya, in which an accelerated rate of growth is a goal of public policy, poses a number of organizational problems. Development planning is not a distinct, defined exercise, but depends upon the general economic system operating in the country. The mission has assumed that planning in Kenya will take place in the context of an economy in which private enterprise and initiative will continue to play a large part. In these circumstances, the main instruments of planning will be a coherent program of public expenditures, and the pursuit of policies designed to stimulate private activity.

A first question concerns the allocation of responsibility for planning functions in the Government. It is important that there should be a coherent connection between the assessment of available resources, the choice of development objectives, and the establishment of criteria for development expenditure and other public policies bearing on development.

The quality of economic planning is, however, determined above all by its implementation. The program suggested by the mission (in Chapter 3 and elaborated in subsequent chapters) is limited not only by financial and balance of payments considerations, but also by Kenya's capacity to provide the personnel and services without which capital investment will achieve little. The limitation is a general one: for example, the supply of extension officers will affect the degree to which agricultural programs can be fulfilled and the supply of qualified teachers will limit the expansion of schools.

Political developments in East Africa are now bringing a re-alignment of responsibility for policy and its execution among different units of government. The possibility of a federal association over the whole area and the introduction of regionalism in the constitution to be adopted by an independent Kenya raise questions of coordination between various government bodies. The desire for economic growth as a national goal has important consequences for the structure of government, since the pursuit of active fiscal and monetary policies and the adoption of common external economic policies require an integration of authority if conflicting interests are to be resolved.

CHAPTER 3 *PROGRAM FOR ECONOMIC DEVELOPMENT*

Measures to Promote Economic Growth
During the Next Few Years

In Chapter 2 we discussed, in broad terms, factors limiting future economic development in Kenya. Some of these factors are fundamental, such as the lack of minerals. Others are man-made and can be influenced more readily by government action. But, there are also favorable factors which should lead to a marked increase in the output of some products in the next few years.

Kenya has yet to reap the full benefit of the work undertaken since the middle of the last decade to develop agriculture under the Swynnerton Plan. Mixed farming in consolidated areas has included the production of tree crops which take several years to reach maturity. The increase in the plantings of coffee and tea during the last few years both by peasant farmers and by estates will yield a greater volume of production of these commodities in the next few years. But investment in sisal has not been maintained and plants already in the ground will soon become overage. Changes in output of many other crops will be influenced more by immediate considerations for production and marketing than by past plantings.

The potential for expanding the volume of production is impressive, but many of the increases will depend on action still to be taken. Expansion of output of some products can be anticipated more definitely (for example, tea and coffee) than of others (for example, meat and dairy products). But expansion in the total output of each commodity will depend on new investment, or on continued progress in the improvement of African agriculture, or on maintenance of production in the scheduled areas. Even if greater output is achieved, the marketing of many export products is likely to encounter serious difficulties which are discussed in Chapter 4. Short-term expectations in world markets are unfavorable for producers of primary products. The achievements of the Swynnerton Plan may be unique in Africa. But economic conditions have changed since it was introduced. Though Kenya African-grown coffee is of high quality and low cost, the surplus of coffee pressing on world markets makes it necessary for a different production pattern to be

41

considered in areas suitable for coffee which have yet to be planted. The scope for the further development of coffee will depend on future arrangements for marketing. In Chapter 4 we envisage a great reduction in new plantings and suggest the greater development of animal husbandry and of alternative cash crops. We do not claim to have found an immediately applicable and equally attractive alternative pattern of production to that enjoyed up to now and we recommend that the Ministry of Agriculture give this matter its attention as one of great importance and urgency.

The output of manufacturing has continued to rise in recent years, but during 1961 there were signs of a falling off in the rate of growth.[1] The prevailing loss in confidence has now affected manufacturing following the decline in construction, but this has been partially offset by an expansion of exports. We believe that there is scope for a limited expansion of manufacturing to serve local and nearby markets (see Chapter 5), but in the present state of uncertainty any projection of a rate of growth over the next four years would be valueless. Likewise, we have made no attempt to project the growth of the economy or the growth in per capita income over the next four years.

The economic effects of the decline in confidence have been following upon each other in the expected order. First of all, the outward movement of funds imposed a strain on financial institutions. As investment projects contracted were completed, an expanding government program buttressed total investment until 1961, when the fall in gross private investment of 28 percent was too great to be covered by the increase in the public sector. The decline in the construction industry and the worries of farmers in the scheduled areas have led to a reduction in staffs and the problem of mounting unemployment which we discuss in Chapter 8. As experience in 1961 shows, the private sector is too big for diminishing activity to be balanced by expansion in the public sector, where serious fiscal and human difficulties impede any marked growth.

During our visit to Kenya many private firms indicated that they were postponing investment projects. Foreign investors and lenders, including governmental institutions, will be disinclined to venture until prospects are clearer. Kenya can do little to alleviate the weakness in international markets for its principal exports. But other depressing factors are political and within the power of the Government—or of the principal political parties—to correct or to influence. Leading politicians told us that they wanted Kenya to develop and at a greater rate than in the past. Broadly speaking, they seemed to envisage a continued role for private initiative provided it achieved development of Kenya's resources.

[1] *Economic Survey 1962*, Government Printer, Nairobi, 1962, Chapter 4.

They wished to ensure that Africans progressively acquired a greater role in the economy and intended to remove racial separatism where that occurred. We have made recommendations for the removal of racial divisions in government activities, particularly in agricultural legislation, since we regard racial separatism as an unsuitable basis on which to build the economy of the country.

During the next four years the main aim should be to lay the foundation for future development. We are convinced that if the period is not to be unnecessarily difficult a first requirement would be the adoption of, and firm adherence to, policies likely to establish economic conditions to promote development. These policies, which we think should be formulated forthwith, can be considered under the following headings:

a. The maintenance of law and order.

b. The maintenance of efficiency in all branches of government. The role of the civil service in Kenya is much more than one of general administration. The development of cash farming by Africans, for example, depends on the work of trained specialists. Until suitable local officers are available, an excessive running down of administrative and professional expatriate staff could jeopardize the efficient running of government and the contribution it makes to achieving economic growth.

c. Fiscal solvency. For many years now Kenya has received financial support mainly from the United Kingdom for the recurrent as well as the development budget, and the extent of this support has been growing. Economic growth in an independent Kenya is unlikely with a weak exchequer. The Government can do much to ensure that the transition period sees the establishment of the fiscal conditions for economic progress. Fiscal prospects call for sustained action over a period of years:

i. To establish a more streamlined administration. A memorandum which the mission addressed to the Minister of Finance of March 30, 1962, included the following remarks: "A thorough reappraisal of government expenditure is required with the aim of eliminating nonessential expenditures and those not supporting expansion of production. Such a review should include levels of government salaries, and the possible merging of services." A commission[2] has examined government expenditure.

[2] A commission under the chairmanship of Mr. S. S. Menneer was appointed in June 1962 "to review governmental expenditure and to advise the Government of Kenya what measures could be taken in that field with a view to bringing the recurrent budget into early balance."

ii. To restrain pressures for the subsequent growth of expenditure. All proposed additions to expenditure should be examined according to need and priority. We discuss this matter in relation to the development program in the next section of this chapter.

iii. To expand revenue by tax changes likely to have the least unfavorable impact on the growth of production. The budget proposals of the Minister of Finance for the financial year 1962/63 represent a good start toward this objective, but we feel that some further changes in taxation will be necessary (see Chapter 10).

d. The promotion of the maintenance and further development of production in private hands to be assisted by:

i. A clear statement of policy toward private investment. This might include reassurances about interference by the state with private undertakings. External investors will be concerned about freedom to transfer earnings and repatriate original capital.

ii. Conditions in which private financial institutions can continue to operate effectively and confidence in the currency is preserved (see Chapter 9).

iii. The opportunity to make reasonable profits. Private business is dependent on prospects to make profits. The Government can ease the path of the businessman by taking action to avoid impediments to production and developments which make costs uneconomic. As long as the present currency arrangements apply, there should be no need for over-all control of imports. Import controls, unless carefully geared to the requirements of producers, can hinder and distort production. Action in the field of labor relations is most important and we note that the Minister of Labour is proposing legislation to improve arrangements for resolving disputes, which also influence business costs. In Kenya, the Government has functions which in many other countries are left to private initiative. Agricultural development is controlled and supported by government departments and statutory bodies. Processing and marketing are undertaken in part by special organizations responsible to the Minister of Agriculture. Arrangements to carry out agricultural policy should be improved, but we are convinced that the development of agricultural production for the market by Africans depends on continued government assistance to farmers and organized marketing of principal products (see Chapter 4).

Pursuit of these policies should also have beneficial effects beyond the private sector. It should encourage other governments and institutions to look more favorably on Kenya's requests for external assistance which will be necessary to meet its development needs.

The Government assists manufacturing industry mainly through the customs tariff. A small amount of finance has been provided and while expectations for the expansion of manufacturing industry depend mostly on private initiative, more effective government assistance, including finance, is required (see Chapter 5). Generally, we do not think that an extension of the role of government in production would be beneficial during the next few years. We believe that the first question to be asked in considering any proposals for transfer of production from private to public ownership should be whether a government body would function more effectively. Where an extension of production is desired and private investment is not forthcoming, it would be necessary first to establish the economic justification for the project and then to consider its priority in relation to other projects pressing for inclusion in the development program. During the first years of independence, the Kenya Government is likely to be overburdened in carrying out its present responsibilities and should be most reluctant to extend its role further in production. In drawing up a suggested program, we have therefore assumed that the scope of government intervention in economic life will be largely unchanged.

Development Planning in Kenya

Development planning is not a new thing in Kenya. At the end of World War II the governments in East Africa, like those of other British dependencies, prepared ten-year development plans covering the years 1946–1955. Financial assistance for the implementation of these plans was provided by the United Kingdom under the terms of the Colonial Development and Welfare Act. These ten-year plans were revised from time to time during their execution and since 1954 the Kenya Government has adopted successive three-year development programs. The present program ends on June 30, 1963. The transport and communications services of the East African Common Services Organization have usually planned for periods of five calendar years. Some of their plans have been reviewed and extended annually.

The Kenya Development Program 1960–63[3] refers only to the public

[3] Sessional Paper No. 4 of 1959/60, Nairobi, 1960.

sector, but also surveys the growth of the economy in general. The recent Kenya plan, however, is essentially a financial plan, and its size and composition have been determined by the expected availability of funds to the Government. It does not cover all public investment: local government bodies and state-owned corporations are included only to the extent to which they were to be assisted by the central government. The plan is not confined to capital expenditure but includes "other sums specifically allocated for projects of a development nature."[4]

From 1956 to 1960 the private sector, including public corporations, accounted for about two-thirds of gross fixed capital formation in Kenya, and we have thought about the desirability of including private investment in government planning activities. We also received many representations to the effect that comprehensive planning of some kind should be undertaken in Kenya or in East Africa as a whole. We, however, feel that during the next few years such a procedure would be of little use for formulating government policy in Kenya. Investment in the private sector will be greatly influenced by the reactions of private investors to the changes in the constitution and in the government of the country. We are making proposals that we consider should encourage development in the private sector but, with so many uncertainties, do not consider that realistic targets could be set for the expansion of the various forms of production in private hands. Furthermore, facing shortages of both financial and administrative resources (particularly specialized manpower), the Government will be fully extended in preparing and executing well-balanced programs for the public sector without the added work of planning in the private sector which could well prove to be largely ineffective. The mission, therefore, considers the more rewarding role for Government in the next few years to lie in planning for the public sector, and in creating conditions and providing services and assistance designed to encourage private investment. We discuss arrangements for development planning in Annex A.

Decisions taken by Asian and European businessmen and farmers will be a critical factor in the progress of the economy during the next few years and it is important that the Government should closely follow changes in the business climate. For example, these decisions will affect government revenue and the ability to carry out development programs. We therefore suggest that the Government should periodically review changes and likely developments in the private sector. Much of the information required will be available in separate branches of Government and in other bodies such as the commodity boards. Centrally, a

---

[4] A note on development planning in Kenya prepared by the Treasury, Nairobi, June 1961, at the request of the mission.

very useful economic survey is already prepared annually within the Treasury, but we think that the Government should take stock every six months of changes in the economy as a whole and especially in the Asian and European sectors.

Resources and Priorities

The central function of the Government in the development effort lies in the preparation and execution of a program of public expenditures designed to stimulate growth and provide essential services. This function is concentrated in the formulation of a development program or budget, described earlier. This budget has assumed significant proportions in relation to economic activity in Kenya, and gross expenditures in it have risen from under £10 million in 1960/61 to £14.7 million estimated for 1962/63.

Any future program for the public sector will be restricted by the limitations on Kenya's available resources. There will be a pressing shortage of funds for development as well as recurrent purposes. Domestic savings are small and limit the capacity of the country to finance any considerable development effort from within. Resources can be supplemented by loans and grants from elsewhere, and the 1960–63 Development Program has been financed mainly from United Kingdom sources. Any program for the next four years will be similarly dependent upon outside help, but funds are likely to be limited in amount, and in any case the balance of payments position will prevent their being resorted to indiscriminately. We shall return to this problem in discussing the financing of our suggested program.

In the past, human factors have not prevented development in Kenya. Resistance to change has hindered agricultural improvement, but skilled manpower has been obtained from abroad and, more recently, trained at home. Africans are now keen to improve their standards of living but are still largely unskilled. The danger is that skilled expatriates may depart before qualified Africans can be found to replace them. The improvement of educational facilities to equip the people better for modern economic life will initially require more expatriates rather than less. Similarly, the extension of cash agriculture will call for more specialist staff. A decline in the number of trained people working in Kenya during the next few years could prevent the effective execution of most development projects and this limitation would then become more serious than it has in the past.

For these reasons we recommend that a development program for the next few years should be framed with sufficient flexibility to permit adjustment in the light of changes in expectations of the supply of finance and of trained manpower. We regard the outline program given in this report as a starting point in the operation of planning. These uncertainties also suggest that the aim should be to avoid large projects only capable of execution over a run of years which, once committed, cannot be adapted to changing circumstances. Fortunately, we see no need for major projects of this kind which are frequently found in the power and transport sectors. The East African Railways are generally well-equipped to meet Kenya's existing needs. Power is privately supplied but no major project is yet required. Some capital works are likely to be needed in these sectors but they should not take a large part of government development expenditures during the period.

While financial and human resources will limit what should be attempted, we believe that the development program should be prepared with attention being paid more to quality than size. In judging programs of expenditure and government action, benefits achieved and expected in the improvement of production rather than the amounts spent are the main criteria. Governments can spend heavily and for long to little effect. Kenya's difficult financial situation makes it doubly important that expenditure should be confined to projects which will yield higher net returns than alternatives.

Political change also calls for a changed emphasis in development. Government and economic activity have been dominated by European ways of life and a natural endeavor to introduce European standards of social and other services. So far, where this has occurred, financial support has been provided partly through taxation, paid principally by the European and Asian communities, and partly through help from the United Kingdom. Maintenance of the standards of advanced countries in these respects would be inconsistent with the task of raising the low level of personal incomes of the mass of the people. Expatriate communities have also brought the desire to modernize. But under existing circumstances, for example, it could be a waste of limited resources to replace serviceable capital equipment with more modern machinery merely for the sake of modernizing.

The Government will not be short of claims for expenditure. For many years now the development program has provided for only a part of the requests from ministries. In the next four years, localization and the desire to bring forward the African people more rapidly to assume the major role in the economy will increase the disparity between aspirations and possibilities. Members of this mission also considered that worthwhile programs for the individual sectors could be drawn up well in excess of what collectively might be financially or administratively attainable.

To arrive at a government program making the best use of limited resources will call for restraint and for the application of suitable criteria in choosing between projects. We suggest that the Government should endeavor to allocate its expenditure to purposes likely to secure greatest increases in income under the circumstances under which Kenya finds itself, rather than to emulate the practices of high-income industrialized countries. Generally, we think that emphasis should be placed on measures likely to improve production rather than on welfare projects. Increased output and rising incomes would enable Kenya to provide more easily for improvements in social conditions which would at the moment be a burden on the economy and hinder growth.

Criteria for expanding social services are difficult to establish. The choice between investments in economic and social services, and between various kinds of social services, is especially difficult. Although the expansion of social services often adds to long-term productivity, their benefits frequently cannot be compared quantitatively. As an alternative, projects should often be judged in terms of the consequences of foregoing them or of the appropriateness of the services they would provide to the level of income of the country.

Recently, projects have been begun to provide relief work for some of the unemployed. We discuss the problem of mounting unemployment in Chapter 8. The solution of this problem lies in the restoration of conditions for the general advance of production. Unless steps are taken soon to revive economic activity, unemployment may continue to increase. The number of people unemployed at present is likely to exceed those for whom useful relief work could quickly be arranged, and the cost would be beyond the financial capacity of the country. Relief projects in agricultural settlement and afforestation have been initiated by the Government. Some projects of this kind can be justifiable on grounds of general priority for economic development, with the level of unemployment a secondary factor. We see little place for unproductive relief works. Unemployment is less of a social burden in Kenya than in industrial countries, in that in Kenya most people still have ties with the land which provides some minimum means of subsistence outside paid employment. The unemployment problem could be in large measure a transitory problem. It should not be a major determinant of the composition of the next development program.

The shortage of well-educated and trained Africans needs to be overcome if the future development of the economy is not to be impaired.

Education improves resources for production, but is also desired for noneconomic reasons. The expansion of education is costly and bears heavily on Kenya's recurrent budget. We have, therefore, placed emphasis on the expansion of secondary education and teacher and technical training rather than on primary education, which has expanded very rapidly in recent years.

Not all productive projects will qualify for immediate implementation. Those promising a higher return should first be favored. This criterion may be difficult to apply, especially in agricultural settlement schemes. The abundance of unskilled labor and the popularity of land ownership may encourage concentration on schemes to settle the maximum number of people regardless of the likely return. The most effective settlement scheme is the one which promises a reasonable standard of living to an efficient farmer and gives priority to men with experience in modern agriculture. The benefit derived from such a scheme over the years is not to be counted in terms of the numbers settled, but rather in the increment to production and its effect on the rest of the economy. The demands of prosperous settlers will boost other activity. Impoverished peasants would be a burden on the whole community.

Preference should also be given to projects likely to yield a quick return over those making a small contribution over a run of years. Some projects of the latter kind can be quickly dismissed by asking if they are really essential for present needs. Many main road projects presented to us in Kenya fall, we feel, in this category. Some people in Kenya would like to have a modern highway from Nairobi to Mombasa, but we do not think that the likely economic costs and benefits have been sufficiently considered. We ourselves do not believe that any possible benefits to be gained from this project in the near future justify it to the exclusion of many other projects of greater urgency and potential. Regard should, however, be paid to the longer term; schemes of afforestation are not to be condemned because their yield comes only in the distant future. But the emphasis should be placed on the most promising projects offering early returns. In this way the foundation will be laid for further development in the future.

Some projects requiring only a small capital expenditure will bring with them a large recurrent burden. Others, to come to fruition, may require much greater expenditure on ancillary services than on the original project. On the other hand, indirect benefits to other sectors should also be weighed in favor of a project. Projects, particularly large ones, should be considered in the context of the program as a whole.

The choice between projects will also be affected by considerations other than directly those of economics. But even projects related to law and order and government buildings, in particular, may have an economic justification. The maintenance of law and order and the efficient functioning of government are vital for the growth of the economy. In Kenya's circumstances, however, the criterion of need should be strictly applied to projects of this kind.

A general aim should be to reduce the cost of individual projects to the minimum, and throughout their work in preparing development schemes, all branches of the Government should review designs and standards to this end.

Suggested Development Program 1963/64–1966/67

The broad aims of a development program during the first years of independence are clear—to increase production and revenue mainly by developing African cash agriculture and to train the people to assume a greater role in the economy. Much has been done in both directions, especially since the Swynnerton Plan was adopted. Political change calls for a much greater effort, but can, as we have seen, bring about depletion rather than accretion of resources. Settlement in the scheduled areas may be regarded partly as an extension of small-scale peasant farming to new areas, and as a response to the desire of Africans for land, but it is also a means of replacing the production of large-scale European farmers who desire to leave. The further development of secondary and specialist education is an immediate requirement to prepare sufficient Africans to assume adequately the major role in economic activity, including government, now filled by Asians and Europeans.

Measures to expand basic services often loom large in development programs. In Kenya, power is provided by a private company and railways and harbors are an East African Common Service. The capacity of these undertakings in relation to the likely growth in demand calls for no major expansion in the next few years. Roads in agricultural areas, however, need to be improved if plans to expand production are not to be frustrated.

A large element in the program can be more correctly described as reconstruction, rather than development. The period of reconstruction will not be successful if it starts with demolition. A mass exodus of the higher and specialist civil servants, farmers, industrialists, financiers, traders, technicians and professional people who constitute the bulk of the non-African communities could only lead to chaos to the detriment of the African people. We hope that conditions will encourage most of them to stay.

Similarly, the program we suggest assumes the maintenance of existing production. The scheduled areas still produce three-quarters of

Kenya's agricultural exports. African production is rapidly providing a greater proportion of export crops but any large reduction in production in the scheduled areas could dislocate the economy. It could make unmanageable an already difficult unemployment situation—European farms and estates are the biggest employers of African labor—and have major repercussions throughout the country.

Even if people stay and production is maintained, budgetary prospects will still impose a severe limit and Kenya is unlikely, over the next four years, to be able to sustain the development effort of the Government at current levels. Judged by annual rate of expenditure Kenya should, therefore, contemplate a development program somewhat smaller than the total of nearly £14.7 million estimated for 1962/63. We suggest a program which, together with the expanded settlement scheme, would amount to about £13.4 million a year and, if the expenditures of statutory bodies are included, would total £56 million for the four years from July 1, 1963. The additional annual cost of services included in the recurrent budget consequent on the implementation of the program is estimated to rise from £0.6 million in 1963/64 to £1.6 million in 1966/67.

The broad structure of the program is shown in Table 1. Another table (Table 4) classifying the program generally in accordance with the ministerial structure in force at the middle of 1962 is to be found at the end of the chapter. The major prior commitment of the five-year program for the settlement of Africans on small-holdings in the scheduled areas, which is now being implemented, has affected the size and composition of the program. When the settlement scheme was announced it was stated that it would be the first charge on development funds provided by the United Kingdom. We have, therefore, regarded this scheme as a firm element in any development program for Kenya for the next four years. Nearly £21 million, or more than one-third of the total program, is planned to be spent on settlement.

It is in the nonscheduled areas that we find the best prospects for expanding and establishing peasant agriculture using modern practices of husbandry. These areas contain more of the land of high potential than the scheduled areas and most of all the land in Kenya. Improvement in the standard of living of the mass of the people, unless Kenya strikes oil, will depend on earnings from agriculture and the complementary development of manufacturing industry. Our suggested program therefore places emphasis on various steps to improve agriculture in the nonscheduled areas. It includes measures to increase the incomes of farms already enclosed, to continue the program of consolidation, to extend irrigation farming and to improve cattle rearing in the lower rainfall areas.

TABLE 1: Suggested Development Program 1963/64–1966/67[a]

(£ million)

	Estimates 1962/63	1963/64	1964/65	1965/66	1966/67	Total	Per-cent
Land Settlement	6.1	5.5	5.2	5.1	5.1	20.9	37
Agriculture, Irrigation and Water[b]	2.8	3.6	4.0	4.2	4.3	16.1	29
Forestry	0.4	0.4	0.4	0.4	0.4	1.5	2
Industry and Geology	0.4	0.2	0.2	0.2	0.2	0.9	2
Tourism and Wildlife	0.1	0.1	0.1	0.1	0.1	0.4	1
Roads and Airports	1.5	0.8	0.8	0.8	0.8	3.2	6
Education, Localization and Training	1.4	1.4	1.2	1.1	1.1	4.9	9
Health	0.2	0.3	0.3	0.3	0.3	1.0	2
Housing	0.3	0.3	0.4	0.4	0.4	1.5	2
Local Government	0.6	0.5	0.5	0.5	0.5	2.0	4
Other Government Buildings	0.6	0.5	0.5	0.5	0.5	2.0	3
Internal Security	0.3	0.3	0.3	0.3	0.3	1.1	2
Broadcasting	Small	0.1	0.2	0.1	0.1	0.5	1
Total[c]	14.7	14.0	14.1	13.9	14.1	56.0	100

[a] All figures rounded.
[b] Excludes provision for trading expenses of African Livestock Marketing Organization which are covered by receipts.
[c] Nearly £2.6 million of works by statutory bodies is included in the suggested program. In this respect the estimate for 1962/63 includes only £130,000 provided by the Government to SCDA.

A major item of expenditure is for field staff in the Departments of Agriculture and Veterinary Services, that is for supporting recurrent expenditure on services which are essential for the improvement of agricultural production. We recommend an expansion of these services, of research, and of facilities for the training of agricultural specialists and farmers. Provision is made for the continuation of land consolidation and enclosure at the present rate and for an expansion of funds and a reorganization of arrangements for the supply of agricultural credit. In the light of experience with small-scale tea growing in recent years, a major expansion of the program at present being organized by the Special Crops Development Authority is recommended. Provision is also made for the extension of cooperative societies, rural water supplies and some irrigation schemes. Measures proposed specifically to improve cattle rearing include tsetse fly eradication, artificial insemination and stock control, and the expansion of facilities for the processing of meat and dairy products. In including programs suggested by the Kenya Meat Commission and Kenya Cooperative Creameries, it is assumed that these organizations can obtain finance which would not be available to the Government for other purposes. The priority to be accorded to the programs of these organizations would otherwise need to be reviewed.

The provision under the heading *industry and geology* is to augment the resources of the Industrial Development Corporation to assist manufacturing industry, and for geological mapping and mineral investigations.

There is no pressing need for major works on airports and almost all the expenditure under *roads and airports* is for roads. Here emphasis has been placed on road improvements required for the expansion of production and not on construction which would be of little direct economic benefit to Kenya in the near future. Nearly two-thirds of the total is for minor trunk and secondary feeder roads for agricultural development (£350,000 alone is for tea roads), and only one-third for main trunk roads.

A broad aim of the program is to train the people to assume a greater role in the economy. Some of the expenditure under other headings (e.g., agriculture and health) is for this purpose, but the major provision is under the heading *education, localization and training*. The bulk of the program is for secondary schools, many of which would have science streams. An expansion of teacher training, trade and technical schools and the Nairobi Polytechnic is also provided for. Limited building of primary schools is envisaged. All the expenditure for education is on buildings. A table showing the recurrent expenditure required is to be found in Chapter 8. The localization and training program, on the other hand, provides partly for scholarships, for the maintenance of training institutes and for the establishment of supernumerary posts. Capital for higher education is not included as the University may well find sufficient support overseas. A much greater problem is likely to be to raise funds to meet its recurrent needs.

The development of *health* and other social services did not justify the same general priority in the program as, for example, secondary education which has been emphasized above. Shortage of staff also limits what may be achieved in this field. Provision has been made for some extension of hospital facilities and health centers, and for staff training. Small amounts are envisaged for community development and social service projects.

Generally, the Government should endeavor to use existing buildings having vacant space rather than build additional accommodation. This may not always be possible in rural areas. Most of the provision for *other government buildings* is for public works nonrecurrent—largely minor new construction and improvement to existing buildings.

The shortage of urban housing is large, but, although its full extent is unknown, it is beyond the capacity of the Government to remedy for some time. Under *housing and local government* more would be spent annually on housing but less on local government than in recent years.

The amount suggested for *internal security* is entirely for buildings for the police and the prisons department. It is divided between training centers, staff quarters and new police stations and prisons. No provision is made for new buildings for the military.

The scope of the program is wider than the Development Estimates in that we have provided £2.6 million for some Kenya Government statutory bodies. We think that the Kenya Government's development programs should embrace the whole of the public sector for which it is responsible. Many of these undertakings play a fundamental part in government programs for agricultural development. Several of the statutory bodies are, we understand, able to make their own separate arrangements for finance and we have included the programs they submitted to us on this basis. We have not, therefore, attempted to assess their priority generally in relation to program as a whole, but have discussed them individually in the sector chapter. In one instance, the Special Crops Development Authority (SCDA), we think the program (for the development of tea production on peasant holdings) is of sufficient importance to justify an extension of direct financial support which is at present being given by the Government. To be undertaken, however, the full program requires major financial support from other sources which has already been sought in part by SCDA.

Financing the Program

Finance for government development programs is usually provided from the savings of the country, supplemented by the savings of others in the form of loans and grants from abroad. In Kenya, the situation during the next few years is expected to be rather different; local savings are small and any considerable development effort will depend on external assistance.

In our assessment of possible finance for the program, major emphasis is therefore placed on external resources (see Table 2). The budgetary situation offers no hope of any substantial contribution from Kenya Government revenues, but amounts can be expected to be generated within the various government agencies, particularly from repayments of loans made by the Land Bank. Before the recent decline in confidence Kenya was able to borrow £2 million and more in the local market, but in the next few years no substantial local borrowings for development purposes can be expected, especially as provision must be made for local loans which will reach maturity and need to be refinanced. The Asian and European communities will remain the dominant financial factor for some time and the principal need is to create conditions for them to regain confidence to use their savings in Kenya and to lend funds to the Government.

TABLE 2: Possible Resources for Development Program[a]

(£ million)

	1963/64	1964/65	1965/66	1966/67	Total
Local loans, funds and repayments available for general development	0.5	0.6	0.6	0.8	2.5
External (already negotiated)	0.8	0.2	0.1	0.1	1.2
Land settlement	5.5	5.2	5.1	5.1	20.9
Finance for statutory bodies, etc., not provided by Government	0.6	0.8	0.6	0.5	2.5
Balance to be financed[b]	6.6	7.3	7.5	7.6	28.9
Total	14.0	14.1	13.9	14.1	56.0

[a] Figures rounded.
[b] £1.5 million per year of this represents expenditure which we consider should be borne by the current budget (in the absence of extended grant arrangements) as soon as possible.

We have concluded that it should be possible to raise £2.5 million from all local sources plus some additional amounts progressively to cover staff salaries at present borne on Development Estimates.

To avoid any major break with current Kenya practice, the present division between the "Development Estimates" and the "Colony Estimates" has been retained. Many items of a recurrent nature included in the Development Estimates are financed by Colonial Development and Welfare grants. As these grants may be expected to fall away after independence, we feel that they should be progressively financed by current revenue. An amount of £1.5 million a year is assumed to be met ultimately in this way. Many of these services of a noncapital nature are, however, developmental in character and fundamental to the improvement in living standards. Much of the expenditure on education (though included in Colony Estimates) and on agricultural extension, for example, is in this category, and we hope that governments and others wishing to assist in the development of Kenya will be willing to provide financial assistance for these services as well as for capital projects.

Some external finance has already been negotiated for the program or can be assumed. This partly consists of support for projects which were started in the 1960–63 Development Program, but the principal amount will be for settlement. In assessing possible additional external finance we considered not only the amount which Kenya might be able to raise abroad, but the extent to which Kenya should incur obligations associated with external borrowing. To repay external loans a country has not merely to raise the funds internally but has also to command the foreign currency in which to make payment. In borrowing abroad, attention should be given to the prospects for developing exports to provide the foreign exchange to cover payments on loans as well as for current requirements of foreign goods and services. In Chapter 2, we have discussed Kenya's external transactions. The country has had a persistent adverse balance of trade in recent years which has been met only in part by earnings from services provided for the rest of East Africa and by capital imports; and, with the decline in confidence, the external assets of the commercial banks have been drawn down. At present the currency board system provides the mechanism for correcting further disequilibrium in the balance of payments (though painfully through deflation). Most of Kenya's public debt is held externally (see Statistical Appendix, Table 25), and past borrowings already impose a substantial burden on foreign exchange resources. In 1961 payments on external debt and pensions were equivalent to about 12 percent of current export earnings.

The burden of repaying loans also bears on the budget. In 1962/63 interest and redemption payments on the public debt are estimated to amount to £4.86 million. Part of this will be met from the earnings of public bodies to whom the funds were re-lent, leaving £3 million to be borne by the exchequer. Net payments on the public debt now take about one-tenth of all receipts from taxation. As payments on some loans already drawn or contracted are not yet due, the amounts to be paid by Kenya on the public debt will rise automatically in the next few years, even without further borrowing for the 1963–67 program. A most unsatisfactory element in present borrowings is the contractor-finance scheme for main roads (see Chapter 7). Kenya has in essence borrowed £4.8 million on short term for road projects which will benefit the economy over a long period but will produce little extra revenue during the next few years when repayment is to be made. A similar obligation has been incurred for a Nairobi housing project (see Chapter 8). Payments to be made by the Government over the four-year period from July 1963 for these two schemes amount to £4.5 million. Kenya (with Tanganyika and Uganda) is also liable to meet payments on loans raised by the East African Common Services should those organizations fail to pay. In many ways, therefore, the cost of debt service will mount rapidly and add to the difficulties of bringing recurrent expenditure down to the level of budgetary resources.

It was suggested to us that in these circumstances Kenya should not borrow more during the next few years. Such a policy would in broad terms confine development expenditure to the amount of grants from abroad. It could also have adverse, rather than favorable, fiscal repercussions, by denying Kenya the benefits expected from promising agricultural projects that have already been started but require further investments to bring them into production. While the budgetary implications should be thoroughly explored in considering the composition of development programs, we do not believe that Kenya's unfavorable short-term budgetary prospects should be the sole determinant of development policy. We think that the aim should be to establish conditions that will enable a progressive growth in incomes to be achieved. In Kenya's circumstances, because of the low level of present earnings, the absence of attractive mineral deposits and the lack of experience in modern agricultural production, benefits from many well-founded development projects are likely to be long-drawn out, rather than immediate and spectacular. In borrowing, therefore, Kenya should seek loans at low rates of interest, repayable over an extended period.

External financial assistance can present other difficulties than the cost of repayment. Loans and grants may require the purchase of goods from the supplying country. If it disturbs trade patterns and investment priorities, this kind of assistance may be of little help to Kenya. While a desirable level of government expenditure may only be achieved with substantial external assistance, care is needed in considering offers of conditional aid.

The size of the suggested program has been limited by an assessment of possible financial resources. The total we have envisaged may not be reached. Only a small part of the amount required for the program (excluding land settlement) is at present assured, and new factors may arise to put the recurrent expenditures beyond the capacity of the annual budget. Changes in the supply of specialists may also call for adjustments to the program. A return of confidence and the resumption of substantial economic growth could provide increased revenues and improved prospects of internal borrowing. In these circumstances, an expansion of development expenditures might be possible in the last years of the plan. Flexibility, including an annual review of progress and expectations, is called for in the execution of any program to be adopted for the next few years.

East African Common Services Organization

We have received tentative programs from various undertakings of the East African Common Services Organization which are summarized on a calendar-year basis below and are discussed more fully in Chapter 7. In addition the Secretariat of the Organization expects to require nearly £100,000 a year for localization and training.

TABLE 3: Summary of EACSO Development Programs

(£ million)

	1963	1964	1965	1966	1967	Total
Civil Aviation	0.1	0.1	0.1	0.1	n.a.	—
Meteorology	0.2	0.1	0.1	0.1	n.a.	—
East African Railways and Harbours						
Railways	9.6	10.3	9.6	8.8	6.7	45.0
Harbors	1.2	0.9	0.8	1.2	1.4	5.5
Total	10.8	11.2	10.4	10.0	8.1	50.5
East African Posts and Tele-communications Department	0.8	1.0	1.0	1.0	1.0	4.8
East African Airways Corporation	0.9	0.8	0.6	0.3	0.3	2.9

The East African Railways and Harbours program of some £50 million consists of approximately £14.5 million for renewals, £11.5 million of betterment and £24 million of new capital expenditure. Of this expenditure, £18 million is to be met from within the Organization, leaving about £32 million to be sought elsewhere. The East African Airways Corporation's program is for the acquisition of aircraft for international services and to replace existing aircraft on internal routes. Special finance has, we understand, been arranged and the aircraft have been ordered.

In our discussion of priorities we have stressed the need for the Kenya Government to concentrate on projects likely to make the greatest contribution to the reconstruction and development of the economy, and we have endeavored to outline a program which meets these criteria and, if things go well, should be financially and physically attainable. But the future holds so much uncertainty that we have suggested that the program finally adopted should be flexible, reviewed annually and not committed too far ahead.

Our role in considering programs for the Common Services is primarily to advise the Kenya Government. The fact that a separate government body is responsible for providing these services in Kenya does not mean that their development should be regarded as distinct from the Government's own program. In the end, common services and territorial services, in broad terms, compete for financial resources at home and abroad. Similarly we think that priorities for the development of the common services should not be regarded as unrelated to priorities for territorial government services and we wish to stress the need for greater coordination in planning (see Annex A).

In considering the programs prepared by the East African Railways and Harbours and East African Posts and Telecommunications we have, therefore, endeavored to be guided by our assessment of priorities for Kenya during the next few years. EARH provides a basic service for the economy. Capacity on the railway and at the ports needs to be sufficient to handle the expected output and requirements of agriculture and industry. Generally we have found that capacity is at present sufficient and we see no need for major development works during the next few years. Investment to expand the railway and port undertaking would be expensive and, with so many uncertainties affecting the expansion of agricultural production over-all in Kenya during the next few years, we suggest that EARH, as well as the Kenya Government, should adopt a flexible approach to capital programing during the period.

Of the harbors program, £2.25 million is for works at Mombasa. A small part of this program is related to the establishment of the new oil refinery; most of the remainder is for the completion of two berths. Construction is not due to be started until 1965 and we suggest that a decision to commit the work be deferred as long as possible and the need then re-assessed.

Of the £31 million railway program, excluding renewals, £11 million is for new lines. Most of this expenditure is on railways in Tanganyika (£6 million) and Uganda (£1 million). We think that the provision of finance for these lines should be considered by the governments of those countries. The balance is for a new railway link between Tanganyika and Kenya, but this is not yet regarded as a firm project as a full economic study has to be undertaken, with £9.5 million for rolling stock, including some dieselization, and £8 million for track works. We suggest that these elements of the program be carefully and periodically reviewed in the light of traffic growth and expectations before being committed. In particular, we think it is difficult to justify capital expenditure to improve (rather than maintain) the operating capacity of the railway at this stage if it is not related to expected increases in traffic.

Our views on the development of EAPT are similar. Most of the expenditure contemplated is for the extension of telephone services, provision for which has been made by extrapolating the recent growth of demand. In the coming transitional period, demand for telephones can be greatly affected by changes in the racial composition and productive activity of the country and we think that only a minimum program should be contemplated to begin with. The program could then be adjusted in the light of experience.

Concluding Remarks

In preparing development programs for the coming years, the Kenya Government starts from a situation of great advantage in that so much has been done. The standards of some services are equal to the best in Africa, and agricultural extension and African education have been greatly expanded in recent years. But an insufficient number of Africans have been trained to assume major roles in economic life. Political change makes it more desirable to expand the training of Africans for these responsibilities; the departure of expatriates who are the managers, administrators, large-scale farmers, scientists and technicians in Kenya, makes it necessary.

During the next few years, emphasis should be placed on improving African farming in the nonscheduled areas to provide the expansion of production to support all other forms of development, and on secondary and specialist education to train the manpower to replace expatriates in the future. Expansion of manufacturing should also be encouraged, but Kenya's greatest immediate advantages lie in agriculture and it is critically important that present production, particularly in the scheduled areas, should continue.

To attain these aims, the retention of the services of many expatriates is essential, but the prospect for doing so is uncertain. The market outlook for many of Kenya's exports is also unfavorable and may restrict the possibilities for expanding incomes even if output increases. The financial position, especially of the recurrent budget, will limit the Government's development effort.

We have therefore suggested the main features of a four-year program, 1963/64–1966/67, but have recommended that expenditure should not be committed far ahead and plans should be recast in the light of an annual review of experience and expectations.

To make our work fit in with present practice, we have, apart from adding capital expenditure by statutory bodies, conformed to the accounting pattern of the Kenya Government's Development Estimates, but we do not regard our suggested development plans for an independent Kenya as merely an extension of past planning. While many programs should be completed and continued, some practices and standards, which may have been appropriate to conditions in which the economy was directed and sustained immediately by expatriates, will no longer apply. Kenya is a country with poor living standards but considerable agricultural potential. At this time of transition to independence, Kenya should adopt realistic and stable policies to maintain current production, and to provide an obviously firm foundation for future expansion—that is, for progressive improvement in the living standards of its people.

TABLE 4: Summary of Development Program Under Administrative Headings

(£ thousand)

	Estimates 1962/63	1963/64	1964/65	1965/66	1966/67	Total
Localization and Training	788	720	620	520	420	2,280
Administration	356	230	230	230	230	920
Irrigation	47	122	181	105	55	463
Board of Agriculture NSA[a]	169	220	220	220	220	880
Finance and Development	534	550	650	900	1,200	3,300
Police and Military	183	200	200	200	200	800
Prisons	86	75	75	75	75	300
Education	565	685	611	620	722	2,638
Agriculture[b]	1,511	1,795	1,856	1,826	1,793	7,270
Water	140	136	145	145	145	571
Commerce and Industry	382	235	235	235	235	940
Health	167	250	250	250	250	1,000
Housing	274	300	400	400	400	1,500
Social Services	5	20	20	20	20	80
Local Government	600	500	500	500	500	2,000
Lands and Surveys	200	180	180	180	180	720
Tourism and Wildlife[c]	82	100	100	100	100	400
Forests	418	370	355	370	355	1,450
Roads	1,386	740	800	800	800	3,140
Airports	134	20	20	20	20	80
Works	550	500	450	450	450	1,850
	8,577	7,948	8,098	8,166	8,370	32,582
Settlement	6,100	5,500	5,200	5,100	5,100	20,900
	14,677	13,448	13,298	13,266	13,470	53,482
Programs of Statutory Bodies, etc.		527	785	641	608	2,561
Total		13,975	14,083	13,907	14,078	56,043

[a] Includes rural piping schemes.

[b] Excludes provision for trading expenses of African Livestock Marketing Organization which are covered by receipts.

[c] Assumes £200,000 special finance.

MAIN CASH CROPS and FORESTS

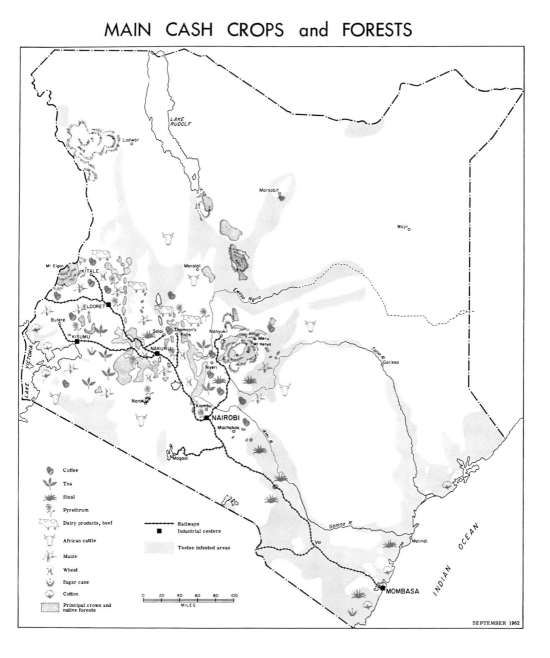

Coffee
Tea
Sisal
Pyrethrum
Dairy products, beef
African cattle
Maize
Wheat
Sugar cane
Cotton
Principal crown and
native forests

Railways
Industrial centers
Tsetse infested areas

0   20   40   60   80   100
MILES

LAKE
RUDOLF

Lodwar

Marsabit

Wajir

Mt Elgon
KITALE
Maralal
ELDORET
Butere
KISUMU
Solai
Thomson's
Falls
Nanyuki
Meru
Mt Kenya
Uaso Ngiro
NAKURU
Nyeri
Tana R
Garissa
Narok
Kiambu
NAIROBI
Machakos
Athi R
Magadi
LAKE VICTORIA
Galana R
Voi
Malindi
MOMBASA
INDIAN OCEAN

SEPTEMBER 1962

MEAN ANNUAL RAINFALL

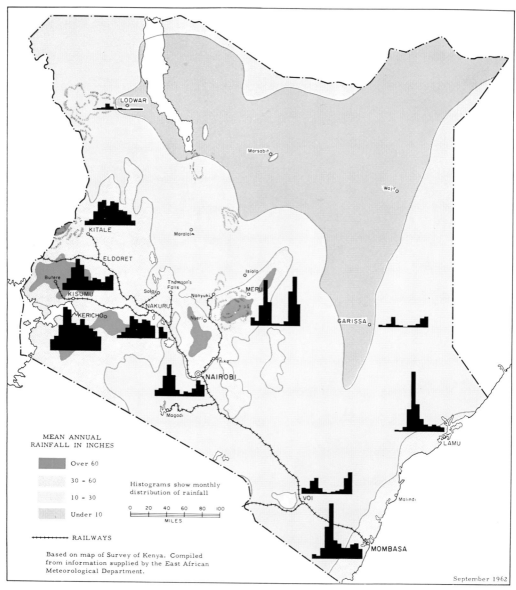

MEAN ANNUAL
RAINFALL IN INCHES

- Over 60
- 30 - 60
- 10 - 30
- Under 10

Histograms show monthly
distribution of rainfall

0 20 40 60 80 100
MILES

++++++ RAILWAYS

Based on map of Survey of Kenya. Compiled
from information supplied by the East African
Meteorological Department.

September 1962

PATTERN OF AGRICULTURE

The Role of Agriculture in Kenya's Economy

After reviewing the resources of Kenya, we have concluded that the country's rate of growth and improvement in the levels of living will continue to depend, in the next few years ahead, primarily on developments in the agricultural sector. It must, therefore, be accorded the highest priority in the allocation of resources, both financial and technical, in the over-all program of development. Primary industries—principally agriculture and livestock—have accounted for approximately 42 percent of Kenya's total product in recent years,[1] and their direct contribution to the economy has ranged from £83 million to £90 million for the past six years (through 1961). Furthermore, primary exports, ranging in value between £25 million and £36 million, have constituted between 85 percent and 90 percent of total export earnings.

Kenya's agriculture has been divided into two distinct sectors, formerly the "European" and "African" areas, now the scheduled and nonscheduled areas. The greater proportion of commercial production has come from the relatively small number of European and Asian holdings, of which there were 3,600 in 1961. The estimated gross income from the scheduled areas in 1961 was £35.9 million. The corresponding figure for the nonscheduled areas, covering an estimated 950,000 African farms, was £10.4 million. The imputed gross value of African subsistence production was £47 million in 1961.

Of the total African population, now about 7 million, it is estimated that more than 80 percent is engaged directly in the primary economy. The increase in gross revenue of African farmers has been of the order of 80 percent since 1956, over and above subsistence production which has also been increasing. The contribution of African farmers to export earnings is increasing markedly, along with their gross revenue, as a result of the establishment of cash crops on consolidated and enclosed African farms which has been a feature of the Swynnerton Plan.[2]

Around 55 percent of total export earnings from outside East Africa

---

[1] For details, see Statistical Appendix, Table 6.

[2] *A Plan to Intensify the Development of African Agriculture in Kenya*, compiled by R. J. M. Swynnerton, Colony and Protectorate of Kenya, Nairobi, 1954.

have been derived from coffee, tea and sisal products over the past seven or eight years, with coffee's share being around one-third of the total (see Statistical Appendix, Table 32). The fortune of pyrethrum has fluctuated, but it is once again of major importance. Earnings from meat and meat preparations have increased very significantly in recent years, but the contribution from wattle bark extract has declined substantially since 1954. Livestock and dairying produced around 25 percent of the total value of agricultural production in 1961. In export trade for that year, livestock contributed around 16 percent of the total receipts from products of agricultural origin.

Although there is a very great reliance on coffee, the economy of Kenya is not at first sight so vulnerable as many other underdeveloped countries because of a too great dependence on a single commodity. Production is comparatively diversified. The export picture does not fully reflect the extent of agricultural diversification, nor does it show the relative values of products to the economy. Many products, such as maize, rice, potatoes, sugar, oats and pulses are produced dominantly, if not solely, for home consumption, while wheat and barley are produced for East African and home consumption. Of the total gross income from crops and livestock products, cereals were responsible for around 15 percent, with wheat and maize being the most important.

Land Use

Although Kenya straddles the equator, nevertheless, due to its physical characteristics, the range of production conditions is wide. There is a comparatively narrow coastal belt with rainfall adequate for tropical agriculture, with a rapid transition to dry semidesert and desert conditions inland until the sharply modifying influences of the mountains are experienced. The highlands of Kenya are characterized by a higher rainfall, lower temperatures, diverse soil types and vegetation.

Of the total area of the country, however, only about 13 percent of 225,000 square miles receives a rainfall consistently above 30 inches annually, and is otherwise suitable for intensive livestock and crop production or mixed farming and plantation industries. Crop production is restricted to some 26 million acres in the highlands, the lands to the west extending to Lake Victoria and the narrow coastal strip. The remainder of the productive land is limited under present conditions to pastoral activities. The large, arid and sparsely populated Northern Province, which occupies 56 percent of the total land area, together with much of the Coastal and Southern Provinces, make very minor contributions to the economy. Kenya's economy rests basically on the lands of the southwest of the country.

The wide variations in climate and altitude, coupled with a variety of soils, largely determine the pattern of Kenya's agriculture, but population density, marketing facilities, tradition and tribal customs have also had a significant influence on the development of a varied pattern of land use. The cropping pattern varies from high altitude wheat, pyrethrum, tea and Arabica coffee through the sisal and cotton of the medium altitudes to the coconuts and cashew nuts of the tropical coastal belt. (For details of production, see Statistical Appendix, Table 10.) This wide variation is not an unmixed blessing. It complicates the problem of farm planning and farm development and, in particular, gives rise to a wide range of research problems with a consequent major need for qualified personnel to deal with problems of plant and animal breeding, selection of suitable varieties, maintenance of soil fertility and pest control, and the like.

A very significant proportion of the soils within the higher rainfall zone is inherently very fertile, being derived from volcanic ash or rock or a basement complex. Nevertheless, there is widespread incipient and sometimes acute phosphate deficiency which, with nitrogen deficiency, constitutes a major barrier to high yield performance. Erosion is an ever-present hazard once the natural vegetation has been removed or excessively exploited by grazing. Major emphasis in farming in the most advanced farming areas is placed on soil conservation measures such as terracing and cultivation along the contours, with careful grazing management where livestock is introduced.

The total area of the scheduled areas was 7.5 million acres in 1961. Census figures include, in addition to the highlands, a small area of the coastal strip, about 0.3 million acres. Census figures reveal that in 1961 the 3,600 farms or holdings vary in size from 20 acres to over 50,000 acres, with more than half the total number being less than 1,000 acres. They are farmed by individuals and partnerships and by companies. The cropped acreage of the scheduled area is around 15 percent or 1.14 million acres. The Ministry of Agriculture estimates that over 70 percent of the total scheduled land is uncultivated and suitable in the main only for grazing. The African or nonscheduled areas are composed of some 120 million acres, of which only 11.65 million acres receive sufficient rainfall in a normal year for the cultivation of crops.

Land Tenure

The tenure of European and Asian settlers, in general, is based on leaseholds. A 1902 ordinance provided for alienation of land on 99-year leases; some freeholds were also given. In 1915, another ordinance created 999-year leases and gave the earlier settlers the opportunity of changing over at higher rents. Many farmers did so and most of the land of the scheduled areas is held on that basis. We were informed that 560,000 acres are freehold; 591,000 are on 99-year lease; and 6,350,000 acres are on 999-year lease.

Land tenure in the nonscheduled areas is much more complex because of the variety of tribal attitudes to it. At one extreme are tribes which control large areas of land which they regard, under their customary laws, as common property, exclusive to the tribe as a whole, no tribal member having individual rights in it. A tribe member has the temporary use of such area as the tribal chief assigns to him and ceases to have any claim to it once he discontinues its cultivation or, as in shifting cultivation, moves to another assigned area. Tenure of this nature is one of the greatest obstacles to agricultural progress.

On the other hand, for many years some tribes have recognized individual rights to land and outright sales have been permitted, though no registered title of ownership exists. Even within the same tribe, however, attitudes may differ. The Kikuyu, the largest of the Kenya tribes, recognizes a form of outright family or individual ownership of land in some areas, but in other districts until recently its members claimed common tribal ownership of agricultural land which resulted from the clearing of forests.

Although reform toward individual land ownership was advocated by a Land Commission 30 years ago, the Native Lands Trust Ordinance, under which the present 31 million acres of African trust land have been administered, made no provision for individual title to agricultural land —though a negotiable title, in the form of registered lease, could be obtained in respect of land set aside for nonagricultural purposes. The customary concept of communal land ownership, however, has been giving place for some years to the idea of ownership with registered title. While such ownership and title represent only one factor in agricultural development, and will not of themselves bring about development, they represent a most important advance.

Extraordinary progress has been made in consolidating fragmented land and in enclosing individual holdings which is a principal feature of the Swynnerton Plan. As recently as 1955, when land consolidation on a large scale began, no African had security of land tenure or negotiable title to his agricultural holding; he had no acceptable collateral to offer against necessary loans for the development of his holdings; and his rights to the land were constantly under challenge in the courts. The 1956 Native Tenure Rules removed those obstacles and the 1959 Land Registration (Special Areas) Ordinance and the Kenya Land Order in Council opened the way to African land development under favorable

The second
kind of madness is far different from this. It comes from me and is to be
desired above all things. It arises whenever a cheerful confusion of the
mind frees the spirit from care and at the same time anoints it with many-
sided delight. It is the state of mind that Cicero desired as a defense against
the evils of his age. The Greek in Horace[8] had the right idea. He was
just sufficiently mad to sit alone in the theater all day, laughing and

103

applauding at a bare stage, because he thought that tragedies were being
enacted there. Otherwise he was sane enough—pleasant with his friends,
kind to his wife, and indulgent to his servants, who could uncork a bottle
without his getting angry. When the care of family and physician had freed
him of his disease, he protested that he had been killed rather than cured,
that they had taken away his pleasures and destroyed his delightful delu-
sions. And he was perfectly right. They were the mad ones themselves,
and needed the medicine more than he did. What sense is there in regarding a fortunate delusion like his as a disease to be purged with drugs?

It is not certain that every delusion and vagary ought to be called madness. A short-sighted man who thinks a mule is an ass is not commonly
considered insane, nor is one who judges popular music to be great poetry.
However, we must grant that a man is pretty nearly mad if he is continually
and extraordinarily deluded by both his senses and his judgment. Take, for
example, a person who thinks he is listening to a symphony orchestra
whenever an ass brays, or a beggar who believes himself to be Croesus.
Nevertheless, when this extreme madness gives pleasure, as it usually does,
it is remarkably delightful both to those who are possessed by it, and to
those who look on and are not mad in exactly the same way. Indeed this
kind of madness is much more common than the ordinary person realizes.
One madman laughs at another; they take turns entertaining each other.
And the maddest one gets the biggest laugh.

If Folly is any judge, the happiest man is the one who is the most thoroughly deluded. May he maintain that ecstasy. It comes only from me,
and is so widespread that I doubt if there is one man anywhere who is
consistently wise and untouched by some madness.

can prove it with a plain example. Is anyone happier than those we commonly call morons, fools, nitwits, and naturals—the most beautiful of names? This may sound absurd at first, but it is profoundly true. In the first place, these fools are free from the fear of death—and that fear is not an insignificant evil. They are free from the pangs of conscience. They are not terrified by ghosts and hobgoblins. They are not filled with vain worries and hopes. In short, they are not troubled by the thousand cares to which this life is subject. Shame, fear, ambition, envy, and love are not for them. If they were just a little dumber and more animal-like they would not even sin—or so the theologians say. Count your cares, you stupid intellectuals, and then you will begin to appreciate what I do for my followers. Remember also that they are always merry; wherever they go they bring pleasure, as if they were mercifully created by the gods to lighten the sadness of human life.

After a life of jollity, and with no fear of death, or sense of it, they go straight to the Elysian fields, where they entertain the pious and leisurely shades. Compare the life of a wise man with that of a fool. Put up against a fool some model of wisdom, one who lost his boyhood and youth in the classroom, who dissipated the best part of his life in continual worry and study, and who never tasted a particle of pleasure thereafter. He is always abstemious, poor, unhappy, and crabbed; he is harsh and unjust to himself, grim and mean to others; he is pale, emaciated, sickly, sore-eyed, prematurely old and white-haired, dying before his time. Of course it really makes little difference when such a man dies. He has never lived. Well, there is your wise man for you.

Here the Stoics croak at me again. Nothing, they say, is more lamentable than madness, and pure folly is either very near madness, or more likely is the same thing. What is madness but a wandering of the wits? But the Stoics wander the whole way. With the Muses' help we will explode this line of reasoning. The argument is plausible, but our opponents should remember the practice of Socrates in splitting Cupids and Venuses,[5] and distinguish one kind of madness from another—at least they should if they wish to be considered sane themselves. To begin with, not every kind of madness is a calamity. Otherwise Horace would not have said, "A pleasant madness inspires me."[6] Nor would Plato have ranked the frenzy of poets, prophets, and lovers among the chief blessings of life. And the oracle would not have called the labors of Aeneas, insane.[7] Madness is really of two kinds. The first is sent up from hell by the vengeful Furies.

conditions on a scale unprecedented in Kenya. Registered titles to land ownership are being issued as fast as the processes of administration permit; there is an urge to grow certain cash crops, a keenness to introduce grade livestock on the enclosed holdings. The following are the latest available statistics (June 30, 1962), on landholding in the nonscheduled areas:

Total area enclosed	2,390,000 acres
Total number of holdings enclosed	292,000
Total area registered for title	1,081,000 acres
Total number of holdings registered	186,000

This progress has also provided the basis for the implementation of the declared policy of government to aim at the progressive abolition of racial and tribal barriers to the holding of land by Africans. Practical effect is being given to the new policy by the settlement of Africans in the scheduled areas, in which they could not previously own land.

It has become increasingly recognized over the years that a sound system of tenure is the key to agricultural development. Whatever may be the merits of joint ownership of land suitable for pastoral use only, registered title is essential to the full development of agricultural land. It provides an incentive to improvement and it furnishes the security needed in order to obtain the loans required for development. The mission believes that an enormous potential has been opened up for African utilization. The extent to which this potential is realized will largely depend on provision by the Government of technical services and supplies to assist the new title owner to develop his farm.

Availability of Land

In general, it can be said that land suitable for development is not a limiting factor in the expansion of the major crops of Kenya. In most cases, the acreages under those crops could be expanded beyond the availability, in the current outlook, of remunerative markets.

In determining the scope for extending particular crops, a number of factors have to be taken into consideration. Altitude is a major criterion as to what can be produced efficiently or to best advantage, but to varying degrees rainfall, the soil and the slope are also determinants. Given suitable conditions of rainfall and soil, coffee of the arabica type can be produced efficiently almost anywhere between 4,800 feet and 7,000 feet. The Department of Agriculture estimates there are 260,000 acres suitable for coffee in the scheduled areas alone, though probably not more than half that area coud be actually planted to coffee without disturbing the pattern of mixed farming. No estimate for the nonscheduled areas was available to the mission, but the amount of suitable land for coffee is very much greater than can ever in the foreseeable future be planted with this crop in the light of world supply and demand.

Tea is grown mainly on acid or slightly acid soils between 6,000 feet and 7,200 feet, where rainfall is adequate in amount and distribution. A departmental estimate of the net acreage which could be planted to tea, including land already planted, without disturbing the present mixed farming pattern is around 123,000 acres. This figure understates the maximum area that is suitable for tea, of course. In the scheduled areas alone, nearly 75,000 acres had been licensed for planting with tea at the beginning of 1961. For the nonscheduled areas, it is estimated that at least 70,000 acres to 80,000 acres could be developed to tea.

The Department estimates the area of land in the scheduled areas suitable for sisal and grazing at 3.5 million acres. Of that total, slightly less than a quarter of a million acres are planted to sisal at present. No quantitative estimate of the extent of the suitable land in the nonscheduled areas is available, but it is known to be very large.

Pyrethrum grows very well above the 6,500-foot level. The Department estimates that around two-thirds of a million acres of land in the scheduled areas are suitable for pyrethrum growing, but only perhaps one-sixth to a third of this total could be put under pyrethrum without disrupting the existing pattern of agriculture. The area suitable for pyrethrum in the nonscheduled areas is not known precisely, but it is undoubtedly very much larger than the acreage required to fulfill world demand in the foreseeable future.

The scope for expanded acreage of other crops, such as maize, sugar cane and cotton, is great, although in the case of sugar cane and cotton the best results would be achieved by irrigation. The area suitable for rice production is large by comparison with that already established, but in this case there is dependence upon the provision of water. Wheat and barley are crops that may have a limited potential because of a shortage of suitable land.

Managerial practices are far more important than the availability of suitable land for the development of the livestock industries. The Department estimates that production could be increased fourfold by better selection and breeding, better nutrition through pasture improvement and controlled grazing of rangelands, better control of diseases and parasites, and limitation of numbers in accordance with grazing capacity. To this must be added, in the case of meat production, the willingness of livestock owners to market their livestock and not retain them for unremunerative purposes.

DEVELOPMENT OF FARMING

Since financial and technical resources available for future development are limited, priorities need to be considered. There is no need to restate the reasons why a very high priority should be accorded to agricultural development. The rate of future development of the economy and the trends in the average level of living of the people of Kenya will be determined largely by trends in production of export-earning and import-saving primary industries. The task of maintaining present levels of production with selective expansion of those products which can find remunerative markets will be far from easy.

Within the agricultural development program, the mission will emphasize that by far the best economic results will be forthcoming from investment in African farm consolidation, enclosure, and development along the lines set out under the Swynnerton Plan. In placing the highest priority upon this it must be remembered that an equally high priority must go to the technical support program, without which the scheme cannot succeed.

There is a very real danger that the combination of pressure for new settlement opportunities in areas already farmed intensively, and the general uncertainty among the non-African farmers and estate owners of the scheduled areas, will lead to a loss of production and export earnings in the years immediately ahead; this loss could seriously retard progress and development of the Kenya economy as a whole. Already there is some evidence of disinvestment on farms and estates due to uncertainty. This comes at a time when further investment in particular industries, such as the livestock industries, tea and sisal, would be to the advantage of the economy. Measures to arrest disinvestment and to encourage selective investment should, in the general interest of the economy, be introduced.

The mission would also emphasize that all the large holdings in Kenya are by no means depriving African farmers or potential farmers of settlement opportunities: to mention two rather clear-cut examples, the livestock ranches in the zones of medium rainfall and the sisal industry. On the other hand, there undoubtedly are large holdings in Kenya that are suitable for subdivision into small farms; and as they become available for purchase (assuming that funds are available) they should be the subject of soundly conceived settlement schemes. A comparatively high priority also should be given to the development of irrigation settlement opportunities. The preinvestment survey of the Lower Tana may well open up such opportunities.

It may well be that the bottleneck in Kenya's agricultural development will not be a lack of high priority projects, or funds to finance them, but rather it will be a shortage of experienced professional personnel to organize and supervise the projects. This means that prime consideration should be given to measures aimed at retaining Kenya's present professional and technical staff, if possible at attracting more to the service, and above all at greatly increasing the flow of personnel into and out of training institutions.

THE NONSCHEDULED AREAS

The present comprehensive plans for agricultural development in the nonscheduled areas are based on the Swynnerton Plan which was introduced in 1954. The purpose of the Plan was to develop a modern system of farming by Africans. The Plan covered all aspects of production from land ownership to marketing of cash crops and livestock. Land consolidation and enclosure, and the granting of title to individual farmers, provided the basis for the development of production for the market under appropriate systems of cultivation.

From many aspects, the Plan has been remarkably successful. In the intensive and semi-intensive zones suitable for mixed farming the results are rather unique in the history of development of underdeveloped countries. What has been achieved in the consolidated, enclosed, and planned districts stands as a model for future development, not only in relation to Kenya, but to many other underdeveloped countries of the world.

Over the period 1954–60 the total expenditure on the Swynnerton Plan has been estimated at £10.9 million. It is difficult to assess all the benefits, some of which cannot be expressed in monetary terms—the higher living standards of the participating farm families, for instance. But it has been estimated that as a result of consolidation and farm development the income from cash crops has risen from £5.2 million in 1954 to £7.1 million in 1960. This magnitude of increase is in no way indicative of what increases in revenue may eventually be achieved when account is taken of the time lag between investment and returns in the livestock industries and such crops as tea and coffee.

Under the Plan, special attention has been given to providing African farmers with holdings of economic size and providing them with the necessary technical advice in farm layout and management. The determination of a minimum sized economic holding is sometimes based on acreage as related to soil, rainfall and topography but in general is related to a realistic concept of what is necessary to provide for £100 in cash income annually for the farm family above what is necessary to meet subsistence requirements and normal debt servicing. The introduction of a cash crop with reasonably assured returns is stressed, not only to provide the cash for the family needs in and above subsistence, but, particularly, to meet repayments of the loans required for planting materials, farm development, foundation livestock, housing and water facilities. The necessary mechanical measures for soil conservation are introduced at the outset. On the assumption that each family would have planted a particular acreage by the end of the 15-year period in the appropriate zone for the crop, a phased 15-year target was set for such crops as coffee, pyrethrum, tea, pineapples and sugar cane. The introduction of improved livestock is part of the scheme. These provide better family nutrition, regular cash income and play an essential role in balanced mixed farming designed to preserve long-term fertility.

The Swynnerton Plan still forms in general the basis of current policy for the development of African agriculture. While in the past it has served the needs excellently, nevertheless many circumstances have changed since it was drawn up and some changes in plans are now necessary.

TABLE 1: Classification of Land in Nonscheduled Areas

Category	Description	Characteristics	Area Square Miles	Remarks
A.	High Potential; arable	25–35" rainfall; soil good	18,197	Includes all the arable land in the non-scheduled areas.
B.	High Potential; grazing	25–35" rainfall; soil mainly shallow; fertility and drainage problems	10,293	The Department would discourage arable farming in this area unless for exceptional reasons.
C.	Low Potential; grazing	20–25" rainfall; bush and tsetse country	14,840	Regarded as doubtfully suited to organized ranching at present stock prices and with indigenous livestock.
D.	Very Low Potential; grazing	20–10" or less of erratic rainfall	147,884	Best use is thought to be for nomadic wild animals or, less so, for strictly nomadic stock keeping.

SOURCE: Land classification made by Ministry of Agriculture and Animal Husbandry.

The emphasis in the cash crops, for instance, needs to be changed. The coffee target of 71,500 acres by 1968, compared with 58,000 acres planted in 1962, needs urgent review in the light of marketing problems. The pyrethrum industry will need to be expanded carefully in accordance with what can be marketed, at remunerative prices, rather than to meet an arbitrary target. On the other hand, greater emphasis in the development of African agriculture can now be placed upon particular crops such as sisal and oil crops. Also, there are certain elements of the livestock improvement program which need review.

Details of changes proposed by the mission are dealt with more fully under the programs for development for particular crops and products, at the end of this chapter. The mission emphasizes, however, that an important basic principle of the Swynnerton Plan might well be restated in relation to future development: "whenever possible schemes should become self-supporting."

Development of the High-Potential Land[3]

Wider application of known techniques could greatly increase the production of both subsistence and cash crops in the agricultural areas that are predominantly African. Approximately four-fifths of the total acreage of high-potential land is in the nonscheduled areas. On such good land, farms of an average size of ten arable acres can, under very good supervision and management, yield a gross annual income of around £390 after the tree crops come into full bearing and the small dairy herd is established. At the time of the mission's visit, only about one-sixth of the high-potential land in the nonscheduled areas had been consolidated or enclosed or both.

Some tribes are agriculturally minded, others are not. But some tribes are in the possession of land suitable for intensive production but will neither put it to a more intensive use nor admit to their lands farmers from other tribes. And as we have mentioned, other tribes have shown the greatest reluctance to move from their home into settlement areas.

In contrast is the progressive attitude of the people in many districts toward land consolidation. This is essentially a voluntary process and the Government has collaborated with the landholders. In 1955, the consolidation and enclosure of the first complete district was undertaken by Government with the voluntary collaboration of the African landholders concerned. Subsequently, other districts have been similarly transformed. Enthusiasm has swept through some tribes to such an extent that, of their own effort and with only official encouragement but not

[3] The classification of the land in the nonscheduled areas is given in Table 1.

assistance, they have agreed upon individual boundaries and have enclosed their holdings over complete districts.

Land Consolidation and Enclosure

It is estimated that enclosed and consolidated farms numbered nearly 300,000 and covered 2.4 million acres of land in the nonscheduled areas at the end of June 1962. Official sources estimate that there still remain to be consolidated 5,200 square miles (3.3 million acres) of fragmented arable land of high potential in the nonscheduled areas. The mission visualizes the consolidation of about half of this area by 1967.

The preparation of a program of land consolidation for the coming years involves a considerable degree of guesswork since consolidation is a process in which execution depends on the voluntary demand of landowners for it and on the availability of sufficient staff.

The mission has provided for the continuation of consolidation and enclosure at the present rate. It has been very difficult to assess the effect of the new program of high-density settlement in the scheduled areas which, as it calls for similar kinds of expertise and is to be given priority, may, in addition to the general factors which will bear on the supply of staff in the next few years, reduce staff available for consolidation. So much experience has by now been gained in enclosure and consolidation that it may be possible to maintain the present rate of progress with a smaller experienced staff. We have therefore provided for the maintenance of roughly the present rates of expenditure on land consolidation (including land consolidation surveys). We estimate that about one-third of the total expenditure of about £1.5 million over the four years 1963–67 may be recovered in land consolidation fees.

In several places in this report we have stressed the importance we attach to the consolidation of high-potential land in the nonscheduled areas. The removal of fragmentation provides the foundation for progress in agriculture. The high-potential arable land in the nonscheduled areas provides the main scope for agricultural development in Kenya.

Farm Development

Although it was believed a fund of £2 million would be required once the Swynnerton Plan got into full stride, it was suggested in the report that the comparatively small sum of £200,000 be set aside as "the start of a Loan (or Land) Bank for African farmers."[4] The ceiling of the loan

[4] *Op. cit.,* p. 55.

for which any one farmer might become eligible was proposed to be £200. We discuss the provision of agricultural credit in Chapter 9.

Estimates of the gross returns attainable under good management and full production, after seven to ten years, based on present prices, indicate an average of around £390, of which around £280 would accrue to the farm family to meet any outstanding loan commitments and to pay for living requirements in and above subsistence (which in the main is provided by the farm). Thus, for example, 10,000 of such farms of an average size of 10 acres would produce cash crops to the value of £3.9 million, a large proportion of which would be from exportable crops. As the land before consolidation would not be producing very much by way of cash crops, it could be said that at least £3 million of this increase would be the result of the farm consolidation and development program.

The mission considers that every effort should be made to raise the farm development program to the level of 5,000 farms per year. The basic credit requirements to achieve this result would be the annual provision of £1 million of short-term (five years) credit, which would need to be extended mainly against potential, with livestock as limited chattel security. Long-term credit would be extended against the security of the land and structure.

The mission is aware, however, that a goal of 5,000 additional farms per year would be difficult to reach as a practical matter. At present there is difficulty in attaining half this rate. Farms need first to be provided by extension officers with a basic layout in order that an appropriate pattern of farming may be adopted. Thereafter, until development work has been undertaken by the farmer, and, for example, pastures established for dairy cattle, the farm will not be ready to benefit from much of the investment which is envisaged. A £1 million development loan from the World Bank, which was to be advanced to farmers by 1963, was not taken up at the anticipated rate: only around one-third of the loan had been used by the middle of the three-year period, 1960–63.

The livestock program for the mixed farming areas has required the development of reticulated water facilities, which allow better control over disease than would communal drinking centers. The objective is to keep the exotic breeds of stock from contact with indigenous disease carriers. It is impossible to work out the costs and benefits of this element of the rural development plan but it can be said that without this water supply the program could not succeed. The Board of Agriculture (non-scheduled areas) has been responsible for the installation of these reticulated facilities with funds provided by Government from various sources, including development loans from the Colonial Development

Corporation and the World Bank. The capital cost is recovered through an annual water rate payable by each holding, village, school, and so on. The amount payable annually appears to be such that the total sum collected over the period for which the loan was obtained (20 years) will be sufficient to repay the full amount of the loan and interest involved. The mission assumes that charges will continue to be made for the water and that necessary maintenance expenditure will be met from these charges. The District Councils are responsible for maintaining and operating these projects.

A development program of piped water supplies costing over £3 million has been proposed by the Water Resources Authority, but the mission sees no prospect of being able to finance so large a program within the next five years. We recognize the great importance of development of water supplies and have provided £600,000 in its suggested program for the next four years for some of the more important projects. This would allow the implementation of schemes in the first two priority classes as proposed, with the exception of an immense scheme for Kiambu, which should be phased over a longer period than five years. We envisage that about £50,000 a year could be devoted to it within the program. We have included expenditures on other types of water projects in our program at about their present level (for details see Table 5).

Development of Lands of Medium and Low Potential

In addition to four-fifths of the high-potential land in Kenya, nine-tenths of the medium-potential land is in the nonscheduled areas. In the absence of irrigation, emphasis must continue to be upon livestock production in areas of medium rainfall. The true potential of these areas cannot be quickly realized since heavy expenditures on water development, fencing, and disease and pest control are necessary, together with the creation of managerial skills. Nevertheless, with cooperative or communal organization, efficient large-scale ranching by Africans could in the long term be achievable. Over the next few years, however, little can be anticipated no matter what measures are introduced. The progressive deterioration of the land and of the stock has not yet been arrested throughout the pastoral areas, and until this is done the rate of increased production from them will at best be slow.

The semidesert and desert regions present a social problem that needs attention, but do not offer attractive possibilities of increased production, except under irrigation in certain areas, within the foreseeable future.

The farm-planning program also applies to the semi-intensive areas, with emphasis on such cash crops as sisal and improved livestock that would be more appropriate than the exotic European breeds which are used in the highlands.

In the semiarid pastoral areas, emphasis has been placed on reducing livestock numbers and improving managerial practices; regular markets were to be provided to enable the reduction of stock to be attained. Improvements in water supplies, controlled grazing and tsetse reclamation are essential features of the program. The Swynnerton Plan stressed that wherever possible, schemes in these areas should become self-supporting in 10–15 years. Similarly, district irrigation boards were to begin contributing to the cost of swamp reclamation and irrigation within five years.

In the purely pastoral zones of lower rainfall, progress has been slow. Although there have been excellent demonstrations of the capacity of badly depleted overgrazed areas to regenerate when livestock are removed or brought under control, and of the economic advantages of rotational grazing with controlled numbers of livestock, nevertheless there is still the task ahead of achieving widespread adoption of the basic principles. But the necessity of improving the utilization of grazing lands is so great, because of its social implication, that this element of the Plan may be justified even though the economic results have been anything but spectacular.

Land Settlement

The African Settlement Board was set up as part of Kenya's Ten-Year Development Plan, 1946–55, to organize settlement schemes in the nonscheduled areas. In the intervening years various boards have successively replaced the original African Settlement Board. Working in conjunction with African District Councils, the boards have provided large sums of money to initiate and develop settlement schemes in the nonscheduled areas, with one or other objective, in all provinces except the Northern. Initially, settlement appears to have been largely a relief measure which would provide fresh fields for those whose original land had deteriorated seriously because of unchecked soil erosion or other reasons. Subsequently this limited objective was broadened in scope; it now includes movement of people in order to relieve intense pressure in regions which are overpopulated, to provide a means of livelihood for landless people, and to afford greater opportunities for progressive African cultivators. As we have already mentioned, there are no longer any legal restraints on the areas where Africans can own or farm land, but tribal restrictions still remain. It is estimated that from 1945 to 1958 the resettlement of about 17,000 families was financed by the government agencies; more recent figures are not available.

The Board of Agriculture (nonscheduled areas) has financed land settlement schemes and a variety of rural development schemes in the nonscheduled areas, among them general agricultural betterment schemes. Expenditures have amounted to more than £100,000 a year under the present Development Program, and we have included the same annual amount as 1962/63 (£116,000) in our suggested program for the continuation of these projects.

Irrigation

As yet irrigation plays a minor role in crop production. There is undoubted scope for considerable extension of irrigated cultivation from small projects using local supplies of water and requiring limited capital expenditure. But the greatest potential is with schemes for intensive irrigation of large acreages.

Government-controlled schemes were initiated originally during the Mau Mau Emergency to provide work for detainees, and therefore they should not be expected to prove economic. Nevertheless, one very important result has been achieved; it has been demonstrated that African families with experience only of dryland farming can adapt themselves to efficient intensive production under irrigation. Irrigation schemes devoted to the settlement of African families in the nonscheduled areas are in operation at Mwea, where 5,000 acres are under rice, at Perkerra, where 1,600 acres have been developed, and at Galole, on the Lower Tana, where a pilot project of 1,200 acres has been developed. There is much yet to be learned about the best approach to irrigation farming, but the results so far are very promising. Exceptionally high yields of rice have been obtained on black cotton soils, with net returns of £130 accruing from four-acre sites.

Irrigation is limited by the amount of water that could be made available for the purpose by the major catchments of Kenya—the Nile Basin, the Tana catchments, the Ewaso Ugiro, the Athi, and the Lumi Basin. These, with miscellaneous catchments, provide a total annual runoff of the whole country of 10 million acre-feet. Forty-five percent of this flows into Lake Victoria and abstractions of water for irrigation purposes are subject to international agreement; it is not expected that a high proportion of the total runoff into the Lake would be available for irrigation development. The ultimate irrigation potential of Kenya might not be greater than 1 million acres distributed as follows: Upper Tana, 93,000 acres; Lower Tana, 400,000; Kenya Nile, 253,000; Ewaso Ngiro

Basin, 75,000; Athi River Basin, 75,000; Lumi Basin (Taveta), 20,000; and Malawa and other minor catchments, 80,000 acres.[5]

The Tana River Catchment

Important investigations of irrigation potential have been made in the Tana River catchments. In the Upper Tana catchment area, it has been established that there is sufficient water and suitable soil available for the development of 15,000 acres of black soil for rice growing and 8,000 acres of red soil for such crops as tomatoes, onions, citrus, beans and fodder for livestock in the vicinity of Mwea. In addition, it would be possible to irrigate nearly 70,000 acres of coffee and to develop other schemes. The total irrigable acreage was estimated to be 93,000 acres. Considerable hydrological data are available to support this assessment.

Mwea-Tebere Project. This project, which embraces 5,000 acres of irrigated rice and provides 1,250 formerly landless tenant families with a very reasonable living, has been a remarkable success. Kenya proposes to extend the present area under this project to 14,000 acres in two phases during the years to 1967, one of 2,000 acres and one of 7,000 acres.

The area of black cotton soil suitable for irrigation and rice growing on and adjoining the project is 15,300 acres. Irrigation supplies from existing sources are more than adequate for this area. The present headworks and structures are designed to meet the long-term water requirements of 15,000 acres of land which can be readily commanded by the main canal.

The mission supports the execution of the first extension of 2,000 acres, and has included the balance of the capital costs (£158,000) for this purpose in the first two years of its suggested program. It is expected that additional recurrent costs will be met from revenues of the project. We advise a cautious attitude toward the proposed second extension for the present, and particularly until research in progress produces rice of the quality which can replace imports more completely or until markets are assured.

Lower Tana Project. Although the irrigation potential of the Upper Tana and the hydroelectric potential of the Middle Tana have been investigated in some detail by well-known firms of consulting engineers, no detailed or comparable study has yet been made of the Lower Tana. The Government of Kenya has drawn up plans for a preinvestment sur-

[5] This analysis of irrigation potential of Kenya is based on information supplied by the Ministry of Works and Communications.

vey of the irrigation potentialities of the Lower Tana, to be followed by the preparation of plans for its phased development.

In the Lower Tana near Galole, there are some 300,000 acres of potentially suitable and commandable soils which could be irrigated. It is contended that sufficient is known about the hydrology of the river to state that some 75,000 acres could be irrigated without storage. Storage sites could open still greater possibilities. The Lower Tana catchment appears to offer Kenya's best prospects for large-scale low-cost irrigation development. Much detailed investigation of soils, crops and crop varieties, crop rotations, the water requirements of crops, economic irrigation design, appropriate storage sites and markets is necessary before this project could be proposed for major investment. Assistance for a preinvestment survey is being provided by the United Nations Special Fund. The total cost of this survey project is still uncertain, but we have included £236,000 in our suggested program to cover Kenya's share of the expenditures, which may be in the order of 35 percent of the total.

Steadily increasing pressure of population in the relatively small proportion of the lands of Kenya where rainfall is adequate to sustain crop production and arable farming is such that all possible outlets for fresh settlement in underdeveloped regions should be explored. If present expectations are supported by the proposed survey, it is believed that the full development of the Lower Tana can provide an assured source of livelihood for upward of 75,000 families on the land, exclusive of a large population representing trade, commerce and services which will follow automatically.

The mission strongly supports the survey which is expected to take three years. It involves the preliminary reconnaissance and the preparation of contour maps of an estimated 3 million acres of desert hinterland, the more detailed survey, investigation and mapping within that region of the most suitable areas, estimated currently at 1.2 million acres and the preparation of a plan of development, determination of area, etc., from the resulting information. It includes hydrological studies of the whole Tana catchment area, which are essential for the ultimate preparation of a planned multipurpose development plan for the water resources of the entire Tana basin. In our view an economic appraisal should also be included as it is an essential element of any complete preinvestment study.

The Galole Project. Originally started about 1955 as a penal settlement for Kikuyu detainees, this farm has been used for the collection of data and information bearing on the possibilities and economics of irrigation farming on the Lower Tana. Its chief use at present is for cultiva-

tion on yearly leases by Kikuyu or local tribesmen who are either landless or in a position only to cultivate on a subsistence basis. The area of
the farm has just been increased from 500 acres to 1,200 acres. It is possible that at some time in the future the extension of the present area may
be desirable for experimental purposes if the development of the Lower
Tana under irrigation farming is undertaken.

Kenya Nile Basin

Kano Plain Pilot Project. The consulting engineers who made an assessment in 1954–56 of the potentialities of irrigation development and
swamp reclamation within the Kenya Nile basin recommended that development of this plain should receive first priority in the development
of the basin as a whole. Irrigation would be provided by pumping from
Lake Victoria, supplemented by gravity flow from Nyando River. The
irrigation potential of the Kano Plain was assessed at 30,000 acres and
development was proposed on the basis of two main cash crops, sugar
cane and rice, in equal areas.

Because of the lack of information on the crops to be irrigated in this
area, the consultants recommended the establishment of an experimental farm to study the growing of sugar cane under irrigation and the
construction of pilot schemes to determine, among other things, the
cropping systems and size of holdings best suited to small-scale irrigated
farming.

The mission strongly supports the proposal to establish a pilot irrigation project on the Kano Plain. The project should be designed to
achieve two main purposes. It should provide basic data essential to ensure eventual development of the Plain on the soundest lines. It is
hoped too that the project will help to overcome the reluctance of many
tribesmen to participate in a development of the Plain under irrigation.
The estimated capital cost of the project is £70,000.

In the Kano Plain area, which has promising prospects for much
more intensive use, particularly with the development of supplementary
irrigation, the attitude of the Luo tribesmen presents a major obstacle.
Although there is no individual land ownership, members of the clan
have cultivating and grazing rights in parcels of land within the area,
as well as rights of communal grazing. Development under irrigation
will involve major reallocations of land rights and property boundaries.
It will further necessitate the movement of some of the inhabitants to
homes elsewhere to provide holdings of economic size for those who remain and reduction in the number of livestock now maintained. The
tribesmen have shown reluctance so far to accept these changes.

Investigations of the Ewaso Ngiro River, which runs northward out of Central and Rift Valley Provinces into the drier pastoral areas of the Northern Frontier Province, indicate that some 100,000 acres could be developed, much of it to fodder crops such as lucerne to be used as an adjunct to ranching.

Our proposals for capital expenditures on irrigation projects outlined in this section total £463,000 for the years 1963/64 to 1966/67 for the Mwea-Tebere first extension, the Lower Tana investigation and the Kano Plain project (see Table 5).

THE SCHEDULED AREAS

The major proportion of the scheduled areas of high potential has been fairly intensively developed on the initiative of the Kenya settler farmer. In addition to developing their individual farms, these farmers have contributed to the general development of agricultural knowledge and the adoption of agricultural techniques suited to conditions in the Kenya highlands. There is, however, a wide variation in farming efficiency as between farms in the scheduled areas which has not been wholly dictated by environmental factors, and there is considerable scope for further intensification. The history of pioneering, as in so many countries, has in many cases been one of clearing first those areas of land which appear the easiest to handle and immediately the most profitable. There was a natural tendency to concentrate too much upon the one crop that seemed at the outset the most profitable and to grow it on the same land until yields fell away. Such monoculture in the past caused much soil deterioration and erosion, and there is still evidence of this malpractice—despite the sweeping powers of control vested in the hands of the Minister of Agriculture and Animal Husbandry.[6]

The efficiency of European farming has been influenced by a number of other factors, such as initial inexperience of a proportion of the settlers, prejudices for breeds of livestock not best suited to Kenya, listening to the wrong advice, not heeding the right advice, and so forth. Increased production on present acreages is undoubtedly held back by the lack of success in finding solutions to persistent farm problems. Research has not yet provided suitable legumes to maintain the fertility of grazing lands, for instance. And there is as yet no satisfactory control for wheat rust, which for some reason mutates very freely in Kenya. There is also a gap between research findings and application of the findings

[6] The Agriculture Ordinance, 1955, gives the Minister the power to determine what crop the farmer can grow and where he can grow it, as well as other powers.

on the farm—the use of artificial fertilizer is a good example. Suffice it to say that the scope for more efficient production in the high-potential lands of the scheduled areas is still large.

Ranching, the chief activity in the areas of medium rainfall, has special hazards—predators, parasites, water limitations and thorn bush encroachment. To control these hazards requires heavy expenditures; hence efficiency of production is related to the scale of operations and managerial ability. Where operations are on a large scale, and management is good, impressive results have been achieved within the past two decades in both sheep and cattle enterprises. There is much scope, however, for increased production within established holdings or extensions. The average wool clip is only around five pounds per wool sheep in the scheduled areas. There is a wide variation in performance, some of which is due to environmental variation, but much due chiefly to management. A big improvement based on existing technology could be achieved.

Further development requires sustained capital investment. With political stability and anticipation of its continuance, the rate of increased production of recent years could be sustained and even increased.

Land Settlement

The development of Kenya's highlands to their present high degree of agricultural intensity is, of course, the result of a land settlement policy that brought Europeans in large numbers into this area, especially between the two world wars. It is due largely to the export earnings from this region that the economy of Kenya has been able to develop at the comparatively rapid rate that it has.

After World War II a European Settlement Board was set up to assist people, with initial emphasis on ex-servicemen, who wished to settle on the land. Large estates, established in the earlier years of settlement, were broken up gradually into smaller units for more intensive development and it became possible for new arrivals with experience of agriculture to settle either as Assisted Owners or as Tenant Farmers on farms of sizes appropriate to their individual means. In the former case the settler purchased the land and, where required, the Board granted him long-term loans for developing it; in the latter the Board purchased the land, leased it to the settler and granted loans for permanent improvements, the settler himself stocking the farm and providing the working capital. He had the option to purchase the farm during the period of his tenancy. The Board obtained its resources from a fund of £2 million in land and cash provided by Government.

By 1960, the Board had settled 493 farmers; 282,000 acres of land were held on lease from it; a further 199,000 acres were held on first mortgages as security for loans advanced or outstanding on farms being purchased from it.

African Settlement in the Scheduled Areas

In 1960 the Kenya Government introduced settlement schemes by which Africans seeking to farm in the scheduled areas could be aided financially both to purchase the land and to develop it. Arrangements for finance were made with the United Kingdom and Federal German Governments, the Colonial Development Corporation and the World Bank. Three types of schemes were introduced:

a. *Assisted Owner Scheme for experienced farmers* with substantial capital; each holding to be sufficiently large to provide the settler and his family with subsistence, the means of meeting his financial obligations and a minimum annual net income of £250.

b. *Smallholder Settlement Scheme for experienced farmers* with some capital; each holding to provide for subsistence, financial obligations and a minimum annual net income of £100 (the target under the Swynnerton Plan in the nonscheduled areas).

c. *Smallholder Settlement Scheme* for Africans with limited capital and agricultural knowledge; to provide subsistence plus a minimum annual net income of £25–40.

Under all three schemes settlers make a down payment of 10 percent of the price of the land, and of the cost of permanent improvements and permanent crops. The remainder of the purchase price and development finance is provided in the form of long-term loans. The aim was to settle at least 1,000 assisted owners, 6,000 experienced smallholders, and 12,000 other smallholders by the middle of 1964. The total cost of the scheme was some £12 million. World Bank and CDC loans are intended to finance development loans to settlers in the first two schemes only.

Actual settlement began slowly. Farms had to be purchased from willing sellers, divided up for settlement in accordance with the pattern of farming envisaged, and road access and other services provided before the new holdings could be sold and the new owners settled. By the end of 1961 about one dozen assisted owners and 150 smallholders had taken up their land.

In July 1962 the United Kingdom Government announced a major expansion of the third or high-density settlement scheme to settle annually 200,000 acres of mixed farming land over a five-year period up to the middle of 1967, with the possibility of the adoption of a further scheme at the end of the period. The first two schemes would also be carried out over five years, instead of about three years as originally intended, to enable staff to concentrate on the enlarged high-density scheme.

It is envisaged that between 50,000 and 70,000 families will be settled under the new program. The target income under the high-density scheme remains very much the same—basic subsistence needs plus a cash income of £25–40 a year. Development loans of an average of £100 per family and subsistence grants of £18 for the first six months will be provided.

The total cost of the revised program over five years is likely to be £25–30 million, of which perhaps about 40 percent would be for land purchase, a slightly smaller amount for development loans, and the balance for subsistence grants, presettlement work and administrative costs. The additional finance is being provided almost entirely by the United Kingdom Government in the form of loan and grant, though the Land and Agricultural Bank is expected to contribute about £1 million from funds obtained from repayments of mortgage loans by European farmers whose farms are purchased.

Only part of the former "white highlands" is contemplated to be subject to the scheme. The area chosen is contiguous with nonscheduled areas and is largely devoted to mixed farming. The areas around Kitale and Nakuru have been excluded, at least for the first five years, with the aim that they would continue to produce grain and dairy products necessary to feed the nonfarming population. In these excluded areas it is contemplated that suitable Africans, and also Europeans from the settlement areas, would have the opportunity to borrow from the Land Bank to buy farms from European farmers who may decide to sell.

When the revised high-density scheme was announced it was stated that the scheme would be the first charge on development funds provided by the United Kingdom.[7] We have accordingly regarded the scheme as a firm element in Kenya's development program for the next few years but, in considering the size and composition of the remainder of an outline program for the period 1963–67, we have given some thought to the possible impact of the scheme on the economy generally and on possible resources for development.

The principal objectives of the scheme appear to be primarily political. There are many landless people and land in the "white highlands" is coveted because until recently it was denied the African people. If

[7] *Kenya Calling*, Kenya Government Information Services, Nairobi, July 14, 1962.

European farmers decided to leave their farms, an uncontrolled influx of African claimants could lead to major intertribal strife. High-density settlement in part of the scheduled areas on the scale proposed is designed to meet African aspirations for land and at the same time provide the European farmer who decides to leave with a purchaser for his farm. The decision to exclude the area around Nakuru and Kitale, besides seeking to maintain production of local foodstuffs, also offers opportunities to European farmers who wish to remain and to Africans who desire to farm on a larger scale.

The economic consequences of the scheme cannot be assessed reliably for some years. They will not be confined to the scheduled areas, and many factors at present unknown to us (including the burden of loan finance) would have to be taken into consideration. It is not only a scheme for the transfer of land ownership. The deliberate replacement of large-scale with small-scale production may mean the destruction of capital assets and the adoption of less efficient forms of production. In some circumstances, a smallholder could increase production on his holding over that previously yielded by large-scale farming, by reason of a greater intensity of cropping and cultivation. Equally a fall in production can be visualized, due to the loss of the benefits of large-scale farming and, for instance, to growing crops less suited to small-scale farming or to poor farming practices. It can mean the replacement of current production with a system of farming which would take time to attain its full potential. It would appear that no great increase in the number of people engaged in agriculture can be expected, as a result of the settlement schemes, because farmers in the scheduled areas have been large employers of labor.

The high-density settlement scheme has many doubtful aspects. Emphasis seems to be placed on the numbers to be settled rather than on the suitability of the size of the holding for efficient production. We think it is just as important for the African farmer that he should be able to farm on a reasonable scale as it is for the highly mechanized commercial farmer. Provision in farm size for the narrow margin of £25–40 net income for a family over subsistence is, in our view, inadequate to cover fluctuations in the price of the main cash product and seasonal adversity. Much will, of course, depend on the extent of the effort of the family, knowledge of good farming practice and extension assistance. The mission recommends that settlers should have sufficient farming experience, or, if not, should receive training before taking up their farms.

At best the scheme can be viewed as a measure designed to remove tension and uncertainty and to arrest the probable fall in production in the scheduled areas which still produce the great majority of the marketed agricultural output of the country. It is not a scheme to change from large-scale to small-scale farming in expectation of economic benefits. Indeed, where conditions are appropriate, we suggest that consideration should be given to ways of organizing African settlement to maintain large-scale farming. The schemes may also have adverse effects on development in the nonscheduled areas, where the principal opportunities for economic development are to be found. The application of specialized manpower to assist in the implementation of the settlement program may seriously deplete the force of extension officers available to encourage sound farm development. The size of the program itself may also be beyond the capacity of the staff available. But, without adequate planning and supervision, settlement schemes of this kind would become a burden on the whole community.

In general, we see a real danger that a combination of pressure for settlement in the scheduled areas, and a lack of confidence in the future among the non-African farmers in the scheduled areas will lead to a decline in production and export earnings in the years immediately ahead. This loss could seriously retard the progress of the country as a whole. Already there is some evidence of disinvestment on farms. We hope that the introduction of the high-density settlement scheme will help to restore confidence, but we think that in any case there is an urgent need for measures specifically designed to arrest disinvestment and to encourage selective investment in the agricultural sector. We have discussed the kind of action we have in mind in Chapter 3. In addition, we think that the formulation of a firm attitude on the role of non-African farms, ranches and plantations in the new Kenya should be an early task of Government.

GOVERNMENT ASSISTANCE TO FARMING

The Agriculture Department's main activities and purposes concern agricultural research, agricultural education of subprofessional status, field extension services and primary marketing. It was obvious to the mission that the Government of Kenya has been well aware of the Department's needs over the years and has met them in large measure. It is equally clear, however, that current provisions fall short of needs, and that progress in agricultural development is being hampered accordingly.

The Kenya Government has built up an efficient veterinary organization over the years. It would have serious economic consequences if this department were to become seriously depleted in either caliber or numbers.

The Veterinary Department provides animal health, meat inspection, laboratory and zoological services. This involves not only diagnostic work, inoculation and vaccination for disease prevention, but also research on diseases, disease prevention and techniques. Tsetse research is a major feature embracing investigations of the tsetse fly itself, preventative drugs, drug resistance and techniques of tsetse control.

Another departmental function is Animal Husbandry and Livestock Improvement, and livestock improvement and animal industry centers have been long established. An artificial insemination service is provided and special attempts are being made to improve the livestock of the small African farmer. Another of the departmental activities is the supervision of a Hide and Skin Improvement Service and an African Livestock Marketing Organization. It also assists in organizing the marketing of dairy and poultry products in African areas.

Agricultural Extension

The agricultural extension service has the final responsibility for securing acceptance and adoption of improved farming practices by the farmers. Its size and efficiency will finally determine the rate at which the changeover from subsistence cultivation to cash-crop and mixed farming will take place. During the first few years of the Swynnerton Plan, additions to the agricultural field staff were in keeping with the progress in land consolidation and enclosure activities. Since then further additions ceased and, in fact, reductions were made in staff. The present aim in staffing in nonconsolidated areas is 1 Assistant Agricultural Instructor (AAI) to 200 families, 1 Agricultural Instructor (AI) per 6 AAI's, and 1 Assistant Agricultural Officer (AAO) per 10 AI's, but wastage among expatriates (Agricultural Officers and Assistant Agricultural Officers) is likely to be abnormally high during the next few years.

The new land settlement scheme in the scheduled areas will make heavy demands on staff. Each field unit of 10,000 acres in the 1 million-acre scheme will require a Settlement Officer, 2 Agricultural Instructors, 4 Assistant Agricultural Instructors, a Veterinary Instructor and 2 Veterinary Assistant Instructors as well as other staff. The mission considers that Kenya will do very well indeed to provide this staff and to maintain the current extension staff of the Ministry of Agriculture. We have therefore made no specific provision for increased extension staff, but have assumed that the additional staff for settlement would from 1964/65 onward be absorbed in the Ministry and have included additional recurrent expenditures for this purpose rising to £112,000 by 1966/67 in the suggested development program.

Localization. Of the four grades of technical staff, the Agricultural Officer grade is intended to be filled by men of full professional status, as a general rule possessing a degree. Postgraduate training in tropical agriculture in Trinidad has in the past been customary. Of the currently approved establishment of 137, 6 posts were held by Africans at the time this report was written. The wise course would, therefore, be to retain as large a number of expatriates of Agricultural Officer status as possible after independence is attained, until adequately qualified Africans are available in sufficient numbers to replace them. The economy of Kenya could suffer seriously if the present high technical standard of its Agricultural Officers were to be lowered suddenly in order to achieve complete localization rapidly.

In contrast to the AO level, there is at present no problem of localization at the Assistant Agricultural Officer grade. It is present policy to train all candidates locally and to localize completely the AAO establishment within five years. In view of the extent of the existing training facilities there should be no difficulty in achieving this goal. The currently sanctioned establishment of AAO's, including research staff and others at that level, is 279. Of this number, 51 posts were held by Africans in December 1961. A large program of local training is in progress to qualify selected Agricultural Instructors for promotion to AAO status; facilities have been expanded also for increasing the annual output of diploma holders for direct recruitment to this grade.

The mission considers that it would be a sound policy, likely to pay good dividends, to retain a small number of the best and most experienced expatriate Assistant Agricultural Officers beyond the five years' localization date. The purpose would be to give newly recruited African officers the benefit of guidance from the expatriates until they themselves have acquired sufficient experience to ensure that no serious fall-off in agricultural production would occur during the years of changeover.

Next to the Agricultural Instructor, the AAO is the technical officer most in contact with the African cultivator. On his greater knowledge and guidance depends to a considerable degree the efficiency of the services rendered by the Agricultural Instructor.

In mid-1961, there were about 50 qualified veterinarians in the Department. As a general principle, the mission would suggest that veterinarians should be relieved of as many nonveterinary duties as possible, including extension responsibilities. We would also suggest that a practical scheme for using private veterinary practitioners in times of emergency be investigated. There are a number of veterinarians engaged in private practice or in ranching. With appropriate arrangements for payment of services, the private practitioners might be given the full authority of a government veterinarian in the event of an epidemic.

Next below Veterinarians in departmental grade are Livestock Officers and Assistant Veterinary Officers. These grades normally require the possession of a diploma. However, it has not been possible to maintain staff of Livestock Officers in recent years without going below this requirement. It is expected that this relaxing of educational requirements will have to continue during the next several years. There are some 320 Veterinary Assistants in the field division who are normal candidates for upgrading through additional training. In-service training procedures should be intensified throughout the field force to increase the qualifications of the extension teaching staff.

Most extension work in the livestock field has been carried on in Kenya as a sideline activity on the part of field officers stationed at provincial and district headquarters and at training centers. The mission considers that there should be specialization using the established techniques of extension, appropriately adapted to African conditions, and that there should be some reassignment of the field staff accordingly. This suggestion applies to veterinary science, animal husbandry, grazing management and livestock marketing. A proposal has been made for the establishment of mobile field units equipped for both education work in animal husbandry and investigational work in veterinary problems. The mission considers this a timely development, and has provided for it in the first year of its capital program.

Agricultural Education

The future supply of local candidates to fill agricultural staff positions can be predicted with a good deal of accuracy because formal agricultural education in Kenya, apart from short courses for practical farmers, is directed to the training of candidates for employment at various levels of government service.

Degree Level Training. The three-year course at Makerere College, Uganda, has qualified students for the degree in agriculture of London University. The capacity of the school is 24 agricultural students admitted annually, and Kenya is entitled to possibly 8 of that total. Due to a lack of qualified candidates, however, the total intake has varied from 10 to 16, of which 4 to 6 students have come from Kenya.

Makerere College is developing a fully accredited veterinary course but, as in agriculture, the most serious problem is obtaining suitable candidates to fill the classes. If the coverage of science subjects were widened at the Royal College in Nairobi, perhaps more students would have the preliminary training needed to take the degree course at Makerere. The mission would also suggest that the Makerere curriculum should place a greater emphasis on animal husbandry.

The holder of a degree in agriculture from Makerere is qualified for immediate appointment as the Assistant Agricultural Officer. Promotion to Agricultural Officer, the highest general level of departmental service, is made after postgraduate training and study abroad. The number of qualified candidates from Makerere is quite inadequate to meet departmental needs for Agricultural Officers, particularly at this time of abnormal wastage, large settlement schemes and localization of the service.

To supply candidates, particularly for research posts, qualified graduates should continue to be sent abroad for postgraduate training. The location and conditions for further training should be decided by an experienced committee appointed to supervise overseas fellowships. There would need to be binding arrangements to ensure that the candidate's overseas training and experience would be used in Kenya in due course.

Diploma Level Training. Egerton Agricultural College, an independent institution, has provided since 1959 a diploma course in agriculture of two years' duration, preceded by training in practical agriculture on a farm. Originally founded for Europeans who wished to take up farming as a career, this institution became nonracial in 1961 and the first class of African and Asian students for the diploma is now in session. In the same year the former certificate course in agriculture at the Siriba Training College of the Department of Education was upgraded to a diploma course of two years, preceded by two terms practical agriculture on a farm.

The holder of a diploma in agriculture is qualified for direct appointment as an Assistant Agricultural Officer. The capacity of the two colleges—a combined output of perhaps 65 diploma holders a year, excluding animal husbandry—is considerably in excess of departmental requirements of Assistant Agricultural Officers and thus the complete localization of this cadre could be achieved within a short period, thereafter leaving a large surplus of qualified candidates, many of whom would be required by private undertakings. The mission considers that the permanent retention of both these colleges on a diploma basis may not be warranted, particularly in view of the inadequacy of training facilities of certificate standard to meet requirements of departmental staff on a lower scale. At an appropriate time Siriba should replace its present diploma course by a two-year certificate course which would qualify students for appointment as Agricultural Instructor and by training in agricultural practices for people outside government. The mission contemplates that agricultural diploma education would then be concentrated at Egerton. Meanwhile, the mission endorses proposals to increase the land area of cultivation, and thus improve the facilities for training in practical agriculture.

Egerton College is also designed to train candidates for the staff of the Veterinary Department. If there is greater collaboration between the Maseno Livestock Improvement Center and Siriba College, as has been proposed, an additional source of candidates would be opened up.

Egerton is located in the wheat growing belt; on the crop side it specializes in cereal crops and it grows a little pyrethrum. It lies outside the coffee, tea and sisal growing regions, and the mission would hope that students be given adequate opportunities to study these crops in their native habitat. The mission noted on a visit to the college that tractor cultivation is stressed. We would suggest that future Assistant Agricultural Officers should have some knowledge of ox cultivation, since it is so prominent in Kenya's agricultural practices.

Certificate Level Training. Instruction at certificate level has been provided by the Agricultural Department since 1949 at a number of centers, but a recent reorganization has concentrated agricultural education of this standard at Embu Provincial Agricultural Training School. Embu is now the only source of supply for the recruitment of Agricultural Instructors, its capacity is insufficient and the mission recommends that additional buildings be provided to make possible the doubling of annual admissions to 100 as soon as possible.

The prescribed standard of admission to agricultural certificate courses is the Cambridge School Certificate, but because of the scarcity of applicants who have passed the school certificate examination, the Department decided to accept students who have studied up to school certificate standard but have failed to pass the examination as a whole. The mission agrees that this step was unavoidable but issues a note of caution that this relaxation should not be overdone to the extent that it might permanently lower the quality of the service.

Farmers Training Centers. These Centers are being established in the principal agricultural districts of the colony in order to provide facilities for giving basic instruction in agricultural techniques, largely by practical demonstration. Groups of cultivators are brought to the Centers for short courses of 10–14 days' duration; separate courses are provided for their wives. In some districts, attendance at a farmer's training course is obligatory before the Department will assist the cultivator in obtaining either a development loan or a grade cow. Thirteen Centers are in operation at present.

At the farmer level, the Livestock Improvement Centers and Farmers'

Institutes play a very important role. Wherever practicable, the mission would integrate training in animal husbandry and veterinary practices with general agriculture, since it is mixed farming which is being encouraged in the intensive areas of Kenya. Five of the operating institutes —Kabianga, Kisii, Maseno, Marimba and Machakos—require expansion in both facilities and staff in order to train more people in animal husbandry and veterinary practices. The mission supports this proposal.

We support plans of the Veterinary Department to equip the Sangalo Livestock Improvement Center and the Ndomba livestock farm to furnish training in agriculture and animal husbandry for the Elgon Nyanza and Southern Embu districts respectively. The Ngong and Mariakani institutes need to be enlarged also. A number of demonstration centers should be developed to service surrounding farmers and to make stud sires and artificial insemination available. Training of Africans in methods of tanning hides and skins and in leather working is being undertaken. In view of the potential for developing this local industry we think training should be expanded to develop rural tanneries.

New Course for Assistant Agricultural Instructors. Subordinate staff, designated Assistant Agricultural Instructors, are employed in most sections of the Agricultural Department. The current sanctioned strength is about 4,000. Departmental employees of this grade are men of low initial educational qualifications. They undergo no set course of instruction or training either before or on appointment. Such skill or specialized knowledge as they may possess is acquired by experience in the course of their normal service. An attempt is made to include some of them in the short courses of instruction given at Farmers Training Centers, but present arrangements are unsatisfactory and inadequate. The mission recommends that the necessary facilities be provided at Farmers Training Centers, so that set courses of instruction, mainly practical in nature, may be given.

The mission's suggested development program 1963–67 includes £198,000 for capital expenditures on educational activities, and additional recurrent expenditures rising to £37,000 per annum by 1966/67 as a result of the recommendations made in this section of the report.

CROP AND LIVESTOCK IMPROVEMENT

A Policy for Mineral Fertilizer

In planning the future development of agriculture, formulation of an effective fertilizer policy should receive high priority. Over the long term, in spite of the availability and use of various organic manures, it will be difficult to maintain the nutrient level of soils, in particular the phosphate level, required for good crop or pasture performance without the application of artificial fertilizers. It becomes necessary to use manufactured fertilizer to ensure the best returns from a wide range of crops and farm pastures, to reduce the costs of producing basic food, cash and export crops and, finally, to preserve the long-term fertility of the soils.

Although a big proportion of the higher potential land is inherently fertile, soil deficiency is nevertheless widespread. This has been well demonstrated by experimentation.[8] A favorable response has been obtained by phosphatic fertilizers over a wide range of conditions and by nitrogenous fertilizers under particular circumstances.

These facts are well known in Kenya, yet the amount of mineral fertilizer[9] being used is very small and the amount being used to best advantage is even less. The gap between knowledge and general application is very wide—and costly. It is estimated that, for every million pounds' worth of mineral fertilizer—the right kind applied in the right quantity at the right time on such crops as maize, wheat, pyrethrum and others as well as pastures—there could be an increased return of £3 million at least to the economy. But above all, the unit costs of production could be very significantly reduced.[10] We feel that it should be possible, eventually, with a comprehensive policy designed to encourage farmers —and in particular the smallholder—to use fertilizer in the right way, to increase the value of their aggregate production by up to £10 million for an increased expenditure of around £3 million.

The cost of the most needed fertilizer, phosphate, to the farmers, particularly the small-scale farmer, appears excessive under present conditions of availability. The mission has studied the retail prices of small packages of fertilizers and the wholesale and bulk lot prices and considers that measures are necessary to reduce the cost to the farmer. We think that a subsidy is needed to inculcate the widespread use of phosphate fertilizer. There is also a need to introduce measures to ensure the availability of the recommended fertilizers in appropriate packages— small packages for the small-scale farmer, etc., and the reduction of the present excessive costs of packaging and distributing small packages. There would need to be adequate safeguards to ensure that the full effects of the subsidy are felt at the farm level.

[8] *The Fertilizer Requirements of the Kenya Highlands,* the final report of the Highland Fertilizer Scheme 1948–1950 by Holmet Sherwood, published by HMSO for the Colonial Office, 1954.

[9] The net imports into Kenya of fertilizers was only 38,500 tons in 1960.

[10] The cost of fertilizer was over 15 percent of total costs on surveyed farms in the Uasin Gishu area producing mainly maize and wheat as cash crops. See *Farm Economics Survey Unit Report No. 3,* 1960, p. 31.

It was suggested to us that nitrogenous fertilizer should also be considered for subsidy. One of its main uses in Kenya is in the growing of coffee. We think that a more logical case could be made for subsidizing the cost of controlling berry disease and rust in coffee, rather than in subsidizing nitrogenous fertilizer since this could have its effect both on the efficiency of production and the quality of the product. The long-term problem of maintaining the nitrogen status of the soil can best be tackled indirectly by intensified research on legumes.

Activity that would encourage the proper use of phosphate fertilizer is also needed. In spite of the evidence in respect to straight phosphatic fertilizers and compounds, it appears that farmers are using mixed fertilizers under conditions where they are not getting the returns to warrant the expenditure.[11] The mission observes, for instance, that the sale of compounds of nitrogen, phosphorous and potash jumped from 1,420 tons in 1958/59 to 5,641 in 1960/61, while the sales of straight phosphorous compounds declined over the same period. The Department of Agriculture is most qualified to advise farmers on the use of fertilizers appropriate to the conditions and crops in Kenya. The Department could itself make available technical information, in easily readable form, on the use of fertilizer.

We cannot overemphasize the need for simple demonstrations for the smallholder. A sum of, say £5,000 per annum, might well be set aside for demonstration of fertilizer benefits on shambas in chosen localities with one half fertilized and the other half not. (This might also be extended to test the additional effects of side dressings of sulphate of ammonia applied some weeks after the maize crop has been planted).

Consideration might be paid to the encouragement of the use of superphosphate from the Tororo factory in Uganda. This is single superphosphate, which, under particular circumstances, provides an added response from its gypsum component. There are large deposits of apatite[12] conveniently situated at Tororo and plans are for the manufacture of 25,000 tons annually of single superphosphate containing 21 percent water soluble phosphate (P_2O_5). If the demand for superphosphate can be increased sufficiently and the output of the plant increased eventually to 100,000 tons it could be produced relatively very cheaply. There ap-

[11] *Farm Economics Survey Unit Report No. 8,* Oct. 1961, pp. 44, 45: "The figures . . . appear to suggest that little advantage was obtained during the survey period by supplementing a basic application of superphosphate to cereals with other, usually more expensive, fertilizers." The figures show a yield of 6.96 bushels per acre of wheat on farms using only superphosphate at a cost of Sh.26.11 per acre against a yield of 5.45 bushels at a cost of Sh.46.94 per acre of mixed fertilizer.

[12] For details see *The Geology of Part of S.E. Uganda,* Memoir No. VIII of Geological Survey Dept., Kenya.

pears to be a strong case on economic grounds for one large efficient superphosphate manufacturing plant in East Africa.

The mission recommends:

a. that a comprehensive fertilizer policy for Kenya be introduced embracing the essential needs outlined above;
b. that there be a direct subsidy on the use of all phosphate fertilizer used in the country, provided it is applied in accordance with recommendations of the Department of Agriculture;
c. that a sum of money, of the order of £150,000 to £200,000 be allocated for subsidy purposes in the first year, expanding to a maximum of £300,000 as fertilizer demand increases;[13]
d. that an Executive Committee be set up to ensure the fulfillment of the stated objectives of the comprehensive policy. This could include the Director of Agriculture as Chairman and officers specialized in research and in extension work together with representatives of the fertilizer industry and distributing agencies.

Crop Research

Research has played a major role in agricultural development in Kenya and research organizations of outstanding quality and proportions have been built up. Research on agricultural problems of common interest and general application to East Africa is the function of the Kenya-based East African Agriculture and Forestry Research Organization. The Research Division of the Department of Agriculture conducts research in soil chemistry, entomology and plant pathology at laboratories in Nairobi, and a network of research stations and substations. This work covers all the principal cash crops.

While Government provides most of the finances required for research, largely from Colonial Development and Welfare Funds, contributions are also made by crop commodity boards, the Empire Cotton Growing Corporation and the Rockefeller Foundation. In 1960 expenditure incurred on research and investigation services on agriculture and livestock by the Ministry amounted to £661,000.

Programs. Despite the wide field covered by current investigations, the mission feels that a number of important problems need increased attention. There is a need for varieties of rice, for instance, to make pos-

[13] In Chapter 10, *Public Finance*, we recommend that the cost of this subsidy be met by discontinuing the rebate to farmers of duty on petroleum fuels used on the farm, which would also leave revenue to meet additional recurrent expenditure which would follow the implementation of the development program we recommend for agriculture.

sible the growing of two crops of rice a year; rice varieties more acceptable to Asian taste could replace the rice now imported. Maize varieties are needed that are better suited to certain environments than those presently grown, unless the synthetic strains now under investigation meet requirements. Inability to control the new physiological races of rust that are constantly appearing threatens the whole future of wheat growing in Kenya. Rather than compiling a catalogue of Kenya research needs—needs of which the Department is well aware—the mission has confined its comments here to programs that in its judgment deserve additional investment funds in the immediate years ahead. The estimated capital cost of the programs (£150,000) is included in our suggested development program.

Development in Low Rainfall Areas. In the many parts of Kenya where rainfall is scarce, such as in many parts of the Southern Province, the harvest is always problematical. Only four of every seven maize crops reach maturity. In drought years the position is even more serious. Investigations have indicated directions in which research needs intensification: the breeding of short-term food crops to fit soil moisture patterns, the possibilities of introducing other food and cash crops, range management studies, the development of fodder crops. To enable this work to be undertaken it is necessary to augment the staff and facilities at the present research center in Southern Province.

Sugar Cane. The paucity of sugar cane research facilities is a major shortcoming of the Research Division. The first requirement would be a station for agronomic research. This would deal with all aspects of sugar cane improvement other than breeding. It should be located in Nyanza Province, the principal sugar cane growing region in Kenya. The second requirement is for a substation in Coast Province for breeding new sugar cane varieties. The sugar cane plant does not flower under Nyanza conditions but arrows freely in Coast Province. Thus new material bred on the Coast would be investigated agronomically at the main research station in Nyanza. Since little progress is being made with a proposal to set up a larger-scale sugar cane breeding station in Coast Province for East Africa as a whole, the mission is of the opinion that Kenya should provide its own breeding station on a smaller scale.

Pyrethrum. Inadequate staff and facilities have limited the scope of research largely to the production of pyrethrum strains with high-yielding flower capacity. A broader program would embrace plant breeding for high pyrethrin content and the study of the biochemistry and physiology of the plant. Application has been made for a Colonial Development and Welfare grant, and if the grant is approved, the entire cost of the proposed expansion would be reimbursed jointly from that source and from the Pyrethrum Board.

Tea. Research into problems of tea growing on a plantation scale is done by the Tea Research Institute, which is financed jointly by the three East African countries. A small departmental station is devoted to the problems of the smallholder tea grower. Tea growing among African smallholders is now spreading rapidly, and some expansion is needed for the results of the work of the Tea Research Institute to be disseminated for the benefit of the small grower.

Legume Bacteriology. Beans, a basic source of protein in Kenya, occupy the second largest acreage among field crops. The protein which they supply is reputedly derived from atmospheric nitrogen by the Rhizobium root nodules. Research has shown that some beans grown in Kenya can carry large root nodules yet fix negligible amounts of nitrogen. Research needs to be undertaken into the process of nitrogen fixation with a view to increasing the protein yield of beans until it is comparable with that of temperate countries.

Also, good livestock performance in terms of meat or milk production depends, among other things, upon sufficient protein in the pasture. Legumes of the right kind with efficient adapted strains of nitrogen-fixing bacteria can provide the means of ensuring this. There is an urgent need for more research in this field. The mission endorses Kenya's policy of seeking technical assistance in legume research from overseas (in this case Australia) where there has been considerable research into the general problems of legumes under comparable conditions to those in Kenya.

Pasture. Different grasses and clover are required for the four main climatic areas in Kenya, and some research has already been done on some of these areas. But much more work is required to produce, by selection and plant breeding, grasses and clovers to suit conditions in each of the regions. For this purpose research staff needs to be strengthened and the facilities improved.

Livestock Performance

Research and Disease Control. Veterinary research is conducted at the Kabete Veterinary Laboratory and at the Naivasha Experimental Station of the Kenya Government which are concerned primarily with applied research. More basic research is carried on by the East African Veterinary Research Organization at Muguga and the Wellcome Institute for Research on Foot and Mouth Disease, which is operated by the

Kenya Government. No contribution is received from the livestock industry for animal husbandry and pasture research.

Physical and operating facilities at Kabete, though good, are crowded. Most animal disease problems are common to the three countries of East Africa, but the more advanced state of livestock and dairying in Kenya means that research work there will tend to cover diseases encountered in Uganda and Tanganyika. The more research can be conducted on an interterritorial basis, the greater the economy of effort. We therefore suggest that discussions be held on an East African basis to consider the desirability of strengthening Kabete as a regional diagnostic institute which might also undertake short-term investigatory work and produce some biologicals for the whole area.

The really big problem for veterinary research in East Africa is disease control. Until certain diseases are controlled, the markets for livestock and fresh animal products will be restricted. Research in animal disease control is also important to human beings since so many of the local animal diseases such as tryanosomiasis, brucellosis and rabies also affect them.

Research in processing animal products is important since the current disease situation restricts the market for fresh products. There are large numbers of low grade and old cattle, sheep and goats and even some wild game which can be converted near the point of origin into edible meat powder. The provision of plant for further research on flavor, nutritive value and utilization is included in the suggested development program.

In the more ordinary avenues of veterinary research, in which excellent progress has been made, the mission would suggest increased attention to certain programs. Animal husbandry research, for instance, has not received the attention warranted by its importance. We recommend that it receive particular attention in future plans. Research in animal nutrition should be intensified with particular reference to nutritive values of forage plants, grazing management and bush control. How to meet drought emergencies is a broader but related problem which requires attention.

Control of external parasites by dipping and spraying requires continuous investigation, particularly from the point of view of efficiency of various chemicals and solutions under the conditions of usage. To induce widespread adoption of dipping and spraying by African stockmen, the techniques must be both effective and economical.

The tsetse species, *Glossina palpalis*, is the primary carrier of human sleeping sickness and the area of highest incidence is the vicinity of Lake Victoria and the Gulf of Kavirondo. The southern portion of this area has been almost entirely cleared of tsetse and it is important that this program should be completed. It is estimated that a total of £100,000 needs to be provided by 1965 for the final clean-up of the fly in Western Kenya, which will then make good land available for settlement. Continued control necessitates the maintenance of boundary lines. The area that will require the closest attention over the next few years is likely to be along the border of Tanganyika.

External parasite control will always be a major operation in the Kenya livestock industry. There are eight or more tick-borne diseases and the resulting loss to the industry is great. Finances in the future are not likely to be sufficient for the Veterinary Department to furnish these services as it has in the past. As an aid to routine parasite control for the smaller farmer, the use of dipping or spraying centers should continue to be encouraged. These centers should be built and operated on a self-liquidating basis under the auspices of District Councils, under the advice of local Livestock Officers, with resident managers who would receive their remuneration from the fees collected. The fees charged should be high enough to pay all operating costs plus the retirement and servicing of any loans taken out for construction and supplies.

Cattle Breeding. The major emphasis should be placed on testing and improvement of the indigenous Boran breed of cattle and the Sahiwal hybrids. For this purpose a limited number of additional Sahiwals will need to be acquired and consolidated with the existing herd. The true Boran has been improved by European ranchers to the point at which its beef producing performance is very high under extensive pastoral conditions. It is a regrettable omission that selection and breeding for milk production were not given the same attention as selection for beef. It has been demonstrated that the Sahiwal hybrids have far better performance in milk production than the native breeds. But whether that would have been the case if the comparison were being made with an improved native strain resulting from an intensive selection and breeding program remains to be proved. The mission recommends that a special committee be appointed to review all aspects of the breed improvement program, particularly in relation to the development of small-scale mixed farming.

In addition to beef and dairy stock, a dual-purpose type of bovine will be in demand by a portion of the African farmers for the foreseeable future. There is believed to be enough exotic dairy stock of high quality in the country to meet the future needs in this regard. The selection of superior sires for dairy production, however, could be improved by expanding the "proved sire" method.

Performance testing, as a guide for selection of beef cattle, has been proved on commercial ranches in Kenya and should have a more important place in the Kenya animal husbandry research and extension program. For the present it should be limited in application to the selection of sires for the artificial insemination study and, because of its established benefits, should be applied as promptly as possible in this direction. It has particular application to the Sahiwal and Boran breeding projects.

Artificial insemination has proved very helpful to the small farmer unable to maintain a bull of good quality. There is established at Kabete an excellent bull stud for the production of semen and the Department has successfully trained artificial inseminators. Over the three report years, 1958–60, the average number of ampoules of semen distributed was slightly over 90,000 per year. The introductory phase of this practice is not over, however, and we support the program prepared by the Department for mobile units to undertake the twofold educational and operational task. It is envisaged that these mobile units will be operated by the Government for three years, after which certain District Councils would take them over and run them on a self-supporting basis. Pending the wider adoption of artificial insemination—the mobile unit previously mentioned could help to popularize the practice among smallholders—the number of "bull centers" which hold good quality sires for the use of surrounding farmers should be increased. These centers normally should remain the responsibility of District Councils.

The Management of Grazing Lands. Forty-five percent of Kenya has been classed as range or grazing lands. This excludes the 33 percent of desert area about which little can be done at the present time. Much of this grazing land has been overstocked and the vegetable cover has deteriorated in some cases to almost total disappearance. Erosion has become serious. The regeneration capacity in some areas, however, has been observed to be phenomenal. A technique of management is required to preserve the vegetative cover and at the same time achieve an effective turnover from grazing livestock.

Certain tribal customs operate against the principles of good animal husbandry, and grazing management and the preservation of natural assets. Among the herdsmen of some tribes, cattle are considered to be the storage-reservoir of individual wealth. They are their savings and investment account and numbers are important, not the condition of the animals. Among some tribes the bride-price is paid in live cattle, more rarely in sheep, goats or money. Thus, the father or older brother must accumulate and have on hand livestock to pay bride-prices for the younger male members of his family. In many cases family clannishness does not permit the scattering of livestock numbers over a sufficiently large area to fit the grazing and water resources.

The result of such customs is the deterioration of grazing lands to the point at which erosion has become very serious. An educational process is necessary, but it will be extremely slow unless supported by demonstrations of controlled grazing, the provision of water supplies and the facilities for the regular marketing of livestock. In some cases legislation may well prove to be necessary.

The critical need for conservative range grazing was more sharply evident in 1961 because of the prolonged drought. The few grazing schemes which were continued clearly proved the success of controlled grazing: the mission observed some large and fat cattle on the Riwa Scheme in West Suk. Likewise, certain of the lightly grazed tsetse fly areas visited by the mission were conclusive evidence that ground cover and forage production could be maintained through periods of critical moisture deficiency if the grazing load were not extremely heavy.

Legislation for controlled grazing by districts was introduced many years ago. The establishment and operation of grazing districts need not impose a continuing financial burden. Grazing schemes could be made self-supporting and, after range recovery, there could be a modest income to government. Administrative arrangements are required to enforce control of grazing. The need varies between areas but, we understand, there has been some decline in enforcement recently. We suggest that the legislation and arrangements for its enforcement be reviewed.

There is an immediate need for range specialists to be reassigned to initiate the grazing districts and to effect liaison between the districts and their grazing boards, and the departmental headquarters. This would entail small additional capital and recurrent costs which are included in our suggested program.

Bush control will probably always be a problem. The encroachment of bush is unending and its dominance over good forage plants serious. Further, in tsetse fly areas it must be destroyed as an initial part of the fly control process. Fire remains the most inexpensive bush control method, and the mission trusts that the search will continue for a system which would preserve the forage cover rather than destroying it, and yet would not be too costly. Techniques developed in countries with similar problems should be studied.

Livestock Marketing. There are now nine or more designated stock routes throughout the country. These have had to be organized and controlled by the Veterinary Department in order to permit movements of stock with a minimum of disease hazards. In conjunction with most stock routes and marketing points there must also be quarantine pastures where animals can be held for observation or, in cases of inoculation, held for the necessary immunization period. These quarantines require a larger resource of grazing, of course, than do the movement routes.

Stock routes and quarantine stations should become self-supporting. Where government support is still the case, the changeover to self-support should be promptly begun. Funds for this self-support might be obtained from a cess on sales.

Credit will be necessary for establishment of new livestock marketing projects. The security of fee collection is already proved in the recent years of operation of the Coastal Stock Route. It is envisaged that the cost of supervision for health, disease and sanitation could continue to be a government expense.

The three present country abattoirs were installed by the African Livestock Marketing Organization (ALMO) and are operated by it. The older established ones are the Baringo Abattoir at Marigar and the Samburu Abattoir at Archer's Post. The new one at Kajiado began operation in August of 1961 as an emergency measure during the drought, but there is definite need for the Southern Province to be permanently served. The Kajiado Abattoir is portable, an advantage which offsets the extra cost. Two more such abattoirs are needed, and have been included in the capital program. They should become self-supporting after about three years of operation.

An additional country marketing installation has been the very successful establishment of outlying saleyards. These all operate on the auction principle and have proved themselves valuable over the years. More such saleyards are being installed by the Department.

Other Animals

The potential for improving African sheep and wool is considerable. Some 1,200 head of good quality Corriedales have been recently placed in the hands of farmers in the Cherangani Hills and the results are encouraging enough so that the Agricultural Officer in that area hopes to increase these numbers by the purchase of 800 head more. Sheep raising under wet high-altitude conditions is, however, difficult. The sheep need to be handled in relatively small flocks with constant attention, and it may take many years to teach the small farmer the necessarily intensive managerial techniques.

The breeds of sheep native to Kenya are poor milk producers but furnish a convenient supply of meat and skins. Crossbreeding has made considerable progress, and a flock-improvement program could make rapid progress if accepted by the small producers.

The mission endorses the proposal to introduce a foreign breed to test out for top crossing. The proposed importation is composed of 10 rams and 40 ewes of the Awasi breed from the Middle East. This is an old breed, native to semiarid areas, which is famous for its milk-lamb-wool production.

In the high-potential areas, a number of breeds have proved their worth, for both wool and meat, but at the present time there appears to be too great a number of breeds with a wide variety in wool quality and conformation. The mission would recommend that the sheep industry standardize its production on the basis of a smaller number of proved breeds.

In the medium-potential areas of 20–35 inch rainfall, where there are the best prospects for efficient wool production, the Merino and the Corriedale have proved themselves. Crossbreeding is unnecessary. Where the hazards of the thorn bush prove too great, improved native sheep may give the best financial results.

The breeds of swine raised commercially in Kenya—Large White and Landrace—are rated among the best pork producers in the world. At present, swine production is subject to quotas and the mission would recommend that this system, along with the attendant marketing restrictions, should be operated more flexibly to enable the small farmer to enter into this kind of production. Specific health inspection requirements for the movement of swine should remain in force, with special emphasis on the prevention of contagious diseases such as foot and mouth disease and African swine fever.

In introducing swine production to small farms, it should be kept in mind that adequate supplies of home-grown maize and a source of animal protein, such as skim milk, are necessary features of the project. The best swine for production by small farmers might be dual-purpose animals rather than a bacon pig.

The production from goats might well be increased by improvement in milk producing capacity and the introduction of the mohair type. Crossbreeding trials with imported milch-goat sires and imported mohair males are worthy of support. The costs of this, and the sheep breed tests would amount to some £3,000.

Suspended bee hives are in evidence throughout most of the non-desert country and the export figures show 97,500 pounds of beeswax and 300 pounds of honey shipped out in 1960, at a value of £19,000. The use of the honey is of much greater value, however, as a home-produced food supply. The mission's program includes a proposal for a clarification plant, collection centers and transportation of honey and wax and for staff to conduct training.

PRODUCTION AND MARKETING POLICIES

The expansion of agricultural production, which will be the major factor determining the general advance of Kenya's economy, depends upon an increase in production for the market. In large part this means increasing earnings from a number of primary commodities in the international market. Economic policy has, therefore, to be geared to the prospects for world trade in the commodities which Kenya produces or could produce. We shall discuss the outlook for several of these individually later in this chapter. The general outlook for international trade for Kenya presents a serious obstacle to a rapid increase in the level of Kenyan incomes. In Chapter 2 we have referred to some of the factors which affect the conditions of world trade in primary commodities. These combine to limit the opportunities for enlarging exports under favorable price conditions.

Confronted with such a marketing problem, the best strategy for a country like Kenya, it has often been suggested, would be to diversify production. Unfortunately, so many commodities are in surplus in present circumstances that it is difficult to find a suitable line of production to follow, and diversification entails considerable burdens of adjustment. In addition therefore to diversifying, Kenya should strengthen her trade drive in all markets that are still accessible. This should include intensifying exploration of the nearest possible markets and the prospects of and requirements for their development, e.g., Bahrein, Aden, Kuwait, Iraq, etc.; also, the possibilities of East-West African trade with particular reference to livestock products, fruits and vegetables.

Secondly, since the scope for increased export earnings is limited, we would recommend that a major emphasis in agricultural planning be placed on import saving. This would include the encouragement of local production where this will be at lower cost than importing, perhaps after an initial period of protection. The uncertainty of Kenya's balance of payments prospects—particularly the doubt whether the country can continue to finance a large adverse balance of trade—however, also argues for special emphasis on production which economizes the use of foreign exchange. There are major import-saving possibilities inside Kenya and, more particularly, inside the East African customs union. The East African countries face similar problems in this field, and are significantly interdependent in a range of products, so that there now appears to be a stronger case than ever for very close collaboration in trade with as near an approach to a common trading policy as can be achieved. Policies of import saving on an interterritorial basis should be explored fully. Quite a range of primary products of significance from the point of view of an import-saving policy are imported into East Africa in appreciable quantities. Food imports into East Africa have averaged over £8.5 million in the last five years. Among the major items were sugar, canned milk and cream, and rice. Other food imports, though comparatively small individually, could be important to Kenya from an import-saving point of view. Imports of animal and vegetable oils and fats have also averaged over £1 million a year since 1957. The urgency of possible import saving also calls for a close look at the category of manufactured goods, which might not only foster industrial development, reduce the import bill, produce internal revenue and create employment, but also might act as a major stimulant to agricultural industries. Manufactured textiles, for example, have a double significance in that vegetable fibers can be produced efficiently in East Africa.

The development of the European Economic Community (EEC) is of particular immediate concern to Kenya's foreign trade policy. The original six countries of the EEC are significant purchasers of Kenya's exports; especially of coffee, although trade in this commodity will be more generally affected by international agreement. In view of the possibility of United Kingdom membership of the EEC, the importance of trade relations with it would be considerably increased. For some products—canned fruit, for example—the common tariff of the EEC might exercise a considerable influence on the direction of trade, while for others, including dairy products and meat, a common agricultural policy will be applicable, which includes provision for import licensing, if necessary, to protect the common internal price from imports. Much will depend on the possibility of Kenya's association with the EEC, and the terms of that association, but the mission would stress that Kenya should weigh carefully the likely economic advantages of association before reaching a decision on this matter.

The marketing of staple foodstuffs and major cash crops in Kenya is organized through statutory bodies that take delivery of products, distribute them to processors, hold reserves to meet seasonal shortages and market surpluses overseas. Prices for major products are fixed by the Minister of Agriculture and the organizations concerned. We feel that arrangements of this kind are essential at the present stage for the maintenance and development of production to meet the needs of consumers in Kenya and to supplement production elsewhere in the customs union. Production is in the hands of a very large number of farmers, many of them unused to producing for the market. A guaranteed market needs to be assured at remunerative price levels, to provide the incentive and to ensure the reward of increasing effort. Outside the scheduled areas, the small volume of output of each farmer calls for complex marketing arrangements, if receipts to producers are to reflect general demand and quality differentials accurately. The advance of African cash farming is largely a recent development, fostered especially by the Swynnerton Plan, and the system of organized marketing was established at a time when existing arrangements were inadequate. These products are basic to the diet of the local people, many of whom are urbanized. To ensure sufficient supplies at reasonable prices is a national responsibility. It calls for an efficient system of distribution, including the holding of reserves to cover bad seasons.

To fulfill these requirements, some system of organized marketing is essential; an organization is essential; and to fulfill national objectives, government intervention is also essential. Although modifications to the present arrangements may be necessary, and we envisage that there would still be a role for the private trader, Kenya should continue to exert control over the production and distribution of major foodstuffs.

East African Relations

The Marketing Board system used in Kenya has come in for a good deal of criticism. There have been complaints in East Africa that the policies of the marketing boards have operated to the disadvantage of Tanganyika and Uganda. In particular, there has been some criticism of the prices that the other countries have been asked to pay for Kenya's products. But many of Kenya's products are competitive with imported products. Statistics produced by Kenya show that, in respect to beef, bacon and ham, butter, cheese and ghee, prices paid by Tanganyika or Uganda have been lower, over any considerable period, than the comparable prices of imported commodities of the same kind.

A rational basis of price determination could be worked out if the three countries could agree on a framework of common principles. It would appear necessary, for instance, to agree on a policy to assist developing and established industries within East Africa. At the same time, it must be stressed that agreed prices should not be so high as to protect inefficient production at the expense of consumers and should, therefore, be influenced where appropriate by world price levels.

A mutually integrated trading policy with Tanganyika and Uganda might include the extension of organized marketing arrangements for key commodities, the strengthening of measures to protect the important developing agricultural industries in all three countries against dumping, disguised dumping, and the impact of heavily subsidized imports of competitive primary products. Negotiations should be placed more on a comprehensive basis and less on a piecemeal or single-commodity basis. In the meantime, Kenya should try to reduce the costs of production and handling of those products which are marketed to Tanganyika and Uganda within the general trade policy agreement.

Work on Economic Matters in the Ministry

There is need for an independent technical body to analyze all the facts that should be taken into consideration, including both farm costs and market trends, in the determination of prices of local marketed products. The MacGillivray Committee recommended that the one-man Market Research Section of the Ministry be expanded and renamed the Economic Section and be given the task of preparing forecasts of production, production costs and market trends, and making these available to the Minister and interested bodies. It also recommended that it should work "in close liaison with the East African Statistical Department."[14]

In the light of the changed prospects for Kenya's principal exports, more attention will need to be given to the economic aspects of agricultural development. Also, if as we envisage, the number of outside advisory bodies is reduced and statutory boards are established for executive purposes, rather than to advise on government policy, greater emphasis should be placed on economic studies within the Ministry.

At present work on economic policy and planning is the direct responsibility of the Deputy Secretary, a senior administrative officer, who also has major responsibilities in the field of financial policy. We suggest that an experienced agricultural economist should be appointed at this level who would be responsible for economic work, including development planning and the preparation of material for the determination of prices.[15] He would be supported by a small economics division which would provide for farm economics surveys and expansion of market research, and would include the Agricultural Statistics Section of the

[14] *Report of the Committee on the Organization of Agriculture,* MacGillivray, Laurie and White, Nairobi, 1960, p. 9.

[15] A recommendation along these lines was made some ten years ago. See L. G. Troup, *Report Inquiry into the 1951 Maize and Wheat Prices and to Ascertain the Basis for the Calculation Annually of a Fair Price to the Producer for Maize, Wheat, Oats and Barley, and Other Farm Products the Prices of which are Controlled by the Government,* Government Printer, Nairobi, 1952, p. 13.

Economics and Statistics Division of the Treasury, which is at present housed in the Ministry of Agriculture.[16]

The agricultural economist would be a member of the planning committee of principal officers in the Ministry which would be serviced by the Economics Division. In Annex A we discuss arrangements for government planning. We consider that the task of planning in agriculture is too great and requires too much contact with the situation at the farm level to be undertaken satisfactorily other than in the Ministry directly concerned. But close collaboration would be necessary with the central planning organization in the setting of over-all targets.

Annual additional recurrent expenditure for the Economics Division, including the expansion of the Market Research Section and the Farm Economics Section, is estimated to be £15,000 and for the agricultural census £8,000.

Agricultural Statistics. The importance of reliable statistics concerning the number and size of holdings, the acreage and yields of the various crops, the rotations practiced, the numbers of livestock, their distribution, and the composition of herds or flocks cannot be overstressed. These statistics are necessary for efficient planning of development, for measuring the effects of particular programs, and for anticipating marketing problems. A census plan for the African sector has been proposed by the Economics and Statistics Division of the Treasury,[17] and we recommend that it be implemented. Because of financial and technical difficulties, it would be a five-year rotational scheme.

Organization

Few underdeveloped countries can compare with Kenya in the magnitude of the organizational arrangements which have been provided by Government to further agricultural development and marketing. Apart from the existence of the normal departments of government, common to most countries, separate Boards of Agriculture have been constituted for the scheduled and nonscheduled areas to promote agricultural development; separate commodity boards have been created for each of the principal cash crops, as well as for some other crops or classes of crops; a separate authority advises on the development of the water resources of the colony; special funds and banks provide development loans and agricultural credit; Government itself guarantees minimum returns to producers of the main cereal crops in the scheduled areas. A

---

[16] The agricultural census work could continue to be undertaken by the main statistical office.

[17] For details see Annex B, *Agricultural Census Taking.*

large number of advisory committees covers most aspects of agricultural development extending into the fields of marketing and pricing policy.[18]

This multiplicity of organizations and procedures is partly a legacy of wartime organization. Circumstances, however, have changed very much since the war and they are changing still as Kenya moves to independence. The organization of agriculture and marketing has not everywhere moved sufficiently with the changing circumstances.

Senior members of the staff of the Ministry are frequently chairmen and members of many of these boards which, depending on their functions, may include provincial, producers' or commercial representatives. Much of the time of senior civil servants is taken up attending meetings of these bodies, but Kenya has also found residents with experience in farming or in managerial work elsewhere who have been willing to serve part time on governmental boards and committees. Such people may not readily be found in the future and there will be many other uses for the services of the available skilled administrators.

There are other reasons than staffing for suggesting that a major review of statutory bodies in agriculture be instituted. The growth of these bodies and the division of functions between them and the Ministry do not, in our belief, follow a consistent pattern of responsibility. Some boards are carrying out tasks which might properly be performed by the Ministry. Often several bodies exist where only one may be needed. Many of them are supported by levies on producers. Although the direct cost to Government is limited, it is the burden on the economy which should receive attention.

Several of these undertakings have as one of their functions that of advising the Ministry of Agriculture; some have their own statutory powers. We think that the Minister should be free to consult whom he wishes, but that generally his principal source of advice on agricultural policy should be his own officers. Civil servants on these boards may also encounter problems of conflicting interest between their roles as departmental advisers to their Minister and as board members. Members of some boards are appointed to represent private interests rather than to serve in a public capacity.

It is easy to see in the present boards' structure the system of organization which divided farming in Kenya into geographic areas on racial lines, with commercial production being undertaken almost entirely in the scheduled areas by expatriate farmers. It is doubtful that this system will be suitable for a new Kenya. We suggest a review of the division of functions between Government itself and statutory boards and advisory

[18] A table listing the functions of agricultural boards and committees is to be found in Annex C to this report.

bodies be undertaken to recommend an organizational structure appropriate to the future constitutional and administrative arrangements, and thus conducive to the efficient conduct of the role of Government in agriculture.

Though we feel that Kenya is heavily "over-boarded," it is of major importance that, in the process of review, the production and marketing of principal products should not be disrupted. We do not envisage that all the boards would be affected by a program of rationalization. In particular, we think that some of the commodity boards, which have regulatory, trade, research and promotional functions for the main crops, have done excellent work. In the next few paragraphs we discuss changes which we suggest should be made in the activities of some of the individual boards.

From an organizational point of view, the most controversial issue involves the function of the Board of Agriculture (Scheduled Areas). This Board administers the guaranteed minimum return (GMR) scheme for cereals, which involves the payment of GMR claims and the provision of short-term finance, through the issue of GMR advances, to farmers in scheduled areas. The basis for this function is the policy that crops classified as "essential" to Kenya's economy are subject to production orders and are thus "scheduled"—a policy that, incidentally, provided the name for a sector of Kenya's agricultural economy. The most recent report on agricultural organization, by the MacGillivray Committee,[19] was restricted in its terms of reference to problems within the framework of the scheduling system. This was unfortunate, for the mission would suggest that the basic system itself is out of date. The mission would point out that while maize, as a classified crop, has been grown in the scheduled areas, under production orders and guaranteed minimum payments administered by the Board of Agriculture (Scheduled Areas), arrangements of this kind have not applied in the nonscheduled areas.

The MacGillivray Committee's recommendation did include, however, that the GMR system should be retained, apparently on the grounds that without the security of crop advances commercial banks would have difficulty in making available short-term credit. The advances made against GMR's are officially limited to "essential" crops, but in practice they are important for other forms of farm development, for example, the establishment of grass leys. The mission agrees with the Committee's concern for the provision of short-term credit. We feel that the difficulties might be overcome by the creation of a crop insurance scheme, financed by contributions from government and producers. Consideration should be given to the possible absorption of the loan

---

[19] MacGillivray and others, *op. cit.*

activities of the Land and Agricultural Bank by the proposed Agricultural Credit Corporation.[20] If these suggestions were to be followed, then there would seem to be little necessity to retain the Board of Agriculture (Scheduled Areas) or the Cereal Producers Board (Scheduled Areas).

On the marketing side there seems to be a very real need for some streamlining of the Boards, their functions, and their consultative obligations. In some cases they can be organized as statutory corporations set up to process (where this is involved) and market farm products and to act in accordance with government policy but with the maximum amount of freedom from politics.

It would be expected that these statutory corporations would conduct their business on strictly commercial lines within the framework of government policy in relation to the products being handled; their management would be chosen accordingly. We have been impressed by the managerial efficiency of certain of the Marketing Boards now operative in Kenya. The mission considers that the Boards associated with the marketing of tea and coffee are fulfilling the marketing function effectively. On the other hand, in regard to meat, it would be advantageous for the Uplands Bacon Factory, now a privately owned company, to be amalgamated with the Kenya Meat Commission and for the single corporation to be responsible for the processing and marketing of all meats, both internally and for export. As the African Livestock Marketing Organization (AIMO) passes through the developmental stage and its operations are put on a commercial basis, as should be the objective, it could be absorbed within the reorganized Kenya Meat Commission. The mission also considers that the Pig Industry Board would no longer be necessary since the Ministry of Agriculture might well administer policies relating to the pig industry and would naturally be in close liaison with the Commission.

The mission feels there would be many advantages in having one strong, well-organized marketing corporation with appropriate operational departments to handle both maize and wheat. The Wheat and Maize Marketing Boards should therefore be amalgamated. Pricing policy would be established by Government on the basis of information supplied by the Market Research and Farm Economics Survey Sections of the Division of Economics, together with information supplied by the marketing authority itself.

The Kenya Cooperative Creameries (KCC), now a cooperative body, might also be transformed into a public corporation, which would have an important role in the more extensive development of the dairying in-

[20] See discussion of Agricultural Credit, Chapter 9, Money and Banking.

dustry, with responsibility for collecting milk products, packaging and processing for internal and external market purposes. It should be responsible for a program of diversification designed in accordance with market trends, and also would engage in a vigorous program of market development. The question should be examined as to whether the role of the Kenya Dairy Board might in future be performed by the reconstituted KCC and the Ministry of Agriculture.

In regard to the marketing and processing of horticultural and fruit products, a thorough investigation appears to us to be necessary, before considering further any proposal for the setting up of a Horticultural and Canning Crops Board. We note that the Government is proposing, with outside assistance, to study the problem of marketing and processing horticultural crops and fruits.

There is still the problem, however the system is reorganized, of deciding a rational basis for the level of prices on certain crops. We cannot agree entirely with the MacGillivray Committee that "the primary consideration is Kenya's capacity to produce at prices which can profitably compete in world markets." We would say that prices should be related to farm costs at a particular level of desired efficiency, but taking into account prices or trends in international markets where transactions are on a strictly commercial basis. The continued acceptance of an eight-bag-per-acre yield for maize set by Troup, for example, should be queried in the light of what should now be the average expectation under reasonably good farming.[21]

The Provincial Marketing Boards. A wide range of criticism of the activities of the provincial marketing boards has been reviewed carefully. We believe, as stated previously, that a system of organized marketing is necessary to encourage small-scale farmers to expand their production of crops for cash. The Nyanza Province Marketing Board in particular performs a very important developmental function in providing the means whereby a large scattered peasant population can sell crop surpluses no matter in what small quantities. This organization acts as agent for crops with guaranteed prices and as trader in regard to other crops. Markets and trading centers have been established where around 2,000 traders, acting in turn as agents of the Board, purchase produce for cash. The Board performs the important service of storage at railhead where produce is fumigated and held until prices are favorable. In the cases where prices are not guaranteed by Government, the Board's sales department fixes its own prices in accordance with its assessment of market prices. The Board also distributes seed at cost, trades in eggs, and runs a

---

[21] See Troup Report, *op. cit.*

ghee factory. It circularizes free monthly bulletins giving advice on marketing matters, including a review of produce values, and performs various other nonprofit services, including the encouragement of cooperatives. The Central Province Marketing Board, which was established more recently (April 1959), performs similar functions, but does not handle nearly so great a quantity of produce as does the Nyanza Board.

At this stage of very imperfect development of a private marketing system, and with the resultant uncertainties regarding both price and the difficulties of moving produce into markets at all, the case for government utilities to perform this function is very strong indeed. The mission considers that the provincial marketing boards are performing a very essential function and that their performance has been excellent. The stage is a long way off when producer cooperative societies could be organized in Kenya to be able to perform the function as efficiently.

Problems have arisen from different systems of marketing in operation in parts of Tanganyika and Uganda contiguous with areas of Kenya in which the provincial marketing boards operate. We suggest that this matter should be discussed within the Common Services Organization. Problems also arise within Kenya because of the need of organization in the areas not covered by the boards. The Nyanza Province Marketing Board, as suggested by the MacGillivray Committee, might well expand into the Rift Valley Province as the needs develop and the Central Province Board might well expand its activities to meet the needs of the Southern Province.

Milk production by smallholders is already presenting a problem which will increase as this source of supply increases. Because it is perishable, rapid collection and movement are required. The small amounts which must be collected to make up full loads for distance hauling require special organization as well as suitable equipment.

The Mariakani Milk Scheme, as it is known, has proved itself an excellent pattern for creamery-type collection and processing for areas of similar size and dispersal of farm units. The plant at Mariakani, sponsored and developed by the Veterinary Services, is self-supporting, even to the new construction and machinery installation being completed in 1962. Since the pattern is already laid and the experience gained, it should be possible to finance additional creameries on a similar basis.

Another established type of milk collection, in the form of rural milk centers, is scattered through the high-potential areas. More of these centers will be needed as the smallholder's dairy production increases and we have provided in our capital program for 60 small milk- and egg-collection centers. In Nyanza and Central Provinces, collection centers have developed to the point of organized provincial marketing operations, and as we have remarked, the Marketing Boards in these provinces could extend their activities to the Rift Valley and Southern Provinces, where surplus milk and eggs are beginning to be offered for sale. In regard to poultry products, the appointment of a full-time poultry specialist should be considered by the Department.

The Hides and Skins Division of the Department has established a lucrative export market for these products. Exports in 1960 were nearly £1.75 million, which ranked well up toward the top of the major items of livestock products sold out of Kenya. The cost to the Government for services was relatively small—£43,000 in 1960—and is reimbursed by a cess on exports.

The Role of Cooperatives. It would be incorrect to infer from the above discussion that the mission is opposed to cooperative marketing arrangements. The success of Kenya's export programs in the past has been heavily dependent, and will continue to be dependent, on cooperative organizations. There are some 600 cooperative societies in Kenya, some of which form the essential link with the small farmer in the marketing of coffee, sisal, pyrethrum and wattle, as well as cereals, fruits and vegetables, dairy products, etc. The profit-making Kenya Farmers Association (KFA), which has about 4,000 members, acts as the trading agent for the Maize Board and plays a related role in wheat. The KFA in 1959 opened its membership to all "bona fide farmers" regardless of race and now includes among its members a number of the cooperatives that service Kenya's smallholders. Because of its monopoly as marketing agent, and its related bookkeeping functions as administrator of the guaranteed minimum return, the KFA has been able to play a convenient role as creditor. It is able to finance purchases of fertilizer, insecticides, and the like as advances against repayment of cash or kind. The large trading companies have argued that competitive marketing would add to the total supply of production and short-term credit and, at the same time, reduce the burden on government agencies.

In the future an increasing proportion of marketed agricultural output is likely to be produced by small farmers. The cooperative form of organization can be a most effective means of arranging processing and marketing and perhaps providing of facilities and supplies for the farmer, thus overcoming the handicap of the small scale of production on the farm. Not all cooperatives have been successful and well managed. The mission considers that a continuing effort is required on the part of the Department of Cooperative Development to encourage the development of cooperatives in both the nonscheduled areas and the new settlement areas, to promote good management within the cooperatives and where desirable to foster the amalgamation of societies into units of

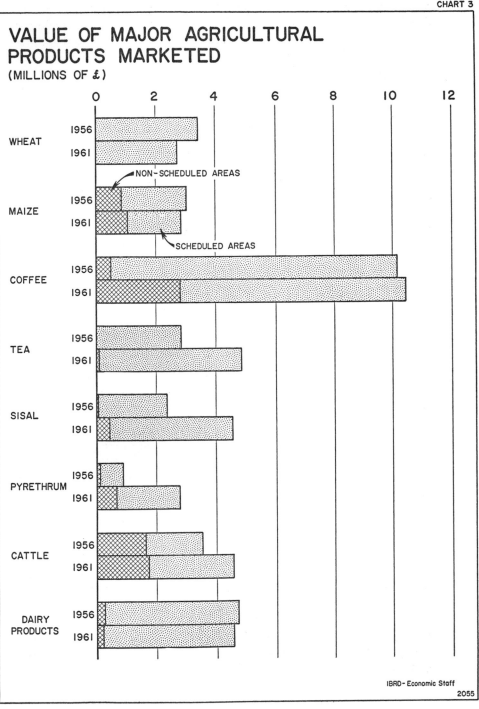

CHART 3

VALUE OF MAJOR AGRICULTURAL
PRODUCTS MARKETED
(MILLIONS OF £)

IBRD- Economic Staff

2055

a size more appropriate to the tasks to be undertaken. In the suggested development program 1963–67 provision has therefore been made for immediate expansion of the activities of the Department and for the gradual extension of the East African School of Cooperation (a joint Kenya-Tanganyika institution) which trains inspectors of cooperatives and staff of the societies.

PROSPECTS FOR INDIVIDUAL COMMODITIES

Coffee

Coffee is Kenya's most important cash crop and export commodity, with an annual value of more than £10 million, although this amounts to a little less than 2 percent of world coffee output. All the coffee grown is Arabica, except for 200 acres of Robusta in Nyanza Province. It is high quality and has been in relatively strong demand, particularly from West Germany, which imports about half of Kenya's coffee. The price at auction is consistently much higher than that of the arabica coffee of Brazil and the robustas of Africa and Asia. Coffee is grown as a plantation crop by Europeans, and as a cash crop on small farms by Africans operating through cooperative societies, membership being obligatory for any cultivator who wishes to plant coffee. The expansion of coffee production by Africans in recent years has played a significant role in the introduction of cash agriculture (see Chart 3). By 1961, African coffee growers were organized in 126 cooperative societies, which operated 160 coffee factories and 245 seedling nurseries. In 1960, there were some 840 holdings in the European areas, ranging from 20 acres to over 50,000 acres. By contrast, in the African areas, there were 105,000 growers with a total acreage of 33,000.

No coffee can be grown in Kenya except under license. The Ministry of Agriculture prescribes the actual areas in which coffee will be grown and the acreage which each cooperative society in the nonscheduled areas will be allotted. The Coffee Board of Kenya, which is a statutory body charged with control of coffee production, issues a bulk license to each cooperative society which distributes the total permissible area among its members. In 1960 the total acreage under coffee was 104,000, of which some 9,800 acres were under supplementary irrigation. The trends in acreage have been sharply upward in recent years. In 1954 the European acreage was 59,000, in 1960 it was 71,000 and in 1962 it was 74,000. The corresponding acreages planted by Africans were 5,300, 33,000 and 58,000. In 1960 the respective cash incomes of European and African producers were £9.4 million and £2.2 million.

It is not easy to assess comparative advantages or relative efficiencies based on costs without taking the quality factor into account. Attempts have been made to assess costs of production and an average figure of around £200 per ton has been estimated by officers of the Department of Agriculture. Estimates of net returns per acre are in the range of £10 to £60, with £40 to £60 being the attainable net return in well selected and managed African areas, where the highest standards of production have been maintained. The average yield of mature African-grown coffee, i.e., trees at five years old and upward, has been estimated by the Department of Agriculture to be 10 cwt per acre, whereas the average for the European acres was less than 7 cwt. The quality of the coffee produced in African areas has tended to be higher than that produced in the scheduled areas but has recently been falling. There are several explanations for this difference in performance as demonstrated in Table 2. From the environmental viewpoint, the African coffee plantings are probably better located, generally speaking, than the European. Some 60 percent of the existing trees on European plantations are old and need replacement—and are from relatively poor quality stock to begin with. African plantings are from good stock and they have been very carefully supervised and the growers are encouraged to use the latest techniques. Finally, most African cooperatives have required producers to meet quality standards and have imposed penalties, in some cases amounting to complete rejection, if the conditions have not been met.

Performance in African areas can vary greatly, however, both in respect of quality and yield, as is evidenced by South Nyanza. The relatively poor performance here appears to be due to a number of factors, among which are the breakdown in the powers of supervision and enforcement of penalties, weakness in the organization, method of selec-

TABLE 2: Coffee Production by Area and Grade, 1960–61 Season

A. EUROPEAN			B. AFRICAN		
Area	Tons	% in first 3 classes	Area	Tons	% in first 3 classes
Lower Kiambu	6,211	3.74	Meru	2,398	33.59
Upper Kiambu/Limuru	1,811	17.20	Embu	1,945	51.17
Thika	4,462	1.55	Kiambu	419	22.98
Ruiru	4,678	4.27	South Nyanza	970	8.39
Nyeri	1,027	9.26	Nyeri	589	39.96
Mitubiri	1,235	6.16	Fort Hall	653	46.40

SOURCE: Kenya Coffee Marketing Board.

tion and delegated power at the cooperative management level. The mission stresses the need to maintain the quality of supervision with sufficient numbers of experienced professional supervisors, and also the need to promote efficiency at managerial levels in cooperatives. There is a strong price incentive to produce quality coffee in that the average price for the top class is around 50 percent higher than the average for all grades. But, in view of the market situation, and the need for Kenya to maintain the high reputation of her coffee, we think that penalties should continue to be imposed upon individuals and cooperatives producing coffee below the specified standards of quality. Shortage of credit can be a problem in the early stages of cooperative organization. At a later stage, however, when the crop is delivered, obligations can be met by deductions; this is a big advantage from the point of view of the lending agency. Coffee is a crop that can finance the general development of the African farm, and has been the key cash crop in farm development after consolidation in many areas.

The mission considers that the Coffee Board and the Coffee Marketing Board, which are responsible for the production and marketing of coffee, are well organized. The crop is marketed efficiently, with quality differentials being worked out on a sound basis and reflected back to producers in accordance with what is determined in the open market. The Marketing Board alone is permitted to purchase coffee from planters; the Board supervises the curing of coffee and the classification of samples by grades and arranges for all sales of coffee whether within or without Kenya. In view of the market situation confronting the industry, there is very great need to maintain quality and all-round efficiency in production and to control the amount and the location of new plantings. Although the Board has the power to refuse licenses, it had not done so when the mission was in Kenya. We consider that this matter is sufficiently important as to call for government directives.

Coffee is a very popular crop and much of the big increase in plantings in the past few years has yet to be reflected in increased production. From Table 3, it can be seen that total output is expected to increase from the 35,500 tons in 1962 to 60,000 tons in 1966. To restrict expansion beyond this period, the Government will need to assume responsibility quickly for enforcing the restriction of new planting to the amount it decides to permit.

The World Market Outlook. At the present time, world surplus stocks are substantially in excess of one year's world demand and the annual rate of production is about 130 percent of annual world consumption. This situation has been caused by several factors. During 1950–57, the relatively high coffee prices stimulated a wave of new plantings. These

TABLE 3: Forecast of Coffee Production, 1962–66

(tons)

	African	Non-African	Total
1962	12,700	22,800	35,500
1963	16,300	23,900	40,200
1964	20,400	25,100	45,500
1965	27,700	26,600	54,300
1966	32,500	27,500	60,000

SOURCE: Department of Agriculture.

new plantings continued generally in the world until 1958 and later in some countries. World production rose by about 1.6 million tons or 72 percent between 1950/51 and 1958/59.

Because plants do not come into bearing for three or four years and only approach full bearing after eight years, the very substantial increases in plantings are only now coming to have their main effect on production and, as the rate of increased plantings has substantially exceeded wastage of old trees, production will continue to rise if most of the berries maturing on the trees continue to be harvested. The recent price trend will tend to curb additional plantings. Policies of uprootings and abandonments in major producing countries are under consideration. Even so, annual production is likely to exceed consumption for some years to come with further depressing effects on prices of some coffees.

Estimates of the likely production and consumption situation in 1965 have been made.[22] These estimates show a range of 4.4–5.0 million tons for world output in 1965 or increases of 25 percent to 40 percent above the output in the 1958/59 season. World imports in 1965 are put in the range of 2.76–2.94 million metric tons, an increase of 10 percent to 20 percent above the 1959 total. In summary, the estimated situation for 1965 is that world imports in that year are not likely to account for more than 60 percent of world production. Allowing for growth of consumption in producing countries and for greater industrial uses of coffee (in fertilizers, oil, feed, etc.) total demand may account for only about 80 percent of current production. In the meantime, in the absence of special disposals measures, stocks will have grown very much.

As the best answer to the problem of surpluses, segments of the world coffee industry have long sought an international coffee agreement, and a five-year agreement was formulated in 1962. There are special factors

[22] *The World Coffee Economy*, Commodity Bulletin Series, FAO of the UN, Rome, 1961.

in Kenya's position as a producer for which she will be seeking due allowance in any coffee agreement. Kenya has only recently become a factor in world coffee production and output from existing plantings will rise very rapidly over the next few years. Kenya coffee is in special demand because of its high quality. The country has a high potential as an efficient producer and has a critical need for export earnings to assist in its development. Coffee is of especial importance to the country's farm development program.

If the world coffee problem is fundamentally a case of oversupply by the major producers, as the mission believes it is, continuance by Kenya of its present rate of planting would not in itself significantly intensify the anticipated disparity between world production and world consumption. However, for there to be an international agreement which would have some prospects of stabilizing prices, control on exports by all suppliers is necessary. The 1962 International Coffee Agreement provides for export quotas by producing countries, for certificates of origin for each shipment of coffee, and restrictions on imports by consuming countries from producing countries not participating in the Agreement. Kenya's basic export quota for the first three years of the Agreement—516,835 bags (30,500 tons)—total exports in 1961 amounted to about 32,000 tons—makes no provision for the expected increases in production shown in Table 3. Exports to "new markets," countries which now consume small quantities of coffee, are not included under export quotas, but only about 1,000 tons of Kenya's coffee exports in 1961 went to these countries. Within the agreement Kenya is likely to be faced with large surpluses for disposal if production forecasts are realized, but Kenya's position outside an agreement which included major consumers as well as producers would be very difficult. In the absence of any agreement to regulate supplies from the major producers to the market, Kenya could find the special characteristics of its coffee insufficient to prevent a major decline in price.

As with other commodities, cooperation on an East African basis is desirable in regard to coffee. Kenya's situation is somewhat unique due to the strong demand for its particular grades of arabica coffee, and there may be scope for arrangements between the East African countries designed to ensure that exports under agreement quotas include as much high-grade coffee as possible. We have mentioned earlier that West Germany takes about half of Kenya's coffee. Italy and the Netherlands are also importers and, if the United Kingdom is added, about three-quarters of Kenya's coffee exports are accounted for. Coffee entering the European Common Market is subject to an import duty of 16 percent, which has been suspended to the extent of 6.4 percent, and to high internal taxes. Trade relations between the East African Customs Union and the Common Market can therefore be an important factor in the marketing of Kenyan, and East African, coffee.

The world supply situation for coffee calls for a reconsideration of the role of coffee in the future agricultural development of Kenya. With Kenya's present quota under the international agreement, any surge in output in the next few years will pose difficult marketing problems. Immediate action is therefore required to discourage new plantings and to limit production of unsalable, particularly low-quality, coffee. Among possible measures to achieve this are quantitative restriction against new plantings, and export taxes as a general disincentive to coffee production. In considering the prospects for the expansion of other commodities, livestock and dairying, later in this report, we have had the need to reduce the emphasis which has been placed on coffee in the development of African production for the market very much in mind.

Tea

Unlike coffee, there are no large stocks overhanging and threatening the world tea market. No sudden upsurge in production of a kind that would demoralize the world market is anticipated from the major producing countries, but plantings and yields are increasing. On the whole, there has been a reasonable balance between supply and demand for many years and tea prices have shown greater stability than those of most other primary commodities.

Kenya's output of 30 million pounds accounts for about 2 percent or 3 percent of world production. Tea plantings have increased substantially over the past decade in Kenya, however, and the industry now ranks with sisal as second earner of export income. The mission considers there is scope for further expansion of the country's tea production.

The political uncertainty frequently mentioned in this report has recently had a considerable influence on tea plantings in the scheduled areas. In 1961, fresh plantings were of the order of 500 acres, in contrast to an average of 3,000 acres annually during 1957–59. Of the total acreage under tea of approximately 37,000 acres, however, 34,500 acres were located in the scheduled areas. Tea plantations employ approximately one worker per acre of tea, and the tea industry as a whole accounts for about 9 percent of the total Kenya labor force.

The estate owners have cooperated in the development of small-scale tea cultivation and manufacturing, and every effort should be made to extend this cooperation in the future. Experience has already proved that tea growing is feasible under smallholder cultivation. A project in the Nyeri district (1,200 smallholdings delivering to a central factory) has demonstrated, for instance, that yields of manufactured tea in excess of 1,000 pounds per acre can be expected after seven or eight years of cultivation. In 1961, development of smallholder tea cultivation was made the responsibility of the Special Crops Development Authority (SCDA).

Estimates of Future Production. The working party which recommended the establishment of the SCDA also recommended a phased tea development plan which would raise the 1959 tea area of 1,600 acres under African cultivation to 10,900 acres by 1966/67. As from 1971/72 when the whole area attained full production, the estimated output of made tea would be 10.9 million pounds per annum.

This plan was accepted and put under execution in 1959/60. Initial difficulties in developing the full area and factory production have now been overcome and though the areas actually planted during the first two years fall somewhat short of the amounts contemplated for those years, the plan will now be developed as intended. Finance has been secured for this purpose from the Colonial Development Corporation, the Federal Republic of Germany and tea companies.

Estimates for the years 1962/63 to 1966/67, taking into account the effects on total production of the acreages planted from 1956 onward, are shown in Table 4.

TABLE 4: Estimated Production of Tea, 1962–67

(million lbs)

	African	Scheduled Areas[a]	Total Production
1962/63	1.20	35.46	36.66
1963/64	2.00	37.50	39.50
1964/65	3.23	38.70	41.93
1965/66	4.83	39.28	44.11
1966/67	7.01	39.68	46.69

[a] This assumes increased plantings 1961–63 of 500 acres annually.

The case for expanding tea plantings rests to a considerable extent on the relative efficiency of the industry in relation to the major exporting countries. Much of the industry in Kenya has been established comparatively recently, and under the influence of the latest technological methods. The costs of clearing land and establishing plantations have increased greatly, but typical costs may favor Kenya substantially in comparison with Ceylon and India, on an average per pound basis. Fortunately also, Kenya tea is no longer hampered by the old belief that it could only be considered a good "filler" type; results in the Nairobi and London markets reveal that the Kenya product is highly competitive in the medium and plain fields.

Proposals for Further Development. The Special Crops Development Authority has prepared two new programs for tea development under African cultivation in the nonscheduled areas. Of the new plans, the mission favors one which would increase new plantings over the current plan by 12,300 acres during the years 1962/63 to 1970/71. This would give a total area of 23,250 acres of African-grown tea by the latter year. Its effect on production of made tea from the present nonscheduled areas would be, other things being equal, to raise it eventually to around 23 million pounds. An estimated addition of 12 million pounds would thus be produced, which, at a price of Sh. 3.8 per pound at the Nairobi auctions, would have a value of £2.3 million per annum. This increase, though large from the standpoint of Kenya, would form a very small percentage of world tea production. While not overlooking the fact that a world surplus of tea might occur at some time in the future, the mission considers that the normal increase in world consumption, the quality and relative cost of Kenya tea, and a continuation of efficient distribution activities justify the implementation of this program. We would stress once again the important need to maintain past standards of supervision of the developing industry since the market outlook is not favorable for a low-quality product.

The Authority's estimate of loan requirements is £1.3 million for field development, and £1.25 million for factory development during the period of our program.

Tea development by the Authority is on an ultimately self-financing basis. Cesses levied on each pound of green leaf supplied to the factory by the grower cover recurrent expenses and recoup development expenditures. Maximum borrowings for field development would be reached in 1971. Thereafter receipts from cesses are expected to exceed annual expenditure. The mission considers that finance should be sought for the SCDA plan described above.

Sisal

In 1961 the sisal industry had become, with tea, second in Kenya in respect of export earnings, its contribution of £4.2 million being nearly 13 percent of the total. In that year, Kenya produced a little more than 10 percent of the world's total production; but this added to Tanganyika's 40 percent gives half the world market to East African sisal.

The expansion of output over recent years has been rapid, the output in 1956 being 40,000 tons (all grades) and in 1961 64,000 tons, an increase of 60 percent. This increase is in no small measure due to the stimulus of the high prices of the early fifties to increased plantings (plants take 2½ years to 4 years to reach maturity).

In addition to its great value as an export earner, sisal is labor intensive, and in the main is grown in the drier semi-intensive farming areas not highly suitable for higher price cash crops. The average labor force employed in the sisal industry is around 25,000. The industry requires permanent settlements with large supplies of water for decorticating.

The total planted area of sisal at the end of 1960 was estimated to be 264,000 acres, mostly in the scheduled areas. The yield of the mature area cut was 0.393 tons per acre. There has been little change in planted acreage in recent years. Most of the output comes from holdings producing more than 750 tons of fiber.

There are no reliable cost figures for sisal in Kenya. The structure of the industry is in many ways similar to that of Tanganyika, and the important fact is that East African production, which is marketed by the Joint Sisal Board, is generally conceded to be comparatively efficient.

It is believed that the future development of the industry could be related to land settlement schemes. The Swynnerton Plan, discussed earlier in this chapter, suggested a program of seven schemes that would produce some 8,000 tons to 10,000 tons a year valued at £700,000. It was suggested that, in certain selected areas, sisal should be developed in plantation form and that "the aim should be to plant up the area in blocks, either a certain acreage being allocated to each family providing the labor or development being as estates on a collective 'basis.' "[23] This development has not taken place.

The last big expansion in estate acreages—of the order of 33,000 acres —took place in the early 1950's. There is room for further development on estates, but future production trends are likely to depend chiefly on the extent to which there has been the necessary reinvestment in replacement plantings, which have been influenced by political and economic uncertainty. Production is not expected to increase much over the next five years.

The Market Outlook. Sisal represented only 16 percent of the world output of hard fibers in the early 1920's, but the proportion had increased by 1956 to two-thirds of the world supply. Since then consumption and production have continued to increase 3 percent per annum. Markets for sisal have proved resilient in the face of new techniques and new fibers for wrapping and binding. It now seems unlikely that a syn-

---

[23] Swynnerton Plan, *op. cit.*, p. 20.

thetic agricultural twine will appear that can compete on a cost basis with sisal unless, of course, the cost of producing sisal increases relatively by a large percentage. Sisal should also compete with other hard fibers, such as abaca, as successfully in the future as it has in the past. In these circumstances, an increase in demand of 2 percent per year is foreseeable. No big upsurges are expected from other sources of supply—Brazil, Indonesia, Angola, Haiti and Mozambique.

The mission therefore feels that there is scope for the expansion of the industry in East Africa. We endorse the proposal to set up a working party to investigate the prospects for the development of the industry among Africans. Should the working party report favorably on the willingness of farmers to cooperate and the availability of developmental opportunities, the functions of the SCDA might be expanded to cover this crop and to implement a plan of development.

The mission considers that, at the same time, the Kenya Government should endeavor to create the conditions for increased investment in the further development of sisal estates and take such measures as are necessary to prevent the decline of this essential source of export income.

Pyrethrum

Pyrethrum was first grown in Kenya before World War II and in the last three to four years production has expanded rapidly. By 1961 the value of exports had increased to £3.1 million. A further large expansion of the industry could take place if markets could be found for the product. Kenya supplies about three-quarters of world production and is an efficient producer.

Production is licensed by the Pyrethrum Board which has pursued a vigorous policy of product research, promotion and market development. These have been major factors in the expansion of the industry in recent years. Pyrethrum is marketed in the form of dried flowers or as an extract. The proportion of extract sales has been increasing and the Board has now completed a second factory giving a total capacity of 12,000 tons to 13,000 tons of flowers.

The most significant development of recent years, in terms of production, has been the increase in small-scale farming. In 1952 there were only 182 growers, who produced about 82 tons of pyrethrum, but by 1960 there were 30,000 African growers most of whom relied on it as their only cash crop. At £10 to £15 per acre it is not a costly crop to establish and returns of £40 and above per acre are readily obtainable. Since pyrethrum produces a harvest in the first year after sowing, its value as a rapid cash earner is of considerable importance on high altitude smallholdings which have just come under consolidation or settlement.

As an insecticide pyrethrum has the advantages of quick knockdown and nontoxicity. This gives it a superiority in use around the home and in the presence of foodstuffs and livestock. It has the characteristics of no residual effectiveness. A synthetic pyrethrum called allethrin is manufactured in Japan at a lower price, and thus presents a major challenge; preliminary tests, however, suggest that the natural product has a more effective knockdown potency.

Production quotas were reduced in 1962 because local production had run ahead of markets and competition from Tanganyika and Ecuador had increased, but in the longer term there might well be a sustained increased demand depending upon the results of research into wider usage. The mission recommends that the policy of controlling production in accordance with estimated demand, while at the same time intensifying research and market development, should continue to be followed.

Dairying

It was estimated that the income accruing to producers of dairy products in 1960 was £4.9 million, of which £193,000 accrued to African farmers. Total sales of the Kenya Cooperative Creameries Ltd. (KCC), the organization which handles 99 percent of exports, were slightly over £4.1 million, of which £1.8 million was from exports and £846,000 from outside East Africa. The supplies of dairy produce to KCC were drawn from about 3,000 farmers, of whom around 1,200 were African. However, about 95 percent of the total supplies came from the scheduled areas, reflecting the very great difference in the scale of operations between small and large producers. Approximately 65 percent of the farms in the scheduled areas have dairy cattle.

The Kenya Dairy Board was formed in 1959 following the collapse of the world market for dairy products. Its duty was to stabilize the industry, as it appeared possible that the low prices realized for exported produce would lead to a collapse of the voluntary cooperative principle and to a scramble for the more lucrative local market. The Board appointed the Kenya Creameries Cooperative Ltd. as its agent in handling, processing and selling dairy products. The KCC, which is a profit-making cooperative, owns nine creameries and five sales depots; it collects and supplies wholemilk to distributors; it manufactures and exports butter and ghee; it produces high-quality Gouda, Cheddar and Tavern cheeses. Other activities are the production of skim and wholemilk powder, condensed milk, casein and ice cream.

In the light of changing circumstances, including high-density settlement in the scheduled areas, it is very difficult to assess the likely course of production within the industry. There is no doubt that the potential for expansion is large, mainly because of the very great scope for intensification. Milk production in Kenya is low,[24] and an attack on the technical problems—breeding, legumes, etc.—should bring very good results.

The dairy industry is very much affected by the general outlook in world trade in primary products. World production in milk products has on the whole tended for a long time to expand at a too rapid rate. Rigidities within the industry in many countries and support or guaranteed price policies have not been conducive to reducing supplies. The future of the industry in Kenya depends upon sound diversification of production, more efficient or lower cost production, the development of relatively nearby markets and close collaboration on import policy with the other countries of East Africa.

A comprehensive plan for development and diversification of the industry was submitted by the KCC for examination by the mission. The plan includes further development of the wholemilk trade by increasing aseptic tetrapak filling, together with the extension of the condensed milk plant, the installation of a new cheese plant and stores, wholemilk powder packing, casein manufacture extension, extra roller driers and new receiving depots in the Central Province and South Nyanza for increasing supplies from smallholdings. At a later stage the installation of spray drying and reconstitution plants is proposed, also the extension of the Nairobi milk plant and new receiving depots. It is understood that the KCC feels that to sell the products throughout East Africa, and so reduce the very considerable import bill, some degree of protection may be necessary against competitive products that are being subsidized directly or indirectly. The mission has examined the proposals and, recognizing the economic, social and technical importance of the dairy industry, and also, the great contribution it can make to settlement schemes, considers that the necessary finance to implement this plan should be sought; the loan requirements over the next four years are estimated to be £550,000.

As already pointed out, we feel that such a plan can only succeed within a general framework of an East African import-saving policy.

[24] In 1958 the average milk yield per cow in gallons was 634 in the United Kingdom, 578 in New Zealand, 368 in Australia, while in Kenya it was 229 (see FAO Year Book for 1959).

The need for further protection against imports should be investigated. At the same time an intensive trade drive in accessible markets should be initiated.

The Meat Industry

The value of exports of meat and meat preparations in 1961 was estimated to be £2.3 million and for hides, skins and fur skins, undressed, £1.6 million. The growth of the export trade in meat and meat preparations since 1957, when it was only £347,000, is due both to the expanding activities of the Kenya Meat Commission and to the development of mixed farming and ranching. Between 1954 and 1960 the cattle population rose by 30 percent and the sheep population by 13 percent. The pig population, after a rapid rise between 1954 and 1958 from 38,000 to 70,000, declined to 50,000 in 1960 due largely to temporary difficulties in marketing.

There is no doubt that meat and meat products of high quality can be produced efficiently in Kenya, and on a cost basis, the country is in a strongly competitive position. However, because of the diseases affecting livestock in East Africa, there are barriers in importing countries in respect to meat from this area. There are transport difficulties as well, including a scarcity of refrigerated transportation, although in this regard the development of the canning industry has been of much importance.

In 1957 the Government canning factory, which had been completed in 1954 but never used, was taken over by the Kenya Meat Commission (KMC), which is a statutory body that carries out a full range of meat processing and marketing functions. To encourage the production of competitive corned beef and extract for export, an agreement to provide technical assistance was made with a large overseas company. A rapid rise in output followed, and by 1960 8.5 million cans of corned beef and 236,000 pounds of beef extract were being produced. Export markets for frozen beef were developed, and export income from meat and meat products increased from £374,000 in 1957 to £2.3 million in 1961. At the same time a large part of the requirements of Tanganyika and Uganda were met. A large increase in hides and skins output paralleled this expansion.

The KMC has been financed largely by the Government of Kenya, by the Standard Bank Finance and Development Corporation Ltd., the Colonial Development Corporation and the Guardian Assurance Co., Ltd. It has a sizable revenue reserve, mainly in the form of a stabilization reserve, and a tax equalization reserve, and is in what appears to be a very sound financial position. The results achieved over recent years indicate that it has been operating very efficiently and has made a major contribution toward the development of the livestock industry of Kenya.

It was originally intended that the Meat Commission should buy in African areas, but for a number of reasons this proved impracticable, and the African Livestock Marketing Organization (ALMO) was established by the Government to encourage sales of stock in the pastoral areas to advance the destocking of overstocked areas, and to ensure the movement of cattle to market without spreading disease. It has been subsidized by the Government because its functions have been much more than pure trading. The Government has contributed more than £90,000 per annum for staff, and traveling, auxiliary equipment, vaccines, upkeep of stock routes, maintenance of holding grounds, and the like. In addition, there was a loss in the 1960/61 financial year of over £17,000 at the Archer's Post (Samburu) Abattoir and over £7,000 at the Baringo Abattoir. In all but the remote pastoral areas ALMO has helped local traders to take over marketing themselves. The mission considers that ALMO itself should be put on a self-supporting basis within the next four years. Cesses on sales of animals might be a feasible means of accomplishing this result. ALMO's share of the surplus accruing to KMC should, now that its loan for stock purchases has been repaid, be spent on the further development of marketing facilities.

Without going into full details of livestock production and consumption trends, it appears safe to conclude that the long-term outlook is reasonably good. There is scope for development of markets within Africa and in nearby regions, although the prospects in Europe are somewhat problematical pending developments within the European Common Market. We would recommend the appointment of two commercially experienced market and trade development specialists to promote the export of meat and dairy products, to be borne by the KMC and KCC.

The Meat Commission placed before the mission a plan for the further development of its facilities over the next five years. This includes housing at processing works, the construction of a cold store at Nakuru, and the construction of an additional canning factory.

The expansion program appears to be one which can readily be justified. The mission thinks that the project is sound and that the necessary financing should be sought. The estimated cost is £557,000 during the period of our program.

The Wool Industry

Wool is a quite important source of export income for Kenya, and the mission considers there may be scope for a further increase in production. In the scheduled areas, the sheep population grew from 357,000 in 1954 to 583,000 in 1960, with production of raw wool increasing from 1.2 million pounds to 2.1 million pounds and the value of exports from £215,000 to £377,000.

Most of the production of wool is from the bigger farms in the scheduled areas. A major proportion of these lie within the medium-potential zone where, despite some major hazards, there are some very efficient production units based on Merino and Corriedale breeds. In order to be successful in this zone, operations need to be on a large scale because of the heavy investment in water facilities and fencing. Thus development of the wool industry need not compete in respect of land resources for African resettlement. There would be scope also for increased production in the high-potential lands parallel with a pasture improvement program. It has been proved in Australia that high-quality wool can be produced efficiently on lush pastures in zones of comparatively high rainfall as a result of, among other things, major advances in disease control. The prospects for the wool industry in the scheduled areas, however, depend on the general future pattern of production there.

The development of the industry among African farmers presents a more complex problem. African sheep have been produced for subsistence rather than for the market. Very few of the indigenous stock are shorn, but they furnish a convenient supply of meat and skins for family use, and are more often bartered or sold than are cattle. Initial experience in developing African sheep production in high altitude areas has indicated some difficulties, but it may be possible in the larger run to teach the farmers in the more intensive mixed farming zones, for example, to handle exotic sheep or dual purpose sheep, admitting the great care and skill required in the use of disease control measures.

Although synthetic fibers have displaced wool for some end uses, no artificial fiber to match the all-round qualities of wool has yet been produced, and there has been a trend toward the blending of wool and synthetics. No spectacular price rises in wool can be expected, but the outlook for wool is sufficiently good to warrant an efficient low-cost producer to engage in a program to expand production.

We recommend that a plan for the efficient expansion of the wool industry of Kenya be formulated, considering economic as well as the technical aspects. Advantage might be taken of such outside assistance as can be provided by FAO and the experienced commercial agency that handles most of Kenya's wool.

Sugar

Kenya's requirements of sugar have been met partly from local production and supplies from Uganda and partly by importing from overseas. In 1961 local production amounted to 33,000 tons, a similar quantity came from Uganda, and 27,000 tons were imported. The sugar millers at Miwani in Nyanza Province and at Ramisi on the coast have their own plantations. Cane is also supplied to Miwani by Asian smallholders. Acreage under sugar rose from 25,000 in 1956 to 42,000 in 1960.

Undoubtedly there is the potential for highly efficient production of sugar cane in Kenya, particularly with supplementary irrigation. In Nyanza soil surveys have indicated that there is a large area suitable for sugar production. With the selection of appropriate varieties and with control of smut, an efficient expansion of the industry could be achieved.

Sugar produced in Kenya has been mill white, not refined, which involves a process of recrystallization. However, a refinery has recently been erected at Miwani. Both mill white and refined sugar have sold at the same price at retail. A specialist recently recommended[25] that the East African sugar industry institute a price incentive to produce a better quality of manufactured sugar, with penalties for sugar of lower quality. This scheme has not, however, been fully implemented. No alteration of the system of pricing, which in East Africa is based on the Commonwealth Sugar Agreement price (increased by a premium equal to a refining margin of Sh.110 per ton), was proposed. Rather, it was recommended that the price payable to millers for mill white sugar should be reduced by Sh.67.20 per long ton. This could mean a drop in the average price to the consumer of approximately 5 percent while the superior product (properly packed refined sugar) would still be available at the old price. In addition it was suggested that a levy of Sh.89.60 per long ton should be paid into a Sugar Quality Equalization Fund which would be used to award quality premiums to those manufacturers who produce sugar of a quality better than a certain minimum standard. We recommend that this scheme should be introduced.

The Market Outlook. It has been estimated that by 1970 world consumption of centrifugal sugar would increase at an average annual rate of perhaps 3.5 percent per year. On this basis it would be 50 percent higher in 1970 than it was in 1950.[26] There is no reason why efficient producers for export should not share this expanded market. However, East Africa as a whole has been importing sugar and there would appear to be room for a substantial increase in production to meet East African requirements. Projections supplied by the EACSO indicate that, after taking into account some production plans in all three countries which have yet to mature, consumption may rise faster than production in the

[25] Report by K. Douwes Dekker to the Department of Economic Coordination, Nairobi, September 1959.

[26] An FAO report by Messrs. Viton and Pignalosa entitled *Trends and Prospects of World Sugar Consumption 1960.*

second half of the 1960's, leaving an import requirement of 33,000 tons of sugar in 1970. Unless new plans for expanding the industry are initiated, the gap will be very much larger since a 119,000 ton level of production by 1970 is assumed for Kenya. Plans for expansion of sugar production should be judged in the context of the general East African understanding on commodity problems which we have already urged. As a potentially efficient producer, we believe Kenya has a strong claim as a supplier of part of East Africa's anticipated requirements. The three East African countries may also still have the opportunity of preferential treatment in some export markets, as they still have an allocation under the Commonwealth Sugar Agreement.

The mission believes that it would not be worthwhile to put up a modern factory to process additional output without an assured throughput of around 50,000 tons of manufactured sugar. We also feel that, having due regard to the import-saving possibility and the market outlook, Kenya should set early plans for an expansion of 50,000 tons. Settlement opportunities for African smallholders must also be kept in mind, and the mission considers that an equitable arrangement might be sought under which investors would set up and run a factory with a capacity of 50,000 tons of manufactured sugar within a selected area, on the condition that one-half of the cane required is taken from settlement farms.

Maize

Maize is the basic food crop of Kenya. Its real importance is therefore not reflected in the value of the marketed crop; by far the highest proportion is consumed on the farm or, at least, locally without being reflected in statistics. The recorded cash income to producers was £2.9 million in 1961, of which £1.1 million accrued to African farmers.

A large proportion of the high-potential areas, where temperatures are not limiting, is very suitable for maize production, and potentially the industry is an efficient one with scope for big increases in production, particularly through the development of hybrid maizes and intensification including the correct use of proper mineral fertilizers. The introduction of new varieties of maize will also increase production in the lower areas formerly unsuitable for maize production. Enough maize can be produced in normal years to meet all Kenya's requirements and any shortfalls in the production of Uganda and Tanganyika. It is also not resource limitations, but marketing difficulties, that would prevent production regularly for export on a considerable scale. The quality of Kenya's maize is high.

The Kenya Government's policy has been directed toward production of a surplus for export only sufficient to provide a safety margin against seasonal fluctuations and the related need to import periodically. Imports of maize, after the abandonment of the East African Cereals Pool in 1953, were very costly for Kenya and Tanganyika. But the introduction of new maizes will affect production, and it is the present depressed price in residual world markets, among other things, which is aggravating the problem of the Maize Marketing Board. The maize exported in recent years, mostly to Europe, has brought a price of little better than £1 per bag f.o.b. and farmers have received little better than Sh.17 at country centers.

Difficulties for the Marketing Board have also arisen because prices paid at country centers, to small producers, are often lower than prices paid to large farmers in the scheduled areas. The reason is that initial payments in the scheduled areas are based on the assumption that the maize will be consumed internally, and thus payments are subject to the guaranteed minimum price; any adjustment is made in the final payment for a season's crop. In areas where the quota system is not used, and where there are thousands of small producers, however, the necessarily more cumbersome system of marketing only allows pricing adjustments to be made in the following year, when it is reflected in that season's prices. The cost of certain additional services which the Maize Board provides to the small producer, including marketing staff and a transport pool, also affects the grower's price. Naturally, the small farmer, not fully understanding the complications, critically compares the price he receives with that received by the large producers.

Another criticism of the maize marketing system involves the price of posho to consumers. The posho price to the consumer is controlled, and posho mills must buy their maize supply from the Board. The high price of maize to the millers is due to two factors. First, the guaranteed producer price, at present Sh.35.6 per bag for the local market, is based on a standard of an eight-bag yield (1,600 pounds per acre), which is extremely low in relation to what an efficient producer can achieve. Furthermore, the Board's price to the miller has to be high enough above the guaranteed producer payment to cover administrative, marketing and storage costs, together with the loss on what is exported. This difference is very considerable. As one result, the price of posho to consumers is high; and as another consequence, the Board has a policing problem in preventing direct sales from producers to the miller. Because of the Board's high "mark-up," the miller can pay the producer a "premium" price and still get his maize cheaper than what he would have to pay the Board.

The alternative to a much closer policing of fixed-price sales would be to make the present legislation much freer and to permit open competition in regard to all locally consumed maize. This would in effect put the Board in the position of setting a floor price for producers and a ceiling for the posho manufacturers. At the same time, it could store surpluses against seasonal variations, distribute to deficiency regions as required and handle exports. In this role it could, in addition, prevent possible exploitative activities of the private traders which are deleterious to producers, to consumers, and indirectly to the economy as a whole.

One question that remains to be answered is how far this would reduce the volume of transactions by the Board and so increase its overhead costs. At present, out of a total crop, which is estimated to be at least 15 million bags, the Board handles only around 2 million bags. Because much of the maize is consumed on the farm, the bulk of the crop does not reach a formal market.

The mission's view, as already stated in its discussion of agricultural marketing, is that some form of organized marketing is essential. The marketing authority will need adequate facilities for the storage without deterioration of the product, prior to its movement to market, and for seasonal reserves of the order of at least one million bags of maize. The mission recommends that the principle of a guaranteed price to producers be retained, but the basis on which it has been established should be independently reviewed, as it appears to be unduly high.

The mission recommends that the Kenya Government should continue to negotiate, within the framework of a general import-saving policy, for a common policy for the organized marketing of maize for East Africa as a unit, to avoid wide fluctuations in supplies and prices, and to ensure stability of the industry in all three countries on a self-sufficiency basis. Pending the success of such negotiations, the Kenya Government may need to limit the movement of maize into Kenya from within East Africa to avoid undue financial difficulties within its own marketing arrangements.

The Other Grains

Wheat. The value of wheat output to producers over the five years 1956–60 has fluctuated between £2.7 million and £3.5 million. The wheat industry has been developed as a strategic import-saving industry within East Africa. Kenya wheat is not exported outside the customs union. The milling industries of Tanganyika and Uganda, as well as Kenya, depend on Kenya wheat.

In the scheduled areas, the industry is an integral part of the mixed farming pattern, although at one time production was at the expense of the long-term fertility and structure of the soil. Now, with an annual acreage of about 250,000, rotational cropping with temporary pastures and livestock is widely practiced. For the past ten years, the average yield has been around 15.5 bushels to the acre. The industry in Kenya has had to stand up against major hazards, the principal one being stem rust.

Although efficient wheat production is generally recognized as a large-scale operation, there is some evidence in the Central Province that smallholder production can be developed under particular circumstances, such as the loan of the necessary machinery during planting and harvesting seasons. We do not, however, expect the acreage under wheat to expand over the next few years. The course of production, apart from seasonal hazards, will be determined by decisions taken by farmers in the scheduled areas.

The quality of Kenya's wheat from the baking viewpoint is not good enough, and some wheat has to be imported for blending purposes to overcome this deficiency. If the rust problem can be overcome, improving the baking quality of Kenya's wheat will take on increased importance: the case for maintaining a wheat industry in Kenya rests mainly on the import-saving possibility, plus the advantages in greater local employment that derive from having it locally produced and processed. We recommend that the present research program on wheat varieties and wheat rust be maintained with increased attention to quality in relation to baking requirements.

Wheat growing is regulated by the Board of Agriculture (scheduled areas), with a guaranteed minimum return per acre. This system should be replaced by some form of insurance, as soon as this is found practicable. The Wheat Board takes over the responsibility for the wheat once it is ready for marketing. This responsibility relates to the movement of wheat to flour mills, to the licensing of mills and to the quantities allocated. The Board has neither financial nor executive functions, but works in liaison with the Ministry of Agriculture.

There is an East African agreement between Kenya and Tanganyika on wheat and flour policy. This relates to the licensing of mills. No new licenses are issued or capacity increased until the consumption of flour throughout the customs union has reached 85 percent of the total milling capacity. There is also an agreement on the entitlement of mills. A committee, with a representative of the East African Common Services Organization, provides the machinery for consultation. Although there have been difficulties, this agreement seems to us to have worked reasonably well.

Barley. Barley provides a substantial cash income to producers in the highlands. This has been variable in recent years, being around £646,000 in 1958 and down to £268,000 in 1961. Malt to the value of around £118,000 was imported into East Africa in 1961. The demand for imported malt comes mainly from brewers who have been concerned about the quality of the malt produced from Kenya barley. An incentive scheme, with licensing according to expectations for getting desired quality, might be worthwhile from the point of view of savings on imports, and we understand that the brewers have now undertaken to purchase the whole crop. We consider that the area which is suited to barley is not large enough to produce an export crop of any consequence.

Rice. Rice production has increased in Kenya over recent years, a major factor being the development of the Mwea-Tebere irrigation scheme. In 1961, the cash income to producers, all smallholders, had reached £384,000 from an acreage of 14,600. In Mwea-Tebere a yield of 43 cwts of paddy rice was obtained over 5,000 acres.

Consumption of rice has increased from around 8,400 tons in 1956 to around 13,000 tons in 1959, but imports are still significant, being around £252,000 for Kenya and £528,000 for East Africa as a unit in 1960. These amounts indicate the scope for efforts to encourage the consumption of locally grown rice. The sindani variety, which comprises around 85 percent of total production in Kenya, is of high quality, and in cooking and consumption tests it has compared very favorably with the imported varieties that appear to be favored among the Asian population.

Rice is now of considerable importance in Kenya, particularly in irrigation settlements. The potential for further development, both in Nyanza and in the Central Province around Mwea-Tebere, is considerable. Production is efficient, particularly at Mwea-Tebere, and although costs are high in certain areas, these could be very much reduced if a two-crop annual rotation can be developed.

Kenya has subsidized rice consumption. In 1959/60, the subsidy, which amounted in total to £22,000, was more than offset by the customs duty paid on imported rice. Under these circumstances, Kenya would find it extremely difficult to find external markets at remunerative prices. Nevertheless, a market research program should be maintained, and rice might be included in the general program of market exploration in nearby areas.

The mission recommends that the Kenya Government should continue its present policy of rice production, which is one of regulated expansion in accordance with what can be marketed. Marketing should be without subsidy, however. At the same time, the reasons for the market preference for rice from other countries should be kept under impartial investigation. Pending this investigation, Kenya might well adjust her production and import policy on the basis of some fixed percentage—say, for example, that local production should account for a minimum of 60 percent of total consumption.

A major complication for rice marketing, however, has been introduced by the low-priced supplies of rice from Tanganyika, which have been marketed in Mombasa with a competitive advantage over up-country paddy of Kenya on account of haulage costs. We recommend that the Kenya Government should continue to negotiate for a common policy in East Africa regarding rice, among several products, which might well be given encouragement and reasonable protection from external competition within the general framework of an import-saving policy.

Cotton

Cotton makes a considerable contribution to the cash income of smallholders in the Nyanza and the Coast Provinces, amounting to more than £500,000 in recent years. Exports of cotton in 1961 were £629,000. There are major fluctuations in yield, but in the past four years the variation in acreage has been small, averaging approximately 100,000 acres. Although a target to raise cotton production to 25,000 bales was suggested in the Swynnerton Plan, this has not been achieved, despite the developmental policy of the Cotton Lint and Seed Marketing Board.

The Board fixes a price to growers, and endeavors to avoid payments from the price assistance fund unless there are very exceptional circumstances. There are reserves of more than £1 million in the price assistance fund, much of this having been accumulated during the "Korean War boom."

Cotton varieties of 1–1/16 inches to 1–3/32 inches staple have been chosen on the advice of the Empire Cotton Growing Corporation to avoid excessive competition from the shorter staple length cotton of the U.S.A. While the outlook in world markets is not wholly reassuring, nevertheless there is the opportunity for expanded production by efficient low-cost producers of a good quality product. It must be borne in mind too that cotton fabrics to the value of more than £3 million are imported into Kenya and over £8 million into East Africa as a unit.

The mission considers that the present developmental policy for the cotton industry, which is designed to achieve expansion, should be maintained. Elsewhere we have supported strongly the case for a pre-investment survey of the Lower Tana with eventual large-scale irrigation development. The prospects for highly efficient cotton production in this area appear at first sight to be good. In the varietal investigations, attention should be paid not only to the types or staple lengths which appear to have the best prospects in the world markets, but also to the needs of a local cotton textile industry.[27]

Oil Crops

Kenya's main vegetable oil product is castor seed, which is produced in the African sector. The value of exports in 1960 was £179,500.

In view of the scope for the increased production of vegetable oils, the imports of vegetable oils were significant. In 1960, the value of net imports of coconut oil into Kenya was £122,000 and for East Africa as a whole £266,000. Palm oil to the value of £456,000 was imported into the three countries in 1960. It is considered that Kenya should aim toward a far greater degree of self-sufficiency in vegetable oil production. For example, production of copra, cottonseed oil and peanut oil can and should be expanded. The coconut improvement scheme, which includes the distribution of better seedlings, should if possible be intensified, together with measures for improving drying techniques or facilities.

The prospects for efficient producers of fats and oils in world market are by no means unfavorable. Since the early 1950's world stocks have fluctuated, but there has been no long-term accumulation, and the trend in world consumption has been about the same as that in production. There would appear to be some excellent opportunities for development of export trade. Particular reference is made to the prospects for castor oil and geranium oil.

The castor oil plant grows under a wide range of conditions of soil and rainfall and could become an important cash crop, in the drier farming areas as well as the higher rainfall districts. With the outlook for increased coffee production far from being reassuring, it is considered that the Ministry should examine the desirability of promoting castor oil as an organized cash crop. The question of whether the oil should be eventually expressed within Kenya need not be resolved immediately but should, nevertheless, be investigated, keeping in mind the scale of operations in relation to economic production and the particular demands of importing countries.

Geranium oil is another product with good market prospects, particularly if types in strong demand are produced. Such a type—the Bourbon variety—has been introduced into Kenya and, despite early setbacks, the mission considers that efforts to develop the industry in Kenya should be intensified.

[27] See Chapter 5.

Wattle

Wattle was the main cash crop in Central Province for a long period of years. Because of extensive felling for building villages and fencing during the recent emergency, bark output from this sector was reduced to about two-thirds of its pre-emergency production. Since then land consolidation has taken place in this region and wattle growing is giving place to other cash crops and to mixed farming. The output of bark from the scheduled areas increased from 19,000 tons in 1954 to 31,000 tons in 1960, but acreages devoted to the crop have declined in recent years.

In view of the unfavorable world market outlook, a policy for the development of the wattle industry cannot be recommended.

Horticultural Crops

Among horticultural crops the most important are pineapples for export and bananas for internal consumption. Though a wide variety of fruit grows in the colony, the export possibilities of fresh fruit are limited. In general, hauling distances are a hindrance and the quality of the produce is not competitive with that of other producing countries. In whatever is grown for export, it is essential that every possible attention should be given to quality.

Pineapples. A small quantity of fresh Kenya pineapples reaches the London market by air and seems to be well regarded. Though the prices obtained are high, disposal by this means is not entirely satisfactory. Only the best pines are selected for export. Since the time taken in transit by air is short, the fruit travels in a ripe condition. Pines rejected for export are by then too ripe for canning use and are a loss to the producer. If export by sea could be developed, the fruit would travel in a much less ripe condition and rejected pines could be utilized. Market research in this area is suggested.

Cashew Nuts. Cashew nuts grow successfully in the Coast Province. Seven thousand tons were produced in 1960; 1,200 tons were processed locally and exported in sealed tins to the U.S.A.; direct exports in the unprocessed state were valued at £250,000. The value of these direct exports, if processed, would have been on the order of £600,000. This would suggest that an expansion of local processing might well be considered, and the development of a suitable nutcracker is being explored with the National Institute of Agricultural Engineering in the United Kingdom. However, a note of caution should be sounded regarding expansion. Although a firm demand for cashew nut kernels is expected to continue, nevertheless the market is a limited one. Apart from the United States, consumption in other countries is small indeed. Furthermore, India is an efficient producer and is endeavoring to increase exports. Market prospects should be kept under close review.

Other Fruits. Strawberries could possibly be a valuable small crop. The industry is now dependent on one variety of plant which is imported and which costs about £330 per acre planted. Gross income is said to be approximately £1,000 per acre and net income about £500 per acre per year. A research effort is being made to produce a good local variety.

FORESTS AND FISHERIES

Forests

Kenya's forest estate—representing about 3 percent of the total land area—ranks as one of the country's most important national assets. Forests fulfill several economic functions, in their role as a conservative land cover, as the source of supply of forest products, and as a revenue earner of high potential. Of the total of 6,800 square miles of forest estate, approximately 5,500 is Crown Land and mangrove and 1,400 is held in the name of African District Councils.

Kenya's past experience apparently has shown that the comparative return is greater from the creation of new forests than from the regeneration of old forests. Thus, forest policy is based on new plantings. Parts of the Kenya highlands are well suited to the growing of softwoods. The Craib "B" Plan,[28] adopted in 1956, set a target of raising Kenya's softwood forest—cypress and pine—from the 92,000 acres existing then to 237,000 acres by 1968. This target called for a planting program of approximately 15,000 acres annually. By 1960, the softwoods forest area totaled 128,000 acres, and the original planting schedule is expected to continue until 1964, when the planting rate will be reduced to below 13,000 acres because of inadequate facilities. Allowing for losses from fellings, drought, fire, etc., it is estimated that, in softwoods, Kenya will have a total forest area of about 225,000 acres in 1968, which would leave a shortfall of about 12,000 acres below the Craib "B" target.

Timber growing is a long-term process, of course, and returns from plantings now being made will not begin to be realized until the 1980's: a first thinning of softwood forests usually takes place after 17 years or

[28] After Dr. Ian Craib, who was invited by the Government of Kenya to examine and make recommendations.

so; a second thinning is made at about 25 years; and the main fellings of mature timber come after 35 years.

During 1959 to 1961, the FAO undertook a study of present and prospective wood consumption in each of the East African countries at the request of the East Africa High Commission. It has been estimated on the basis of the FAO report and on present planting programs in the three countries that there would be an over-all deficit in available production of the order of eleven million cubic feet per annum by the year 1980, although Kenya would have a surplus of some four million cubic feet.[29] Consequently, the mission would deem it desirable for Kenya to accelerate its planting program.

The mission would recommend the establishment of two new forest stations, which in Kenya are centers for producing seedling plants for the planting program as well as being foci for general forestry activity for surrounding areas. The cost of two additional stations, including establishment of the necessary labor community and relocation of resident families, would be on the order of £30,000 in capital expenditure and an increase in Forestry Department recurrent expenditures of about £3,000 a year. These two stations would in effect bring the planting schedule for the next few years closer to the original Craib "B" program. For the next few years, say 1964 to 1967, the mission would envisage increased plantings of perhaps 1,000 acres a year over acreages now scheduled for those years.

The success of the forestry program is uncertain because of expected difficulties in staffing. The mission does not envisage that effective localization of the professional forestry staff can be achieved quickly; recruitment at present depends on sending suitable candidates overseas for the necessary university training. It is hoped that a new diploma course in forestry at Egerton College will provide a supply of diploma holders from 1964 onward with which to localize the forester cadre. We would stress that African officers on first recruitment will often be without any previous practical experience of forestry, and that it will be important to retain or secure the services of experienced expatriates.

Fisheries

There would seem to be little demand at this time for any major development of Kenya's fisheries industry. The export of fish and fish products is small and the likelihood of developing an appreciable export trade would seem not to lie in the immediate future. The profitable

[29] Report of the Committee on East African Forestry.

species in general are found beyond Kenya's territorial limits, and thus are open to competition from other, more advanced, fishery countries.

The demand for fish in Kenya is small because the bulk of the people are not traditionally fish eaters. Any increase in demand for ocean fish could be met without difficulty, though provision of proper fishing craft and gear would be needed as well as possible expansion of the shore organization and facilities for processing and marketing. The resources of Lake Victoria, on the other hand, are reported to have been seriously depleted by overfishing and conservation measures, rather than increased exploitation, may be called for.

Lake Rudolf, in the Northern Province, is a large and practically untouched fisheries resource; it is thought to have a potential sustainable yield of 20,000 tons of Tilapia and Nile Perch a year. This lake is some 300 miles from the railway and accessible only over desert tracks. However, production of processed fish—dried, smoked, etc.—could be instituted if the demand for fish should increase in inland or export areas and reasonable means of access were established. It is believed that the cost of development of a fisheries industry in this area would be such as to make it unattractive as a near-term prospect.

The other principal fishing resource appears to lie in the Domestic Fresh Fish Pond Scheme. The latest estimate places the number of these farm fish ponds at about 7,000. Production is said to average around 60 pounds of fresh fish annually for a pond of about 100 square yards in area. Farmers have no difficulty in disposing of any fish surplus above their own requirements. The Domestic Fresh Fish Pond Scheme is now largely confined to North Nyanza. Plans for expanding and extending it to other areas appear to be largely in abeyance at the moment due to the contention of the medical authorities that the fish ponds have caused an increase in the incidence of malaria. Malaria control measures are well known and easy of application though somewhat costly, but the return in the expansion of fish production should far offset this expenditure. The mission therefore commends the extension of this fish pond scheme.

SUMMARY OF PROPOSED EXPENDITURES

The mission's proposals for capital expenditures in the field of agriculture and animal husbandry are summarized in Table 5. Suggested capital outlays for the years 1963/64–1966/67 total £9.3 million, and comprise expenditures by the Ministry of Agriculture and Animal Hus-

TABLE 5: Proposed Capital Expenditures on Agriculture 1963/64–
1966/67

(£ thousand)

	Estimates 1962/63	1963/64	1964/65	1965/66	1966/67	Total
Under Ministry of Agriculture:						
Agricultural and Animal Husbandry Education	25	77	69	36	16	198
Agricultural Research	14	37	38	37	38	150
Animal Husbandry Field Services	–	13	–	–	–	13
Livestock Research and Disease Control[a]	34	50	50	30	–	130
Livestock Improvement[b]	25	23	18	15	19	75
Livestock and Animal Products Marketing[e]	13	28	28	28	28	112
Rural Development: non-scheduled areas	116	116	116	116	116	464
Tea Development: field expenditures[d]	130	267	316	280	242	1,105
Cooperative Development	–	25	10	10	10	55
(Items not continued)	54	–	–	–	–	–
Total	411	636	645	552	469	2,302
Under Other Ministries:						
Irrigation	40	122	181	105	55	463
Water Development	215	286	295	295	295	1,171
Agricultural Credit	511	550	650	900	1,200	3,300
Forest Development	38	15	–	15	–	30
(Items not continued)	100	–	–	–	–	–
Total	904	973	1,126	1,315	1,550	4,964
Statutory Bodies:						
Kenya Cooperative Creameries	–	100	155	170	125	550
Kenya Meat Commission	–	77	180	200	100	557
Special Crops Development Authority—Tea Factories	–	250	250	171	283	954
Total		427	585	541	508	2,061
GRAND TOTAL		2,036	2,356	2,408	2,527	9,327

[a] Includes proposals for tsetse control, and research into animal products.
[b] Includes proposals for animal breeding, management of grazing and artificial insemination.
[e] Includes proposals for abattoirs and collection centers.
[d] Most of this amount likely to be financed outside the Development Budget.

bandry, by other ministries operating in this field and by statutory bodies. In this chapter, we have recommended projects to be undertaken by the Ministry of Agriculture and Animal Husbandry costing £2.2 million. The largest item on this amount is for field development by the

Special Crops Development Authority, most of which we expect will be financed from special sources. Proposed expenditures on irrigation, water development, agricultural credit and forest development are shown separately since other ministries are responsible for them under the present division of government functions; they amount to about £5 million. In addition, we have considered the development plans of various statutory bodies, and have included in Table 5 the expenditures for which we think finance should be sought.

We have already indicated in Chapter 3 that many recurrent expenditure items are charged to the Development Budget in Kenya, and this is particularly true of expenditures for agricultural purposes. We stated that we thought the present practice should be modified, but to simplify the presentation of our proposals we have set out in the first part of Table 6 those items of recurrent expenditure at present contained in the Development Budget which we think should be continued over the next four years. In certain places, we have specifically recommended reductions in these expenditures. We envisage that total outlays for these purposes by the Ministry of Agriculture will decline from £1.1 million in 1962/63 to £1.0 million in 1966/67, and outlays by other ministries from £0.9 million to £0.8 million.

On the other hand, the execution of the proposed capital program would add to recurrent expenditures, and again for the sake of simplicity these have been treated collectively as development expenditures. It should be noted that we have also recommended new items of expenditure, particularly the fertilizer subsidy, which we regarded as current in nature and have included in our estimates of the current budget. The second part of Table 6 shows the implications of suggested new projects for recurrent development expenditures on agriculture, which rise by £0.3 million a year over the 1962/63 level by 1966/67. In total, recurrent development expenditures for both continued and new purposes are estimated to be £0.2 million higher in 1966/67 than in 1962/63.

Taking both capital and recurrent development costs together, our suggested program contains aggregate expenditures for agriculture, animal husbandry, forest and water development of £17.5 million for the period 1963/64 to 1966/67.

TABLE 6: Proposed Recurrent Development Expenditures 1963/64–
1966/67

(£ thousand)

	Estimates 1962/63	1963/64	1964/65	1965/66	1966/67
EXPENDITURE ON EXISTING ITEMS					
Under Ministry of Agriculture:					
Agricultural Field Services	490	490	490	490	490
Agricultural Education	78	78	78	78	78
Agricultural Research	187	187	187	187	187
Artificial Insemination	29	29	29	29	29
Tsetse Control	50	50	50	50	50
Stock Control	68	68	68	68	68
Animal Husbandry Field Services	71	71	71	71	71
African Livestock Marketing Organization[a]	102	100	75	50	25
Total	1,075	1,073	1,048	1,023	998
Under Other Ministries:					
Consolidation and Land Surveys	398	380	380	380	380
Irrigation	7	7	7	7	7
Board of Agriculture (nonscheduled areas)	89	70	70	70	70
Forest Development	100	100	100	100	100
Supplementary Forest Development	211	211	211	211	211
Forest Development: District Council Schemes	44	44	44	44	44
(Items not continued)	25	—	—	—	—
Total	874	812	812	812	812
NEW PROJECTS					
Under Ministry of Agriculture:					
Agricultural Field Services	—	—	22	67	112
Agricultural and Animal Husbandry Education	—	14	28	34	37
Agricultural Research	—	7	14	21	28
Animal Husbandry Field Services	—	33	33	33	33
Livestock Improvement	—	15	23	23	23
Livestock and Animal Products Marketing	—	8	14	23	23
Cooperative Development	—	—	20	40	60
Total	—	77	154	241	316
Under Other Ministries:					
Forest Development	—	2	2	3	3
Total under Ministry of Agriculture	1,075	1,150	1,202	1,264	1,314
Total under other Ministries	874	814	814	815	815
GRAND TOTAL	1,949	1,964	2,016	2,079	2,129

[a] Excluding provision for trading expenses offset by receipts.

CHAPTER 5 *MINING AND MANUFACTURING*

MINING

No mineral wealth of great consequence has been discovered in Kenya. Explorations for petroleum are still being carried out, however, and further drilling may show the presence of oil in commercial quantities. Aside from this possibility, the prospects for increasing export earnings from mining look dim. There are, of course, producing mines of various sorts in Kenya—soda ash is the most important—and there are a considerable number of mineral locations that deserve a more careful investigation. Further possibilities may be uncovered by the "reconnaisance" survey of Kenya's geological potential that is now being carried out by the Department of Mines and Geology. This survey had covered about half the country at the end of 1961 and is scheduled to be completed in 1966.

Kenya's recent experience with mining operations has been rather discouraging. Over the 20-year period from 1940 to 1960, for instance, gold production decreased from over £500,000 a year to barely £100,000 a year. In 1952, the country's largest gold mine was exhausted and in 1957 another important producer ceased operations; the current output comes from a number of small operators. Though minor discoveries continue to be reported, there are no indications that gold will make any significant recovery in the next few years.

Kenya also has had a disappointing experience with copper. A decade ago, the Colonial Development Corporation (CDC), at the request of the Kenya Government, put up the bulk of the capital and loan funds for a promising copper venture. The Macalder-Nyanza Mine began producing copper in 1951 and copper cement in 1956; gold, silver and zinc concentrates were also recovered from the ores. The financial results of this operation have been so unsatisfactory that the CDC has written off £3 million of its investment. It has therefore been decided to extract the readily available, higher-grade ores and then to close the mine. The value of Kenya's mineral production will decrease as the copper ores are depleted. As recently as 1960, copper contributed £413,000 out of a total mineral production of £2.5 million. Since soda ash accounted for £1.4 million in that year, the production of all other minerals—excluding gold and copper—totaled only about £550,000.

146

However, the mission would urge the Government to maintain a positive policy toward the mineral sector. An immediate case in point is the current search for geothermal steam. An exclusive license to prospect for geothermal steam was originally held by the East African Power and Light Company; but after a drilling test to 3,800 feet at Naivasha failed to produce commercial quantities of steam, the Company allowed its license to lapse. The Mines and Geological Department then took over the search and assigned one of the Department's technicians to pinpoint what are known as "hot spots." This one-man survey was scheduled to be completed by the end of 1962, at which time drilling would become essential to probe any promising locations. The mission is, of course, in no position to say whether drilling should or should not be carried out, but if the prospects for locating geothermal steam are promising enough, Kenya may want to request assistance from an appropriate external agency. If suitable drilling equipment is made available, it could also be used to probe other mineral sites, such as the concealed coal field that is believed to exist at MacKinnon road, about 50 miles west of Mombasa, and the concealed gold veins believed near Lake Victoria in Nyanza. The services of a geothermal expert also may be needed, and if this expert is procured, he could advise on the possibilities of exploiting carbon dioxide and geothermal steam for the production of power.

As a general policy recommendation, the mission would suggest that the Government should maintain the staff of the Mines Department at a high level of technical competence, should encourage genuine prospectors in their search for mineral wealth, and should consider providing some financial support to encourage genuine prospectors to follow up discoveries where the prospects are promising but where "risk money" is lacking.

Oil Exploration

Legislation creating a "special oil prospecting license" was passed in 1960, with the granting of licenses left to the discretion of the Governor. The legislation sets only the broad requirements that licenses must:

a. cover definite areas that are defined as to size and location;
b. specify an obligation to drill and to expend a minimum sum of money; and requires a progressive reduction of the size of the prospecting area, accompanied by increasing expenditures per unit of land area.

The maximum duration of such a license is ten years.

The broad provisions of this licensing law are in keeping with the general trend in the petroleum field. Government negotiators are left with wide leeway to set the specific terms of licenses. As Kenya policy has recognized, countries without oil must offer licenses that are favorable in comparison with the terms offered by the major oil-producing countries. A license currently in force calls for a 12.5 percent royalty on crude oil production and a 6.25 percent royalty on natural gas. The appropriateness of such terms can best be assessed through normal communication channels with the petroleum industry. The most important fact to the mission is that Kenya's oil prospects are being explored. Some explorations, including gravity survey work, were carried out some years ago by Frobisher Ltd., in the northeastern tip of Kenya, north of the second north parallel and east of 40° 30′E. Two prospectors are currently active in other parts of the country. The Mehta Oil Company holds a license covering the southeastern part of the country, between Voi and the 39° 30′ meridian, and has started drilling. The most extensive explorations are being carried out by BP-Shell Petroleum Development Company of Kenya, Ltd., a joint venture of the British Petroleum Company and Shell Oil. This Company holds two licenses which encompass most of the region east of 39° 31′E and south of the second north parallel. BP-Shell has over the past ten years spent approximately £8 million looking for oil in East Africa, and the Company is currently drilling for oil on Pemba Island (off the East African coast) as well as in Kenya.

After carrying out extensive seismic, gravity and aeromagnetic surveys in its concession area, BP-Shell planned a drilling program that called for four test holes. The first three holes were drilled by a contractor using equipment with a maximum depth of 6,500 feet. For the fourth hole, the Company transferred a rig from New Guinea (duty-free admission of equipment was granted the Company) that has a drilling depth of 14,000 feet. The area being investigated is difficult to reach but a wharf near Lamu has been constructed.

The major technical requirements of the ten-year BP-Shell license are as follows. The Company agrees to spend £20 per square mile of concession the first six years; £40 the following two years; and £80 the remaining two years. At the same time, the concession area is to be reduced in proportion to the increase in spending: after six years, the original area must be reduced by half and after eight years the concession area is to become one-fourth its original size. The licensee has the right to select whatever area he wishes to surrender.

The spending requirement amounts to a legal obligation on the Company. Permission may be granted the Company to underspend in the first two periods; any overspending can be offset against future requirements. Payment by the Company of the minimum contractual expenditure, assuming permission to vary expenditures had not been granted, would constitute complete compliance. The drilling requirement is a depth of 15,000 feet by the seventh year. Finally, the licensee agrees to apply for an oil mining lease within two years of any discovery of oil in commercial quantities.

Other Minerals

Asbestos. About 100 tons of anthophyllite asbestos are mined annually in West Suk. The extent of the deposit is unknown. Most of the output is sold within East Africa and no difficulty is encountered in disposing of surplus abroad. Interesting deposits worthy of further investigation are reported at Taita Hills and near Mtito-Andei.

Beryl. Beryl has been found in several areas in association with mica and other minerals. Some further investigation appears warranted north of Nanyuki, but inaccessibility of the area is a limiting factor.

Carbon Dioxide. At Kagwe and Esegeri, in the Rift Valley, carbon dioxide is found under pressure, and dry ice and carbon dioxide gas are being produced.

Diatomite. This material has been found in various parts of the country and production appears capable of greater expansion.

Graphite. An important discovery appears to have been made near Meru, but no investigation of the find has yet taken place. At current market prices of £100 to £140 per ton, the deposit—if and when proved —could become an important export earner. The market for high-quality graphite, though not unlimited, appears favorable.

Gypsum. Several substantial deposits are known and being worked. Gypsum and local limestone are used in cement production and for building and agricultural purposes. Due to the heavy cost of internal transport, no export market can be envisaged.

Iron Ore. At Bukura, a lode estimated to contain 17 million tons has been tentatively established and there is a known hematite ore body in the Homa Mountains of perhaps some 10 million tons. Similar deposits are believed to exist in other parts of Nyanza. However, no deposit with sufficiently large reserves to warrant serious interest has been found. There are also deposits of pyrites.

Kaolin. Adequate quantities for local consumption by the ceramics and refractory brick industries are being produced. Deposits known and suspected appear to be adequate for Kenya's needs.

Nickel and Chrome Ore. Deposits located in an area 150 miles north of Kitale contain 1 percent to 3 percent nickel, and there is high-grade chromite in the same region. Investigations carried out by a South African mining concern between 1956 and 1958, by means of mule transport, were abandoned owing to inaccessibility coupled with smallness of deposit.

Niobium—Rare Earths. A number of deposits are known and one near Mombasa contains considerable quantities of niobium. Work is continuing on methods of extracting the metal economically.

Soda Ash. The Magadi Soda Company was formed in 1911 to exploit the 12-mile wide natural soda deposit on Lake Magadi. In 1924, Imperial Chemical Industries took over the management and now controls the Company. In 1960, 127,000 tons of soda ash were produced, the great bulk of which was exported. The main use of soda ash is in the manufacture of glass but it is also used in soap and paper manufacture. Output is regulated by overseas demand and no substantial contribution to increased export earnings may be expected unless demand increases correspondingly. The Magadi Company also produces some 17,000 tons of crude salt per annum by solar evaporation. The output of salt is entirely consumed in Kenya and Uganda. Salt is nevertheless imported into Kenya.

Others. There also are deposits of columbite, kyanite, tantalite, uranium, lithium, meerschaum, mica, mullite, pumice, silver and vermiculite, but their total contribution to national production is not significant.

MANUFACTURING

Manufacturing industries in Kenya were set up initially to process agricultural products. The development of agricultural production, following World War II, promoted a complementary expansion of processing factories and the establishment of a wider range of industries to supply the internal market. By the mid–1950's manufacturing industry had come to provide nearly 10 percent of Kenya's Gross Domestic Product.

In the last few years, the value of the output of manufacturing industry has conformed closely with changes in the total GDP. Since 1955 the value of manufacturing output, at current prices, has risen somewhat less than 5 percent a year,[1] from £17.4 million to £22.7 million in 1961. But since 1958 employment and investment in manufacturing have been

---

[1] These estimates are based on the annual survey of employment and of wages and salaries paid to employees and assume that the relationship between wages and the product of manufactures and repairs as shown in the results of surveys of industry remain constant. *Domestic Income and Product in Kenya,* Government Printer, 1959.

much reduced. Employment in "manufactures and repairs" fell from a peak figure of 57,000 in 1957 to 42,500 by the middle of 1961; at that time manufacturing provided approximately 7 percent of the total employment in Kenya. Complete estimates of investment in manufacturing industry are not available, but expenditure on new machinery and equipment and commercial vehicles by the private sector has fallen from £9 million in 1957 to £7.5 million in 1961.

A comparison of the estimates of Gross Domestic Product and employment statistics prepared for each of the East African countries for 1960 shows that Kenya is the most industrialized of the three countries. Kenya's output figure for manufacturing and repairs of £21.6 million compares with £7.3 million for Tanganyika and £5.9 million for Uganda. As a percentage of total Gross Domestic Product, including the subsistence economy, the figures become 9.7 percent for Kenya, 3.9 percent for Tanganyika and 4 percent for Uganda. Of Kenya's 52,300 manufacturing and repair employees, 42,600 were Africans; this figure compares with 18,300 Africans employed in Tanganyika manufacturing (including electricity) and 24,600 in Uganda.

THE STRUCTURE OF INDUSTRY

Information about the structure and production of manufacturing industry is incomplete. The last census of industrial production was taken in 1957, when a survey was made of industrial establishments which employed five or more persons. The results require careful analysis as the census included mining and quarrying, electricity supply, building and construction as well as manufacturing and repairs. Table 1 summarized the results of the census of manufacturing establishments by principal industrial groups. As this table shows, manufacturing industry in Kenya is principally engaged in the production of consumer goods or in the processing of agricultural and forestry products for export. There are also many establishments for the repair of machinery and equipment, but industries manufacturing capital goods are of little importance.

Nairobi is the principal center of manufacturing industry and 40 percent of all of those engaged in manufacturing in 1957 were employed in the capital. But apart from Nairobi, and a smaller group of industries in Mombasa, industry in Kenya tends to be located away from the towns. This pattern is attributable to the importance of primary products processing (e.g., sawmilling).

Manufacturing is mainly undertaken by private concerns; investment has been partly by local businessmen and partly by overseas firms (especially British companies). The Government, through the Industrial Development Corporation, has provided some financial assistance to private firms. Some industrial activities are entirely government owned: the railway workshops (which dominate the category—shipbuilding and rolling stock repairs) employ over 3,000 people and statutory bodies are important in the processing of foodstuffs.

TABLE 1: Manufacturing Establishments in Kenya, 1957[a]

Industrial	Number of Establishments	Number Employed (thousands)	Gross Production (£ million)	Net Output (£ million)
Foodstuffs	161	9.8	17.0	2.7
Beverages	44	3.0	5.2	3.1
Tobacco	1	1.1	6.4	n.a.
Clothing and textiles	77	1.4	1.4	.4
Jute, sisal and coir products	3	1.5	.7	.3
Shoes, including repairs	47	.9	.9	.3
Sawn timber	75	8.2	1.6	.6
Furniture, joinery, etc.	140	2.2	1.2	.5
Printing and publishing	60	2.1	2.2	1.3
Chemicals and soap	50	3.5	4.8	1.9
Clay and concrete products	20	1.9	.7	.3
Cement and other mineral products	19	1.6	2.8	1.3
Metal products	71	2.4	2.8	.7
Machinery, including repairs	42	1.5	1.1	.4
Shipbuilding and rolling stock repairs	9	6.5	2.6	1.2
Motor repairs and motor bodies	172	4.7	3.4	1.4
All other manufacturing	47	1.5	1.8	.7
Total manufacturing	1,038	53.8	56.6	17.1

[a] Includes repair shops, refers to all firms employing five or more persons.
SOURCE: *Kenya Survey of Industrial Production*, 1957, East African Statistical Department.

The structure of manufacturing industry shows a preponderance of very small plants. Nearly 60 percent of the establishments in 1957 employed less than 20 people. This is probably because repairs are included in the definition of manufacturing. Most of the people engaged in manufacturing are, however, employed by larger businesses, and 75 percent of those working in manufacturing were in establishments employing 50 or more people.

FACTORS AFFECTING THE GROWTH
OF MANUFACTURING

The potential for industrial development in Kenya is limited at the outset by the small extent of the country's presently known natural resources. The available raw materials are mostly primary agricultural products which, though requiring processing for market,[2] do not offer known prospects for any major new industrial developments, and though explorations for minerals continue, prospecting so far has not opened the possibility of establishing any large metal or chemical complexes. The situation in regard to power would reinforce the negative outlook for any major industrial developments; Kenya is without coal and its water resources, though far from being negligible, do not have any compelling potential as a *force majeure* of cheap power.

Another limiting factor is the composition of Kenya's human resources. The enterprise, capital and skill for manufacturing have been almost completely provided by European and Asian settlers. The mass of the African population is still poorly educated, and even rudimentary industrial skills have not been handed down from one generation to another. Progress in education will help, of course. It is also true that the presence of a large unskilled labor force can provide scope for industries that require labor with little training—provided that the capital and management can be obtained. For the normal range of manufactured products, however, labor productivity is a major factor. Wages in Kenya are low in relation to rates in the industrial countries. But if labor is inexperienced and unaccustomed to the discipline of factory life, low wage rates may not always yield low labor costs per unit of output. And it is labor costs per unit of output, rather than wage rates, that will largely determine what products can profitably be made in Kenya.

A major factor in unit cost, in most cases more important than labor costs, is the quantity of product that a factory of a given size manufactures. The level of output of course depends on the size of the market. There are several aspects of the potential market for goods manufactured in Kenya. Obviously, there is some sort of market for the wide range of goods that are now imported. While there undoubtedly are opportunities for entrepreneurs among this range of goods, the mission would caution that a too enthusiastic approach to import substitution, from the standpoint of national policy, would be self defeating. Local

---

[2] The essential processing of primary products before export overseas—including such activities as coffee, tea and pyrethrum processing—is treated in this report as part of the agricultural sector and prospects are covered in Chapter 4.

consumption of many imported goods is so small that the unit cost of manufacture, if the goods were produced in Kenya, would be greatly above the imported price and most of Kenya's agricultural products have to be sold competitively in markets overseas.

In a broader sense, the market for Kenya-produced goods begins with the local population of 7 million people, extends to the 25 million population of the East African customs union, and expands outward, through the port of Mombasa, which is favorably situated to serve markets along the African coast and the Indian Ocean.[3] The per capita income level within this marketing area is admittedly low; clearly there are many industries that could not be profitably established in Kenya. But though people in Kenya have low incomes, they offer in the aggregate a substantial market for some products, e.g., cotton textiles. The relevant factors are the size of the market in relation to the output of factories operating on an efficient scale, and we believe there is scope for the expansion of some forms of manufacturing. On the other hand, some industries already have expanded beyond the current level of demand and some others may depend on continued government assistance for their survival. Before going into what the Government might do to encourage industry, we will take a closer look at the composition and prospects for the principal manufacturing industries, excluding the essential processing of primary agricultural products.

PRINCIPAL MANUFACTURING INDUSTRIES

The Food Industry

In 1957, there were 53 establishments engaged in grain milling. The two largest companies, with maize and wheat mills at Nairobi, Nakuru and Eldoret, are both locally owned. The grain mills work under licenses issued by the Department of Agriculture, and buying and selling prices are also set by the Department. The mills supply Tanganyika and Uganda, as well as Kenya, with flour. Kenya annually consumes about 1 million bags of wheat and about 90 percent is locally grown. African consumption has been growing but still amounts to less than half of the total. Bread is the usual end product, but there is a large output of biscuits. Production of biscuits has risen to 6.5 tons per day. Biscuit manufacture is protected by a customs duty of 25 percent, but local demand is still met partly by imports (120 tons in 1961).

Except in years of crop failure, Kenya produces an exportable surplus of maize of at least 50,000 tons. The industrial potential of maize is not

[3] There is a wider market for some specialist goods, largely the product of cottage industries (e.g., carvings).

as yet being exploited in Kenya. A distillery was recently established, for instance, but it will use molasses rather than maize as a raw material. Local industrialists have investigated the possibility of manufacturing breakfast foods, but the introduction of unknown products of this kind to African consumers would be both costly and lengthy. Another possibility for exploiting maize might be the manufacture of starch.

Slaughtering and meat packing are mostly in the hands of the Kenya Meat Commission and the Uplands Bacon Factory. The production of butter, cheese and ice cream is similarly dominated by Kenya Cooperative Creameries. These activities were included in our discussion of agriculture (Chapter 4). There are protective duties on imports of bacon and ham, and on dairy products and substitutes.

Kenya's requirements of sugar have been met principally by imports. In 1961, 33,000 tons of milled sugar came from Uganda and 26,000 tons of refined sugar were imported from outside East Africa. A sugar refinery has been recently erected by one of the two companies engaged in sugar milling, one in Nyanza and one at the coast. Their production of milled sugar is limited by the output of cane and amounts to about 30,000 tons a year. The possibilities of expanding sugar growing are discussed in Chapter 4. There is a small chocolate and sugar confectionery industry.

In 1957 there were four establishments engaged in fruit and vegetable canning and jam making. Pineapple products account for about two-thirds of this production, and unlike the industries previously described, most of the output is exported. In 1961, exports of canned pineapple and concentrate amounted to £475,000. The bulk of these shipments went to the United Kingdom. At the time of the mission's visit, the two principal manufacturers had plans to increase their sales to the United Kingdom, and they were also diversifying their activities. One is turning to fruits (figs, plums, strawberries, peaches and guavas) and the other to vegetables (beans, peas and tomatoes) for sale mainly within East Africa.

The oil-expressing industry has been expanding its production of coconut, sesame, palm and groundnut oil, but Kenya remains a large importer of coconut oil. The manufacture of margarine has been increased to the point where local demand is now met. Other industries processing local foodstuffs include coffee roasting and packing.

Beverages and Tobacco

The first brewery was established 40 years ago. There are now three producers with breweries in Nairobi and Mombasa (and Dar es Salaam). The largest concern is substantially owned by local shareholders; the other two are partly owned by United Kingdom and Dutch associated companies. The industry has expanded rapidly to meet the growth of demand, which in recent years has come especially from Africans. African-type beer is still brewed by municipalities from small grains, but many Africans in urban areas now drink malt beer. Though beer is subject to excise duties, there is a higher customs duty on imported beer, which assists the local industry. Imports amount to only about 1 percent of local production. The production of malting barley, however, is insufficient to meet the full requirements of the breweries; most of their raw materials are imported. Bottles for beer and soft drinks are manufactured in Kenya. Output of soft drinks, aided by an import duty, has been expanding rapidly.

Tobacco manufacturing is assisted by a customs duty much higher than the excise duty on local production. Production was started by a United Kingdom company in 1905 and Kenya now supplies nearly all its requirements of cigarettes. Most of the leaf used is grown in Tanganyika and Uganda.

Textiles

Textile manufacture in East Africa is subject to industrial licensing. The principal plant is in Uganda and, though inquiries for textile licenses in Kenya have been frequent, the industry is still small. The industry consists of plants producing cotton and rayon knitwear, woven blankets, clothing from imported piece goods and sisal products.

Imports of textile products that Kenya manufactures, apart from knitted underwear, are still large: in 1961, for example, Kenya imported more than 2 million cotton and rayon blankets and about 2 million shirts. Imports from outside East Africa of piece goods, of cotton and synthetic fibers, amounted to more than 100 million square yards. Generally, the industry is assisted by a 33 1/3 percent ad valorem customs duty with higher specific duties on the lowest priced imports.

From these statistics, it would appear that there should be considerable scope for the development of Kenya's textile industry. Though the population has a low per capita income, the market for cotton textiles in particular is substantial. As we have already suggested, the relevant factor determining the feasibility of a factory is not over-all purchasing power, but rather the size of a specific market in relation to the unit cost of output from a specific factory. In terms of the textile industry, the consumption of a number of standard products is larger in Kenya than the required output of efficiently operated plants.

Processing local sisal is an important segment of the industry. Output consists of bags, piece goods, rope, twine and matting. Output of jute-sisal bags amounted to 2.5 million in 1960, a year in which 3.7 million jute bags were imported.

Shoes

There is one large factory and many small establishments scattered throughout the country. Factory production includes leather, rubber, plastic and combination shoes and is supplied with leather from the firm's own tannery. Output has been expanding at an annual rate of about 10 percent over the past few years, and imports are small in relation to local production. There is a 25 percent ad valorem duty on imported footwear with higher specific duties on the cheapest shoes. Two other tanneries process hides and wild game skins, mostly for export.

Sawmilling, Woodwork and Matches

There are some 60 sawmills. The decline in the building industry in the last three years has seriously affected output and profitability—sales in 1960/61 amounted in value to less than half of the figure reached in 1955/56. Cedar slats (for pencils) and cedar oil are exported. Much of Kenya's indigenous timber is of poor quality and the country's softwood plantations have yet to mature (forestry is discussed in Chapter 4).

Furniture is manufactured by the Ministry of Works, by smaller private factories, and by a large number of Asian craftsmen. Along with sawmilling, the decline in the building industry has adversely affected the joinery and furniture industry.

There is one match factory which aims to supply the whole of the East African demand, but sales have been affected by serious competition from external suppliers. The industry is assisted by a differential between the customs and excise duties of Sh.7 per 7,200 matches.

Paper, Printing and Packaging

The manufacture of paper is confined to the production of kardus for packing materials, and wrapping paper from used paper. Imported paper is used to produce stationery, paper bags and toilet paper. Several firms produce corrugated containers and industrial paper bags, largely from imported materials. The possibility of pulping local timber has been investigated and it is the mission's opinion that a detailed feasibility study should be undertaken. A study by FAO estimates the average annual consumption of paper in East Africa to rise from 21,000 tons in

1955–59 (Kenya 13,500 tons) to between 64,000 tons and 80,000 tons in 1980.

In addition to the Government Printer, there is a well-established printing industry that produces newspapers, periodicals and undertakes jobbing printing.

Soap and Chemicals

A large soap factory opened in 1958, and there are many small ones. There is as yet no detergent plant. Kenya's chief chemical products are soda ash from Lake Magadi (see Mining) and wattle extract (see Chapter 4); production of wattle extract has been affected by the decline in world demand. By-products from the oil refinery being erected at Mombasa could extend the range of locally made chemical products.

Clay, Cement and Concrete Products

A wide range of brick, tile and precast-concrete products is manufactured in Kenya, and imports are small in value. There are two cement plants, one near Mombasa and the other near Nairobi. Production first started in the early 1950's and by 1957 Kenya became self-sufficient. Since 1959, with the fall in the local demand for cement, a large part of the output has been marketed outside Kenya. In 1961, 100,000 tons went to Tanganyika and 80,000 tons were exported to Mauritius out of a total output of 340,000 tons. Plant capacity of the two firms exceeds 500,000 tons.

Metal Products, Machinery and Engineering

Firms in this group are engaged in a wide range of manufacturing as well as repair work. Plant facilities include foundries and rolling mills. The chief products (by value) in 1957 were holloware, steel drums, metal cans, metal doors and window frames, and heavy motor vehicle bodies. Other activities include designing and erecting machinery and plant. Most of the materials used by the industry are imported, but a substantial export trade has developed in some products, notably hurricane lamps, metal containers, aluminum holloware and worked aluminum, and metal doors and windows. Some of the products are protected in the home market by customs duties (e.g., 33 1/3 percent on enamel holloware and 25 percent on hurricane lamps, with a higher specific duty on the cheapest products in both cases).

GOVERNMENT POLICY

The basic policy of the three East African territories, in relation to manufacturing, is to make East Africa as a whole self-sufficient insofar as it is possible and economic to do so. Government policy has been to encourage by all reasonable means the development of private industry. The chief mechanisms through which this policy has been implemented include customs and excise duties, industrial licensing, funds and land for industrial development, and industrial research. Government policies and performance in fiscal and economic matters can have a decisive influence on investment in industry and these are discussed elsewhere in this report. Here we are concerned with government behavior which specifically affects manufacturing industry.

Customs and Excise Tariff

Except for a small number of items, uniform rates of customs and excise duties are charged throughout the three East African countries. The tariffs are administered by a single department which is part of the East African Common Services Organization. Revenue from tariffs, less 6 percent for the pool, is paid to the territories as collected. The excise tariff consists of seven main items; the customs tariff has 177 principal items. Since East Africa is within the "Congo Basin" Treaties area, the same rate of customs duty is applied irrespective of the country or origin of the goods. There are six main levels of customs duties applied at present:

a. Luxury rate: 66 2/3 percent ad valorem. This rate applies to goods such as wines and cosmetics.
b. Protective rate: 33 1/3 percent ad valorem. The protective rate applies to dairy products, macaroni, tomato puree, clothing and piece goods, holloware and jewelry.
c. General rate: 25 percent ad valorem. This rate is primarily for revenue purposes, though where there is local production it can be protective in effect.
d. Motor vehicle rate: 15 percent ad valorem. This rate applies to all types of motor vehicles and parts other than tractors.
e. General assisted rate: 12½ percent ad valorem. This rate is a reduction in the general rate designed to assist producers.
f. Items admitted duty-free. Many items of machinery are admitted duty-free and in reclassifying raw materials the aim has been to

rate them duty-free. Chemicals, metals, building materials and tools are duty-free.

There are many exceptions to these standard rates. The exceptions frequently take the form of specific duties: either for revenue purposes (e.g., on spirits, cigarettes and petrol) or as an alternative to ad valorem rates to provide greater protection to local industry against the cheapest imported goods. Specific duties are so important that in 1960, 63 percent of the total amount of customs revenue raised in East Africa was collected in this way. There is also a list of suspended duties which may be imposed quickly by the government concerned in time of need. Kenya has imposed such duties on a range of processed foodstuffs and on bottles to help local producers.

Customs duties are a major means of raising revenue in all three territories (see Public Finance, Chapter 10). For them to adjust customs duties to encourage the development of local industry may add to their fiscal difficulties. Concern with budgetary problems has been prevalent in recent discussion in Kenya of duties on industrial materials.

All three territories refund all or part of the customs duty paid by industrialists on many materials. (For imports that were eligible for drawback of customs duty by registered manufacturers in Kenya in 1961, see Table 2.) The duty is paid at the time of importation and, after the goods have been used, the manufacturer can claim a refund from his government. In Kenya, but not in Tanganyika and Uganda, the drawback payments to industrialists depended on amounts voted annually to the Department of Commerce and Industry for this purpose. This led to difficulties at the time the mission was in Kenya, because drawbacks claimed were outrunning the sum voted. Once drawbacks of duty on specific goods are approved, refund of duty should not be subject to complications of this kind and in July 1962 Kenya arranged for payments to be made directly out of revenue. It was suggested to us that manufacturers should be relieved of the burden of financing the initial payment of customs duty on materials at the time of entry by rebating the duty on such goods and making their use subject to customs control. This we do not favor: it would increase the administrative burden on the Customs Department and could lead to abuse.

We understand that the policy adopted in Kenya has been to grant drawback to industrialists who are unlikely to be able to compete with imported goods if they have to pay the full duty on their materials. This implies that, where they can stand it competitively, policy is to tax imported materials used by industrialists. But all the evidence we reviewed indicated that, on the contrary, the Government wished to encourage industries to use imported materials, provided that the materials were not available locally. We think that practice in relation to customs drawbacks should be regarded as an extension of general customs tariff policy. Here the aim has been to rate raw materials duty-free in the tariff and not to load costs of production with import duties. We think that in general this policy is appropriate for Kenya.

Where a raw material is produced under favorable conditions in

TABLE 2: Imports into Kenya by Registered Manufacturers Eligible for Customs Duty Drawbacks, 1961

Industry	Material on which Drawback is given	Extent of Drawback	Estimated Annual Cost (£ 000)
Printing	Printing paper for specified products	100%	8
Canning	Sugar for canning pineapple, tropical fruit and jam for export and sweetened condensed milk	100% customs and excise	7
Insecticides, disinfectants, etc.	Kerosene and other oils and materials listed	100%	3
Soap	Perfume and essential oils	⅝ of duty	8
Brushes	Fiber	70%	2
Can manufactures	Cans for manufacture of specified goods, if for export; if for sale locally	100% Duty in excess of 25% ad valorem	11
Knitwear	Rayon fiber	25%	6
Blankets	Waste materials and fiber used as weft fillers	100%	13
Footwear	Textiles	Duty in excess of 25% ad valorem	7
Tires	Specified materials for manufacture of cycle tires and tubes	100%	20
Metal containers	Paints, lacquers and thinners	100%	(under £400)
Fabricated metalwork	Aluminum plates, etc., for aluminum tankers, tanks and vessels	100%	4
Matches	Splints and splint timber	100%	2
		Total	91

Kenya or East Africa, industrialists would normally find it advantageous to use the local product. Some departure from free entry may, however, be necessary in these circumstances when manufacturers may be attracted to outside supplies, for instance, in times of abundance, or because prices are determined by artificial factors. There are often other reasons for an industrial material remaining dutiable in the customs tariff. It may be a general purpose product. Only a small proportion of the quantity imported may be taken by industrialists for processing, or manufacturing may represent a new use for the product. The customs duty would then be determined by the nature of the principal or original demand for the product, and industrial users would seek a refund of duty.

We suggest that the general intention of the Government should be to refund to industrialists sums paid in import duty on materials used where manufacturing is conducted on a substantial scale and makes a significant contribution to the finished product. But refunds might not be granted if the materials were freely available in the customs union. They might also be refused on goods subject to high revenue duties, though here the aim should be to introduce countervailing excise duties on the manufactured product.

Duties on imported goods may more frequently assist rather than impede local manufacturers. Though the original intention in imposing most duties in East Africa was to raise revenue, local manufacturers of such products would automatically be assisted in meeting external competition, unless excise duties were imposed. As we have seen, manufacturers in East Africa have also been deliberately assisted by the imposition of duties on some products which are specifically protective in purpose.

We have indicated that the potential development of manufacturing industry in Kenya (and East Africa) is limited by its physical and human resources and by the extent of the market. Nevertheless, we believe that there is scope for the expansion of some manufacturing industries and for the establishment of some others. In time, as production expands, particularly in the primary sector, a larger market should provide the opportunity for the growth of manufacturing industries. There may also be specific opportunities for the integration of the development of primary and secondary production (e.g., sugar and cotton).

The expansion of agriculture is being achieved with much government assistance, particularly in providing finance and services to growers. Similarly, some forms of manufacturing industry which could be established advantageously may need governmental help, especially in their early years. As many of the opportunities for industrial development in Kenya are likely to be found in production for the East African market, the initial need may be some form of assistance in meeting external competition, to divert consumers from the imported products which they have bought in the past to the new local manufactures.

This is not to suggest that all will be in need or that all in need will be worthy. Some industries producing for the home market will not be worried about imports (e.g., industries producing goods which are costly to transport). Some other industries, if located in Kenya, are likely to have much higher unit costs of production than the price of imports. Assistance should, therefore, be selective in character. It could be in the form of subsidies, import quotas, or protective customs duties. If subsidies are provided, the extent of the assistance is clear and prices of the product are not raised. The effect of import quotas is arbitrary; they do not encourage efficiency in local production and they reduce the consumer's freedom of choice. Protective customs duties are much less certain in their effect, and it is often very difficult to decide the extent to which a duty should be changed. But, increased customs duties can yield revenue to the extent to which the product is still imported. They have been the means used by the customs union, and in the present fiscal situation of all three governments, we do not consider a major change in practice advisable.

We suggest that protective duties should only be applied after examination has established that they are necessary and that it is desirable to protect the production of the local industry from external competition. When it is decided to give protection, the duties imposed should be appropriate to the situation; if the industry can meet local needs, they should be adequate, or, if the industry needs assistance to expand to supply local demand, tariff quotas or import quotas might be considered as alternatives to a straight protective duty. To give some continuity of financial conditions within the industry, protective duties should be imposed for a short term of years, after which the need for them should be reappraised. In the case of a new industry, such protection should be contingent on agreement to establish production.

In considering applications for protection, attempt should be made to arrive at the net benefit of the industry to the economy; the extent to which it will meet internal demand, the net addition to employment, the likely use of locally produced materials, the extent to which it will require services, the extent to which protection is needed and for how long, and its likely effect on prices and on production of the country's main exports.

Customs and excise tariff policy has been discussed with attention directed primarily to Kenya, but where we have referred to the local or internal market, we have had the customs union area in mind. It might be an advantage, but not a necessity, for a uniform policy of granting refunds of duty on imported materials to be adopted by all three governments. But an extensive divergence in protective duties could transform the customs union into an unworkable free trade area. We found some parochialism in the approach of the territories to matters of customs policy and import control. Without a separate central government for East Africa, this is probably inevitable. The Triumvirate of the Common Services Organization for Commercial and Industrial Coordination is served by a Tariff Protection Committee of officials. To foster the development of manufacturing industry, we think it important that this Triumvirate should review its industrial policy, including the criteria which it instructs the Tariff Protection Committee of officials to apply in examining applications for protection.

Industrial Licensing

Assistance to manufacturing industry in East Africa has also taken the form of making some industrial production subject to license. In 1948 the three territories agreed on a common policy as regards industrial licensing and enacted parallel legislation which was revised in 1952/53. The legislation provides for the orderly promotion and development of licensed industries. As of the end of 1960, the following groups of industries had been licensed: cotton, woolen and synthetic textiles including blankets; steel drums; glassware including sheet or window glass; metal window and door frames; and enamel holloware.

The East African Industrial Council, established in 1943, is charged with advising the Common Services Organization upon questions of policy relating to industrial development. The Council's policy, and the licensing law, have been the subject of controversy from the beginning. In 1949, the Council granted to Nytil Textiles (formed by the Uganda Development Corporation in conjunction with Calico Printers Association) a quantitatively unlimited, as well as exclusive, license for the production of cotton yarn and cotton piece goods. The decision gave rise to sharp criticism as it granted a five-year monopoly to one concern, but there was good reason to believe that without such concession the industry would not have been established at that time.

At the expiration of the exclusive period in 1954, the Council stated that it would consider favorably applications from qualified and experienced manufacturers for the establishment of vertically integrated textile industries that would use, as far as possible, East African cotton. It added that it would, however, not consider favorably any applications

for the manufacture of cotton piece goods where these would be competing unfairly against the existing licensee. Licenses for weaving were
granted (usually with a proviso requiring the introduction of spinning
within a few years from the commencement of production). The Council
has stated that few serious applications were received during the 1954–
59 period and that revived interest on the part of potential manufacturers was shown only when in early 1958 a protective tariff was introduced covering local manufacture of piece goods.

Some branches of the textile industry have not developed as much as
might have been expected. The difference in quantity between local
production and imported supplies of blankets and some other textiles is
large and, as we have stated, provides scope for the expansion of the industry in East Africa. The principal reason for the limited development
of the textile industry may be that, since the present wide range of protective duties on textiles was introduced, investment has been discour-
aged by political factors.

No difficulties appear to have been encountered in either scheduling
or licensing other commodities. Many industries, notably cement, beer
and soft drinks, have been set up without licensing.

The value of industrial licensing has been questioned and its abolition recommended.[4] On the other hand, according to statements made
to us, some scheduled industries may not have commenced operations in
East Africa without the assurance which licensing provided. But a license does not in itself provide protection against external competition.
Much depends on the way in which such legislation is administered.

We are not however convinced that the extension or continuation of
licensing is likely to promote the growth of efficient industrial establishments in East Africa: all it does is to limit competition among local man-

[4] The report of the Economic and Fiscal Commission, February 1961, speaks of
licensing as "an agreed form of restriction on the free development of the Common
Market Area" (199, p. 64) and advocates discontinuation "because there neither exists
an agreed general plan of development nor is (such a plan) generally thought to be
applicable."

The IBRD report on Tanganyika (pp. 240, 241) states that "on balance, the policy
of industrial licensing has contributed little, if anything, to East African industrial
development and that its probable contribution to future development is equally
limited." While suggesting that consideration be given to abolishing the system it
recommends that no new industries be placed on the schedule.

The IBRD report on Uganda (p. 253) draws attention to the interterritorial difficulties besetting endeavors to establish an over-all development program (without
which licensing cannot function to best advantage) to the growth of non-scheduled
industries and to the trend for licensing to create monopolies. While admitting that
even a single concern in an industry is not *ipso facto* monopolistic, it feels nonetheless
that the weight of argument is in favor of abandoning licensing.

ufacturers. While the licensing system may lead to the establishment of some capacity in an industry in East Africa, it may also act as a deterrent to the future growth of that industry. We therefore think that industrial licensing should be abolished. There is, however, the question of the rights of existing licensees. We recommend that no further classes of product be subject to licensing and that products subject to licensing be de-restricted as rapidly as commitments allow.

Industrial Research

The East African Industrial Research Organization (EAIRO) owes its existence to the exigencies of the Second World War. It contributed scientific data leading to the establishment of the first paint factory, a caustic soda factory, and a pilot plant for the extraction of pyrethrum. Recent contributions made by EAIRO include work on the conversion of rock phosphate into fertilizer, extracting hecogerin (the base for cortisone) from sisal waste, and the use of wood-producer gas in combination with fuel oil for cheaper power generation. The Organization's current budget provides for an expenditure of about £50,000, which is contributed by Kenya, Uganda, Tanganyika, the United Kingdom, and from charges made to industry for work performed. Twenty-five percent of the work has been for governments of East Africa, 40 percent for statutory boards, and the balance for private concerns. Current studies include dehydration of vegetables, and improved methods of processing coffee and of drying sisal.

The Materials Branch of the Ministry of Works was established in 1949 and now consists of seven well-equipped laboratories operated at a recurrent cost of £122,500. It acts as the official technological organ of all East African territories and performs work also for governments of neighboring countries and for non-governmental bodies.

We support the recommendation made by the Commission headed by Professor A. C. Frazer,[5] that an Industrial Research Council should be established to bring together scientists and technicians of private industry and those of the East African governments, thus establishing liaison which to date has been missing.

Industrial Land

The availability and cost of land as well as services plays an important part in attracting industry. Crown land reserved for industrial purposes

[5] *Report of the Commission on the Most Suitable Structure for the Management, Direction and Financing of Research on an East African Basis,* East African High Commission, Nairobi.

and services by rail is most likely adequate for Nairobi (1,000 acres), Kisumu and Thika, but possibly inadequate for Mombasa (35 acres) and Nakuru (4 acres).

Land is available to industry on 99-year leases. The price of the land is established by reference to prevailing market prices. One-fifth of the assessed land value is paid by the lessor as a lump sum, and on the remaining four-fifths a yearly charge of 5 percent is made by way of rental; this rental is not subject to variation during the 99-year tenure.[6] The purchaser is also required to pay the cost of utilities and essential services (currently £2,000 per acre in Nairobi, substantially less in other areas). Moneys received by Lands Department are used to develop further areas.

Financial Assistance for Industrial Development

Government finance for industrial development is provided by the Industrial Development Corporation (IDC), which was established by the Industrial Development Ordinance of 1954 "to facilitate the industrial and economic development of the Colony by the initiation, assistance or expansion of industrial, commercial or other undertakings or enterprises in the Colony or elsewhere." The IDC took over the assets and liabilities of its predecessor, the East African Industrial Management Board, which had been established in 1944 to supply certain essential products during the war period.

The Corporation is financed by government loans. Up to June 30, 1960, it had received £466,000 from the Kenya Government; and losses of £65,000 had accumulated to that date. In 1960, its investments were distributed between four undertakings—two hotels, a soap maker and a coastal fishing enterprise. In addition, it had £71,000 on deposit with the Land and Agricultural Bank and £53,000 on deposit with the Savings and Loan Society, Ltd. In the last two financial years 1960/61, 1961/62, the IDC has had a further £79,000 of loan money from the Government. In 1960/61, it made loans for undertakings engaged in making buttons, canning, fluorescent lighting, and cashew nut processing; and it increased its investments in the hotel business. The Corporation has been limited in part by its financial resources, but it has not played a significant role in fostering industrial development. It has, for instance, no full-time staff. We know that the Kenya Government has been reviewing the role of the Industrial Development Corporation and is

[6] Example: A five-acre plot in Nairobi is currently worth £9,500. The purchaser pays one-fifth (£1,900) as lump sum and 5 percent on four-fifths (£180) by way of annual rental.

likely to obtain additional financial resources to expand its activities. We suggest that the opportunity should be taken to reorganize the Corporation and to build up its reputation both inside East Africa and abroad.

An industrial investment organization can play an important role in promoting the development of manufacturing industry. Industrialists with sound projects may have difficulty in obtaining sufficient capital. A central organization of standing could not only help in this respect by providing funds itself, but could also encourage the supply of funds from elsewhere, including external sources. Such an organization would need to be equipped adequately to appraise projects submitted to it. It might also encourage the establishment of new industries by commissioning studies of industrial development possibilities that seemed promising and by acting as a source of information concerning industrial development in the country. Its investments should be well placed, and resources provided for the organization should be justified on grounds of general priority. It is difficult to assess the financial needs of an industrial investment organization in its first years of operation. We have included £800,000 for industrial development in the outline program suggested in Chapter 3, which we hope will be raised mostly from external sources, but the amount appropriate for this purpose will need to be reviewed in the light of progress made.

The Industrial Development Corporation has also administered a fund of £25,000 supplied by the United States Government to provide loans to Africans to establish or expand industries. Not all undertakings need be large in order to be efficient and there should be scope for small establishments, especially where the product needs to be tailored to the requirements of individual consumers. A private company has also assisted Africans to form and manage private companies. The first venture consisted of four factories recently constructed outside Kiambu for the manufacture of furniture, glue, locks, bolts and metal brackets and cheap radio sets. The company drew up standard company documents and accounts and offered its services as managing agent and as auditor for individual companies.

CONCLUDING REMARKS

Manufacturing industry in Kenya expanded rapidly in the postwar period and by the mid-fifties had come to provide nearly 10 percent of the Gross Domestic Product. Since then the value of the output of manufacturing at current prices has risen by about 5 percent per annum,[7] but the number of employees has fallen. Potential industrial development is limited by the small extent of mineral resources so far discovered, the quality of labor and the size of the local market in the customs union area. The development of some industries has not been as great as might have been expected and there is scope for the expansion of some industries producing consumer goods, particularly some textiles. In time the growth of local demand, especially from the transformation of African agriculture, should provide further opportunities for the expansion of manufacturing. Kenya may also be well placed to continue to build up an export trade in manufactures to neighboring countries.

The expansion of manufacturing, as of other forms of production, depends partly on the establishment of a favorable climate for investment. Specific governmental assistance is also required, especially to encourage the growth of industries which could be well located in East Africa to displace imports. We have made suggestions for consideration by the Kenya Government and the Common Services Organization about policies for customs drawback on imported materials and protective duties and their administration. We have also reviewed other forms of government assistance to manufacturing industry. Whilst we believe that most finance for investment should continue to come from private sources, a reorganized Industrial Development Corporation providing finance and information could play an important part in stimulating industrial expansion.

[7] These estimates are based on the annual survey of employment and of wages and salaries paid to employees and assume that the relationship between wages and the product of manufacturing and repair as shown in the results of surveys of industry remain constant. *Domestic Income and Product in Kenya*, 1959.

CHAPTER 6 *TOURISM AND WILDLIFE*

Tourism

There are considerable opportunities for the expansion of the international tourist trade in Kenya. Tourism can be an important foreign exchange earner and, at the same time, help stimulate domestic income and employment in related industries. Accordingly, governmental policy should be directed toward its active encouragement and some expenditure for this purpose may be regarded as of high priority.

Kenya's range of scenic attractions, its beaches and mountains, the Rift Valley, a varied and pleasant climate, brilliant flowers and trees, the numerous natural recreation spots, and the diversity and number of wild game still to be found in Kenya, offer a potential attraction to tourists difficult to match in any other region of the world. With the growth of international sea and air travel, and having in Mombasa a first-class seaport and in Nairobi an excellent international airport, the accessibility of most of Kenya to tourists from all over the world has become relatively easy.

Kenya has numerous national parks and game reserves, varying in size from the Nairobi National Park of 44 square miles to the Tsavo National Park of well over 8,000 square miles. Among these national parks and reserves are the Masai-Amboseli Game Reserve, the Masai-Mara Reserve, the Meru and Samburu District Reserves, the Uaso Nyiro National Park, the Marsabit and Ngong National Reserves, the West Chylulu National Reserve, and two mountain parks of Mount Kenya and the Aberdare Mountains. The Tsavo National Park is the main stronghold for big game in Kenya readily accessible to tourists. The Marsabit National Reserve in the Northern Province is the most remote and by far the wildest and most rugged, containing many types of animals not found in reserves in more accessible areas. The Masai-Mara Reserve, combined with the Serengeti Park in Tanganyika, probably contains the largest variety of wild game to be found in East Africa.

Kenya's main natural attractions for the tourist provide a good base for the development of tourist services. The number of tourists is not yet great, but has become of increasing importance in recent years. While the mission has no reliable data on the subject, indications are that tourist expenditures in Kenya have been increasing materially and were es-

170

timated to be on the order of £2.5 million in 1960 with expenditures by other travelers raising the total to something in excess of £4 million.

A basic step in the development of tourism in Kenya has already been taken through the creation of a Ministry of Tourism, Forests and Wildlife,[1] and in the support given the Trustees of the National Parks, the District Game Parks, and to the East African Tourist Travel Association, which advertises Kenya and East Africa to the rest of the world.

While the development of the tourist industry in Kenya will require government support and encouragement and the expenditure of some government funds, the greater part of the industry should remain in the private sector. The primary role of the Government should be to take the lead in the creation and maintenance of an atmosphere conducive to drawing visitors to the country, the provision of some assistance in the establishment of representation in principal foreign centers of population, the provision of basic facilities in Kenya required to make local travel and sightseeing reasonably easy, safe and interesting, and in the enactment of such legislation as may be needed to ensure safety of travelers and preservation of national points or things of interest. While some public funds would naturally be devoted to such general purposes, it would also be reasonable to expect commercial tourist interests, who would benefit from an increase in the trade, to make important contributions.

Tourist policy should aim at increasing the volume of middle-income tourists as well as what has been called "the luxury trade." The expenditures per person of the former group while in Kenya might be substantially less than of the latter, but the aggregate number of middle-income persons participating in tourist travel throughout the world today so greatly exceeds the present number of de luxe travelers that the aggregate income to be derived from the larger group should far exceed that from the heretofore more sought-after de luxe group. As the flow of middle-income tourists increases, some increases in expenditures, both public and private, will be needed to provide additional facilities and amenities.

In order both to define the public role in tourism and to provide private interests with a better base for their own plans, the Government should itself prepare a tourist amenities program. Such a program would consider each national park, game preserve and similar area of tourist interest, and would establish the needs of each for hotels, lodges, motels, shelters, observation points and similar amenities. On this basis,

[1] Although these three matters come under the purview of a single ministry in Kenya, the mission deals with forests in its consideration of agriculture (see Chapter 4).

private interests and local government bodies could construct, equip and operate many such facilities, with the central government providing credit where necessary.

To make such an amenities program meaningful, attention will have to be paid to tourist infrastructure—to roads primarily, or solely, for tourist purposes, to water supplies, to lookout points and the like. Private investment in tourist facilities is only likely to take place if the provision of such infrastructure, either by the central or local governments, has been assured.

Of particular importance is the construction and maintenance of access roads. At present the roads in national parks are constructed to earth standards and are often impassable during the rainy season. While indispensable to an increase in tourist capacity, the cost of roads can be very high: all-weather roads are estimated at £800 a mile, with roads of lesser standards proportionately less. Accordingly, their construction can only be economic if there is reasonable prospect of relatively heavy traffic. The construction of roads should, therefore, be coordinated with the provision of other facilities and amenities.

Furthermore, the expanded supply of augmented tourist capacity must of course be balanced by a continued augmented demand in the form of increased numbers of tourists. For this, a carefully planned publicity campaign will be essential. Potential tourists must be made aware of Kenya's tourist attractions, its advantages in terms of accommodation and facilities and, above all, be assured of public policies for the development of safety of travel within the country. While overseas publicity would best be coordinated under government sponsorship, the participation of major private interests should be actively sought.

Wildlife

Kenya's wildlife, as we have stated, is an important tourist asset. Kenya is one of the few countries remaining in the world where wild animals can still be seen in their natural habitat. There has long been world-wide interest in Kenya's wildlife and, in recent years, a growing concern over its possible extinction. The mission believes that additional measures will be needed for the protection of wildlife if the latter is to be of continuing long-term value to the country.

Kenya's game has been exploited in the past through sport hunting and trophy collecting, through slaughter for food, skins, ivory and other game products for personal use or commercial sale, through the trapping of live specimens for sale abroad, and as a tourist and photographic attraction. Some attempts to determine the income realized from these sources have been made, but complete and reliable data are not available and estimates based on such data as exist are likely to be misleading. However, it is known that licenses were issued for game shooting to the value of £40,000 in 1960. Wild animals, skins, tusks, and other animal parts and products were exported to an estimated value of £248,000 in 1961 (see Table 1). Reports of "safari firms" (supplying transport, guides, professional hunters, equipment, etc., to tourist hunters and photographers) and from other firms engaged in selling clothing, shoes, and other equipment and supplies direct to safari tourists, indicate that substantial amounts of money have been expended in Kenya by tourists

TABLE 1: Exports of Game Animals and Game Animal Products, 1961

Kind	Unit		Value (£)
Live animals (not for food)	number	11,389	93,416
Ivory	cwt	719	60,140
Hippo teeth	cwt	10	266
Rhino horn	cwt	9	3,729
Trophies	—	—	76,413
Crocodile skins	cwt	112	14,043
Total			248,007

SOURCE: *Annual Trade Report,* East African Customs and Excise, 1961.

primarily engaged in "big game" viewing, photographing, or shooting. Apart from all these forms of direct income, it is, of course, the abundance of wildlife which in general attracts tourists to Kenya, so that virtually all tourist income in Kenya may be regarded as being indirectly derived from the existence of its wildlife.

Steps have been taken in the past to protect wild game through the establishment of measures designed to protect certain species and to control the slaughter of others, and through the inauguration of measures to provide water and food to diminish deaths of wildlife from thirst and hunger. The rapid decrease in numbers of wild animals in Kenya in the past half century, however, can be taken as a measure of what can and may happen in the next few years if more comprehensive and more energetic steps are not taken to prevent their further destruction. The mission endorses action taken toward the establishment of wild animal reserves, of experimental "game crop" farms and of game protection schemes in appropriate areas, and of further research into the value of local fauna as feed, the possibilities of improving the local meat supply from that source, and the ancillary supply of skins and other items for market, all as a means of conserving and protecting the wildlife of Kenya as a valuable economic and cultural resource.

The mission considers that the problem of enlisting the cooperation of local people toward the preservation and profitable exploitation of the big game population is crucial. To stimulate further local interest in areas where some beginnings have already been made, the following steps by the central government are suggested:

a. Establish a policy of dividing between the central government and local governments (with specific reference at this time to existing District Councils establishing and operating game reserves) all fees collected for licenses to hunt game in their areas, and a substantial proportion of all fees collected by landowners for "land use" from hunters for hunting over lands in those districts.

b. Assist in the execution of bady needed road construction in the Masai-Amboseli Game Reserve.

c. Provide funds to the local District Council for road construction in the Masai-Mara Game Reserve.

d. Assist the Meru District Council in arranging for the construction of a lodge in the Meru Game Reserve.

Park rangers, guards, wardens or similar officials will be required in all areas devoted to the preservation of game to enforce the game laws. They should be provided by local governments in reserves under their jurisdiction and by the central government in the case of national parks or national reserves. Operations of the two groups should be coordinated, and a general uniformity of policies and regulations controlling all parks and reserves established. Similarly, throughout Kenya, steps will be necessary to control trade in wild animals and wild animal products and by-products, and to eliminate illegal trapping or killing of wild game in all areas.

Public Expenditures on Tourism and Wildlife

Mass tourist movements depend on delicate psychological factors and extended publicity campaigns so that sizable increases in tourism cannot be expected for some time after it has become clear that political and social stability has been assured and until publicity campaigns have had time to take effect. Thus, it is as much in the field of policy as in expenditure that public initiative can invigorate the tourist trade in the coming few years. We have also made clear the large role of private en-

NATIONAL PARKS and GAME RESERVES

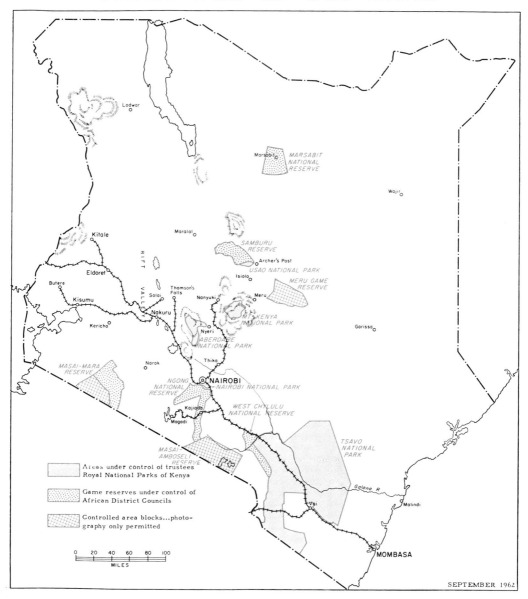

Lodwar

Marsabit *MARSABIT NATIONAL RESERVE*

Wajir

Kitale Maralal *SAMBURU RESERVE* Archer's Post *USAO NATIONAL PARK*

Eldoret *RIFT VALLEY* Isiolo *MERU GAME RESERVE*

Butere Thomson's Falls Meru

Kisumu Solai Nanyuki *MT. KENYA NATIONAL PARK* Garissa

Nakuru

Kericho Nyeri *ABERDARE NATIONAL PARK*

Narok Thika

MASAI-MARA RESERVE NAIROBI *NGONG NATIONAL RESERVE* *NAIROBI NATIONAL PARK*

Kajiado *WEST CHYLULU NATIONAL RESERVE* *TSAVO NATIONAL PARK*

Magadi

MASAI AMBOSELI RESERVE

Galana R.

Voi Malindi

MOMBASA

Areas under control of trustees
Royal National Parks of Kenya

Game reserves under control of
African District Councils

Controlled area blocks...photo-
graphy only permitted

0 20 40 60 80 100
MILES

SEPTEMBER 1962

terprise in the tourist trade so that the scope and need for public investment should be relatively limited.

In present financial circumstances and despite the potential for the growth of income from tourism, the mission does not believe that the Kenya Government can significantly expand its expenditures for this purpose unaided. In the financial year 1962/63 it was planning to make outlays of the order of £180,000 on tourism and game.[2] Of these expenditures £83,000 were charged to the Development Estimates and included grants for the development of the national parks, lodge accommodations and for capital and research expenditures by the Game Department. We understand that the Government has been formulating a program along the lines suggested above and entailing increased expenditures, with a view to obtaining private financial support for it. If this support is in fact obtained, a larger program of development expenditure for accommodation, roads and ancillary tourist facilities, much of which might be put on a self-liquidating basis over a reasonably short period, would be justified.

We accordingly recommend that for planning purposes a figure in the neighborhood of £100,000 a year be allocated for the development of tourism and wildlife, but we also suggest that this allocation be kept under periodic review in the light of the considerations stressed in this chapter. Future policy and expenditures must depend upon the responses of citizens, investors and tourists to the limited initiatives which are within the Government's present capacity.

[2] This excludes a portion of the administrative costs of the Ministry of Tourism, Forests and Wildlife, which we have not attempted to allocate among the separate purposes.

POWER

Electricity is supplied by the East African Power and Lighting Company Ltd. (EAPL) and its associated company, the Kenya Power Company Ltd. (KPC). Both companies operate under exclusive 50-year bulk supply licenses granted by the Government. The EAPL is responsible for the generation, transmission and distribution of electricity in Kenya with the exception of the generation and transmission of bulk supplies to the Nairobi area which is the function of the KPC.

The EAPL is a public company maintaining share registers both in London and Nairobi. Paid-up capital as of December 31, 1961, amounted to £8.2 million. The Government of Kenya, which sold its Nyeri Electricity Undertaking to EAPL in 1960 and accepted shares in exchange, ranks as the largest single ordinary shareholder with 150,000 stock units (2.5 percent of the capital) with only one other holding in excess of 1 percent. A large number of assurance companies, banks and investment companies own between 10,000 and 25,000 shares each.

The financial position of the EAPL is strong. Loan capital consists only of about £2 million debenture stock. Dividends have been progressively increased to the current rate of 10 percent but additions have been made annually to reserves. As the bulk of £10 million worth of plant and equipment has been purchased since 1947, normal annual depreciation provision ranges near £0.75 million.

The KPC was formed in 1954. A large hydroelectric station had been constructed at Owen Falls in Uganda and a bulk supply from this source was found to be the most satisfactory means of meeting the growing demand for power in the Nairobi area. Power for consumers in Nairobi had been supplied by hydroelectric and thermal stations in Kenya. For economy of operation it was decided that the bulk supply of power to Nairobi from both sources should be operated by one authority, and the KPC was incorporated for this purpose. Its capital of £100 is held one-third each by the Government of Kenya, EAPL and Power Securities Ltd. of London.[1] The 50-year license issued to the KPC provides that upon expiry or prior revocation all assets of the company revert to the

[1] Sessional Paper No. 75 of 1955, Government Printer, Nairobi. Kenya Power Company Limited (Shareholding and Licensing) Agreement, 1955.

Government and that the two electricity companies sell their 66 2/3 shares to the Government at £1 per share. (The Government would be responsible for meeting outstanding debentures and other liabilities and commitments.)

EAPL sold its Tana and Wanjii hydroelectric plants, including the 66 kv lines, to KPC for a total of £3.3 million. The cash payment was made by KPC out of the proceeds of an issue of £7.5 million 5½ percent debenture stock. The balance of the cash was used to build the 132 kv transmission line to carry Uganda power from the border to Tororo to the main Nairobi grid, and a bulk-supply contract was negotiated with the Uganda Electricity Board.

Licensing enables the Government to regulate bulk prices of electricity to distributors and requires the company to seek government approval for any issue of debentures, loans or permanent finance. Charges made by the KPC are designed to provide payment of interest on debentures, redemption thereof and to leave a small surplus to cover minor additions.

Prices charged for electricity sales to the public are subject to government approval and are geared to meet the financial needs of the supply companies.

Sales of electricity in Kenya over the years 1956–61 have increased at an average annual rate of about 10 percent. In 1961, sales rose by 6 percent. In the last quarter of the year, unprecedented floods closed Kenya hydroelectric stations supplying Nairobi for a short time, but the decline in the rate of growth of consumption of power is more attributable to general business conditions than to physical factors (see Table 1).

There are two separate main supply areas, the coast area centered on

TABLE 1: Production, Import and Sales of Electricity

(million kwh)

| | Kenya Generation | Imports from | | Power Station Use and Transmission Losses | Total Sales |
		Uganda	Tangan-yika		
1956	245	—	23	46	223
1957	268	—	23	49	243
1958	214	90	24	61	267
1959	212	129	22	62	301
1960	221	160	21	67	336
1961	215	191	20	69	357

SOURCES: *Kenya Trade and Supplies Bulletin* and *Uganda Electricity Board, Annual Report.*

Mombasa (extending to Likoni in the south, Malindi in the north and ten miles inland from the coast) and the Nairobi area (extending through the 132 kv line to Tororo, Nakuru, Gilgil, Thomson's Falls, Njoro, Kisumu, Kericho, Nandi Hills and Miwani). Eldoret is being connected to the bulk supply to Nairobi. Kitale, Nyeri and Nanyuki generate their own electricity and are self-contained.[2]

The supply for the coast area is generated mainly at Kipevu (oil fired steam) backed up by small supplies from Tanganyika and 7 mw of diesel plant. Recent installations at Kipevu (5 mw and 12.5 mw) were financed from internal resources, but finance for a further 12.5 mw steam unit costing £750,000, required in 1963/64 to supply the new oil refinery, has not been obtained. In the absence of any major new developments on the coast, present and planned installations appear adequate. They would increase generating capacity to 49 mw, whereas the forecast of peak demand in 1966 amounts to 28 mw.

Power for the Nairobi area is obtained up to 30 mw by bulk supply from the Uganda Electricity Board and up to 24 mw from local hydro sources, backed up by 27 mw of thermal standby plant. The peak demand in 1960 was 53 mw but was projected by EAPL to rise to 80 mw by 1966 (see Table 2).

TABLE 2: Estimate of Maximum Demand

(megawatts)

	1960 Actual	1962	1963	1964	1965	1966
Coast Area	15	17	23	25	26	28
Nairobi	49	54	59	61	64	68
Nairobi and up-country	53	61	68	70	74	79

SOURCE: East African Power and Lighting Company Ltd.

Thus, total projected demand would seem to be within the limits of present capacity. However, the latter is not entirely satisfactory. First, assured Kenya hydro power amounts to only 18 mw due to recurrent drought conditions. Next, some of the standby thermal plant, though postwar, cannot be considered reliable. Finally, thermal plant is more expensive to operate (12½ EA cents per unit against 7 cents for Kenya hydro and Uganda power) because of transporting oil from the coast. Consequently, EAPL believes that present supplies will soon be fully

[2] Kitale has 900 kw, Nyeri 2,000 kw and Nanyuki 1,600 kw of installed plant.

TRANSPORT

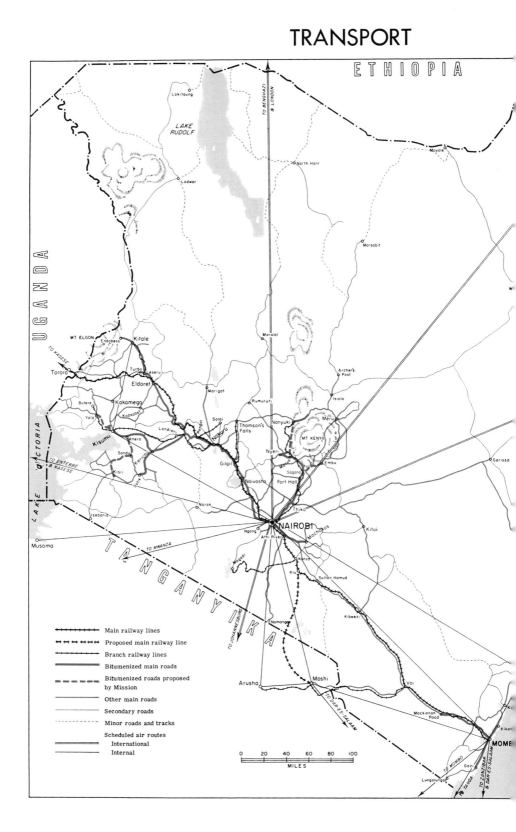

SOMALI

REP.

TO ADEN, KARACHI
& BOMBAY

TO KARACHI
& BOMBAY

Garsen

Lamu

Malindi

INDIAN OCEAN

ASA

committed and additional sources of power will have to be made available. The alternatives under consideration are to take more power from Uganda or to erect a major hydroelectric station at Seven Forks, in Kenya.

The first stage of the Seven Forks hydroelectric scheme in Kenya, which provides for the generation of 40 mw, is estimated to cost £7.2 million. The full scheme for generating 230 mw would eventually cost £24 million.

The bulk supply contract between the KPC and the Uganda Electricity Board runs for 50 years from the beginning of 1958. From the beginning of 1964 and until the contract runs out, the KPC will pay a minimum of £397,500 a year, equivalent to a demand of 30 mw at £13.25 a year per kilowatt (the present contract rate is £11 a year per kilowatt and in 1961 total payments amounted to £290,000). At the same time, the KPC can increase its demand up to a maximum of 45 mw, but this would require additional transmission facilities between the Owen Falls and the Kenya border as well as in Kenya. The estimated cost in Kenya of reinforcing the transmission line and substations is £340,000.

The installed generating capacity at Owen Falls is 120 mw and this can be increased to 150 mw. The peak load in 1961 was about 74 mw, including power transmitted to Kenya. The Owen Falls station should be able to meet additional demand in Uganda and increased requirements of the Nairobi area of Kenya for some years to come. No large new consumer of power is expected to require connection to the Nairobi system during the next few years. The increase in demand forecast by the EAPL of about 7 percent a year is modest, but the current rate of growth of consumption is smaller and the forecast should be reviewed in the light of present expectations.

Kenya wishes to develop the Seven Forks site. The Uganda Electricity Board should be able to provide more power for Kenya from Owen Falls for the near future. It would, however, seek a more favorable price to Uganda than is included in the present contract. We cannot see the justification for proceeding with the Seven Forks scheme at this stage and consider that it should be possible for both electricity undertakings to negotiate an increase in the supply of power to Kenya from Owen Falls to their joint advantage.

TRANSPORT AND COMMUNICATIONS

As Kenya approaches and achieves independence and assumes the accompanying heavy demands for funds for both capital and recurrent expenses, care should be taken that new works in the field of transport and communications make a maximum contribution to the economic development of the country. To ensure this, efforts in this field should be closely related to the priorities established in other parts of the economy. Accordingly, the priorities within the transport sector should be with respect to those projects likely to promote the development of agriculture and other income-producing activities.

Furthermore, to maximize the return from existing transport and communications activities, experienced technical and administrative staffs must be maintained. Staffs presently employed are, in general, composed of European and Asian personnel of such caliber. Many, however, may be lost when independence is achieved. In realization of this fact, all of the major undertakings dealing with transport and communications in Kenya are reported to be greatly concerned with the problem of finding local qualified personnel to replace departing expatriates. This is the essence of the problem of "localization." It is discussed in Chapter 8, but deserves special mention here because of its serious impact on government undertakings in the field of transport and communications. If the management is inexperienced some serious adverse economic results can be expected, and if technical operations cannot properly be carried out, services may have to be curtailed.

Some services have already been curtailed where replacements for departing personnel have not been found. The situation will undoubtedly become worse in the near future unless steps are taken to induce key personnel of present staffs to remain or at least to defer their departures until satisfactory replacements can be found and trained, and energetic steps in this direction should be taken. "Localization" in the field of transport and communications is likely to be slow and difficult, but if a substantial number of the present expatriate staff departs there appears no alternative but to accept the cost of finding trained replacements, largely from expatriate sources, or suffer the dangers resulting from the deterioration of services.

In Kenya the principal transport facility provided and maintained by, or under the jurisdiction of, the Kenya Government is the network of roads. Airports are also nationally owned and maintained. Railways, harbors, telecommunications, postal services, and some aviation and related services are all provided and maintained under the East African Common Services Organization (EACSO).

The operation of these services, through the East African Common Services Organization, jointly for Kenya, Tanganyika and Uganda, poses a somewhat difficult problem of evaluation in relation to the economy of only one of the three countries. This becomes especially true when some of these common services operate under an agreement between the three countries that imposes on the EACSO a mandate that they should be "self-sustaining."

In preparing national programs for investment in transport and communications, as in other sectors, care must be exercised to provide for the use of funds in a manner calculated to be of the greatest benefit to the economy of the country. Where a common service enterprise is concerned, each country should examine the common service programs and proposals both from the viewpoint of its own interest and of the interest of East Africa as a whole; indeed, the two interests are interrelated. An important matter for Kenya in this respect is to coordinate the programing of the various means of transport operating in Kenya, regardless of nominal ownership or current status, to provide adequate service at the lowest cost in support of Kenya's own national economy.

The Common Services Organization has required comparatively little direct financial assistance from the three countries for the "self-sustaining" services. Revenues have tended to cover recurrent costs and capital has been provided either by or with the assistance of the United Kingdom. As the countries become independent, however, they will assume the United Kingdom's responsibility in this respect, as well as retaining their contingent obligation to pay the debts of these undertakings.

The adequacy of their services and the suitability of the charges made by these undertakings are also a matter of great importance to the economy. Insufficient railway transport and inappropriate tariffs could hamper economic growth.

ROADS

In terms of the transport network as a whole, the short-term economic function of the roads should primarily be to augment the railroad system in the haulage of freight. The network of primary and secondary all-weather roads in Kenya, especially those needed for agricultural development, requires augmentation and improvement. The only good bituminized roads are those from Nairobi to Kericho and Kisumu, to Eldoret and Kitale and to Nyeri, and sections at each end of the Nairobi-Mombasa road. The greatest deficiencies from the point of view of development are roads for agriculture, including those necessary to move new tea harvest between farms and factories. Connections with Uganda and with Tanganyika, including Mwanza on Lake Victoria, and other internal trunk roads are, we think, of lower priority.

There is some indication that the increase in road traffic will of itself call for an augmentation and upgrading of the road system. The annual increase in vehicles during the years 1954–60 averaged 10 percent and was 15 percent in 1960, so that by the latter year the number of vehicles registered in Kenya was nearly 90,000, an increase of nearly 12,000 over 1959. According to a traffic count, 35 miles of roads, all bitumen, carried over 2,000 vehicles a day; 60 miles of roads, all bitumen, carried between 1,000 and 2,000 a day; 183 miles of roads, all bitumen, carried between 500 and 1,000 vehicles a day; and 295 miles of roads, bitumen and gravel, carried between 300 and 500 vehicles a day.

Roads and road traffic in Kenya are the responsibility of the Kenya Government, although some responsibilities for road maintenance and construction rest with local authorities.

All trunk and secondary roads in Kenya excepting those in forests and parks are selected, constructed and maintained under the supervision of the Kenya Road Authority, established by Ordinance No. 64 of 1950, and appointed by the Governor. The Road Authority is at present within the portfolio of the Minister of Works and Communications. It is responsible for establishing priorities for construction and maintenance of roads supported by Road Fund grants; and for the expenditure of Road Funds. It advises the Minister on legislation in relation to road communications. Actual maintenance operations and construction work are undertaken by the Ministry and local authorities. In general, the Ministry is responsible for the maintenance of many trunk roads and local authorities for other roads. Funds for these works are provided on a grant basis. To control the activities of agencies doing the actual work, and to assist local agencies such as African District Councils in their engineering work, the Ministry employs a number of inspectors on a permanent staff basis.

Capital Programs

Construction of roads has in the past been financed from resources available to the Government for general development purposes. In addition, funds have been obtained specifically for construction from the World Bank and under contractor finance arrangements.

In 1960, the World Bank provided a loan of £0.9 million to the Kenya Government for a project costing £1.56 million for construction and improvement of roads under a special program of the Kenya Government for the development of African agriculture. This was a part of a larger loan, of which the major portion was intended for development of agriculture itself, with the road project an essential segment of the over-all program.

A £4.8 million "contractor finance" scheme was started in 1959 with

work on the main road from Nairobi to Nyeri. Other roads recon-
structed under this scheme are Mau Summit to Eldoret and to Kericho
and Kisumu. Construction contracts were awarded for work to be done
on a deferred payment basis. All told some 250 miles of main road will
have been built at an average cost of about £19,000 per mile. Up to June
30, 1962, payments made under this scheme amounted to £450,000. The
estimate for 1962/63 is £214,000, but during the following four years the
full amount of the contract will come due for payment. Payments are
estimated to rise to a maximum of £1.7 million in 1965/66. In entering
into schemes of this kind the Government is in fact financing, by means
of short-term loans, roads which can only be expected to yield returns to
the exchequer over a long term of years. The heavy burden of payments
in the next few years will be difficult to manage and will limit ability to
finance projects having a higher national priority. Offers of contractor
finance may also lead to the adoption of projects which on grounds of
general priority would not qualify for inclusion in the Government's development programs. The mission strongly recommends that contractor
finance should not be resorted to for further road construction. This
matter is also discussed in Chapters 3 and 10.

The Road Authority has prepared a program of capital requirements
which may be summarized as follows in the two periods 1963 to 1966 and
1966 to 1968:

		£ million
a.	*July 1963 to June 1966:*	
	Main trunk roads	7.9
	Lesser trunk roads and feeder roads	2.2
	Main and district roads in munici-	
	palities and roads in townships	.4
	Total	10.5
b.	*July 1966 to June 1968:*	
	Main trunk roads	3.3
	Lesser trunk roads and feeder roads	3.4
	Main and district roads in munici-	
	palities and roads in townships	.3
	Total	7.0
	Grand Total	17.5

The mission considers that the program as prepared should not be
adopted at this time and that it should be reviewed to eliminate, curtail
or postpone all but the most urgent items. In establishing a revised program, priority should be given to improvement of road surface drainage
works, culverts and bridges which have been shown to be inadequate to

carry the flow from heavy rains, followed by construction of roads required to assist in agricultural production and processing. The opportunity should also be taken to review the class to which each road should be constructed. A limited amount of work to standards below those envisaged may be justified. This could increase burden of maintenance, however, and should therefore be kept under constant surveillance. The revised program should be subject to the annual review and modification recommended for the 1963–67 program as a whole.

Specifically, the mission considers that the main roads listed in the Authority's program as priorities 5 to 9 inclusive in Group A, will contribute more to an increase in agricultural production and essential movement of agricultural products than will those listed as the first four priorities (Mombasa road and international roads) and recommends that they receive higher priority. These five are Marua-Nyeri-Nanyuki road, Kisumu-Yala road, Sagana-Embu road, Ahero-Sondu road, and Sondu-Kisii road. We also consider that the Leseru-Turbo section of the main road to Uganda, which serves the intensively cultivated farming area of Turbo and Eldoret, should similarly be given high priority. In the secondary (feeder) roads category, except for emphasizing the importance of tea roads, the mission is not in a position to recommend firm or detailed priorities as between either areas or individual roads. In this group, changing developments in different parts of the country, will require a flexible plan rather than the establishment of rigid priorities. The method used by the authority of nominating a list of roads in each area, with work to be performed on selected items, or substitutes, as funds are found, satisfies this criterion.

The improvement of the Nairobi-Mombasa road and the international road between Nairobi and Tanganyika is not included in the road program we envisage for the next four years. We believe that these projects have much less claim than interior roads needed to support the development of agriculture. We are also satisfied that a larger road program to include them, to the exclusion of other development projects, is not justifiable. The Mombasa-Nairobi road is discussed in Annex D.

Municipalities receive 100 percent grants from the Road Authority for construction and maintenance of main trunk and secondary roads within the municipal areas to the geometric standard of the rural extension of the road. Higher standards or special conditions may form the basis for additional assistance. Some municipalities have indicated a need for an increase of their present annual expenditure, which is only partially covered by recent increases of local taxes (principally rates on properties). The requirement for Nairobi, caused by the rapid growth of the city and resulting serious traffic problems, has been indicated as in excess of £700,000 over five years or something over £140,000 a year. Assuming the present ratio of Nairobi's maintenance costs to the costs of other municipalities (about 4:1) can be applied, the total for all municipalities including Nairobi would be about £180,000 a year. In addition, Mombasa has the special problem of improving the road to the new oil refinery. With the heavy demands for other development expenditures, we suggest that amounts to be provided for municipalities by the Government (and for townships) be reduced to a total of approximately £150,000 for the years 1963–67, an annual average under £40,000. It is further suggested that all road improvements within municipalities become the financial responsibility of municipal authorities, except for special projects serving government installations or forming parts of trunk highways which in turn form parts of a national network.

The following shows the principal elements in the road program we suggest for the years 1963–67.

	£ million
Trunk roads	1.25
Lesser trunk roads and feeder roads in nonscheduled and county council areas	1.59
Roads in municipalities and townships	0.15
Bridges, etc.	0.15
Total	3.14

Maintenance

Government expenditure on road maintenance is in the form of grants to the Ministry of Works and the local authorities which carry out the work. The basic rates per mile per year for road maintenance grants used by the Road Authority in their plans and estimates in 1959 were as shown below and reflect the traffic density. Gravel roads require in addition periodic regraveling at a cost of up to £500 per mile about every four years. The bitumen rates include the cost of periodic resealing but not interest or amortization costs.

	Vehicles per Day	*Basic Rate per Year (£)*
Class I gravel roads	0–50	43
Class II	51–100	66
Class III	101–200	89
Class IV	201–300	150
Class V	300+	270
Bitumen roads (1 lane)		200
Bitumen roads (2 lanes)		265

It is understood that in forecasting revenues and recurrent expenditures the Road Authority has assumed an increase of 5 percent a year. This rate is less than the annual increase of vehicles during the years 1954–60, which averaged 10 percent, and was 15 percent in 1960, but the decline in the European population may well affect the amount of road traffic. At present, revenues—which are derived from fees for drivers' and vehicle licenses and from some gasoline and diesel fuel taxes—are barely sufficient to cover recurrent expenditures, with no surplus available for capital expenditures. Because of the budgetary situation, arrangements for meeting maintenance costs should be decided annually by the Government rather than by allocating receipts from specific taxes to the Road Fund.

All expenditures incurred by the Authority in the performance of its duties are charged to the Road Fund which, in addition to the statutory revenues mentioned above, receives capital funds allocated by the Government. During 1961/62, some £1,822,000 was received from the statutory sources. At present, 3,740 miles of trunk roads and 6,400 miles of secondary roads have 100 percent maintenance grants from the Road Fund. In 1962, only some 925 miles of the total of more than 10,000 miles of trunk and secondary roads had bituminous (paved) surfaces; the others are for the most part surfaced with gravel or murram. Many of these nonbituminous roads are of low-grade construction, difficult to traverse, and subject to temporary closure in wet weather.

A part of the expenditures on minor roads in African District Council areas is also covered by the Road Fund. In those areas 5,700 miles of minor roads leading to farming or village areas receive grants from the Road Fund of 20 percent of costs; the balance of the cost is provided by the ADC's from their own revenue. The Road Authority contributes also £5 per mile toward the maintenance of 10,000 miles of "administrative roads" in outlying areas (about 4,800) and in the sparsely settled Northern Province (around 5,400).

The principal expenditures by local authorities from their own resources for maintenance and betterment of roads are reported to be about £0.6 million in 1961, divided as follows:

a. African District Councils	£183,000
b. County Councils	25,000
c. Municipalities	434,000
(Note: A part of these municipal expenditures may be related to private streets and, therefore, recoverable.)	
d. Small townships	4,000

In addition, European farmers may have expended on access roads in the County Councils areas an amount of the order of £75,000.

Mechanical transport and plant used in road work appear to be minimum in quantity but adequate for the present because of the care and efficiency with which they are used. The renewals fund appears sufficient to meet requirements for essential replacements for the near future, assuming that present standards of operation and maintenance are continued.

Traffic control is an essential element in keeping maintenance costs at the minimum consistent with the actual traffic densities on given roads of specific structural standards. On highways of the higher classes, there will need to be a rigid control over the speeds at which vehicles may travel and over the loads (per vehicle and per axle or wheel) that they may carry. Total load control is essential to protect bridges from structural damage; axle or wheel load control is needed to protect the road itself from foundation or surface damage; and speed control is needed to reduce the damage to the road caused by the pounding effect of heavy loads when carried at excessive speeds as well as to protect the lives of occupants of vehicles traveling on highways, especially on those sections where curvatures or gradients occur. We recommend that the existing legislation and arrangements for its enforcement be reviewed.

Staffing and Training

The staff of the Kenya Road Authority is largely administrative. The Ministry of Works has in the past provided the Road Authority with laboratory research assistance, has supplied field inspectors, and has carried out major road projects, all with funds provided by the Road Authority. It is assumed that this system will be continued. Technical supervision, advice, and assistance are provided to local authorities through an "Inspectorate" of the Ministry of Works, operating on behalf of the Road Authority.

Localization and training schemes under the Ministry of Works were established early in 1961, to train professional officers, to equip existing staff to fill junior supervisory posts, and to train young candidates for employment as technical supervisors. The success of the first scheme will depend principally on the output of Africans from secondary schools, as indeed will many other programs of localization as we stress in Chapter 8. The second scheme, for promotion beyond the foreman level, will depend on basic educational qualifications of the candidates. The third scheme, consisting of the roads branch's own training school located between Embu and Meru, is designed to train technical supervisors by actual work on the construction of a new road in progress in that area while the students continue with their studies. Currently, for the entire Ministry of Works the number of trainees is approximately 150. The estimated cost of these training schemes for all branches of the Ministry of Works is approximately £120,000 a year beginning in 1962.

Since its inception in 1956, some 300 trainees have been turned out from the training school operated by the Road Authority. Beginning in July 1961, the school began to take in trainees designed to take charge of the ADC road organizations, replacing officers of the Ministry of Works, most of whom were sent overseas for further professional training.

EAST AFRICAN RAILWAYS AND HARBORS

General

The East African Railways and Harbours Administration (EARH) is a "self-contained" entity of the East African Common Services Organization. It operates railway services (about 3,500 miles of line with some 285 stations); inland waterway services (some 4,200 route miles using 75 harbors on Lakes Victoria, Tanganyika, Kioga, and Albert and on the Nile); road haulage services (some 2,600 road miles on specific routes in Tanganyika and Uganda); and harbor services at Mombasa, Dar es Salaam, Tanga, Mtwara and Lindi along the coasts of Kenya and Tanganyika. It is operated as a unified enterprise under a single general management.

In general, the financial position of EARH has been sustained through the years in satisfactory condition. Revenues have been sufficient to provide for adequate maintenance, and have provided for the accumulation of special reserves for normal replacements of equipment and structures, for betterment expenditure needed for improvement of operations and for a rates stabilization fund. Revenues have, of course, depended on traffic flow as well as on rates charged. In 1961, the total traffic moved on railways, lake marine and road services of EARH was reported as:

   a. 5.1 million passengers; a decrease of 4.2 percent from 1960 and a decrease of 14 percent over 1950. Revenue from passenger traffic fell by 3.7 percent to about £1.9 million in 1961.
   b. 4.1 million tons of freight and 1,621 million ton-miles of freight traffic; a decrease of 1.8 percent over 1960, but an increase of 33

percent over 1950. Revenue from goods traffic fell by 0.3 percent to £16.2 million in 1961.

The staff employed by the entire EARH organization in 1961 totaled about 50,000, of which Africans numbered some 44,000, Asians 4,200 and Europeans about 1,500. Africans are mostly in the lowest pay and grade scales (Division III) and Asians in the middle scales (Division II). Wages were raised in 1960, principally after labor disputes in Tanganyika.

Railways

General Description. The main lines of the East African Railways in Kenya run from Mombasa to Nairobi, Nakuru and Kisumu and to Uganda. Other lines run to Tanga and Arusha in Tanganyika, to Nanyuki, Thomson's Falls, Magadi, Solai, Kitale and Butere. The railway in Kenya is the principal means of transport to and from the coast, carrying the overseas traffic of both Kenya and Uganda.

There has been a general improvement in operating performance by the railways during recent years. For example, net ton-miles per train-hour have increased by 25 percent since 1955. All railway services seem to be well managed, and are in general of a high standard.

There are three passenger classes on the railways, the third tariff decreasing slightly with distance. Passenger revenue in 1961 was £1.9 million from fares and £0.5 million from mail, parcels, etc. The balance between passenger traffic receipts and expenditures is marginal.

Goods Traffic. Section 21 of the East African Railways and Harbours Act, under which EARH operations are conducted, provides that "the administration shall be administered on business principles and, so far as is not inconsistent therewith or with the principles of prudent finance, cheap services shall be provided by the Administration to assist agricultural, mining and industrial development in the territories." The Railways Administration has met this objective by establishing special freight tariffs favoring the traffic of some of the specified industries.

The present railway tariff on freight consists of seven standard and four special class rates. With the exception of the maximum scale, the rates are generously tapered so that over long distances the charge per ton-mile is considerably less than the ton-mile charge over a shorter distance. This is particularly important in those areas where traffic has to move over long distances, as is the case with most exports and imports. Generally speaking, agricultural products, move either at special rates or at one of the lower rates; the lowest rates are applied to basic agricultural products while processed agricultural products are charged at somewhat higher rates. The highest tariff rates of all apply to high-value consumer goods, especially luxury articles, and to petrol. Cheap rates are established for the carriage of livestock. Cattle cake is charged at a special low rate as are fertilizers for use in East Africa; timber for fencing is charged at a lower rate than timber used for other purposes; baling and fencing wire is also rated lower than the same wire used for other purposes. The rates for insecticides are especially designed to benefit the farmer who buys his dips and sprays in bulk.

The density of goods traffic varies markedly between the various railway lines. Trunk lines carry much more traffic than branch lines. For example, the line from Mombasa to Nakuru carries 8 million gross tons a year and the line from Dar es Salaam to Dodoma some 2.2 million tons. Many branch lines carry 500,000 tons or less. While the relationships between branch-line and main-line traffic volume are intricately interwoven, and the cost of operation of each is sometimes difficult to establish, it can be inferred from the quoted figures that the cost per ton-mile for haulage would be less on trunk lines than on many branch lines. Main-line revenues may, in effect, be supporting some unprofitable branch lines.

The mission suggests that the EACSO should review the functions of branch lines which earn revenues persistently below operating expenditure to decide whether these lines should be closed. Such a review should include the availability, cost and convenience of other means of transport and the likely effect of closure on main-line revenues. Proposals for construction of new branch railway lines should be subjected to searching economic review before being accepted.

The EARH relies on charging enough for the carriage of goods, which move at rates above the average cost of movement (18.83 cents per ton-mile in 1961), to permit it to support the movement of other more favored goods, principally the products and requirements of agriculture and some domestic industries.

So long as government policies provide that the EARH will assist certain industries with cheap transport where possible and at the same time carry on its operations in a business-like and self-sustaining manner, it is necessary that a sufficient proportion of the total traffic carried on the railway should consist of high-tariff products. If the proportion of this traffic to the total of all traffic carried should fall appreciably, the railway would find itself in an unprofitable position, and would be required to raise its agricultural and industrial tariffs, or to raise the general level of its rates. This situation has not yet arisen because the railways have had a considerable measure of protection from competition of road transport along parallel routes in Kenya, and to a lesser extent in Tanganyika, although not in Uganda.

Protection of the railway's financial ability to afford assistance to agriculture and other industries through preferential tariffs is now effected in Kenya in part by the control of road haulage operators through licensing and in part by the ability of the EARH to lower its own rates to a level at which road transport cannot compete. Control of road licenses has restricted the direct competition of motor haulage operators with long-distance rail carriage of goods. The policies governing transport licensing however differ between the three territories served by EARH.

It is the view of the mission that control of highway transport as a means of assisting in the maintenance of railway revenue may in the long run have little to recommend it. It could deprive the economy of benefits to be derived from the development of the most efficient transport system. The policy of using differential rail tariffs for stimulating agriculture or any other industry involves the application of haulage charges by the railway which may be far below the real cost of transport. As a general policy, the mission believes that railway tariffs should be based on costs of service rendered and that, if subsidies are to be granted to agriculture or other industries, such assistance should be by direct, rather than indirect, methods. On the other hand, and in the light of all the administrative and financial problems likely to confront the Kenya Government and the Common Services Organization over the next few years, we think that changes in the control of road transport and in railway rating are not sufficiently urgent to call for early attention. Moreover, it seems to us that changes which might radically affect the operations and finances of the East African Railways and Harbours should not be introduced without very careful assessment of the benefits to be achieved.

Future Programs. The EARH has prepared a comprehensive but tentative program for the development of the system from 1963–67 which is summarized in Table 3. Excluding betterment and renewals covered by internal funds, the program would require about £20 million of capital funds. It provides for diesel locomotives; rolling stock and strengthening of drawbars and couplings; improvements to ancillary installations such as signal equipment; and construction of several branch lines.

It has been noted that substantial amounts are included to replace existing locomotives and goods wagons and to acquire locomotives and rolling stock of improved type and capacity. The EARH recognizes the need for stringent control of expenditure and decisions to replace equip-

TABLE 3: EARH Forecasts of Capital Expenditures on Railways, 1963–67

(£ million)

Purpose	Total 1963–67	
New Lines		
Kalembwani-Moshi	2.20	
West Nile (Uganda)	1.00	
S.W. Tanganyika	6.00	
		9.20
Civil Engineering (existing lines)		
Regrade, re-alignment, relaying	3.68	
Operation (yards, sheds, depots, passenger and freight, signal and communications)	5.48	
		9.16
Rolling Stock		
Locomotives	4.63	
Goods wagons	10.44	
Brake conversion and other items	1.00	
Work shops and machinery	2.30	
		18.37
Water Transport		
Ferry and terminal bulk oil carrier		1.15
Staff Quarters		0.37
Grand Total		44.98

ment are subject to survey boards. However, East African countries are finding it difficult to finance development programs, and the general rate of growth in railway traffic in the next few years is very uncertain. Now is therefore not a good time to acquire expensive equipment, unless it is essential to replace worn out or otherwise unusable stock or is needed to meet expected traffic requirements. It is therefore suggested that the policies of EARH in writing off equipment be reviewed as a possible means of reducing the cost of equipment programs by deferring some replacements. This suggestion is made here because of the size of EARH activities, but we would recommend that a similar re-examination of replacement policies should also be undertaken by all government departments and statutory bodies using capital equipment.

Although for the purpose of long-term planning, railway traffic is forecast by the EARH to increase at an annual rate of about 3 percent a year from 1962–67, this forecast is very uncertain. A major increase in the capacity of part of the main railway line—Nakuru-Nairobi-Mombasa—may be required in the future, but the growth of traffic is not ex-pected to make this necessary in the 1960's (see Annex E). The building of a new line from a take-off point on the main line near Nairobi through to Moshi, bringing Nairobi within about 500 miles of Dar es Salaam by rail, as planned in EARH programs, also deserves consider-ation at a later date. On Lake Victoria, the construction of a wagon ferry has been proposed to accelerate and simplify the transfer of wag-ons and goods between Kisumu, Mwanza and the other principal centers around the lake. This project could increase flexibility and reduce op-erating costs. In the next few years, however, the first objective in plan-ning expenditures should be to maintain the railways in good operating condition with sufficient revenues, rather than to expand the system.

The internal resources of EARH may in future be insufficient for its replacement programs. Transfers from revenue to betterment funds amounted to £500,000 in 1960 and declined to about £250,000 in 1961. There is pressure for higher wages, and increased costs from localization must be provided for. The Rates Stabilization Fund (£1.3 million in 1961) is not available for development purposes.

In these circumstances the EARH may wish to place greater reliance on external resources to finance capital expenditure, and we understand that the EACSO has already authorized it to seek external funds for the 1963–67 program. The East African countries, who would be the guar-antors of future external loans for the Common Services, will however, wish to weigh the merits of such programs against their own commit-ments. Development in Kenya will increase dependence on borrowed funds, and further loans for development of the EARH should be justi-fied by the same criteria of urgent need and expected return which we suggest be applied to domestic projects. The capacity of the EARH is generally sufficient to meet present demands. Any expansion of the sys-tem should reflect clear expectations of increased traffic above present ca-pacity.

Harbors and Shipping

In 1948, the Kenya and Uganda Railways and Harbours Organization and the Tanganyika Railways and Port Service, which were then sep-arate undertakings, were amalgamated. As a result of this merger, the operation of the five principal maritime ports of East Africa is a com-mon service of EACSO, assigned to a single department of EARH.

The old Arab harbor, now used only for coastal and other minor ship-ping, lies on the north side of Mombasa. Kilindini, to the west of the city, is Kenya's only important port. It has a fine deep water harbor, with eleven principal berths in operation and two incomplete. Cargo-handling equipment includes modern cranes of adequate numbers and types for current operations. Construction of an oil refinery has begun on the west of the harbor at Port Reitz, with one new berth being built capable of accommodating super tankers up to 70,000 tons dead weight.

Cargo handling in Kilindini is provided on the quays by the Landing and Shipping Co., local contractors in which EARH acquired a controlling interest in 1960; on shipboard, cargo is handled by four local stevedoring companies.

The total amount of cargo loaded and unloaded at Mombasa was more than 20 percent greater in 1961 than ten years earlier. Traffic did not, however, increase steadily during the 1950's. Exports declined after the Korean War and import cargoes fell temporarily in 1958–60. The temporary decline in imports was partly due to the replacement of cement imports by local production. At present the port is handling about 1.2 million tons of petroleum fuels and 1.6 million tons of other cargo a year (see Table 4). Also, a total of more than 80,000 passengers are embarked and disembarked each year.

Except for a small permanent staff, dock-workers are normally supplied for work at Kilindini through the Mombasa Port Labour Utilization Board. Although it is understood that shipowners claim from time to time that the cargo-handling organization has insufficient mechanical equipment, stores and supervisory staff, and that the time taken in ships

TABLE 4: Cargo Handled at Mombasa (Kilindini)

(thousand dead weight tons)

Year	Imports	Exports	Total[a]
1938	462	548	1,010
1948	1,117	738	1,855
1950	1,209	754	2,079
1951	1,349	905	2,267
1952	1,494	904	2,411
1953	1,515	765	2,287
1954	1,526	792	2,325
1955	1,744	833	2,584
1956	1,760	880	2,652
1957	1,711	888	2,614
1958	1,621	909	2,541
1959	1,564	993	2,568
1960	1,633	1,002	2,651
1961	1,739	1,020	2,772

[a] Includes transshipments.

waiting for loading or unloading is excessive, these claims do not seem to be fully justified. The total time for unloading and loading averages about three days, while the waiting time between unloading and loading, which averages less than half a day, appears to be no more than normal for such operations in other ports. The maximum delay, which occurs at the end of the month, may in part be due to the provisions of shipping contracts, and to that extent might be decreased. The harbor itself appears to be well managed.

Coastal traffic for many centuries was carried by Arab dhows. Coastal traffic is now small. The Southern Line Limited, which operates five 500-ton to 700-ton ships and one 2,000-ton ship for cement in bulk, is the only shipping line now operating solely between East African ports, and the Seychelles, Mauritius and Madagascar. The tonnage shipped in 1960 on the Southern Lines amounted to about 160,000 tons of which cement accounts for 100,000 tons, petroleum 30,000 tons, and the balance in general cargo including some sisal. Cement and oil cargoes are profitable, but a loss is made on general cargo. Cement is now shipped in bulk through pneumatic handling from silos installed in the factory near Mombasa, and at Mombasa and Dar es Salaam. The company is encountering competition from dhows and small motor schooners, which are not compelled to use the expensive installations at Kilindini and other ports. Competition from motor vehicle operators along the coast is also increasing. The improvement of the roads along the coast and the rail connection with Dar es Salaam, which is to be completed in 1963 may further reduce the movement of freight by coastwise shipping, except for bulk shipments such as cement and petroleum. Road and rail transport are able to provide services without the two expensive terminal transshipments that are generally necessary for transport by sea.

The operation of inland waterways transport services in East Africa is also a function of the EARH. Although when taken in the context of the EARH over-all operations these services do not comprise a major undertaking, they form an important link between the three territories, and provide useful "feeder routes" to the railway system. Kisumu, the most important port on Lake Victoria, was the terminus of the original Uganda Railway, and is now the center on which the marine fleet is based. The services, both goods and passenger, connect a large number of relatively small ports in Kenya, Tanganyika and Uganda, the largest being Kisumu itself and Mwanza in Tanganyika, both handling more than 100,000 tons of cargo a year. In 1961, the combined passenger and cargo revenues amounted to some £0.7 million.

Estimates for the years 1963 to 1967 of capital expenditure, under what the EARH considers to be a minimum program for port develop-

TABLE 5: EARH Forecast, Capital Expenditure on Harbors, 1963–67

(£ million)

Purpose	Total 1963–67	
Wharves, Quays and Jetties		
Mombasa—Completion of berths 13 and 14	1.50	
Dar es Salaam—Two deepwater berths	1.00	
Dar es Salaam—Refinery facilities	0.30	
		2.80
Floating Plant and Machinery		
Dar es Salaam—2,000 hp. tug	0.22	
Mombasa—2 each 70' pilot cutters	0.06	
Dar es Salaam—2 each 45' pilot launches	0.03	
		0.31
Shore Plant and Machinery		
Mombasa—4 cranes, berths 11 and 12, etc.	0.09	
Renewals	0.50	
		0.59
Land and Buildings		
Mombasa—Renewals sheds 7 and 8	0.37	
Additional staff quarters	0.05	
Miscellaneous works	0.90	
		1.32
Grand Total		5.56

ment are summarized in Table 5. The program calls for a total capital expenditure of some £5.6 million, of which about £2.3 million is for specified port works in Kenya, and about £1.5 million is for miscellaneous items, including staff quarters, some of which are assumed to be in Kenya. Outside Kenya, the two most important items in the program are two additional deepwater berths and harbor works in support of an oil refinery in Dar es Salaam for which £1.3 million is allowed.

We think that a critical review looking to a downward revision of the program should be undertaken. Capital expenditure on East African harbors should be limited for the next few years to that required for safe operation, to complete projects already carried to a point where failure to complete would cause serious loss of funds already spent, or to prevent excessive delays in traffic under normal conditions.

CIVIL AVIATION

The scheduled internal airlines in Kenya, Uganda and Tanganyika are operated by East African Airways Corporation (EAAC), which also operates external lines to or from certain foreign countries. Two independent air transport companies provide chartered services. Airports in Kenya are constructed and maintained by the Ministry of Works and Communications. Five airports in Kenya are sufficiently equipped to be used by EAAC aircraft, of which only one (Nairobi airport) is now equipped for jet services. The control of air services in the three countries and the operation of all airports are in the hands of the Directorate of Civil Aviation, a branch of the EACSO. Meteorological services are maintained by the EACSO.

Civil Airlines

EAAC is a self-sustaining public corporation, created by an Order in Council during the year 1945. The general duty of the EAAC is to develop air transport services within East Africa and to operate such services to the extent feasible outside East Africa. It is managed by a board nominated by the East African Common Services Organization. Financial supervision is provided by the EACSO. The governments of the countries are expected to meet losses if they occur.

At the present time, internal lines are operated by EAAC between Nairobi and Malindi, Mombasa, Kisumu and Kitale in Kenya; Dar es Salaam, Moshi, Arusha, Mwanza, Musoma in Tanganyika; and Jinja, Entebbe, and to some other places in Uganda. Foreign services have been greatly developed since 1950. They are operated under agreement with BOAC, Central African Airways and South African Airways. The principal foreign services are to London, Aden, India and South Africa. It is understood that the revenue of these foreign services at this time is sufficient to carry part of the costs of the internal operations of the corporation in East Africa.

Financial forecasts for the next years to 1967 are fairly balanced. Traffic was 18.5 percent higher in 1960 than in 1959. The average passenger load factor was 61.5 percent. The increase in revenue over 1959 has been: 62 percent for external services; 13 percent for internal services; 35 percent for operations as a whole; 25 percent for freight; and 23 percent for mail.

The staff of EAAC in 1960 was as follows:

	European	*Asian*	*African*
Flying crews	100	—	—
Cabin crews	39	6	4
Engineering and supplies	129	193	222
Other	254	282	530
Total	522	481	756

Engineers in lower scales and commercial agents are now trained in Nairobi, including African candidates. At present it is understood that no Africans are being trained as pilots or as engineers or officers in the higher scales. Serious consideration is being given to training pilots and engineers locally, but expenditure of about £500,000 would be needed for the purpose and as yet no specific progress appears to have been made.

No very important change is contemplated in the structure of the present East African air services, except for further development of internal routes. It is expected by the EAAC that the increase in traffic per year will be stabilized at a rate of 3.5 percent after 1962. The replacement of present planes on internal services by faster and heavier aircraft is planned in 1962/63.

Airports

While the Ministry of Works and Communications of Kenya is responsible for decisions as to all improvements and works required at national airports in Kenya, for their financial programing and for construction, the Directorate of Civil Aviation (EACSO) is in charge of their operation (and of those in Uganda and Tanganyika); furthermore, the airlines naturally have a vital interest in the condition and operation of airports. In consequence, there is a need for constant coordination between EAAC, the Directorate of Civil Aviation and the Kenya Government.

Nairobi airport is now one of the most modern on African routes. The runway was extended to 13,500 feet in 1962, in order to facilitate the operation of large jet aircraft, bringing the total expenditure up to over £3.5 million. A radar tower and instrument landing system were completed in 1961, as was a livestock holding station for the reception of animals imported and exported by air. The number of passengers handled has increased very rapidly from 168,000 in 1958 to 242,000 in 1959 and 311,000 in 1960.

A major extension of facilities at Nairobi airport, consisting of the construction of an additional taxiway and apron and major extensions to the airport buildings, is being proposed. The total cost is estimated to be about £1 million. From the information at our disposal, we do not believe that any of this work will be necessary during the next few years, and we have therefore not considered including any part of it in the suggested program for 1963–67 to the exclusion of other projects. In any event, the future use of Nairobi airport for international traffic will depend in part on technological changes and the pattern of air movements. Several international flights are handled within two limited periods—northbound traffic at night and southbound in the morning. Delays in the arrival of some of these aircraft could lead to bunching. But for most of every day Nairobi airport traffic is light. Close collaboration between international airlines and East African authorities is desirable to promote a better use of airport facilities provided partly for international service at great cost to these low-income countries.

Four internal airports are equipped for local scheduled services: Mombasa, Kisumu, Kitale and Malindi. Some improvements will be necessary at Malindi to accommodate the heavier airplanes which, as noted above, EAAC is acquiring. Night flight facilities will likewise be required at Kisumu. Kitale is planned to be the fifth airport to be equipped for that purpose. In addition to these five airports, there are in Kenya 36 airstrips used for chartered, private, or special government-operated flights and 44 more used for government communications only. A program of capital expenditures for the next four years suggested by the mission is summarized in Table 6.

TABLE 6: Mission's Proposed Program of Capital Expenditures on Airports, 1963/64–1966/67

(£)

	1963/64	1964/65	1965/66	1966/67
Kisumu				
Lighting	20,000	—	—	—
Passenger bridges and traffic tower	—	3,500	—	—
Malindi				
Hardstandings, strengthen runway, air traffic control	—	16,500	15,500	10,000
Other	—	—	4,500	10,000
Total	20,000	20,000	20,000	20,000

There are no passenger "embarkation" taxes collected at Kenya airports as is done in some countries. A tax of Sh.7.5 per locally embarking passenger, as collected in London, could yield a yearly revenue of £37,500 at Nairobi airport on the basis of 100,000 passengers a year, and lesser amounts from other air embarkation points. These amounts, collected by air companies as passengers check in for departure, if applied to airport purposes, would materially assist in airport operations or maintenance and would cost the Government very little for collection. To the extent found feasible by comparison with competitive airports, revenues from air navigational service charges and landing fees at all Kenya airports might be increased in correlation with increased costs of operation of airports.

Operational Control of Civil Aviation

The Directorate of Civil Aviation is a department of the EACSO, not self-sustaining, responsible for the control of all operational ground services to aviation, including air traffic control and telecommunications for licensing aircraft and air personnel and for making recommendations concerning air legislation. During the four years, 1963/64–1966/67, the Directorate is forecasting capital expenditures of some £250,000 in all three territories; about 10 percent of this amount could be assumed as applying to Kenya. Recurrent expenditure is forecast at £700,000–£800,000 a year, with about one-third being spent in Kenya. While these are relatively modest amounts, we nevertheless urge as tight a rein on expenditures as consistent with safe operations.

A long planned Radio (VHF) Area Cover Scheme has come into operation, enabling the center controllers to have direct static-free speech with the pilots of aircraft. The planned coverage is not yet complete and additional relay stations are proposed.

It is necessary now to have high-level holding and let-down procedures for jet aircraft. VOR (very high frequency omni-range) used in this process was installed two years ago at Nairobi and Entebbe airports and is planned to be installed at Dar es Salaam and Mbeya.

Traffic control procedure, growing more and more difficult with the ever-increasing demands of the jet age, has been considerably improved this year through the installation at Nairobi airport of radar surveillance and ILS (instrument landing system) equipment. A powerful unattended radio beacon has been installed at Lodwar. Its servicing is difficult and expensive, however, because of its location. Other radio beacons are planned. The recent use of teleprinters has eased the work of staff and is planned to be developed further.

The telecommunications section of the Directorate requires vastly improved technique for dealing with messages concerning the movement of jet aircraft. Six thousand messages per day have to be transferred manually from one circuit to the next relay circuit. This manual link, in a process which is otherwise all electric or all mechanical, is the cause of major operational delays in communications. A semi-automatic link, although expensive, should be seriously considered. High frequency air-ground communication is now centered in Nairobi with Tabora as the relay station. Traffic on these frequencies has declined considerably with the introduction of the VHF Area Cover Scheme. Air search and rescue operations are carried on throughout the area.

A considerable increase in messages to more than 50,000 words a day is now possible due to a direct teleprinter link with the United Kingdom. A second duplex channel of information has been necessary to permit the normal use of the main channel for aircraft movement signals.

The staff establishment of the Directorate of Civil Aviation, which includes personnel for administration, air traffic control, communications, engineering and trainees, totals 405, of which 220 are handling communications and 7 are trainees. There is a shortage of technical officers, in spite of the efforts made by the Directorate to rectify this situation during the last few years. The majority of the vacancies are in grades which still require overseas recruitment for lack of qualified local candidates.

Air traffic control courses have been organized in recent years for training school certificate recruits and for improving the training of air traffic control assistants and radio superintendents. The ultimate aim is to qualify the officers concerned for an Air Control Certificate and an Aerodrome Control Rating. Steps have been taken also to train some traffic control officers to form the nucleus of watch-keeping officers for the radar surveillance and instrument landing systems.

As yet, the staff available for these services is not sufficient and it is reported that there are no African candidates with adequate technical education. The Telecommunications Operational Training School, operated by the Directorate, is greatly handicapped by the low educational qualifications of available recruits. Eighty-two out of 130 candidates have failed proficiency examinations during the last year. It has been estimated that £150,000 will be necessary to accelerate training and localization within the Directorate in the next few years. Both traffic control and radio training are reported hindered by lack of qualified candidates.

In the field of licensing and air registration, technical examinations and practical tests for various personnel licenses are undertaken by the staff of the Directorate. The staff also surveys aircraft undergoing overhauling, for the renewal of certificates of airworthiness.

Meteorological Services

The introduction into regular commercial service of faster, high-flying, long-range jet aircraft has faced the Meteorological Department with a number of problems, both as regards staffing of its forecast offices and observing stations, and as regards meteorological telecommunications. In the past, a substantial contribution toward the cost of aviation forecast services has been met by a contribution from the United Kingdom. However, this assistance may not be maintained far into the future and, if the services are to be maintained, the three East African countries should consider now the method of financing to be adopted. In 1962, a mission was jointly organized by the International Civil Aviation Organization (ICAO) and the World Meteorological Organization (WMO) and its terms of reference include recommendations on methods of financing.

Like the Directorate of Civil Aviation, the Meteorological Department is an interterritorial service of EACSO, and is not financially self-supporting. Official contact with the Kenya Government is maintained by the Regional Meteorological Representative, Kenya, through the Ministry of Works and Communications.

There is a forecast office for each territory situated at the main airports, Nairobi, Entebbe and Dar es Salaam. There is also a Main Meteorological Office, being the interterritorial Meteorological Analysis Center, situated in Nairobi, which is also designated as one of the Master Analysis Centers for Africa by the World Meteorological Organization. Although understaffed, the Meteorological Analysis Center, now operates on a 24-hour basis for the collection, analysis and dissemination of weather reports, forecasts, warnings and inferences.

The Kenya Regional Forecast Office provides forecasting services for the whole of Kenya for aviation interests (including some service for the Royal Air Force), agricultural interests and the general public. Situated at Nairobi airport, it is the only aviation forecast office in East Africa maintaining a 24-hour service. In Kenya, there are three 24-hour observing stations, at Nairobi, Mombasa and Kisumu, and 13 others operating for 12 hours a day. In addition, there are four more part-time stations (not staffed by the Meteorological Department) which transmit observations by telegram once or twice daily to the Kenya Forecast Office. As a result of the continued increase in the volume of air traffic, the total number of forecasts issued for all purposes by the Kenya Regional Forecast Office now exceeds 100 a day.

In addition to forecasting, the Meteorological Department handles much climatological data, particularly with respect to rainfall, and also engages in various types of research. Shortage of funds and staff have limited this work.

While nearly all meteorological telecommunications were formerly handled by the Directorate of Civil Aviation, since early in 1962 this has been the responsibility of the Meteorological Department at its Meteorological Communications Center, attached to the Meteorological Analysis Center. Meteorological broadcasts from other countries are received by radio-teleprinter, and a selection of the information is passed on to the Regional Forecast Office by land-line teleprinters. Provision has also been made for radio-teleprinter broadcasts from Nairobi, and for the transmission of weather charts by radio facsimile.

The total staff establishment of the Meteorological Department includes 14 professional staff, 33 Technical Officers and 241 Technical Assistants. Recruitment in the Meteorologist grade has become well-nigh impossible, and three out of eight posts remain vacant. Meteorologists are recruited from the ranks of physicists and mathematicians in a very highly competitive market, and salaries offered in East Africa are insufficient to attract candidates to a career with no prospects, and in the face of uncertain political developments. Recruitment of short-term expatriate Technical Officers is not over difficult, but at present there is little prospect of recruiting many Africans into this grade, as all candidates with sufficient academic qualifications can go on to university.

EAST AFRICAN POSTS AND TELECOMMUNICATIONS

Posts and Telecommunications are operated as a common service according to the East African Post and Telecommunications Act, 1951. It is a self-contained service, with its own sources of revenue. In the end, responsibility to meet shortfalls in revenues would rest with the three countries.

Services Provided

There were 230 post offices in operation in Kenya at the end of 1961, an increase of 75 over those of 1946. The Postmaster General estimates that £50,000 a year will be required for new post offices over the next few years.

In 1961, compared with 1960, the number of money orders issued increased by 5.8 percent, the number of postal orders issued decreased by 4 percent. Money orders paid increased by 5.6 percent and postal orders paid by 9.31 percent. Special services rendered to the territorial governments, such as collection of customs duty on items moving by mail and sale of revenue forms and stamps, amounted to £211,000, of which £150,000 was with respect to the Kenya Government.

The general level of inland telegram traffic has been declining. The number of messages fell 12.3 percent in 1960 when compared with 1959 and 47 percent when compared with 1949; however, there was an increase of 3.4 percent between 1960 and 1961. The number of international telegrams fell by 3.7 percent and 2.0 percent in 1960 and 1961 respectively as compared with the previous year. International Telex, introduced in Nairobi in July 1960, has shown an encouraging growth of traffic but this service must be extended to other main centers in East Africa before any real growth in Kenya can be expected.

The development in telephone service during the past years has been as follows:

	1938	1949	1959	1960	1961	% Increase 1949–60
Automatic exchanges	—	9	—	58	65	622
Telephone stations	—	14,680	—	71,313	74,941	410
Trunk calls (million)	0.4	1.4	2.6	4.4	3.2	129
Local calls (million)	8.8	22.1	62.8	68.7	77.3	250

Long-distance calls actually increased by 4.8 percent in 1961 but, because trunk calls of less than 25 miles are now included with figures for local calls, this is not readily apparent from the table. Waiting lists showed 3,274 unfilled service applications at the end of 1961 for the three territories; of these 2,014 were in Kenya. In several areas potential subscribers have had to wait two or three years before receiving the service requested.

International radio telephone service has been extended so that by 1961 it operated to 73 countries. The hours of service have been progressively extended in several towns and operator trunk-dialing facilities provided between Nairobi and Kitale and between Dar es Salaam and Mwanza. One new automatic exchange and five new manual exchanges were installed. Six existing exchanges were converted to automatic working and three manual exchanges were replaced to give increased capacity.

Finance and Development

During the last few years, the Administration of East African Posts and Telecommunications has been able to operate on a commercial basis, and to remain entirely self-supporting except for the capital situation outlined below. At the same time, the service offered to the public has been progressively improved and modernized to the satisfaction of those users who could be furnished with service. In 1961, there was an operating profit of about £800,000 and a net revenue surplus of just over £175,000. The outlook for the coming few years is not so favorable. The Administration itself forecasts net revenue deficits for the five years, 1963–67, although the Administration expects them to decline from about £150,000 in 1963 to a very small amount in 1967. We feel, however, that in view of the pending possible departure of a substantial number of current users of PTT services, normal revenues may not cover unavoidable operating expenditures. In this event, an early increase in charges may be needed.

The raising of fresh capital to meet the Administration's planned program of development is its principal difficulty. The debit balance in the capital account already stood at £2.8 million at the end of 1961. The Administration has now prepared what it considers to be a minimum program, which would be able to keep pace with the present rate of demand for telephones, new post offices, etc. (see Table 7). This program provides for normal development of all items, and is designed to remove the backlog demand by substantial completion of the auto-

TABLE 7: Capital Expenditures on East African Posts and Telecommunications, 1963–67[a]

(£ thousand)

Purpose	1963	1964	1965	1966	1967
Telegraph System	15 (7)	13 (6)	9 (3)	9 (4)	6 (2)
Telephone:					
Trunk Networks	128 (73)	203 (63)	297 (96)	274 (68)	206 (87)
Exchanges	35 (13)	207 (67)	217(130)	262 (78)	389(319)
Exchange Networks	170 (99)	250(125)	214(122)	259(107)	237(155)
Subscribers'					
Apparatus	81 (41)	94 (44)	84 (39)	92 (42)	89 (44)
Buildings	209 (74)	130 (29)	121 (88)	133(100)	95 (46)
	638(307)	897(334)	942(478)	1,029(399)	1,022(653)
Replacements, etc.	200	200	200	200	200
Grand Total	838	1,097	1,142	1,229	1,222

[a] Amounts for Kenya alone shown in parentheses.

matic telephone network about 1970. In all, the Administration program would entail capital expenditures of some £5.5 million between 1963 and 1967. In view of the economic prospects facing Kenya, we urge that these estimates and programs be reviewed carefully and reduced or postponed in line with revised requirements as shown by a new survey.

Personnel and Training

The total staff of the PTT at the end of 1961 was 7,067 which included 534 Europeans, 1,547 Asians and 4,984 Africans. Although not obvious in the above data, "localization" has long been the official policy of the Post and Telecommunications Administration. Considerable progress has already been made and has been accelerated recently. It would appear to be well in hand as compared to other localization operations.

The Central Training School has been in existence at Mbagathi since 1949 and all Post Office training schemes are concentrated there. The recurrent expenditure of the Central Training School rose from £89,000 in 1960 to £184,000 in 1961; these figures include the cost of localization. Total training costs are expected to amount to about £300,000 in 1962 and about £337,000 in 1963. There were 1,192 students trained in 1961, of which 493 were in engineering, 477 in postal operations and 222 in telecommunications. The Central Training School can now provide courses for a total of 240 students.

By persisting with its training programs, the Administration has been able gradually to reduce recruitment of expatriates (formerly drawn mainly from the British Post Office) except for those required to fill the few grades in which very special qualifications were needed. The increasing availability of African candidates is reflected in the following total recruitment figures:

	Europeans	Asians	Africans
1951–59	709 (15%)	1,395 (30%)	2,586 (55%)
1960	62 (19%)	84 (25%)	184 (56%)
January–August 1961	14 (14%)	16 (15%)	107 (71%)

The entire cost of localization, an expensive item, has so far been borne from the Administration's limited resources. The cost of supernumerary posts, however, estimated at £50,000 for a full year, and the cost of the Central Training School, estimated at £300,000 in 1962, without including the necessary capital expenditures, appears beyond the ability of the Administration to meet adequately from its own funds, and some external help appears necessary if it is to be continued at its present rate.

RADIO AND TELEVISION

Until June 1962, the national broadcasting services (apart from a British Armed Forces station of limited coverage) were provided, in sound alone, by a department of government at a net direct cost on revenue account of about £171,000 a year, after taking account of receipts from license fees and a limited amount of advertising. Services were provided from stations in Nairobi, Kisumu and Mombasa in three main and fourteen vernacular languages. This organization with all its assets and staff was then transferred to a newly created public corporation, the Kenya Broadcasting Corporation, which is controlled by a board on which the Government, the general public and commercial interests are represented by three members each, under an independent chairman. The commercial interests (a locally registered company comprising an international consortium of commercial television, cinema and press interests) in return for making capital available for the establishment of a television service and providing general consultative and agency services, receive, under a 15-year contract with the Corporation, fees expressed as commission on net advertising revenue.

The gross direct cost on revenue account of operating the sound services as a department of government was £358,000 in 1961/62. Their transfer to an independent corporation, with the recasting of estimates in a quasi-commercial form created a need for increased provision on revenue account, for such purposes as the funding of staff superannuation and equipment depreciation liabilities. New charges were generated for land rents and duties from which a government department is immune, and for services formerly provided by the Government centrally, such as for building maintenance, legal advice and audit. The total of additional costs arising in this way approach £100,000 a year. The Government was, however, unable to increase its total allocation from current revenue to broadcasting and accordingly the amount of government subvention for the first year was fixed at £171,000.

Even with certain financial concessions from the Government, the Corporation was obliged to budget initially for a deficit on recurrent account of £92,400 in the first year (1962/63), during which the newly established television service was to be in operation for only nine months. The forecast deficit was to be met by borrowing. The Corporation has already made significant progress toward reducing the forecast deficit without any reduction in transmission times or program quality. But for the present, and particularly in the light of the current depressed state of the country's general economy which limits potential commercial revenues, it seems unlikely that, with the amount of government support pegged to its current level, the Corporation would be able to close the gap completely in the immediate future without severe reductions in the essentially non-viable services in vernacular languages, the maintenance of which is important in the present stage of constitutional development.

For reasons of economy in management and operation, the new television service forms an integral part of the Corporation's organization. From experience elsewhere there is no great doubt that, costed as a separate entity, it will, within a relatively short time, show a surplus even after meeting all its capital charges. This surplus must be applied first to the deficit arising on the sound services. There is also little reason to doubt that with its own revenues from licensing and advertising the Corporation will be able to maintain substantial sound broadcasting services with government support at its present level, or even if the amount of subsidy were to be reduced. The doubt is simply whether all the existing sound services in a total of 17 languages can be maintained in their present form.

The capital needed to establish a television service and to carry the forecast deficit for the first year is estimated at £250,000, and is being borrowed from banking sources. The extension of the television service (which will initially cover an area of, very approximately, 60-mile radius of Nairobi) to the western and coastal areas of dense population is estimated at £60,000 in each case. The phasing of further borrowing for this purpose must depend upon developments in the financial circumstances of the Corporation which must in turn depend upon the general economy of the country. Assuming that the political climate is reasonably stable and that the Corporation's budget on recurrent account is brought into balance in the year 1963/64, by whatever means, it would be the aim to carry out at least one of the proposed extensions of the television service in that year. Each of the proposed extensions is expected to prove self-supporting from commercial revenues and to show a surplus once established.

Both the Corporation and the Government wish to use radio and television for education. Broadcast school programs could greatly help in the problem of national shortage of teachers. Efforts have been made to interest international aid authorities, and there seem to be real prospects of obtaining it for this purpose. Such development could therefore take place independently of the Corporation's general budget, at least for an initial period. The capital requirement for the establishment of a schools service is estimated at £26,000 and the subsequent recurrent cost at £10,000 a year.

CONCLUDING REMARKS

Whereas present capacity is sufficient to meet present demand for electricity, some deficiency is likely to occur in coming years in the Nairobi area. The mission believes that additional supplies should first be obtained from Owen Falls in Uganda. When the need for additional power is foreseen, suitable arrangements with the Uganda Electricity Board and additional transmission facilities would be required. We do not think that the Seven Forks project will be justified in the next few years.

Emphasis on new works in the field of transport and communications should be aimed first toward assisting the economic development of the country through development of agriculture and other income-producing activities.

Railways will remain for a long time the backbone of freight transport, especially for long-haul traffic, and should be maintained in effective operating condition. Major expenditure to extend the capacity of the system in Kenya is not expected to be required in the next few years.

The mission believes that the program of railway works planned by EARH for the years 1963–67 is too large under the economic conditions facing the countries it serves. A complete review of all new works, and of assumptions as to useful life of equipment and structures which are planned to be replaced under the program, is suggested.

Road and highway networks need substantial improvement and extension to facilitate farm to market movement of produce and distribution of goods. For the next few years, we feel that the emphasis in road programs should be placed on construction required for the expansion of agricultural production.

Airways and airdromes should need only minor improvements, while in the field of posts and telecommunications an expansion of the telephone network and an increase in postal services will be desirable when consistent with the course of demand and the availability of resources.

The trained administrative and technical staff needed for management and operation of transport and communications, especially in the higher positions, are now drawn largely from expatriate sources. There is serious risk in attempting a too-rapid transition from the existing staff to a new staff composed of less well-qualified persons. The replacement of expatriates by local people should be gradual, and such replacements in the more responsible positions should be made only through the appointment of capable and well-trained individuals.

CHAPTER 8 *SOCIAL SERVICES AND MANPOWER*

MANPOWER

The human resources of a country are one of the major determinants of its economic performance. To achieve growth, a country's people must be willing to exert themselves in seeking out economic opportunities and they must develop new skills in translating their effort into fruitful production. The quality of human resources is thus conditioned by the attitudes, attainments and physical capacities of the population. We have referred previously to the role that the Kenya Government has and can play in developing these human attributes by stimulating incentives and improving productivity, particularly in agriculture. In this chapter we discuss education, health and housing which have important influences on the labor force. We first turn to a more direct look at Kenya's human resources and some problems of utilizing them.

A person's occupation in the traditional society of Kenya was determined largely by his status in the community: production was a collective activity, in which there was no direct relation between the individual's effort and material reward. Organized employment was introduced with the immigrant communities. Africans were employed as laborers on European farms, where they frequently cultivated part of the land for themselves, or in the towns, where they usually only stayed for a short time. The growth of a modern labor force has been a gradual process and is still under way. This transition presents many difficulties that have still to be overcome.

There were about 620,000 people in Kenya in 1960 working outside the traditional sector of the economy (see Statistical Appendix, Table 3). Some 500,000 of these were adult male wage earners comprising probably about one-quarter of the able-bodied adult males in the country.[1] About 270,000 people were recorded in agricultural employment, and including those cultivating their family holding, roughly 80 percent of the male labor force still made their living on the land. Since many women play a significant role in cultivation, the concentration of the economically active population in agriculture would have been even more marked. The national accounts statistics—though figures on the subsistence sector are subject to some uncertainty—suggest that a high

[1] *Reported Employment and Wages in Kenya, 1948–1960.*

210

percentage of the work force contributed only about 40 percent of Gross Domestic Product in recent years. While a shift of labor to nonagricultural occupations may be expected over the long run, accompanying the process of economic growth, it seems clear that immediate improvements in the productivity of labor in agriculture would yield a significant expansion of output.

About 350,000 people were employed in other branches of activity in 1960. Though still small in total, this number had increased during the 1950's as the economy diversified and the public services expanded. The numbers engaged in private industry and commerce rose from 134,000 in 1950 to 194,000 in 1957, a period of particularly heavy investment in manufacturing industry. The expansion of the public service was also rapid in these years, with employment increasing from 107,000 in 1951 to 167,000 in 1957. From 1957 to 1960, however, employment in these sectors showed little change. At the end of the decade, 52,000 people were working in manufacturing, 39,000 in commerce, and 21,000 in building construction. In the public sector, the Kenya Government was by far the largest employer, accounting for 100,000 people, while the East Africa High Commission and the East African Railways and Harbours employed another 29,000.

The 38,000 Asians and 23,000 Europeans recorded as being employed in 1960 comprised about 10 percent of the total. The numbers represent about one-fifth and one-third respectively of the total population of these groups; by contrast less than a twelfth of the African population was included. Almost all of the Asians and Europeans were engaged in nonagricultural occupations; they filled most of the professional, technical and administrative positions both in public and private fields, as well as providing the entrepreneural function for many undertakings. Twenty-one thousand of them were employed in the public services, while commercial and manufacturing concerns were the most important private employers, accounting for some 24,000 jobs.

It is difficult to assess how far human resources are likely to place a general limit to growth in Kenya. The present availability of data is small—chiefly the Annual Enumeration of Employees and the Ministry of Labour's records of vacancies, applications, engagements and terminations of jobs. The demand for trained manpower cannot be measured with any accuracy until a comprehensive manpower survey is undertaken. We understand proposals have been made to undertake a manpower survey in Kenya. However, the mission considers that this is not an urgent need at the moment since the manpower situation may be expected to change rapidly, making the task of conducting a survey difficult and the results ephemeral; there is believed to be an indeterminate number of itinerant workers, particularly since the end of the Emergency, with only a varying interest in paid employment, and a projection of the future trend of economic activity would also be hazardous. We believe it to be more important to improve sources of continuous and current information. In considering in what way the Government can play a fruitful role in assisting the development of manpower resources, attention should first be focused on determining the extent of present knowledge of Kenya's manpower, of coordinating existing sources of information and analyzing them, and of identifying the significant remaining gaps. This stock-taking function requires the drawing together of many strands, and should be geared to the needs of development planning; it would therefore be appropriate for it to be performed within the planning organization. Such preliminary work would, in any case, be necessary in preparation for an eventual comprehensive survey.

Localization

The approach of independence has added urgency to Kenya's problem of developing its manpower resources, since this movement has been accompanied by a desire to substitute more local people, particularly Africans, for expatriates in the civil service and in other employment. The process of substitution, generally known as "localization," is most pressing in the public service, although it cannot be treated in isolation.

In the middle of 1962, the composition of the civil service reflected the limited extent to which Kenya Africans had entered the higher and more specialized posts of government. There were only 18 Africans among the 89 civil servants in the top administrative grade of the central government from the rank of Assistant Secretary upward; there were 181 Africans in the 374 posts of the Provincial Administration from District Assistant and above. There were 180 Africans among the 3,000 professional and senior technical staff; 381 among the 1,900 of executive grade; 2,600 among the 4,700 of clerical grade and 1 among the 418 of secretarial grade.

The objective of localization is to modify the composition of the civil service to reflect more accurately the proportion of the main racial groups in the population.[2] The rate at which the replacement of expatriates by Kenyans can be accomplished is uncertain, depending partly on the political objective set, and partly on the willingness of expatriates to remain in the service of Kenya after independence. In any

---

[2] Establishment Circular No. 15, March 16, 1961.

case, it seems clear that the supply of candidates and the standards set will be the critical limits to what can be achieved.

At the time of self-government, certain expatriate officials of the Overseas Civil Service will have the choice of premature retirement on compensated terms under the Overseas Aid Scheme.[3] It has been estimated that, if 25 percent of the officers eligible to retire were to do so (which may be regarded in the light of experience elsewhere as a conservative assumption), there would probably be more than 1,500 vacancies in the senior ranks of the civil service. The problem is to move toward meeting the requirements of such a change. A major difficulty is that the number of trained and potential technical personnel is limited by the output of the secondary schools. We recommend later in this chapter that high priority should be given to the expansion of secondary education, but this will not yield immediate results.

Responsibility for localization rests with the individual ministries, although the programs are coordinated through a special section in the central administration. Training has been proceeding along several lines.

a. There are a number of departmental schemes through which specialist instruction is given in local training schools. These cover a wide range, some of which, such as the agricultural colleges, have been discussed elsewhere in the report.

b. Training within the Government is being effected on-the-job, by the creation of training grade posts, or of direct appointment to substantive posts under temporary supervision of a supernumerary. Provision of 557 additional posts is made in the 1962/63 estimates.

c. Direct training for administration, through courses in Kenya at the Royal College and the Institute of Administration, is being financed by the Government, including the cost of bursaries, to prepare specific categories of higher civil servants. The former makes use of existing academic facilities to train senior officials in economic, financial and diplomatic affairs. The Institute of Administration, constructed with assistance from the United States Government, trains for administrative officers and executive posts.

d. Graduate and professional training, including courses overseas which are not available locally, is arranged and financially assisted by the Government. Many of the overseas courses are

[3] *Service with Overseas Governments,* October 1960, London, HMSO, Cmd. 1193; see Chapter 2, paragraph 24.

organized in cooperation with host governments. Efforts have also been made to attract other Kenyan students at overseas universities to the civil service by informing them of the opportunities available.

The civil service had been open to all races since 1955, and the training and appointment of local people were proceeding before the formal introduction of the present policy. It is difficult to assess how far needs can be met by present programs, particularly since it is uncertain what demands on staff will result from future constitutional arrangements. The time required to gain the training and experience is an unavoidable limitation to achieving the objective of localization and at the same time maintaining standards of administration upon which so much of the development of the country will depend. We acknowledge the desirability of accelerating programs of training, but we have noted already the continuing need for expatriate staff, especially in specialized posts for the next few years. In the transition to a localized civil service, the role of expatriates is perhaps at its most valuable, since they can impart knowledge and experience to officials soon to be promoted. We hope that efforts to maintain conditions of service which will encourage essential expatriates to stay for this interim period will be considered together with programs to train their replacements.

Insofar as we have observed the operation of departmental training schemes, they are discussed in the relevant chapters of the report. Capital works for this purpose should only be undertaken in the light of continuing needs for training establishments and the possibility of utilizing existing buildings.

In relation to the training and promotion of existing civil servants, we note that there had been a large increase of Africans in executive grade posts by the end of 1961. We do not know how many of these would be suitable for promotion, but we consider that a desirable policy would be thorough selection procedures based on a systematic assessment of capabilities rather than insistence on traditional academic qualifications. These policies can contribute to the easing of the supply problem; but in addition, it is important for the morale of the service that existing staff are not superseded by inexperienced, rapidly trained candidates. In this respect, it may be valuable to expand the work of the aptitude testing unit of the Ministry of Labour so that selection, where not based on previously accepted qualifications, is put on as objective a standard as possible. It may also be necessary where an inadequate knowledge of English is an obstruction to localization and training programs to institute short, intensive courses so that this need not cause delays and frustration.

Training outside the Government poses a number of special problems. Kenya's economic development can be retarded by lack of skilled entrepreneurs as well as of unqualified public officials, even though the immediate need may be to retain the momentum of present development programs. Government, the East African Common Services and private enterprise will inevitably be competitors for the limited supply of trained manpower as localization progresses. The mission would regard it as undesirable for the Government to attempt to claim a disproportionately large share of the training facilities, or of the output of students. We feel, for example, that financial support should not be diverted from training for management at the Royal College to that for government at the Institute of Administration. Since there will be a great financial need to simplify the administration, we do not think localization in general should be designed to maintain the full complement of the present civil service.

Many students go abroad for courses to prepare themselves for specific jobs after their return. There may be a concern that some returning students will not be "qualified" for positions available in Kenya. Steps could be taken to overcome unnecessary doubts on this matter. First, students planning study overseas could be provided with vocational information to help them choose programs suited to opportunities in Kenya. Selection of the place and course of study for students receiving Kenya government bursaries should be strictly supervised with the same objective in mind. It might be of value to circulate information within Kenya describing unfamiliar academic programs to inform local employers of the varied supply of trained men becoming available to them.

The Kenya Government is estimated to have spent £580,000 on localization in 1961/62, and has budgeted for more than £800,000 in 1962/63.[4] In view of the uncertain and rapidly changing position of the needs and progress of localization training schemes, we have not attempted to specify what outlay of funds would be necessary or justified in this field, and the amounts included in our program of expenditures in Chapter 3 are notional. We have assumed, however, that external funds might be provided for this purpose which would not otherwise be available, if greater outlays are required.

Unemployment

While Kenya faces a shortage of trained local manpower at the higher levels of government and private business, the country also suffers from a serious general problem of unemployment and underemployment.

---

[4] Excluding institutional training by Departments.

The recent decline of economic activity has aggravated this problem by curtailing available wage-employment. But the problem is structural in origin, deriving from the pattern of peasant subsistence farming which hinders the full development of agriculture, and the disparity between the increasing demand for wage-employment and the limited expansion of jobs for largely unskilled workers. The employment problem has been described in two official papers[5] and the mission concurs with their conclusion that the main part of the solution lies in the concentrated development of agriculture and the development of skills appropriate to the country's needs.

It is difficult to assess the magnitude of unemployment in Kenya, even in the strict sense of those depending on and seeking wage-employment who are not able to find it. The Ministry of Labour's Employment Services records show only those who register for jobs and are unable to find them at the end of the month. There is little incentive to register—though a system of priority work-seekers cards has been instituted—and many people seek work directly from employers. Thus, although the Enumeration of Employees showed that the number recorded in employment fell by over 30,000 between June 1960 and June 1961, there were only 200 more unplaced work-seekers reported at the Public Employment Offices over that period. The fall in recorded employment was equivalent to more than 5 percent of the total. This reflected, above all, unfavorable business conditions and declining confidence in the private sector, where the numbers engaged fell by about 8 percent for agricultural occupations and by about 10 percent in industry and commerce. The mission observed that labor mobility among jobs has been declining in Kenya and we therefore presume that loss of employment is becoming an increasing hardship as people gradually divorce themselves from the security of a traditional rural community.

Under these circumstances, there will no doubt be increased pressure on the Government to take emergency measures to relieve unemployment, especially that of a short-term nature. Though it may be socially and politically difficult to resist these pressures, we think that the arguments against temporary relief measures under present conditions are serious ones. First, we regard the task of selecting areas, people and industries that are subject to special hardships as a result of the decline in economic activity as being very complicated. Construction is at present one of the most depressed industries, for instance, but unless relief projects are carefully chosen they may divert work from commercial

[5] A. G. Dalgleish, *Survey of Unemployment,* Government Printer, Nairobi, 1960; *Unemployment,* Sessional Paper No. 10 of 1959/60.

firms. Short-term measures are unlikely to achieve any tangible results in introducing the itinerant worker fully into the wage economy, while they cannot serve the dismissed employee for long if employment in general does not expand again. A more fruitful way of assisting the stabilized worker would be to assist in restoring conditions favorable to economic growth. Secondly, the financial resources of the Government are very limited so that to support relief schemes would require the diversion of funds and supervisory talent from other projects. This situation calls for the greatest care in using resources in their most productive uses, and the costs of mounting temporary schemes where overheads are heavy in relation to the productivity of inexperienced labor would entail a disproportionate loss of benefits from other projects that are foregone.

In this connection we would mention the employment opportunities which have been provided by the location of military bases in Kenya. We recognize that the retention of these bases by an independent government or the United Kingdom is likely to be based on noneconomic factors, but we would stress the impact their immediate withdrawal would have on employment. It has been estimated that more than 5,000 workers derive employment from the bases, who at the present state of the economy would be unlikely to find other occupations.

While we have concluded that the potentiality for the greatest increases in total output over the next few years lies in the development of agriculture, the nonagricultural sectors will have a complementary role to play as rising incomes provide a widening market for a diversified range of products. After a return of confidence and investment, the growth of secondary and tertiary industries will require an efficient labor force and this is a concern of government. If labor productivity remains low even in relation to low wages, entrepreneurs will not be anxious to increase the number of workers they employ.

Wages and Industrial Relations

The creation of a modern labor force is a complex process, requiring basic changes in behavior and cultural attitudes from those of traditional society. The objective of encouraging these changes is to secure the commitment of the worker to a wage-earning environment, in which conditions are such that he is induced to work efficiently.

General wage levels have not yet become sufficient to support the worker and his family in an urban environment, although this is the declared objective of the Government's minimum wage policy. The level of wages was stressed as one of the basic conditions for stabilizing labor by the Carpenter Committee.[6] Following the recommendations of that committee, the declared policy of the Government has been to move toward a minimum level of wages sufficient to meet the essential needs of a worker's family, although progress has been limited to take account of "economic and other circumstances." At present, the system of statutory minimum wages consists of two standards: a "youth minimum wage" applying to anyone under 21 years of age and to women, and an "adult minimum wage." The wage levels are based on the Nairobi Wage Earners' Index and a separate housing allowance. The index establishes the basic minimum wage at the youth level; a factor is applied to reach the adult wage. This factor is at present 1.45, and it is intended to increase it to 1.67 of the basic minimum as conditions permit. Minimum wages apply in 13 towns in Kenya, and the rates in effect from January 1962 are shown in Table 1. It has not yet been considered feasible to introduce a family minimum standard, which the Carpenter Committee recommended be assessed at 2.5 times the basic minimum wage.

TABLE 1: Statutory Monthly Minimum Wages (Effective January 1, 1962)

(E. A. Shillings)

Area	Minimum Wage		Housing Allowance	
	Over 21	Other	Over 21	Other
Eldoret	107	74	26	13
Kisumu	103	71	22	11
Kitale	103	71	25	12.50
Mombasa	107	74	30	15
Nairobi	107	74	26	13
Nakuru	103	71	24	12
Nanyuki	102	70	24	12
Nyeri	102	70	24	12
Thika	104	72	24	12
Kericho	90	72	20	10
Machakos	88	70	30	15
Naivasha	86	69	30	15
Thomson's Falls	85	68	25	12.50

Average earnings for Africans in employment have in fact risen markedly. From 1954 to 1961, they rose 70 percent in industry and commerce, 55 percent in agriculture and 90 percent in the public service.[7] Two in-

[6] Report of the Committee on African Wages, Nairobi, 1954, para. 49.

[7] Average earnings are based on the Estimated Wage Bill derived from the Enumeration of Employees, which contains an imputed valuation for rations and housing that is particularly significant in the agricultural sector.

dices are available to measure price changes in Kenya, but the one that refers to labor and artisans—the Wage Earners' Price Index—is available only from the end of 1958. The Nairobi Cost-of-Living Index was constructed to measure the cost of living standards among European families, based upon a budget survey conducted in 1939. Judging by the cost of living calculations for minimum wages, prices affecting low income groups rose by 15–20 percent from 1954 to 1961, and this reduced the rise of average real earnings. The over-all average earnings for Africans in reported employment were Sh.127 a month in 1961; there was, however, a wide variation between the public services (Sh.188), industry and commerce (Sh.173), and agriculture (Sh.65). Almost one-third of the earnings in agriculture represented the value of benefits received in kind.

Average wage levels do not yet fulfill the requirements for a stabilized work force, and the mission believes that the Government should pursue the policy of raising statutory minimum wages toward a family standard as rapidly as conditions permit. Collective bargaining and enlightened management practices in a number of industries have, however, resulted in the establishment of basic wages well in excess of the legal minimum, and in other improved terms of employment. Several companies operate job incentive schemes, and an increasing number have introduced superannuation funds. Working hours are regulated by statute in certain industries, and by collective agreements in others.

The institutional development of industrial relations, regulated by a number of ordinances, has advanced rapidly in Kenya.[8] There are some 68 trade unions in the country (with a total membership of about 80,000), most of which are affiliated with the Kenya Federation of Labour (KFL). There are also a number of employer organizations, linked in the Kenya Federation of Employers (KFE). The legislation provides for conciliation and arbitration of trade disputes by the Labour Department. Arbitration has in the past been compulsory for essential services —water, electricity, health, communications and fire services—but we understand this provision is to be repealed. There are more than 125 consultative and negotiating bodies in various industries, and a joint industrial council has recently been set up between the KFL and the KFE to coordinate these arrangements. Training in industrial relations is arranged by the Ministry of Labour, and by the KFL (under the auspices of the International Confederation of Free Trade Unions with which it is affiliated).

[8] Trades Union Ordinance, Trades Disputes (Arbitration and Inquiry) Ordinance, Essential Services (Arbitration) Ordinance.

CHART 4

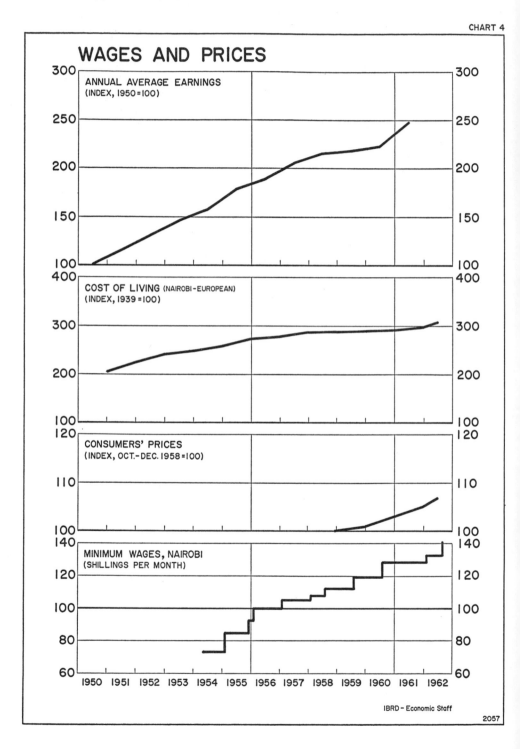

WAGES AND PRICES

ANNUAL AVERAGE EARNINGS
(INDEX, 1950=100)

COST OF LIVING (NAIROBI-EUROPEAN)
(INDEX, 1939=100)

CONSUMERS' PRICES
(INDEX, OCT.-DEC. 1958=100)

MINIMUM WAGES, NAIROBI
(SHILLINGS PER MONTH)

IBRD - Economic Staff

2057

The increased sophistication of the organization of industrial relations has not led to a marked reduction in trade disputes, nor in the resulting loss of work. The number of work stoppages and man-days was lower in 1961 than in the two previous years, but frequent strikes again disrupted many of Kenya's important industries in 1962. The Government has been making efforts to secure general agreement between trade unions and employers on the conduct of industrial relations. We would stress the significance of good relations between labor and employers as a condition for increasing private investment in the country's development.

EDUCATION

The contribution of education to expanding knowledge as basis for economic growth is now widely recognized. The future development of Kenya will require an increasing supply of trained manpower, and a widening range of specialized skills. Education is, however, an expensive undertaking; for example, average income per head is about £30 in Kenya, but it costs more than £200 per pupil to build a secondary day school. In the country's present financial situation, the central problem of policy in this field is to devise an education program appropriate to the manpower needs of the present stage of development, but which is related to the resources available and the demands of other types of expenditure. Until recently, educational facilities were provided separately for the principal racial groups. Some schools are now moving over to a nonracial basis and we have assumed that this process will continue. But we have addressed ourselves primarily to the problems of the education of Africans who form by far the largest part of the peoples.

An educational system is like a pyramid, with relatively large numbers at the base of elementary schooling and smaller numbers at each step of more advanced training higher up in the structure. (The shape of the pyramids for Kenya's primary and secondary schools is illustrated in Chart 5.) Policy must take into consideration not only the number of students at each level of the pyramid at a certain time, but how many students will be prepared for successive higher levels of the pyramid in succeeding years. For some time, there has been a surge of African pupils into the first four years of school—the "lower" primary standards—with the result that some primary schooling is now regarded as normal for the majority of children in most parts of Kenya. Many beginning pupils are overage, but it is estimated that the equivalent of 90 percent of the boys and some 50 percent of the girls of the starting age group enter pri-

CHART 5

EDUCATIONAL PYRAMIDS OF PRIMARY AND SECONDARY SCHOOL PUPILS, 1962

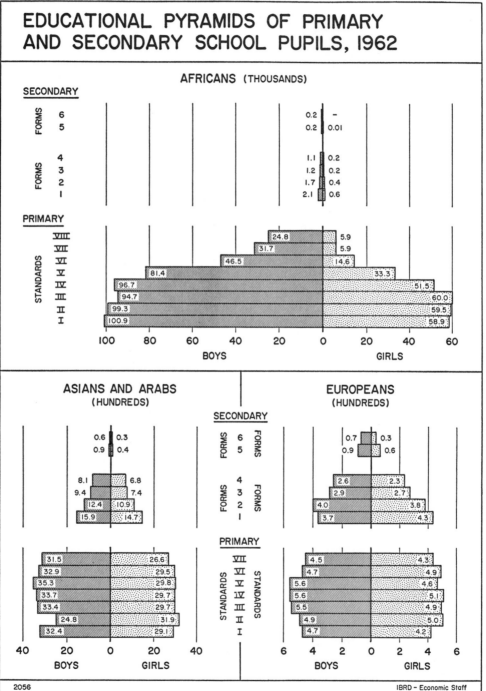

2056

IBRD - Economic Staff

mary school. Although the enthusiasm for education in Kenya and the striking advances that have been made are in many respects admirable, they pose a major problem since the increasing enrollments in primary school will generate pressures to provide continuing education for these pupils. As a result of the expansion of primary schooling which has already been achieved in recent years, the number of pupils expected to complete this stage may increase by more than six times by 1966, representing more than three-quarters of their age group (see Table 2). The mission does not believe that post-primary education can be expanded in proportion with this tremendous output from primary schools. Besides the financial limitations, expansion of secondary education is likely to outrun the prospective supply of teachers. Therefore, the mission urges policies of restraint toward further enlargement of primary education in Kenya during the period immediately ahead.

Apart from the pressure of increased expectations for secondary education in the future, there are other important reasons why the Kenya Government should now place particular emphasis on the secondary level of the system. This will be necessary in order to quicken the output of people ready for employment or for higher levels of training. The developing economy will require many local, middle-level trained people, entering employment directly from secondary school or with brief additional training. Training for the highest skills will also demand an increased output of secondary students, and the facilities and staffs in higher education are at present underutilized.

TABLE 2: Analysis of African Pupils Completing Primary School (1962 actual numbers, 1963–67 tentative forecasts)

| | | Pupils Completing Primary School Previous Year | |
Year	Estimated Population: Age 16[a]	Number[b]	Percent of Age Group[c]
1962	133,000	20,900	15.7
1963	136,500	29,200	21.4
1964	140,500	59,400	42.3
1965	145,000	106,700	73.6
1966	150,000	143,200	95.5
1967	155,000	135,200	87.2

[a] Population data are rough; these figures are adjusted from estimates from the Ministry of Education.

[b] Starting in 1964, the length of the primary school course will be reduced from eight to seven years; this explains the temporary fall in the number of pupils completing school in 1967.

[c] Since many pupils are over-age, the percentage figure (based on a single age group) may be overestimated.

Secondary school expansion is also urgently needed to increase the meager supply of teachers. Education is a heavy consumer of its own product. When schools are expanding as rapidly as they are in Kenya, there is a bottleneck because the need for teachers within the system exceeds the number of teachers who are likely to be produced from the current flow of students over the next few years. An accelerated output of properly qualified teachers, in other words, depends on a prior expansion of schooling. This bottleneck of teachers may have a restricting effect on the speed with which facilities can be expanded. If serious consideration is not given to the quality of teaching staffs, education might well lose some of its force as a catalyst of economic and social development. There is an almost total lack of Kenyans qualified to teach in expanding secondary schools, and in view of the attractive alternative opportunities for suitable candidates this is likely to prove the most difficult problem in education in the immediate future.

When this report was written, budgetary responsibilities for education under Kenya's new constitution had not been decided upon. In the past, however, secondary schools have been supported mainly from central funds; primary schools, while they have depended on central funds, have been considered the responsibility of local governments. It has been proposed that responsibility for secondary education be shifted to regional authorities.[9] In any case there is a good argument for transferring the costs of primary schooling to the local District Councils, or other local authority.

PRIMARY EDUCATION

Kenya's school system has a thrust that could not have been developed overnight. Previous decades of work by religious bodies helped to create a zeal for education among the Kenyan population, and ministry policy during the past decade led to an impressive expansion of primary schooling throughout the country. Goals for African education in Kenya, set down by the Beecher Committee in 1949, have been more than fulfilled. During the past decade the enrollment of African primary pupils rose from one-third to over four-fifths of a million, although wastage is high and more than 80 percent of these pupils were in the first four years of primary schools.

This progress in African education, though rapid, has been uneven as between the 30 school districts and as between the sexes. In the more

---

[9] Statement by Secretary of State for the Colonies, July 17, 1962.

populous areas, lying, broadly speaking, northward from Nairobi and including central and northern Nyanza, steady progress has been made toward a universal seven years of education, at least for boys. Though in a few districts there is apathy toward the education of boys, in a clear majority of the districts at least three-fifths of the boys begin school. The propensity to send girls to school is more uneven among localities, and there is noticeable apathy toward the education of girls in a number of the districts. The proportion of boys to girls in Standards I and II ranges as high as ten to two in some districts and as low as ten to eight in others.

Senior primary sequences or "streams" have been added to the more progressive African primary schools at a rapid rate in recent years.[10] African enrollment in the upper standards increased twentyfold between 1955 and 1961, rising from 7,600 to 156,000. Kenya must continue to strengthen this link between the mass education at lower levels of primary school and the selective requirements of the secondary schools. The difficulty will be to formulate a program of expenditures that will be adequate to the needs of this phase of education, but will not jeopardize other programs of higher priority. In the mission's opinion, it would not make good economic sense to invest scarce resources in pursuing a primary school goal of "seven years of schooling for all" during a period when there is a critical need for a good share of these scarce resources at the post-primary level.

The mission believes the adoption of compulsory attendance laws in the near future would only add to the problems of the primary schools and could seriously hinder all higher scales of schooling in Kenya. The growth of African education has occurred without assistance from such regulations, and to introduce compulsory school attendance for all children would, if the rules were enforced, increase primary attendance beyond the point at which the school system could cope. The mission recommends that compulsory attendance laws be postponed, and the compulsory attendance rules that apply to Europeans and Asians should be rescinded.

The Grant System for Primary Education

Under the grants-in-aid program, central funds have been made available for both capital expenditures and operating expenses of primary schools. Support for capital expenditures, in general, has been confined

[10] As larger numbers of pupils continue in school, the distinction between "lower" (i.e., I–IV) and "senior" (i.e., V–VIII) primary standards will disappear. Standard VIII is gradually to be dropped in African schools, and primary schools will thus be based on a seven-year course.

to sparsely settled and poorer areas and to lagging projects such as schools for girls. The mission views this as a sound policy, especially since most of the cost of building primary schools—many of which are mud and wattle—can be contributions in kind or labor.

Support for noncapital expenditures has been based on what is known as the "Vasey Formula," which calls for the Government to pay two-thirds of the operating costs of primary schools in excess of the funds collected from tuition fees. The mission believes that a progressive shift of these recurrent costs to local authorities should be instituted. The most compelling reason for a shift is the necessity to allocate a greater proportion of the Government's funds to post-primary education. But the mission would also argue that, as a general principle, central support of noncapital expenditures should be limited to improving the quality of education while local funds are relied on for the quantity of education. There would be some exceptions to this rule, of course. Certain minimum operating grants might be needed in some districts to ensure any schools at all; yet even in sparsely populated districts, central grants in part might be made conditional on improvements in attendance rates, especially for girls. Operating grants may also have to be made to former all-European primary schools. The mission assumes that the fees charged by these schools will be higher than average. To encourage them to maintain maximum enrollments on a nonracial basis, all government support should be on a per pupil basis.

We consider that Kenya should retain the fee system in primary schools. Tuition fees account for approximately one-half the total expenditures of the primary school system, and in most districts the fees are willingly and well paid. If primary fees were to be abolished, the implications for public budgets would be awesome. As a corollary to the rapid reduction of operating grants-in-aid, we endorse the Ministry of Education's plan to raise primary fees. As fees increase, a more liberal policy will be called for in remitting fees in hardship cases.

Primary Expansion Policy

Ministry projections of lower-primary streams in the next few years are predicated on the assumption that the increase in pupils at this level has tapered off to the point where future needs are largely dependent on the growth of population. It has been assumed that the annual intake of European and Asian pupils into Standard I will remain fairly constant at about 800 and 7,000 respectively, and only minor expenditures for extensions to existing schools will be required. The Ministry estimates the normal increase in the African school population can be met by an increase in lower-primary class units of the present size at an annual rate of 2.5 percent. Such an increase would mean a net addition of approximately 1,300 class units during the 1963–66 period, rising slowly from 260 in 1963 to 275 in 1966.

African education in Kenya is in a transition stage during which the normal expectation of pupils is shifting from four to seven years of school. The idea of primary school as a continuous passage of seven years has gained wide acceptance in some of the more progressive school districts. Because these districts also tend to be the more populous districts, the continuation rate beyond the fourth year is reaching significant proportions for all of Kenya. In 1961, for example, over half of the African boys who completed Standard IV moved on into Standard V, as did 40 percent of the girls. In recent years boys have tended to remain for the full primary course once they reach Standard V; the drop-out rate for girls at the senior-primary level has been a moderate 25 percent over the three or four years. The number of pupils who will be continuing on in school after Standard IV will increase sharply over the next few years, and school officials will be faced with difficult decisions of priority in deciding how fast to expand senior-primary streams. Though senior-primary enrollments will expand rapidly, efforts should be made to prevent this expansion from absorbing an undue share of funds. The expansion already accomplished has lowered quality standards and special effort is needed to neutralize this tendency.

The time is rapidly approaching in Kenya when bold experiments in primary education are called for. The mission suggests, for instance, that Kenya might consider a double-shift system at the primary level where conditions are favorable. In some countries two streams of students—one in the morning, one in the afternoon—are taught in the same classroom and sometimes by the same teacher. The system is generally associated with high pupil-teacher ratios, such as are found in Kenya's Standards I through V. The ratio of pupils to all teachers, both trained and untrained, in the lower-primary standards is 50:1 and the number of pupils for each trained teacher is close to 65. The ratio of pupils to teachers in Standard V (in 1961) was on the order of 60:1 at a time when the ratio throughout the senior-primary streams was only 30:1. If the shift system were to be introduced in the more populous districts, there would be a sizable reduction in the net requirements for new classrooms and teachers over the next few years. The Ministry could also reduce the need for teachers by encouraging the consolidation of small schools into one larger school and the consolidation of small classes into a larger class of several grades taught by one teacher. Thirdly, the biennial entry system, which has been successfully tried in Uganda, could be introduced in some of Kenya's new primary schools. According to this system, entrance groups spanning two years are admitted to Standard I in alternate years and only alternate standards are taught in a given year—Standards I and III one year followed by Standards II and IV the next. Finally, the more populous districts might also be encouraged to consider the merits of automatic promotion in the lower standards, to eliminate the pile-up of repeaters such as has been the case in Standards I and IV.

Kenya should aim to reduce the potential increase in expenditures at the primary stage to a point where primary expansion would not threaten the higher priority programs at the secondary stage. If enough of a reduction cannot be achieved by the measures suggested below, Kenya may be forced to concentrate even more strongly on primary schools in the most populous districts, where the return from educational expenditures is greater than in more sparsely populated districts, which at any rate usually require an operating subsidy from the Government.

The net addition of teachers and classrooms needed will depend on the extent to which the double-shift principle and other methods of making more efficient use of school facilities are adopted. We think that only a limited contribution by the central government to this expansion is justified. In our program we recommend capital expenditures of £70,000 per annum for the financial years 1963/64 to 1966/67 mainly for schools for Africans in urban areas, which will add approximately an additional £90,000 each year to the recurrent budget (see Tables 4 and 5).

The Primary Teacher Supply

It is difficult to predict primary teacher supply. Most likely, however, the demand for educated males elsewhere will be a drain on teaching staffs, and any larger complement of female teachers will, in itself, lead to a higher wastage rate due to marriage and maternity leaves. The output of primary teachers will have to be drastically speeded up to meet both replacements and even modest additions to school staffs.

There are 42 teacher training centers in Kenya now, and most of them are inefficiently small. In our opinion training for present numbers could be concentrated into perhaps half as many centers, each of which could be large enough to provide a diverse student body and to make the best utilization of scarce staff. Some consideration must be given to accessibility, however, for it is known that people are more likely to enter a school, especially a training college, if it is located nearby.

Teacher Support and Curriculum in Primary Schools

With demand for senior-primary teachers steadily rising, it will be almost impossible to improve the quality of lower-primary teachers, and this will reflect on the standard of early education most children receive. This situation might be ameliorated by enriching school experience during the first years. Since so many primary teachers—especially at the lower-primary level—will have no more than a full primary education themselves, their responsibility for planning classroom work should be reduced to a minimum. The best place for lesson planning, it seems to the mission, would be in the Ministry of Education. The mission believes that it is imperative that the Ministry take on increasing responsibility for guidance of teaching by an expanded program of syllabi construction for the primary classes. This program should include the preparation of school materials that are more closely related, in terms of subject matter and illustrations, to the experiences of Kenya children; we think that carefully prepared elementary science courses could replace much of the so-called craft training at the primary level. Most of what is worth learning in the usual school farming lessons—excepting the few schools with enthusiastic teachers and good land—would be better learned in simple science courses. Such courses could include lessons on conservation and similar topics that would be of later importance to Kenya citizens whatever their occupations.

There is a widespread opinion in Kenya that the primary schools should be expected to make children ready for specific jobs. In the mission's opinion, however, it would be shortsighted to expect the schools to prepare pupils fully for particular types of agricultural or industrial work if at the same time they are to receive a good general education. In Kenya, where three-fourths of the parents are at present illiterate, the objectives of the presecondary schools should be primarily that of teaching numbers, the bare essentials of geography, history, and science, and crucially important, a common national language.

A part of the past educational effort in Kenya has gone to waste for lack of a common national language. Knowledge of a common language will be required by a considerable part of the population over the coming years if educational and consequent economic development is to be realized. If any advance is to be at all rapid, that language in Kenya should be English. It has been demonstrated in the Asian schools that English can be used for teaching all subjects from Standard I on, and there is no pedagogical reason to refrain from extending this practice to all schools. To implement such a policy, a program to train teachers in

English is imperative. The mission recommends that a schedule of short vacation courses at training colleges be instituted, although the content of these should be carefully investigated to reflect the complex problem of teaching in a borrowed medium; it may prove desirable to make salary increments dependent on proficiency in English.

POST-PRIMARY EDUCATION

Secondary school is composed of a four-year course (Forms 1–4) leading to the School Certificate Examination, followed by two further years (Forms 5–6) for students who are preparing for university study. From the output of Form 4 must come not only candidates for Form 5 classes and subsequent training, but also teachers and recruits for the middle level of jobs that are traditionally filled directly from secondary school. Of course, there is no way of predicting with accuracy how many Form 4 completers will be available for, or will choose, a particular vocation. The supply in a given year will depend on, among other variables, what percentage of the pupils pass their Cambridge School Certificate examination. Yet educational planning must be based on such imprecise predictions as the percentage of passes on examinations to be given four, five and six years hence. The projections we make for expansion of secondary schools, therefore, must necessarily be subjected to a very careful re-evaluation from year to year; but the projections will give a good idea of the financial implications of the policies that we are recommending for secondary education.

The continuation rate of African pupils from senior-primary to secondary school was roughly 13 percent in 1961. Given the rapid expansion of primary schools, it would seem to be out of the question to make provision in the regular school system for the further education of a similar proportion of those who will complete primary school in the next few years. Standard VII will remain terminal for the majority of Kenya youth for some years to come. Educational planning should, therefore, also consider problems of mobilizing this group (see the discussion below on trade schools and vocational training).

Secondary Education

Although entrants to secondary school in Kenya doubled between 1957 and 1961, the total enrollment in Forms 1 to 4 numbered only 21,800 in 1961: 6,300 Africans; 2,700 Europeans; and 12,800 Asians, Goans and Arabs.[11] There has been a striking relative increase in at-

[11] Includes students in unaided schools, which are excluded from figures given in Chart 5.

tendance figures for African girls in recent years, but the total for all of Kenya in 1961 was only 1,100. Thus the problem of secondary education can be stated quite simply: there is a critical need to expand enrollments at this level of schooling as fast as teachers and funds can be found.

We suggest, as a feasible target, that enrollment of African pupils in Forms 1 to 4 should be more than doubled in the next five years, based on expanding entries into Form 1 as shown in Table 3. It is expected that the number of European pupils in these forms will decline and, although there will be more Asian pupils in secondary education, that only about the same number will be in government-supported schools.

TABLE 3: Analysis of African Pupils Entering Secondary School

| Year | Pupils Completing Primary Schools Previous Year | Pupils Entering Secondary School | |
		Number	Percent of (1)
	(1)	(2)	(3)
1962	20,900	2,706	12.9
1963	29,200	3,180	10.8
1964	59,400	3,990	6.7
1965	106,700	4,440	4.1
1966	143,200	4,800	3.3
1967	135,200	5,200	3.8

It is estimated that an additional 262 class units (of 30 pupils each) will be required to accommodate this school population, of which 41 may become available in formerly European schools. The cost of construct-ing the remaining classes required—one-quarter of these in boarding schools at a cost of £9,500 per class and three-quarters in day schools at £6,250—amounts to £1.56 million and comprises the largest item in our recommended program for education. The output of pupils of all races from Form 4 will be determined largely by the numbers already in school, but is expected to rise from the 3,200 or so actually completing in 1961 to over 6,000 in 1966. Considering that it will be difficult to maintain a uniformly high quality of students in the face of increasing numbers, pupils passing the Cambridge School Certificate would prob-ably rise from the 2,400 passing in 1961 to only something over 4,000 in 1966.

Information is not available with which to measure the incidence of secondary attendance by districts as was done for primary schools. The generalization can be made, however, that districts with large senior-primary enrollments supply a majority of secondary pupils. Secondary students have tended to come from parents who themselves have had an education and an unusually large proportion of students have come from parents who are not engaged in agriculture. Past patterns no doubt will change somewhat as the output of senior-primary streams expands. Not only will there be a larger pool of partially educated individuals from which to choose, but the pattern of abilities will be broader. At the secondary level, a person's educational development and his aspirations are more significant than the district in which he lives.

A pass in the Preliminary Examination (KAPE), which is normally taken at the end of primary school, is a prerequisite for entry to secondary school, and this examination is scheduled to be made uniform for all children irrespective of race. The secondary level of education is where the strongest movement toward racial integration will undoubtedly take place in Kenya and where pupils from different tribes and ethnic groups are most likely to be brought together. The process of social adjustment in these schools, especially in boarding schools, will give the future leaders of Kenya a chance to know and understand each other. The mission assumes that racial integration will be accomplished by maintaining the present high-quality secondary schools and admitting qualified students to them on a nonracial basis. Schools will continue to vary in quality, but every effort should be made to assign the most able pupils to the best schools. Opening new secondary schools should be contingent upon the existence of at least two streams of study.

It would be quite unrealistic in the mission's opinion to plan to give Form 5 education, leading to the Higher Certificate, to all pupils passing school certificate, or even to all those with good passes. There are many demands upon this scarce cadre and not all of the vocations suitable for them call for this particular type of academic education. The mission estimates that entrants to Form 5 classes, which it believes should be limited to Class I and II passes, can be expected to rise from about 600 in 1962 to around 1,100 in 1967. Of these, Africans entering Form 5 would be expected to double in the next five years, and rise from about two-fifths of the total in 1962 to over one-half in 1967. Thus about 20 percent of African students completing Form 4 would continue in school. Most of the others would be Asians, underlining the fact that Asians will continue to make up a large, and only slowly diminishing, part of the trained personnel of Kenya for some years to come, though the African share will grow and at an accelerating rate. There is already a fairly adequate supply of buildings for these classes, and it is estimated that the increase in enrollment in government schools from 1963 to 1967 could be accommodated by the addition of 12 new class units at a capital cost of £168,000, with the size of the class gradually increasing to 25 pupils (see Table 4).

We also suggest that in the future some secondary schools previously considered European be converted to Form 5–6 schools and operated on a nonracial basis. The mission acknowledges that the separation of Forms 5–6 from Forms 1–4 would deprive some schools of the stimulus of a group of advanced, more mature students, but we feel that other gains outweigh these losses. It should be possible to ensure a higher quality of preparation for university, a better utilization of existing facilities, and establish a more equitable method of recruitment for Form 5 by reducing the variations in opportunity among students from different areas.

The Secondary Teacher Situation

Secondary schools face the most difficult staffing problems. The proportion of secondary teachers with a university degree has been declining rapidly. Over the coming decade only a small number of teachers with university degrees can be recruited from the local population; even local nongraduates qualified to teach in secondary schools will be scarce. The expansion of secondary education envisaged in this chapter would require more than 400 additional teachers (on a basis of 1.5 per class) over the years 1964 to 1967, without considering replacements for the present staff. To achieve this will depend largely upon the ability to retain present expatriate teachers and to increase their numbers, which will be a major problem despite programs for the supply of teachers from Britain and the United States. The minimum task for Kenya itself will be to maintain the local supply of nongraduate teachers to at least their present ratio to pupils. This will hinge mainly on the possibility of recruiting trainee secondary teachers, but the mission recommends, within the provision for teacher training, the allocation of funds to expand capacity sufficient to supply about 140 teachers a year by 1967.

The most uncertain aspect of the teacher situation concerns the proportion of Form 4 completers who will pass the Cambridge School Certificate examination. A drop below a level of about 40 percent Class I and II passes would be a serious blow to the output of secondary teachers with adequate qualifications.

Science-Technical Streams

The Ministry would like to convert the trade-school facilities at Thika into a 320-pupil technical secondary school and to replace it with trade-school facilities at Nyeri. It is also thinking of constructing another 320-pupil technical secondary school at Kisumu. The mission would offer its serious reservations concerning proposals for extending a network of technical secondary schools. A new system of such schools would be extremely expensive to construct and operate; they would be difficult to staff; there is the further risk that they would fail to enlist the interest of students and that places would go unfilled. Furthermore, the mission believes that technical training could be more effectively mobilized outside the regular school system. This argument would also hold for any excessive amount of technical training below the secondary level: there cannot be provision in regular schools for training more than a small portion of the many pupils coming out of the senior-primary schools. We recommend an alternative approach by which science-technical streams would be added to regular secondary schools. Every secondary school should have a strong science program. The mission assumes that the present vacant places in Asian technical secondary schools would be filled by Africans—and bursaries would encourage this development.

Generally, however, we think that in Kenyan conditions the time of entry to secondary schools is too early to begin full technical education, and a principal advantage of having scientific-technical streams in regular schools would be the flexibility offered to students wishing to shift between programs. The mission would suggest that transferring to the scientific stream at, say, Form 3 should not be in any way a block to entry into the Polytechnic or the Royal College.

Trade Schools and Vocational Training

Kenya needs a diversified system of training for skilled jobs, but there is need to consider the most appropriate form this training should take. We have already given our reasons for believing that a new system of separate secondary technical schools should not be pursued. The mission endorses the Ministry's plans that the present trade schools, with courses shortened to two years, be preserved, that a new school at Eldoret be opened in 1963, and that two new schools be built by 1967. We include provision for these latter schools (£104,000) in our program of expenditures for 1963/64 to 1966/67. These trade schools might be linked more closely with an expanded Ministry of Works apprentice program. At the technician level, the mission approves plans for the further development of the Kenya Polytechnic to allow an extension of courses offered there—chiefly in engineering and commerce—although attention should be given to ensuring coordination with work at the Royal College.

Education should not be considered solely in terms of the regular school system. A complex and extensive sector of training has been supported and operated by various public and private bodies which have supplied most of the trained men for some occupations. The existing trade program of government departments has been closely related to job requirements. There are available experienced training officers, classrooms, hostels and equipment. We think that these programs should be expanded, with the programs and content of the training schedule being coordinated by the Ministry of Education. Encouragement should be given to private firms to expand their responsibility for vocational training, and the possibility for building up cooperative training programs in which a joint responsibility is taken by Government and private employers should be explored. It might be feasible, for example, in agreement with Uganda and Tanganyika, to expand part of the railway school into a transportation school for training of candidates for all of East Africa. As a unilateral Kenya action, the training now given by veterinary schools, the Kenya Meat Commission, and private firms might be brought together into a coordinated training program. It is the mission's conviction that the programs of the ministries, plus the on-the-job training programs of statutory boards and commissions, combined with those of private firms, should continue to form the major part of vocational training.

Post-Primary Bursaries and Fees

Though pupils beyond senior-primary stage tend to come from higher income families, most incomes are too small to pay for a child's schooling. As the number attending after primary school grows, pressure for increases in bursaries becomes greater, largely on grounds of equity. Capable pupils should not be eliminated from school solely on personal financial grounds. Even with careful selection, the total cost of bursaries can become enormous if allowed to become "automatic." It becomes imperative to find ways to control these costs, and the mission would recommend that the entire bursary program be reviewed with this in mind: both means tests and ability-selection procedures should be improved and systematized. Bursaries should be graduated to give the maximum incentive effect.

It is suggested that when fee schedules are established for various types of schools or courses, the prestige courses for which there is little difficulty in obtaining applicants could have fees raised substantially. On the other hand, for programs of vital importance in development but to which applicants do not come forward plentifully, fees might be lowered. The mission approves of the present policy of waiving fees in teacher training programs, as well as meeting other costs of students at teacher training colleges. As an incentive measure (with minor cost-saving features also), a system of conditional bursary assistance for regular Form 5–6 students in the form of loans rather than grants might be considered. Loans might also be offered to post-Form 4 teacher trainees.

HIGHER EDUCATION

Kenya shares in the benefits and costs of the three constituent colleges of the University of East Africa: the colleges at Makerere, Uganda and Dar es Salaam, Tanganyika, as well as the Royal College in Nairobi.

The mission is not in a position to evaluate any specific plans for the University; this subject is now being investigated by a special committee. We are of the general opinion that large government expenditures on higher education should not have an exceptionally high priority at this point in Kenya's history, and that strenuous efforts should be made to avoid an increased burden of recurrent costs. In particular bursaries of all types should be scrutinized seriously, and we recommend that they be put on a loan basis as soon as possible. The mission assumes that the capital requirements of higher education will, under existing conditions, be met from abroad and from local private donations.

The problem for the future will be to avoid too much duplication in programs and to avoid setting up programs for which training could be obtained more cheaply abroad, or for which there will not be sufficient students to occupy the facilities fully. The mission is of the opinion that arts degree programs should be developed at each college along with professional training in a limited number of specialties, to the bachelor's level. Some special programs should eventually be transferred to a more appropriate place below the university level. Whenever laboratories or other equipment are not fully utilized, they should be made available for nondegree programs of other schools or agencies. Furthermore, in the fiscal circumstances of East Africa, enrollments at the university colleges should not be limited to those who can be accommodated in hostels. The mission believes that residential quarters in local communities could be found by many students. Further, it is suggested that more students could be accommodated at less cost if accommodation in hostels were made more Spartan in character and if the space per student were decreased by doubling occupancy per room or per dormitory.

The mission would recommend that, as far as can reasonably be done, higher education be put on a comparative cost basis: as a general principle, new courses of study would be started only when the cost per student would be less than the cost (including transport and living expense) of sending students to overseas universities. If this policy were adopted, it would probably lead Kenya in the direction of more training programs for technicians rather than professionals. At the technician level of training, which is above the secondary school level, Kenya relies chiefly on the Polytechnic. The Polytechnic has met these responsibilities well and the mission would recommend that its program be given a relatively greater priority than it now has.

The mission would suggest that in time an Institute of Education be established, preferably at the Royal College, to maintain and improve the quality of education by systematic instruction and research. This Institute would coordinate the training programs for the various kinds of teachers and engage in research that would concentrate on the specific problems of education in Kenya. We do not feel, however, that this is of such immediate urgency as to warrant being included in our present program.

Finally, we have included provision (on the recommendation of the Ministry) in our program of £4,000 per annum to meet the local costs of an adult education scheme.

SUMMARY OF PROPOSED EXPENDITURES

The recommendations we have made in this section would entail capital outlays of about £2.6 million during 1963/64–1966/67 (see Table 4).

TABLE 4: Proposed Capital Expenditures on Education 1963/64–1966/67

(£ thousand)

	1963/64	1964/65	1965/66	1966/67	Total
Primary	70	70	70	70	280
Secondary					
Forms 1–4	452	380	339	389	1,560
Forms 5–6	42	42	42	42	168
Trade and Technical	52	50	100	152	354
Teacher Training	65	65	65	65	260
Adult Education	4	4	4	4	16
Total	685	611	620	722	2,638

Arising from the proposed capital program would be additional recurrent expenditures totaling more than £1.1 million by 1966/67 (see Table 5).

TABLE 5: Additional Recurrent Costs of Proposed Program for
Education 1963/64–1966/67: (Increments to 1962/63 Expenditure)

(£ thousand)

	1963/64	1964/65	1965/66	1966/67
Administration[a]	20	40	60	80
Primary	90	180	270	360
Secondary				
Forms 1–4	162	298	419	558
Forms 5–6	15	30	45	60
Trade and Technical	25	50	75	85
Teacher Training	10	20	30	40
Total	322	618	899	1,183

[a] Estimates of increasing administrative costs resulting from the program based on information received from the Ministry.

HEALTH

Present Health Conditions

Modern medicine has achieved control over diseases which once periodically decimated Kenya's inhabitants. Cholera and plague and others are now almost negligible as immediate threats to the health of the country. The application of new control measures and drugs have achieved dramatic cures and reduced the dangers of current epidemics. For example, it has been possible by a program of spraying to exterminate the tsetse fly in most of Nyanza Province and so limit the incidence of sleeping sickness to the point where control is in sight. As a result Kenya does not now face an overwhelming problem of dealing with specific diseases common in many other tropical and subtropical countries. There are no adequate statistics to make possible an accurate assessment of the health of the people, although it seems that the infant mortality rate may still be very high in places, but the country as a whole is reaching a stage of high birth rates and declining death rates.[12]

[12] The Ministry of Health estimates the infant mortality rate for Kenya as a whole to be about 190 per 1,000 live births, and the birth rate to be 40–50 per 1,000 population.

Nevertheless, a formidable pattern of diseases is still to be found in Kenya, some of which are endemic, others now occurring in epidemic form. As might be expected in a country with such a range of natural conditions, there are marked regional variations in the incidence of particular diseases. Knowledge of the extent of diseases is incomplete. The returns from hospitals and the notifications of the main infectious diseases do not give a complete picture, and these data are still influenced strongly by improved methods of detection and by increasing readiness to seek medical aid. However, an outline of conditions may be discerned. Respiratory diseases and tuberculosis are still prevalent, particularly in Central Province, and these diseases are the main causes of death among Africans in government hospitals. Outside the higher altitude regions, tropical diseases are more common; malaria, bilharzia, hookworm and leprosy being chief among them in Nyanza Province. Bilharzia and hookworm are known to be endemic there, as in many other parts of the country, and it has been estimated that about 8.4 per 1,000 of the population of Nyanza suffer from leprosy. A similar pattern of disease is found in the Coast Province, where there is also a high incidence of filariasis.

In addition to the persistence of endemic diseases, the increasing incidence of other diseases also poses another aspect of the health problem which has gained in significance. Epidemics of certain infectious diseases now appear to occur more frequently; notably poliomyelitis, which has tended to break out in a three-year cycle. Cases of tetanus admitted to government hospitals have risen markedly, and this has become one of the major causes of mortality in these hospitals: of 707 tetanus cases admitted in 1959, 327 or 46 percent died. Kala-azar has spread from the Northern Province to become endemic through an area extending along the foothills of the highlands southeastward from Turkana as far as Machakos. The resurgence of diseases such as gastroenteritis, meningitis and typhoid in Central Province during the Emergency, seems to indicate the dangers of overcrowding under conditions where water supplies and sanitation arrangements are inadequate.

Poor environmental conditions—the problems of hygiene, malnutrition and lack of education in health matters—increase the deleterious effects of disease. Overcrowding and inadequate housing and sanitation have become serious with the rapid concentration of population in urban surroundings, both in the main towns and in the new villages of Central Province. The bulk of the food of the rural family in Kenya is produced on the shamba, beyond the control of hygiene measures. Water supplies derived from springs, wells, dams, boreholes and rivers are a frequent health hazard, being related to the incidence of many of the important tropical diseases. Evidence of multiple nutritional deficiencies—of calories, proteins, iron, riboflavin, icotonic acid, vitamin A and iodine—has been collected. These deficiencies, which result from inadequate dietary patterns, appear particularly in children in the post-weaning period aged one to five years, but are more serious in some areas than others. The pastoral tribes live mainly on cows' milk, meat and blood, but the bulk of the population subsists chiefly on vegetable foods, cereal flour, maize, millet and bananas, supplemented by beans, green vegetables, cassava and sweet potatoes. Various tribal customs limit the use of available sources of protein; these restrict the consumption of chicken, eggs and fish in different parts of the country. The comprehensive nutritional and dietetic survey being undertaken in Kenya, with the cooperation of WHO, FAO, and UNICEF, should increase knowledge of this problem.

Medical and Health Services

General responsibility for health matters in Kenya rests with the Ministry of Health of the central government, although many important functions are fulfilled by local government bodies, and supplemented by private organizations.

The central government is responsible for organizing and administering the government hospital service, which forms the core of the clinical facilities in Kenya. This service is based on an integrated system of cottage and district hospitals, provincial hospitals and a central consultative hospital in Nairobi, with a full range of modern facilities. In the capital, besides the headquarters of the Ministry, there is a general hospital and specialist institutions, which include the main mental hospital, an infectious diseases hospital with a poliomyelitis and respiratory wing, an orthopedic rehabilitation center, a medical research laboratory, a division of insect-borne diseases, and radiological department. The expertise focused in Nairobi is available to receive difficult or infectious cases referred there by the supporting hospitals. In addition, the laboratory and pharmaceutical services provide supplies for the whole of Kenya, including a range of vaccines, some of which are exported.

There are five provincial hospitals at Kisumu, Machakos, Mombasa, Nakuru and Nyeri, administered by the provincial medical officer, each with about 250 beds. These institutions act as general hospitals for their own districts but also serve some of the specialist needs of the district and mission hospitals. The provincial hospitals have two medical officers with higher qualifications on their staffs, and provide specialist as well as general services, clinical laboratory and diagnostic X-ray services. Below the provincial level there are 32 district hospitals and about 21 subordinate centers. The Medical Officer of Health is responsible for the management of the district hospital, in addition to his other functions in connection with the local health services. The cottage hospitals, under the charge of a hospital assistant, provide simple medical care. There were over 7,000 government hospital beds in 1960, or roughly 1 per 1,000 population.

The government hospital service is augmented by hospitals operated by the Protestant and Catholic missions in Kenya. There are 35 mission hospitals with over 25 beds each, most of which have qualified resident medical and nursing staffs. In addition, there are several other smaller institutions which provide in-patient medical facilities, contributing to a total of 2,200 beds from this source. The missions have played an important part in introducing medical services to the African population of Kenya, especially in the rural areas. They have tended to emphasize curative aspects of health. Standards in these hospitals have varied, although frequently the uncertainty of their financial support has resulted in their not being maintained at comparable levels to government hospitals, especially in standards of accommodation. In addition, there has been disparity in the fees charged by mission hospitals, which in many cases are higher than at government hospitals. A committee appointed to consider the relation of the mission services with the Government recommended measures to achieve coordination of these points.[13]

There are also private hospitals operating in Kenya. In the main towns there are a number of private general hospitals varying in size. Nairobi is served by two private general hospitals and two maternity homes. In the rural areas, hospitals have been built by various agricultural and commercial enterprises for their employees. There were about 1,150 private hospital beds in Kenya in 1960.

The total complement of hospital beds in Kenya was about 11,000 in 1961, or roughly 1.5 per thousand population. Separate institutions cater for the different racial communities, however, and there are fewer beds per thousand of the African population. Kenya ranks among the less developed countries in the supply of hospital beds. As a result, there has been frequent overcrowding, which endangers health standards. It has been estimated that between 800–900 more beds are needed in existing hospitals to reduce bed-occupancy rates to accepted levels. In addition, there are shortages of special hospital beds, particularly for mental patients and for those maternity cases which require urgent attention.

[13] *Report of the Committee Appointed to Consider the Role of the Medical Services Rendered by the Missions in Relation to Those Provided by the Central and Local Government.* Sessional Paper No. 8 of 1960/61.

Various local government bodies, assuming the status of Health Authorities, take responsibility for ambulances, maternity services, environmental sanitation, as well as dispensaries and health centers.[14] These services are under the supervision of the Medical Officer of Health, supported by a Health Inspector and Public Health Nurse. As central government employees, they ensure that a uniform policy is pursued throughout the rural areas. An important part of the health services is provided by the local authorities through a network of health centers. "The aim is to bring medical aid and the forces of preventive hygiene completely in touch with the home . . ."[15] The program now depends on local initiative and largely on local finance. The local health authorities provide most of the capital and recurrent costs of health centers, but the central government assists them with a capital grant (usually of £1,000 per center), and a recurrent grant-in-aid. The health centers are located in large villages or small towns. The target is to build 300 centers, to give a coverage of 1 to approximately 20,000 population, at the rate of 20 to 30 a year. So far about 140 have been completed, but only 14 were finished in 1960, progress having been slowed up by shortages of trained staff and finance.

Health centers generally contain various facilities, although the services offered are as far as possible adapted to local conditions. Primary emphasis is directed toward the preventive and promotive aspects of health, but at the present stage of development of the health center program, the pressure on the curative facilities is great as in most areas they are serving a larger population and more extensive area than 20,000 people or 5–10 mile radius for which they were designed ideally. This pressure has been met temporarily by the formation of health subcenters or rural clinics, operating a few of the facilities of the full centers and drawing on their staffs. Nevertheless, these centers fulfill an important role in providing a wide coverage for preventive health measures, which is a primary goal of health policy. Mobile health units staffed by the center pay regular visits to areas beyond the center's immediate sphere. Among the nomadic tribes such as the West Suk and Masai, an entirely mobile health unit is used, as far as possible following a regular cycle of visits to coincide with the movements of the people.

Staffing these centers poses a formidable problem. Although they are under the direction of the district Medical Officer of Health, considerable responsibility is delegated to the center staff, which operates as a

[14] These include 27 African District Councils, 6 Urban Health Authorities, and 4 County Health Authorities.

[15] A. J. Walker, "A Health Center Policy for Kenya," *The East African Medical Journal,* February 1950, p. 86.

team. A Hospital Assistant has general supervisory and administrative control, as well as being responsible for curative activities. A Health Inspector or Health Assistant is concerned with environmental health work and the investigation of infectious diseases in the field and health education work in the center. A midwife operates the maternity section and arranges for domiciliary midwifery services and health education for mothers. A graded dresser capable of elementary diagnosis and treatment deals with most out-patient work. Occasionally, laboratory assistants may be posted to investigate specific diseases in connection with control programs. The team lives in the district where it works, and the center associates itself with community activities. This decentralized health strategy makes heavy demands upon the supply of staff and on the supervisory duties of the Medical Officers of Health, whose main activities are concentrated in the district hospital. The primary justification for this approach rests on the gains to be made from a decentralized approach to preventive health. But it is implementing preventive health measures which poses the most acute staffing problem, and which is most likely to suffer from the demands of curative work.

Preventive Health Services

Health education work is focused at the Ministry of Health under the control of the Health Education Officer. All medical auxiliaries are trained in the elements of health education, and courses are provided for Health Inspectors to provide a background for staff destined for field work. In addition, the Ministry operates a mobile demonstration unit to assist local authorities in giving public instruction on preventive measures against special diseases. It also produces education materials and demonstration models for special exhibitions and for use by health centers and in schools.

The main problems of health education lie in bringing the program close to the people. The low level of literacy among the adult population limits the use of printed matter so that the health authorities have attempted to introduce education in hygiene into community life through the health centers and schools. Teams from the better established health centers pay regular visits to schools providing them with a rudimentary school health service, but health education is often left to the Medical Department staff. A center has been set up at Kitui to instruct farmers and their wives in improved hygiene and husbandry practices as potential community leaders.

Environmental health matters are the responsibility of Health Inspectors as part of the local health service, under the general supervision of the Chief Health Inspector in the Ministry of Health. Their main functions are concerned with the setting and maintenance of health standards for sanitation, water supplies, housing and food production, and particularly to recommend economic methods appropriate to different local conditions. Strenuous efforts have been made to introduce pit latrines in rural areas, especially for newly constructed houses. Protection of water supplies through the construction of concrete standings, storage tanks, etc., has been emphasized and there appears to have been an increasingly positive response to this need. Bylaws and regulations governing food shops and eating houses have been adopted by most communities, but the present staff is not adequate to make complete inspections.

Some measures have been undertaken to counteract nutritional deficiencies—by the distribution of dried milk provided by UNICEF, and by encouraging the production of protein-rich foods, through innovations such as fish ponds. Fish ponds present their own problem of water-borne diseases, and require adequate precautionary measures. A common feature of the problems of environmental health is the decisive influence of the attitudes of the people, and the need for education before the importance of protection is realized and adequate control within the reach of the limited available health staff.

Staff

Doctors. There were approximately 670 registered medical practitioners, 56 licensed doctors and 26 preregistration interns in Kenya in April 1962. There was thus 1 doctor to every 10,000 of the population. The supply was largely concentrated, however, in private practice in the main towns. The ratio of doctors to population in rural areas is less favorable, perhaps in the range of 1 to 40,000 or 50,000 population.

Two hundred eighteen of the registered doctors were on the Ministry's establishment, of whom only 34 were African. Another 44 doctors in the government service were licensed or serving their internships, 7 of them African. All specialist grade staff were expatriates. The supply of qualified medical practitioners does not meet present staff requirements for government hospitals and the public health services, falling short by about 60. Mission and plantation hospitals are also understaffed. Training and recruitment of additional African doctors will be slow and hopes for the development of medical services in Kenya will continue to depend on non-African doctors. The mission, therefore, believes the interests of the country to lie in assuring conditions of work for expatriate personnel as attractive as possible to induce them to remain in their present positions.

Nurses. There were about 3,100 nurses and 1,400 midwives of all grades in Kenya in 1960, of which about 1,350 were Registered Nurses or 1 to every 5,300 population. The status of Kenya Registered Nurse (KRN) is recognized as the equivalent of the State Registered Nurse in the United Kingdom. There were about 190 matrons, nursing sisters and psychiatric nurses of this or higher rank on the government establishment in 1962. One hundred thirty of these were on expatriate terms. Recruitment to these ranks has proved difficult recently—there were over 20 unfilled vacancies on April 1, 1962—and extensive use has had to be made of married women employed on temporary terms. This supply will be particularly uncertain in the future as it will depend largely on the movements of their husbands. There were also 13 staff nurses having passed their KRN examinations, gaining experience before becoming eligible for appointment to these ranks.

The bulk of the nursing staff in Kenya is filled by enrolled assistant nurses, about 900 of whom were in the Kenya Medical Services in 1962. Recruitment at this level is easier as it requires only an intermediate standard of general education, and a surplus of applicants over available places has allowed a probationary period before selection.

Other branches of medical work, particularly the radiological and laboratory services and in the field of public health, suffer from staff shortages. Many senior posts are still filled almost entirely by expatriate personnel: all 20 of the qualified Health Visitors, 4 of the 5 Pharmacists, 27 of the 28 Health Inspectors and 13 of the 20 Laboratory Technologists. Vacancies exist in these grades which cannot be filled, and there is also difficulty in securing an adequate supply of trained people for more junior posts as a result of the competition for them from commercial employment at higher salaries.

Training. The only training for doctors now being carried out in Kenya is for post-graduates serving their internship or training as Registrars at the King George VI Hospital. The demand for appointments by Kenyan students exceeds the places available, which are filled a year in advance.

Kenyan medical students take their studies at Makerere College or overseas. There were about 165 medical students at Makerere in 1961, who would be expected to qualify by 1966, about 45 of whom were Africans. This rate of output is unlikely to provide an adequate supply of doctors for Kenya. Besides the existing shortages of medical practitioners in the Medical Department, replacements for normal retirement and to meet the expected demands for the localization of the medical serv-ices will be pressing. The Medical Department will also be competing with private practice for the limited supply available in the country. Since little can be done to influence output during the immediate years ahead, Kenya will depend upon expatriate doctors to maintain the pres-ent ratio of doctors to population. The Ministry recognizes that the country will need to rely also on a cadre of Medical Assistants in the next few years.

The longer-run problem of increasing the number of doctors for Kenya is aggravated by the scarcity of suitable students for medical training. Makerere College is unlikely to produce more than 15 to 20 Kenyan doctors a year. The majority of Kenyan medical students go abroad for their basic training and for specialized courses, mainly to In-dia and the United Kingdom. There are recognized disadvantages to relying on overseas training: the studies may not be appropriate to Kenya's needs and there may be delays in students returning to the country immediately. Consideration has been given to developing an undergraduate medical school in Nairobi at the King George VI Hospi-tal. In view of the difficulty of increasing rapidly the number of entrants for medical training in Kenya, the mission does not believe that a large expenditure of public funds on undergraduate clinical teaching is at present warranted, although it may deserve consideration in the future.

Training for the higher grades of Medical Auxiliary Staff in Kenya is concentrated in Nairobi, at the Central Hospital, and the Medical Training Center, which provides free education and accommodation for the student. There has been no difficulty in finding recruits for KRN training, and an expansion of facilities would be necessary to increase the output. The supply of students for other subjects has been inade-quate, particularly for health inspector work, or has been rapidly re-duced during training by the attraction of careers in private enterprise or by scholarships for study abroad. Negotiations have been held in or-der to secure recognition of training of various auxiliary grades at the Medical Training Center. The provision of training in midwifery for KRN's would allow them to qualify as nursing sisters, which has until now required examination in the United Kingdom. This development would be provided for by the construction of the proposed obstetrics block at King George VI Hospital (see Table 6). In view of the heavy demands on the supply of school certificate holders—the minimum qualification for many medical technicians—in the next few years, the mission does not believe that any appreciable expansion of training facilities for other parts is called for at the moment. Some direct meas-ures to alleviate the high rate of wastage of students in training may be appropriate. A review of the adequacy of facilities may be needed if a greatly expanded supply of candidates should become available.

Training for junior grades takes place mainly in hospitals. An intermediate educational standard is required for candidates for Assistant Nurse, Assistant Midwife and Health Assistant, and there have been more applicants than can be accepted for training for these posts. There has been considerable wastage from some of these ranks, particularly after girls get married, and increased output will be necessary to satisfy present and future needs. Since training in Nairobi is being concentrated at the KRN level, there is expected to be the need for expanded facilities for Assistant Nurses elsewhere. The mission therefore supports the proposal to provide training and accommodation for them at Mombasa. It seems likely that the limitation to a rapid increase in the output of staff at this level will be the lack of teachers, nursing sister tutors being heavily burdened with clinical duties.

The health center program will make additional claims on the training of staff. Shortages in certain posts may be anticipated as a result of wastage. It would therefore be desirable to improve the present rate of training of supporting staff, particularly those engaged in promotive health work, but we do not believe that this would warrant additional facilities. Present capacity for training Assistant Health Visitors is not fully used, and more Health Inspectors and Health Assistants could be instructed at the Medical Training Center. Health center work also requires a distinctive approach under rural conditions in a team unit. A contribution to this purpose is being made by the construction of a training health center to provide instruction for staff at Karuri near Nairobi but in a rural setting, with assistance from the Rockefeller Foundation and WHO. The experience gained from this venture may suggest lines for the future development of training.

Finance

The estimated gross expenditure of the Kenya Government on health in the financial year 1962/63 was about £2.8 million. Expenditures by the various local government authorities are difficult to aggregate but were perhaps in the region of £1.5 million. Total public outlays on health were therefore the equivalent of approximately 2 percent of Gross Domestic Product, or about Sh.11 to Sh.12 per capita of population.

Kenya Government expenditures on health cover the expenses of the Ministry; the Government also makes grants to various private and local government bodies in the health field, and grants-in-aid to the recurrent

and capital budgets of private and mission hospitals and charitable social organizations. Hospital construction and improvement grants are
usually given on a matching basis. Contributions are made to the Hospital Funds for the non-African communities, to which individuals are
required to make payments to offset hospital fees. In addition, the Ministry of Local Government makes a grant to public health authorities to
support health services in their area. This practice was originally instituted to encourage local authorities to assume the full responsibilities of
Local Health Authorities, and it was proposed to provide matching
funds for approved net expenditures. Financial stringency has since led
the Government to place a ceiling on the amount of the grant available,
passing the financial burden of expanding health services in the localities on to the local authorities.

The Ministry of Health receives revenues at a current level of about
£600,000 a year. The main sources for these are hospital and dispensary
fees and reimbursements from the local authorities for staff and services
rendered. Fees at government hospitals have been reviewed annually in
the light of the supply and demand for beds. Fees were raised to their
present level in 1961 and the Ministry believes that for the time being
they could not be increased further without affecting the number of patients needing hospitalization who are able to meet the charges for undergoing treatment.

The Government's forecast of capital expenditures for health for the
financial year 1962/63 amounts to £167,000, or £145,000 net of appro-
priations-in-aid. These expenditures for 1962/63 are expected to involve
an additional recurrent cost of about £20,000 per year. We envisage capital expenditures of about £1 million over the years 1963/64 to 1966/67
or an average of £250,000 a year (see Table 6). Outlays on capital projects of this scale would, when completed, require an additional £90,000
a year for current payments (set out in Table 7). Such a program would
meet the most urgent geographic and specialist needs for extending government hospital institutions, to provide essential accommodation for
staff, to expend the coverage of medical services in cooperation with the
local government through the health center program, to assist private
hospitals in raising their standards to a level comparable to government
hospitals, and to finance research and other activities of the Ministry.

Expenditures on health that improve the productive capacity of the
population, like those on education, may be viewed as investments, although the returns from them are not easy to calculate or to realize. It
is clear that, gauged by international standards, opportunities for improvements in health exist in Kenya. However, in considering this
among other objectives of public policy, the mission has been conscious

TABLE 6: Proposed Capital Expenditures on Health 1963/64–1966/67

(£ thousand)

	1963/64	1964/65	1965/66	1966/67	Total
Government Medical Institutions:					
Acute Mental Hospital	60	50	—	—	110
Health Education Center	30	—	—	—	30
Obstetrics Block	—	40	56	—	96
District Hospitals					
a. Homa Bay	60	—	—	—	60
b. Ukwala	—	—	20	60	80
Clinical and Teaching					
Laboratory	—	—	20	—	20
Nurses Training School	—	50	—	—	50
Hospital Improvements	10	20	50	85	165
	160	160	146	145	611
Staff Housing	40	40	50	50	180
Grants-in-Aid:					
Health Centers	20	20	25	25	90
Nongovernment Hospitals	20	20	20	20	80
Research	10	10	10	10	40
Total	250	250	251	250	1,001

TABLE 7: Additional Recurrent Expenditures on Health 1963/64–1966/67[a] (Increments to 1962/63 Expenditure)

(£ thousand)

	1963/64	1964/65	1965/66	1966/67
Government Medical Institutions:				
Acute Mental Hospital	—	24.0	16.0	16.0
Health Education Center	0.5	0.5	0.5	0.5
Obstetrics Block	—	—	24.0	19.0
District Hospitals				
a. Homa Bay	15.0	8.0	8.0	8.0
b. Ukwala	—	—	—	15.0
Clinical and Teaching				
Laboratory	—	—	4.8	2.3
Nurses Training School	—	5.8	2.0	2.0
Hospital Improvements	2.0	8.0	8.0	10.0
Staff Housing	9.0	6.0	7.0	8.0
Health Centers	4.0	8.0	8.5	8.5
Total	30.5	60.3	78.8	89.3

[a] Includes initial equipment costs.

of the need to keep expenditures, for current as well as capital purposes, within Kenya's present limited financial means. Under these circumstances we do not believe a general expansion of hospital facilities can be undertaken, nor that very large expenditures in the range of £800,000 should be concentrated in the construction of a proposed new provincial hospital. We agree that there is an urgent need in meeting particular deficiencies, and the program suggested would provide about 200 additional mental patient beds and about 100 maternity beds (even excluding those in new health centers) as well as between 100 to 200 general beds. This would allow some small progress toward improving the ratio of beds to population, but will need to be concentrated in underserved areas such as are found in Nyanza Province. It is assumed that adequate staff will be available to support an expansion of hospital facilities of this magnitude, and the mission regards that this is a necessary condition before attempting expansion. Improvements to existing hospitals, particularly replacing substandard ancillary buildings, are regarded as having high priority, but only those most essential to ensuring adequate standards of service should be undertaken. We expect about £165,000 will be available for this purpose from 1963/64 to 1966/67. Expenditures for the construction of a health education center and clinical laboratory in Nairobi have also been provided for.

Expenditures to support programs for the training of staff have been accorded priority to meet future personnel needs in line with the discussion in the previous section.

The mission regards the program for assisting local authorities in the construction of health centers as well suited to the needs of extending both preventive and curative medicine into the rural areas of Kenya. We therefore approve the provision of funds to continue partial capital grants in support of construction toward the objective of a total complement of 300 for the country at about the present rate, provided adequate trained staff are available. The capital program also makes provision for the cost of building centers in Mombasa and replacing a government dispensary at Karatina. The total amount of these expenditures would be £90,000 over the period 1963/64 to 1966/67.

The Government assists nongovernment hospitals by making grants to meet a portion of the capital costs involved. The mission recognizes that other bodies make an important contribution to medical services, but we believe that the Government should not make general commitments to provide finance for these projects since funds will not be adequate to meet all claims that may be made on them. In deciding each case on its merits, funds should only be expended on those of recognized value when funds would not otherwise be available, and the proportion of the assistance may be varied according to the needs and the supply of other resources. The committee studying the medical services stressed that an expansion of hospital facilities should not be embarked on without a corresponding expansion of the preventive and promotive health services.[16] As the scope for enlarging the medical services is limited, we do not propose increased expenditures be allocated to this purpose.

The mission believes that there should be a strict limit on the amount of housing which the Ministry should provide for medical staff under present financial circumstances. Those facilities should only be provided where the presence of staff in the vicinity of the hospital at all times is essential. In particular, other sources of accommodation should be sought for staff in the Nairobi area.

Expenditures on research represent a continuation of the approximate level of expenditures undertaken under the three current schemes, on the expectation that assistance from overseas can be attracted for such work.

HOUSING

The traditional house of Kenya is a thatched, mud and pole, circular hut which is seen all over the country, although the design and the local materials used differ from place to place. More than three-quarters of the population of the country still live in the rural areas in this kind of accommodation. Sometimes the structure of the hut has been improved —by more permanent roofing materials such as corrugated iron—and roughly painted, or else the old materials have been adapted to a more practical rectangular construction, particularly for homes on newly consolidated holdings. Such housing in rural areas does not require government action if adequate environmental health measures (discussed earlier in this chapter) are taken, and if care is taken in the siting and planning of new building.

This report has already referred in Chapter 2 to the rapid development of towns in Kenya in recent years, and the concentration of population that has gone with it. Nairobi is perhaps the most striking illustration of this tendency, the number of people living there more than doubling between 1948 and 1961.[17] While many of the residents at a particular time may not be permanent, the increase in the urban popu-

[16] Sessional Paper No. 8 of 1960/61, p. 18.

[17] The population of Nairobi was 119,000 in 1948, and estimated at 297,000 in 1961. Cf. East African Statistical Department, *Economic and Statistical Review*, December 1961.

lation has expanded the need for new housing. Until the recent slow-down in economic activity, new residential building in the main towns of Kenya has been constructed at a rate of more than £3 million a year in response to this demand (see Statistical Appendix, Table 40). The bulk of this accommodation has, however, been provided on a commercial basis for the middle and higher income groups, particularly for residents of European or Asian origin. Some large employers—the Government and private and public enterprises—provide accommodation for their workers.[18] Social groups have also made considerable communal efforts to house poorer members on a financially viable basis—for example, the Ismaili community.

The provision of housing for lower income groups, almost all of them African, in and around towns, has not been adequate to meet the enlarged needs of this part of the population. Probably the majority of the African residents of the main towns are migratory workers. It is usual for an African coming to town in search of a job to lodge with a relative, already living there, who looks upon it as an obligation to take him in. Several samples of housing conditions have been made, but the extent of overcrowding in present accommodation and the demand for new in towns throughout Kenya is not known. The seriousness of the problem is recognized in Kenya, but the mission suggests that a country-wide survey should be undertaken to assess the relative needs in different areas, and to provide a basis for implementing government housing policy, in particular in relation to rent structures and the type of housing required.

Ministerial responsibility for housing now resides in the Ministry of Health and Housing. The main functions of the Ministry in this field are to supervise the structure of rentals charged by local authorities and the control of expenditure on government staff housing (see below). In addition, the Ministry administers the Central Housing Board, which is the principal instrument of the central government for promoting the building of housing. The Board provides finance to local authorities for housing and associated services, to assist them in preparing plans, letting contracts and supervising projects. The Board employs a small technical staff including an architect and an engineer.

The Board had approved about £4 million in loans by the end of 1961. Most of these were made to local authorities for the construction of housing, which is carried out by contractors approved by the Board. Local authorities also borrow from the Board in order to re-lend to em-

---

[18] Employers are obliged under the Employment Ordinance to provide housing for employees earning less than Sh.200 per month, or to pay a cash housing allowance in addition to the minimum wage.

ployers up to 80 percent of the costs of building housing for their employees. Funds are provided to local authorities to develop sites and install facilities—roads, sewerage, drains and water supply—either in the form of loans, or as matching grants for services for local authority housing schemes where these services are not charged against rent. The resources of the Central Housing Board are a revolving Housing Fund, derived from a free grant and loans from the Kenya Government amounting to about £1.5 million at the end of 1960, and a loan of £2 million from the Colonial Development Corporation. The Board's loans for housing schemes are made at a rate of .25 percent above the rate at which it borrows, currently 6.75 percent as against 6.5 percent, repayable normally over 40 years, and made against the security of the rates and revenues of the local authority. The Board is fully lent at the moment, and depends for additions to its resources on allocations from the Development Fund which are now far below its previous rate of lending. Furthermore, the Board is now faced with repayments on the CDC loan over the period to 1985, while its own loans to local authorities are of longer term. The scope for further government encouragement of housing is, therefore, limited by present budgetary considerations, or by the possibility of attracting more funds from overseas.

In allocating its limited resources to the heavy demands made on them, the Central Housing Board has applied a number of criteria. The size of the local authority contribution, the technical suitability of the housing scheme and its financial structure have been important considerations. An accurate assessment of needs, however, has not always been possible, and as already stated, the mission regards this as an important step in approaching the housing problem.

The main responsibility for providing adequate accommodation where this is not available through private enterprise lies with the local authorities. The physical conditions of the area, the financial capacity and policies of the local authority as well as housing conditions have varied from place to place, but some general observations may be made. Encouraged by the Central Housing Board, attempts have been made to develop purchase schemes, by which the tenant pays for his house over a period of years. These schemes are designed to give the owner a stake in the area, and to stabilize the population there, and it is hoped that more people will be able to afford to purchase their homes in this way as incomes rise. At the moment, even the modest deposits necessary are beyond the means of many families, and rental schemes continue to play a major part in housing schemes despite difficulties of rent collection and maintenance. Although a large proportion of urban residents are temporary migrants, who leave their families behind at their traditional homes, there is a significant demand for single accommodation. Houses have been designed and built with self-contained lodging rooms to meet this demand, and to provide the main tenant or owner with a supplementary source of income. Considering the early stage of urbanization and the levels of income reached by Kenya, this feature of the housing problem seems likely to be a continuing one, although on this point the proposed survey should shed some light.

If precise knowledge of the lack of housing in Kenya is incomplete, it would seem clear that in aggregate it far exceeds the present capacity of the economy to satisfy. Applications by local authorities to the Central Housing Board may be in the order of ten times the present availability of funds. A rough calculation suggests the investment required to provide the inadequately housed people with a minimum of permanent accommodation in the main town areas alone may be more than £5–7 million without considering the increased number of people attracted there and the rate of population growth. The mission considers it unrealistic at Kenya's stage of development to attempt to divert resources on this scale from other fields of investment to housing of this kind during the next four years.

A further aspect of the problem is the inability of large numbers of low income people to pay an economic rent for local government housing even when it has been constructed. Continuous efforts have been made by various branches of the Government to find materials and draw up designs which would reduce building costs as much as possible, and by the Central Housing Board to keep a close check on the carrying out of contracts. This work is valuable, but requires persistence and cannot be expected to yield spectacular new gains. Costs of building and rents charged vary between towns, but a subsidy element is common, and would certainly be necessary if all the underhoused were to be accommodated at present standards and rents. The mission doubts the wisdom of attempting to meet general low income housing needs by means of subsidies. This would impose a large added burden of taxation which the country is ill-placed to take on. It would also confer discriminatory benefits on certain town dwellers which would require invidious systems of allocation. The ability of workers to pay an economic rent would be expected to increase as minimum wages move toward the goal of a family standard supported by increases in urban production. There may still be a role for the selective use of subsidies where important external economies are to be gained—for example, where commercially valuable land becomes available through slum clearance and rezoning of land use.

The general policy for meeting urban housing needs might also move along other lines. The provision of publicly built housing cannot meet all the demands for accommodation on the basis of present costs. The mission considers therefore that an approach should be made toward the construction of houses by "self-help" methods; that a greater part of the investment required for building be found by the people themselves.

For such an approach to be successful, substantial government action will be required to create conditions to encourage private construction and to meet the minimum social requirements of a healthy and productive environment. There are obvious dangers in allowing uncontrolled slums, which have already appeared outside local authority boundaries, but these dangers will increase if steps are not taken to meet unfulfilled housing needs. Efforts should be made to encourage improvement in the standards of housing by providing facilities for building, and maintaining hygienic conditions. This might involve the allocation of adequate land for self-constructed houses within the zoning arrangements of town plans, and its division into defined plots with clear title. The basic urban amenities—roads, water, sanitation—should be arranged as far as possible on a scale appropriate to the contribution that the inhabitants can make toward their cost and maintenance, but allowing scope for future improvements. A part is also played by the development of community facilities to encourage civic pride in local development. Technical assistance should be directed to helping in the supply and use of better materials and designs, information on which should be widely advertised. The practicability of making funds available to plot owners should be investigated to increase the incentives to build to improved standards.

The Government also has been an important supplier of housing for its employees in the past. The mission approves the expressed policy of the Government to play a more restricted role in this respect.[19] Since the construction of additional housing should be related to special needs of the particular ministry—i.e., requiring the presence of an officer on the spot or in remote areas—the program suggested by the mission in Chapter 3 contains no general allocation of funds for staff housing, but includes them under ministerial headings.

A change in government housing policy poses a problem for the allocation of existing quarters. The mission feels that in general civil servants occupying staff housing should be expected to pay an economic rent for their accommodation. To do otherwise would give a discriminatory benefit to the tenant, at the expense of the taxpayer. Considerations of

---

[19] Cf. Sessional Paper No. 77 of 1956/57, Nairobi, 1957; Sessional Paper No. 4 of 1959/60, Nairobi, 1960.

equity would suggest that conditions of civil service housing should be brought into line with private citizens as soon as practicable.

The mission has envisaged expenditures by the Government of £1.5 million for housing and ancillary services during the years 1963/64 to 1966/67. In line with the argument in this section we would suggest that in the future more of these funds should be devoted to assisting local authorities in the preparation of sites for private construction than in direct building of housing.

In the previous chapter, the mission has discussed contractor finance arrangements for constructing roads. We understand that a similar means of financing has been used for building some housing in Nairobi, and that the Kenya Government has guaranteed to meet the difference between the payments due to the contractors and the receipts of the Nairobi City Council from the housing scheme. The Government will need to find £1.2 million over the period 1965–70 for this purpose. Kenya has again been financing a project which is essentially long term in yielding revenue by short-term borrowing, and must now meet its obligations at a financially difficult time.

The Currency System

The East African Currency Board, originally constituted in 1919 to provide for and control the supply of currency to Kenya and Uganda, now covers also Tanganyika, Zanzibar and Aden. The Board, which originally operated from London, has been located in Nairobi since August 1960. Its members are a Chairman (at present Secretary General of EACSO), an independent central banking expert (at present an Adviser to the Bank of England) appointed in a personal capacity and the senior Treasury Official of each of the participating governments. The evolution of new constitutional relationships between the U.K. and the East African countries has led to the Board acquiring, in practice, a large measure of autonomy.

The Board has an obligation to issue and redeem its currency, the East African shilling, on demand by any person against the delivery of sterling in London at a fixed rate of exchange (EA Sh.20 = £1) subject to a commission charge which may not exceed ½ percent (the Board's current charges for buying and selling sterling are ⅛ percent and ⅜ percent respectively). To avoid unnecessary direct dealing with the public, it is empowered to fix a minimum limit of value (at present £5,000) for such transactions: in practice, applications for the issue and redemption of currency are made only by the commercial banks in the light of their day-to-day requirements. A cushion against short-term fluctuations in demand for sterling is provided by virtue of the fact that most commercial banks in East Africa are branches of London banks. These banks find it convenient to hold reserves of their branches at the head office, where they can be invested profitably at short term in the London market: thus the reserves of Kenya's banks are available in London to meet any short-term excess of sterling purchases from abroad over sales. Without such a cushion the Currency Board would be called on to meet the gap by selling sterling in exchange for local notes, thus reducing the volume of currency in circulation.

Public confidence in the Board's ability to meet demands for conversion into sterling rests primarily on the extent to which its currency liabilities are covered by external assets. The Board's holdings of sterling assets have been such as to permit the issue of currency against member

257

governments' securities (i.e., make a fiduciary issue) without loss of confidence in the currency.

The need to retain such confidence necessarily imposes a limit on the size of the fiduciary issue. The size cannot be precisely defined, however, and it is likely to change from time to time as developments in the country and in its external trading experience affect the willingness of people to retain the local currency.

In 1955, the East African Currency Board was authorized to issue up to £10 million of currency against the securities of the member governments. This figure was doubled in 1957, and in December 1961 the Board held £15.8 million of local securities. Kenya was allocated £5.8 million of this fiduciary issue and had taken up nearly £4 million in long-term securities and was using the remainder from time to time to take up or discount short-term bills.

Total assets of the Currency Board at June 30, 1961, amounted to over £67 million or about £8 million greater than the value of currency in circulation. Investments at ruling market prices amounted to £38 million, of which £30 million was in issues quoted in London. Most of these securities were U.K. Government issues. In addition, the Currency Board held £26 million in U.K. Treasury Bills, giving a total holding of sterling assets of some £56 million or 95 percent of total currency liabilities. Since interest is earned on its securities—and since the cost of a currency note is only a small fraction of its face value—the Currency Board is an earner of income. Part of the annual profit is distributed to member governments. In recent years, Kenya has received about £350,000 per annum and, as at June 30, 1961, the Board had an income distribution reserve of £1.25 million. The mission suggests that the Board should continue to maintain adequate capital reserves to provide resources for the eventual establishment of central banking facilities.

Most of the Board's sterling assets are short- and medium-term securities, redeemable in less than five years. It is, however, holding some securities which will not reach maturity until the second half of the 1970's and local purchases include long-dated issues of all of the territories. To preserve the liquidity of the currency, the Board should continue to concentrate its investments in short- and medium-term securities and, as a matter of policy it should not, as a general rule, acquire securities with a term longer than ten years. Liquidity of the Board's assets is of paramount importance, not only because of the need to maintain a strong currency in time of uncertainty about East Africa's political future, but also because of the possibility of governments considering increasing the fiduciary issue as a means of raising development capital.

The Board is now authorized to cover its liabilities with non-sterling assets to a maximum of £25 million. In addition to the maximum fiduciary issue of £20 million, the Board is empowered to support seasonal agricultural credit, by rediscounting bills and making short-term advances to the commercial banks, to a maximum of £5 million at any one time. Thus if the authorized fiduciary were fully taken up and crop financing were supported to the maximum extent, the Board could under existing arrangements have more than one-third of its liabilities covered by local assets.

Until World War II the sterling cover amounted to less than 50 percent and in the great depression the East African territories were given power to raise sterling loans to provide for the redemption of currency. During the last few years, however, there has been a loss of confidence in the future of the East African territories—with a concomitant withdrawal of funds, principally to London, and a great reduction in the sterling balances of the commercial banks. In the early years of independence we believe it to be of primary importance that the East African currency should continue to be backed by sufficient sterling assets. A major decline in the proportion of the Board's sterling assets could impair confidence in the stability of the currency and lead in the end to a much smaller volume of external funds for investment.

The Board's sterling assets, which are equal to about four months' imports for East Africa, at present form most of the foreign exchange reserves of the member countries. After independence, Kenya and the other members could gain access to additional resources to meet short-term fluctuations in external payments by joining the International Monetary Fund. The Currency Board has set aside about £4 million to meet initial subscriptions to the Fund and the World Bank. But principal reliance still would need to be placed on their own foreign exchange reserves.

One of the advantages of the Currency Board mechanism is that it provides a built-in, automatic means of adjusting external payments. Because most imported goods—and most external transactions—are paid for in sterling, a deficit of payments would normally be reflected in an excessive demand for sterling. The Currency Board would meet this demand by selling sterling assets, and currency in circulation would decline by a corresponding amount. This fall in circulation, in turn, would have a parallel effect on purchasing power and also on demand for imports. We assume that the countries will wish to retain this "self-balancing" currency system, with full sterling convertibility, until decisions are taken on political association in East Africa.[1]

In developed countries, central banks exert their influence on the

[1] The eventual establishment of central banking in East Africa, which would make possible a "managed" currency system, is the subject of an inquiry commissioned in 1962 by the Tanganyika Government.

total flow of credit and money in the economy in an attempt to promote growth over the long term and to stabilize income over the short term. The amount of credit the commercial banks may extend to the public through loans and investments is influenced by three means. Central banks normally hold, or control, the reserves of the commercial banks. Changes in reserve requirements, as prescribed by the central bank, in turn can exert a powerful control over the amount of assets a commercial bank can devote to lending. Secondly, by changing the basic rate of interest at which it supplies short-term funds to commercial banks, a central bank can make loans less or more costly to the public. Thirdly, central banks can influence the money market by buying or selling government securities.

There are dangers and limitations to the effective use of full-scale monetary management in circumstances such as those of East Africa. Credit control influences the disposition of resources; it does not create real resources. The supply of credit cannot be increased indiscriminately without generating pressures of demand to which in Kenyan conditions supply cannot quickly respond. Expanded purchasing power would then lead either to an increase in imports and a drain on reserves, or to price inflation and rising money costs in the domestic economy. Much of the income of the area is dependent on foreign trade: that is, on markets beyond the scope of domestic action.

In a more general sense, however, as the principal financial institution, state-owned yet apart from government, a central bank could be a source of expert advice to the Government on financial policy and, in its relations with the money market, the means of encouraging the development of local financial institutions and of guiding their operations to meet the broad economic interest of the country. A central bank could help in the raising of loan funds for government purposes both at home and abroad; a central bank of repute might be especially useful in interesting overseas institutions in lending to Kenya.

But the establishment of a central bank, whatever its functions, assumes the existence of a central political authority. We have already discussed several aspects of economic cooperation among the East African countries, particularly the customs union and the common services. Experience has shown, however, that it has not always been possible to resolve conflicting interests and approaches into an agreed general policy. The difficulty of evolving a single monetary policy in harmony with the individual economic objectives of separate governments would allow little scope for a central bank to function. Although the idea of an East African federation has been supported by all political groups, no decisions to implement it have as yet been taken.

Nevertheless, we hope that the Currency Board will assume a wider role in banking matters in East Africa. As a further step, we recommend extension of the activities of the independent central banking expert, referred to at the beginning of this chapter. He would be appointed as financial adviser to advise the three Ministers of Finance on currency and banking matters. He should, therefore, visit each of the capitals frequently. One of his tasks would be to prepare the way toward the eventual establishment of central banking facilities, and it might be an advantage if at some stage he became Chairman of the Currency Board.

The Currency Board has recently started to provide clearing-house facilities for the commercial banks, but the financial assistance which the Currency Board could provide to financial institutions in various ways would not be very great. The financial adviser, in consultation with the Ministers of Finance, might also, however, through regular contact with the local head offices of commercial banks, help to ensure that within the limits of their financial resources the practices of the commercial banks were aligned with current economic policies.

The Role of Commercial Banks

Banking facilities in Kenya are provided by commercial banks, building societies, hire purchase finance houses, some government organizations (e.g., the Land Bank) and by the Post Office Savings Bank. A small stock exchange has provided facilities for the marketing of long-term East African Government and company securities. Insurance companies have invested substantial sums in both government and private issues. A market for short-term government securities was also developed in the 1950's, particularly with the support of the commercial banks and the Currency Board. Short-term finance for government purchases of wheat, maize and sugar has also been provided by a special organization—the Cereals and Sugar Finance Corporation—which obtains its funds by issuing bills on the London and local markets and by accepting deposits from government and commercial organizations.

There are nine commercial banks operating in Kenya, five of them with head offices in Europe, three with head offices on the Indian subcontinent and one with its head office in Tanganyika. The majority of the banking business is handled by three banks with head offices in London and East African headquarters in Nairobi. These banks provide the usual range of facilities offered by commercial banks, including current, deposit, and savings accounts and short- and medium-term credit.

Bank deposits are the principal element in the money supply in East Africa, particularly in Kenya where demand deposits amount to more than half of the total for East Africa, including Zanzibar. Figures for the end of 1961 show demand deposits in Kenya amounting to £41 million and in East Africa as a whole to £77 million. In contrast, the volume of currency held by the East African public (excluding Aden) was unlikely to have exceeded £50 million—or £2 per capita—at that time. Thus it is not surprising that changes in deposits with commercial banks have been more important in relation to economic activity than fluctuations in the volume of currency (although seasonal variations in the demand for currency have been rather pronounced, there has been little movement from year to year).

In recent years there has been a substantial withdrawal of funds from East Africa, accompanied by a fall in bank deposits and a rise in borrowing from the banks. The changes since 1956 can be seen in Table 1, which lists the major items of the balance sheets of the commercial banks in Kenya. As the table shows, there has been a marked deterioration in balances held abroad and a consequent decline in the liquidity ratio of the commercial banks. The year 1960 was particularly critical for the banks: during that year balances held abroad deteriorated by £15 million to a net position of indebtedness (to head offices) of £6.6 million.

TABLE 1: Commercial Banks in Kenya

(£ million)

December 31	Balances due from		Total Liquid Assets Incl. Cash	Loans and Advances	Deposits		Liquidity Ratio[b]
	Banks Abroad[a]	Banks in E. Africa			Total	Demand	
1958	8.6	1.7	13.4	34.3	52.2	40.0	26
1959	8.4	3.2	13.9	37.5	56.9	44.0	24
1960	−6.6	6.4	2.8	42.2	50.2	40.3	6
1961	−1.0	6.7	8.7	39.0	52.5	41.2	17

[a] Information from one of the banks refers to its operations in the whole of East Africa.
[b] Liquidity ratio = total assets (balances due from other banks abroad and in East Africa and cash) expressed as a percentage of total deposits.

Much of the short-term finance provided by the commercial banks is for trading, and in 1960 the banks encountered a succession of unfavorable developments. There was a loss of confidence following the Lancaster House Constitutional Conference early in the year, but orders for imported goods took time to work themselves out. Commercial imports rose by more than £7 million and, even though exports rose by nearly £2 million, the net effect was a substantial deterioration of the balance of trade. No estimates of Kenya's balance of payments with the rest of the world are prepared, but there was probably a deterioration in current external transactions as well as an outflow of private capital.

The deterioration in Kenya's external position was met in the first place by the commercial banks' own reserves in London and the head offices provided sterling to give their East African branches time to make adjustments internally. The commercial banks raised interest rates and then took direct action to bring down advances: new advances were restricted to a minimum and others were called in. Opinion in Kenya is that this measure, rather than the increase in the price of credit, turned the tide in the banks' favor. The position of the banks showed a marked improvement by the end of 1961. Advances had been reduced by £3 million; deposits had risen by £2 million; indebtedness to banks abroad had fallen to £1 million; the liquidity ratio had risen from 6 percent to 16 percent.

Until recently the Government and the Currency Board appear to have played little part in influencing the quantity of the distribution of bank loans. Apart from the amount of agricultural credit which the Board may now advance, it also discounts Treasury bills for the commercial banks. But the supply of commercial bank credit in East Africa still depends primarily on the policies of the commercial banks in the light of their resources and the demands of the public. The banks themselves meet from time to time to concert action on major matters. Since the ratio of advances to deposits is still considered to be abnormally high, no great re-expansion of credit is to be expected until the banks' balances with their head offices become substantially more favorable.

Statistics showing the distribution of commercial bank credit are limited to broad categories. Out of a total of £39 million at the end of 1961, £4.7 million was provided for industry, £7.2 million for agriculture and £23.4 million for all other purposes. During 1960 the banks reduced advances made to industry and for other purposes substantially, but funds provided for agriculture rose by about 12 percent. Loans and advances made by the commercial banks are normally for a maximum of 12 months, but three- to five-year loans have been made to farmers and for commercial buildings. The banks finance farmers over the crop season,[2] though this form of credit is not as significant as in Uganda. Neverthe-

---

[2] Seasonal credit is also provided by the Government in the form of advance payments to farmers on account of guaranteed minimum returns and other payments on the purchase price of cereals (see Chapter 4).

less, at the end of September 1961, seasonal advances accounted for nearly 30 percent of the total agricultural credit provided by the commercial banks.

Most commercial bank credit has been extended to the Asian and European communities, owing to the limited extent to which the African people have entered the money economy. But it will become increasingly important for arrangements to be made for the provision of credit to African farmers and businessmen. During the last two years, the commercial banks have made advances to African farmers and to African cooperatives for the development of farms, including tree crops, rather than for seasonal purposes. The amount so far financed in this way is very small compared with loans and advances to European farmers.

Over the years, the commercial banks have helped to promote economic activity in East Africa; in particular, they supported European farmers for many years until farming became established. In order to avoid the possibility of conflict between policies which the commercial banks feel they should adopt and those which the economic situation of the country requires, there should be close collaboration between the banks and public authorities. We have referred to this matter earlier in connection with the appointment of a financial adviser.

Agricultural Credit

Loans to farmers in the scheduled areas for long-term development are made by statutory bodies: the Board of Agriculture, the Land Settlement Board and the Land and Agricultural Bank. The Board of Agriculture is concerned with land development and conservation loans and provides short-term finance to farmers growing crops subject to a minimum return guaranteed by the Government. The purpose of the Land Settlement and Development Board was to assist European farmers to settle and develop their holdings, and its activities are now declining with the change in settlement policy. The Land Bank provides mortgage funds. Its capital has been built up by successive loans from the Treasury to nearly £3 million and it has about £3.5 million out on mortgage. It pays interest on its loan funds but is not required to amortize them. Its annual resources for new loans have been about £0.5 million—£0.2 million from repayments and £0.3 million from new government loans. The Land Bank lends up to 60 percent of its valuation of the land. We are impressed by the efficiency with which the Land Bank has conducted its operations and the small administrative staff which it has found necessary for its purposes. It has only recently become empowered to make loans outside the scheduled areas, and its activities need to be reconsidered in relation to the likely pattern of development of an independent Kenya.

The African Land Development Board (ALDEV) has been the principal source of credit to African farmers. Funds are now available from the Land Development and Settlement Board for specialized purposes. Some credit is also supplied by the commercial banks, cooperative societies, traders, etc. Similarly, the activities of the commercial banks and government bodies in providing credit are reinforced for European farmers by cooperatives, the Kenya Farmers' Association, traders, etc. Long-term loans for agriculture have also been made by the CDC, the World Bank and the development corporations of the commercial banks.[3] Funds have been obtained by the Government to provide credit for specific agricultural projects, but present arrangements provide more funds for land purchase and layout than for farm development.

Progress with land consolidation and African farm settlement provides the scope and the need for the provision of more agricultural credit if a progressive expansion of African farm production is to be achieved. The commercial banks, however, find it difficult to transact credit business with many African farmers who have yet to understand this method of finance. Moreover, to administer the small amounts for which most smallholders would be creditworthy is costly. The commercial banks are also unlikely for some time to have the resources greatly to expand loans to agriculture.

Existing organizations for government agricultural credit, though numerous, are unlikely to provide the volume and quality of credit which is needed if African agriculture is to expand in the way we envisage. We also feel that there are an unnecessary number of government institutions providing farm credit. Their activities overlap. They are not suited to conditions likely to be found in the future as the administration of African and European agriculture becomes progressively integrated as we feel it must. The present statutory bodies also place a burden on agricultural extension staff who should be relieved of the task of supervising loans. Their role in farm planning and knowledge of farm production prospects make it important that they should continue to work closely with government agricultural credit organizations.

The time is propitious for a complete reorganization of arrangements for the provision of agricultural credit, and we recommend that an Agricultural Credit Corporation be set up in Kenya to fill the gaps left by commercial organizations and provide funds on terms which are suita-

[3] Barclays Overseas Development Corporation Ltd., National and Grindlays Finance and Development Corporation and Standard Bank Finance and Development Corporation Ltd.

ble for the average farmer. It would supply all types of agricultural credit where facilities are not sufficiently provided by commercial banks and other financial institutions outside government.

It would be expected to conduct as much of its business as practicable on a strictly commercial basis. However, to foster agricultural development under the circumstances of Kenya, it should provide some funds on easier terms than those applicable to loans from the commercial banks. In particular, African farms and cooperatives are, in some cases, likely to need special terms and security arrangements. Loans would often need to be made on the potential of a farm after development work had brought it to the stage where advantage would be gained from the injection of further capital (e.g., from the introduction of dairy stock after the establishment of pastures). But the extent of credit advanced on noncommercial terms to any borrower would be limited. At the same time, a standard of loan responsibility on the part of the farmer or the cooperative should be developed and insisted upon. There is scope in this regard in educational programs and in the training of cooperative managers.

It has been suggested that the Government should remain noncompetitive with other sources of credit. "Loans made . . . are to be made only to individual farmers and groups of farmers who cannot obtain needed financial assistance at reasonable rates and terms from private and cooperative credit sources."[4] Kenya is, however, unlikely to find the commercial banks with sufficient resources to meet the demand for agricultural credit except seasonal credit, which has in the past been supplied by them. The organization should, therefore, undertake a proportion of the truly commercial limited-risk business. This would also assist it to attract outside loan moneys or deposits to enlarge the total amount of credit available for all purposes.

This should not be taken to mean that private commercial organizations should not be welcomed into the agricultural field. So great is the need that there is room for all and every encouragement should be given to them. The situation in which only the most creditworthy few are able to get credit is not one to promote the rapid development of agriculture.

The Agricultural Credit Corporation should take over the agricultural credit responsibilities of all government bodies in this field with the possible exception, because their work is so specialized, of the Special Crops Development Authority and the Settlement Board which should establish close working relationships with it. The Corporation

[4] M. H. Williams, International Credit Administration Consultant, U.S.A., *Report to Kenya Government on Agricultural Credit in Kenya*.

would acquire the relevant assets and liabilities of existing organizations including the Land and Agricultural Bank. Medium- and long-term credit for agriculture would be provided on a strictly commercial basis with the pledging of titles as occurs at present in the case of Land Bank loans. The commercial banks would, however, continue their role in the provision of seasonal credit, now with assistance from the Currency Board, and would be encouraged to provide longer-term credit as in the past. Loans on less conventional terms are made at present by the Settlement Board and by ALDEV. We envisage that such operations would continue, supplemented perhaps by loans giving the lenders a lien on the produce, where the farmers are unable to pledge title. To manage this type of business, it is important that the Corporation should acquire staff to ensure that loans are made only to the good farmer and applied to the purpose agreed. Where circumstances are propitious, the Corporation might consider using cooperative societies as a channel for the supply of credit, but many cooperative societies in Kenya are insufficiently developed as yet to be the normal channel of operation for the Corporation.

The Corporation should provide for its current costs and the charges on its capital in its loan terms. The extent to which it would lend on noncommercial terms should be determined by the Government, and might be reflected in the conditions attached to funds supplied to the Corporation.

The greater provision of agricultural credit forms a major part in our proposed program for the expansion of African agriculture. It would call for the investment of substantial long-term monies, but for some time the limit to the development of African farms is likely to be set by the size of the technical staff available. We think that the planning of 5,000 additional small farms a year would be the maximum which could be achieved with the present technical staff but, in the next few years, both political developments and the priority given to high-density settlement in the scheduled areas may be expected to reduce the extension staff working in the nonscheduled areas. On average, a ten-acre mixed farm would require, over a period of years, at least £200 for buildings and watering facilities and £100 for foundation stock, equipment, fencing and planting materials for tree crops. Farm buildings and watering facilities require long-term finance; five-year loans are suitable for the acquisition of other assets.

In its development program, the mission is suggesting that £3.3 million be provided for loans for small farms and for other purposes (for cooperative societies and for development in the scheduled areas outside the settlement schemes) over the years 1963 to 1967, partly from the repayment of sums already advanced by government bodies. The expected return in expanded production is discussed in the chapter on agriculture. We would hope that outside institutions would regard this kind of investment as an appropriate way in which to assist the economic growth of the country. We would also hope that in view of their role in providing agricultural credit the commercial banks would progressively develop the practice of making funds available to the Corporation.

Post Office Savings Bank

The East African Posts and Telecommunications Administration operates a Post Office Savings Bank in each of the three territories. These savings banks and the commercial banks provide convenient means of deposit for small savings, and the African people are coming increasingly to deposit their savings, rather than to hold them as in the past, in the form of cash. At the end of 1961, the total of deposits in the Kenya Post Office Savings Bank was £6.3 million (the Tanganyika and Uganda Post Office Savings Banks held about £1.5 million each [see Statistical Appendix, Table 24]). It is impossible to assess deposits by race, but we understand that more than 50 percent of the total had been deposited by Europeans, about 40 percent by Asians, and perhaps 5 percent by Africans.

Each account has a possible maximum of £5,000; interest is tax-free and at present amounts to 2.5 percent per annum. Since 1957 the total of deposits has been falling because of the withdrawal of funds by the European and Asian communities. The decline was exceptionally rapid in 1960 when, as a result of a rise in withdrawals and a fall in new deposits, it fell from £8.5 million to £6.8 million. The Post Office Savings Bank has invested its resources principally in gilt-edged securities in London. To repay deposits, securities have been sold, some below their original purchase price. By the end of 1960, the Kenya Post Office Savings Bank had accumulated a deficiency in its reserve accounts of over £500,000, which is a contingent liability of the Government. The Bank has also an annual working loss of about £40,000, which is reimbursed by the Government. Balances are withdrawable either on demand or at short notice; the Bank has been a short-term borrower but a long-term lender.

The revival of confidence in the future of Kenya is, in the mission's view, the major factor required to correct the position of the Post Office Savings Bank. Some changes should, however, be made in investment policy to make it less vulnerable in the future to a large withdrawal of funds. The liquidity of the Post Office Savings Bank is in the last resort the responsibility of the Government. As deposits can be drawn out in the time it takes to undertake the necessary checking, we recommend that a considerable proportion of resources be held at short term, perhaps in Treasury Bills. The schedule of securities held by the Kenya Bank at the end of 1960 showed a holding of long-dated securities of East African Governments, as well as of British Government and local government stocks, and of Colonial and Commonwealth Government stocks. There were no holdings of short-term securities. The current market value of the investments was £1.5 million less than the purchase price. The decline in interest rates on the London market in 1962 will have relieved the situation somewhat since then. But if the bank, when it acquires additional resources, concentrates on short-term investments, it should in time be able to hold long-term securities to maturity or until opportunities for selling without loss occur. The suitability of the rate of interest paid on deposits should also be reviewed from time to time.

In September 1959 the Government introduced Kenya Savings Bonds with the aim of attracting the African small saver. They were issued in comparatively large units of £5 and in the event subscriptions have come mostly from Asians and Europeans. From the beginning of 1960 until the middle of 1962 receipts were small and more than half of the total originally subscribed (£132,000) was repaid. We were told that savings certificates are not issued by the Post Office Savings Bank because they are unpopular with the public. They have, however, the advantage of retaining money for a certain period of time and we should like the use of this means of attracting small savings to be reviewed.

We would hope that as the earnings of the African community increase, the Post Office Savings Bank would benefit. The number of African accounts rose remarkably in the past decade from 100,000 in 1951 to 301,000 in 1960, but, as has been said, the total amount deposited by Africans is relatively small. The Post Office Savings Bank should in time become the principal means of canalizing African small savings for use for government purposes.

Other Financial Institutions

Mortgage loans for residential and commercial buildings have been provided by five building societies in East Africa. Their resources have been obtained from shareholdings and loans and deposits, and the last three years have been difficult because over £2 million in deposit was withdrawn at short notice. As mortgages could not be called in—indeed, loans on mortgage were increasing rapidly—the building societies needed to obtain additional funds quickly. They were assisted by the Kenya Government and the commercial banks and then massively by the Colonial Development Corporation, which was empowered to make funds available as necessary up to a maximum of £4.6 million to maintain the societies in operation and to supervise their general management. An embargo was placed on new mortgage loans and the short-term aim is to restore financial stability of the undertakings. Table 2 summarizes the changes in the principal assets and liabilities of the building societies since 1958.

TABLE 2: Building Society Assets and Liabilities

(£ million)

Financial Years of Individual Societies Ending	Deposits Including Shares	Special Loans	Bank Over-Draft	Mortgages Outstanding	Invest-ments	Cash in Hand and in Commercial Banks
1958	7.6	—	—	6.9	.3	.9
1959	9.7	—	—	8.0	.5	1.8
1960	9.1	.7	.6	9.5	.5	1.1
1961	7.3	3.2	.7	11.8	.5	.04

Finance houses making loans for the hire purchase of plant and machinery and motor cars have met similar difficulties, and one hire purchase house closed down its operations in East Africa. Their problems, however, have been rather different from those of the building societies in that their investments were for much shorter periods of time. The finance houses also have not suffered from having resources withdrawn on demand. They borrow from the commercial banks at the minimum lending rate (currently 8 percent) and take deposits subject to three and six months' notice on which interest at the rates of 6 percent and 7 percent is paid. Part of their lending operations also have been supported by government guarantees, e.g., by the Kenya Government for its car loan scheme. Hire purchase finance for motor vehicles is also provided by some of the distributing organizations.

General insurance and life insurance are provided by some 130 firms operating in East Africa. Most of them are branches of large United Kingdom undertakings, and East African business forms only a small part of their activities. Others are Indian, South African and Australian firms, and a few are incorporated in East Africa.

No separate statistics are available for Kenya. Income from premiums paid in East Africa in 1960 amounted to £10.6 million. Claims amounted to £3.6 million. Income from premiums was distributed as follows:

Percent

Fire	14
Accident	5
Employers' Liability	3
Motor Vehicle	22
Marine	4
Life	52

The insurance houses have been investing a substantial proportion of their resources in East Africa or in East African securities in the London market. At the end of 1960 a total of more than £24 million had been invested in this way, of which nearly £12 million was held in East African Government and local government securities.

In the 1950's income from premiums for all types of insurance rose from £3 million in 1950 to £10.9 million in 1959. The rise was particularly great with respect to life insurance where premiums received jumped from £1.4 million to £6.3 million. The decline in confidence has had some effect on life insurance business where there has been a demand for policies payable in London and an increase in applications for surrender of existing policies. Income from life insurance premiums in 1960 declined by £800,000 or 13 percent. The companies themselves changed their investment policies and are making no more mortgage investments at present.

Concluding Remarks

In this chapter we describe the major facilities available for the provision of currency and credit in Kenya. We suggest that the operations of the East African Currency Board should be developed step by step toward the establishment of a central bank. We see no immediate need for a central bank and consider that decisions on future political cooperation in East Africa should come first. It is most important that confidence in the currency should be retained. In present circumstances this must depend on the maintenance of adequate external assets plus free convertibility into sterling.

Kenya has a well established pattern of banking and financial institutions, most of which are branches or subsidiaries of British and Asian houses. They were established primarily to serve the Asian and European communities and so far conduct only a minority of their business with the African people. As the African community enters the money economy, however, some adjustment to existing policies and facilities will be required. Changes are especially necessary for the provision of credit to African farmers. We recommend the establishment of an

Agricultural Credit Corporation to add to the facilities provided by the commercial banks and to integrate the activities of the various governmental undertakings operating in that field at the moment.

The effect of the decline in confidence of the expatriate communities in the last few years pervades any survey of financial institutions. It has left them in no position immediately to play a large part in encouraging the growth of the economy. The need of all of them is, in fact, to improve liquidity and to increase resources. A return of confidence, however, particularly if it brought repatriation of funds transferred from the country in the last two years, could markedly change the situation.

There are some fundamental factors which make financial institutions in East Africa especially vulnerable to changes in confidence. The extent of credit which is customarily being used is great, particularly in trading. Little capital has been required to open a trading business, business standards have been insufficiently high, credit in the past has perhaps been too freely available. As one person put it, "Kenya is a borrowing country." Thus when confidence wanes, finance houses find it difficult to obtain repayment of loans and the period of adjustment can be unduly prolonged.

In addition, the bulk of the African community may not easily understand the modern financial system operating in Kenya and appreciate the obligations attached to the provision of credit facilities. This problem, however, is one that experience and education will remedy. There is evidence of a widespread use of banks for the safe deposit of savings which will lead in time to a greater use of banking facilities.

The Post Office Savings Bank has met difficulties from the withdrawal of deposits, and we have suggested that as deposits start to rise again it should first of all improve the liquidity of its assets by investing in short-term securities.

In addition to the institutions that have been described, there are other organizations that have made long-term loans to assist in the development of production. Some of these are international and state organizations (e.g., the World Bank and the Colonial Development Corporation). Others are private development corporations affiliated with the largest commercial banks and private investment trusts. If Kenya is to command the volume of credit required from outside sources to stimulate economic growth, these organizations, as well as the undertakings described in this chapter which provide short- and medium-term credit, will look for the necessary reassurances in the conduct by the Government of the country's financial policy as well as at the intrinsic merits of the projects which they are examining.

CHAPTER 10 *PUBLIC FINANCE*

In Kenya there are three levels of government that provide services for the population, and for which support must be found: the East African Common Services Organization, the Kenya Government and the local authorities. The framework of the constitution agreed in London in April 1962 introduces a further level of government in the form of regional authorities. The detail of the functions and responsibilities of the central government and the regional authorities was discussed by the Secretary of State and the Kenya Government in July 1962. The outcome of these discussions was unknown to us at the time of writing and we have been able to give no consideration to the effect of the new constitution, particularly to any fiscal functions to be assumed by the regional authorities, in this report.

East African Common Services Organization

The East African Common Services Organization operates certain services on behalf of Kenya, Tanganyika and Uganda. It has no taxing power. Some of its services are approximately self-supporting out of their own revenues: the East African Railways and Harbours, the East African Airways Corporation and the East African Posts and Telecommunications Department. Until 1961, most of the finance for the other services was voted annually by the separate governments of East Africa; now the Organization's revenues are allocated out of specific tax receipts. Forty percent of the annual proceeds, within the three territories, of the income tax charged to companies on profits from manufacturing and finance and 6 percent of the annual revenue from customs and excise duties, are paid into the Distributable Pool Fund set up by agreement between the three territorial governments. One-half of the annual receipts of the pool, after deduction of the costs of the two revenue collecting departments, is used to meet the cost of the services which are not self-supporting; the other half is distributed equally among the governments of the three territories. This system, within limits, removes the financial dependence of many East African common services on amounts to be voted by the parliaments of the three territories. It is due to be reviewed before June 1963.

As the revenue from the taxes mentioned above is much greater in

Kenya than in the other two territories, distributions from the pool also have the effect of transferring part of these revenues collected in Kenya to the other territories.

The services of EACSO which are not self-supporting are also assisted by various grants from the United Kingdom Government. In recent years the revenues and expenditures of the non self-supporting services have risen from about £4 million in 1956/57 to estimates of more than £5 million in 1961/62.

Kenya Government

The (central) Kenya Government is, by the magnitude of its income and outlay, by far the most important of the three levels of government disposing of some £40 million a year or the equivalent of one-fifth of Gross Domestic Product at market prices. Table 1 presents data for recent years, divided into Colony (current) and Development categories. Development expenditure is not confined to capital items but includes, for example, expenditure on salaries of some staff whose work is of a developmental character. The form of provision of finance seems also

TABLE 1: Kenya Government Net Revenue and Expenditure (Excluding Appropriations in Aid, Interdepartmental Transfers)

(£ million)

	Revenue			Expenditure			
	Colony	Develop-ment	Total	Colony	Develop-ment	Total	Deficit
1956/57	28.5	4.2	32.7	29.8	7.8	37.6	−4.8
1957/58	30.1	5.5	35.6	30.6	5.9	36.5	−0.9
1958/59	31.1	6.0	37.1	30.9	7.9	38.8	−1.7
1959/60	30.5	7.4	37.9	30.4	8.0	38.4	−0.5
1960/61	27.9	8.8	36.7	33.5	7.3	40.8	−4.1

Note: Deficits on Development Account were financed by short-term borrowing until long-term finance was received. The deficit on Colony Account in 1960/61 was met from previous surpluses, and United Kingdom Overseas Aid Scheme and grant-in-aid assistance.
SOURCE: Economics and Statistics Division, Kenya Treasury.

to have been a factor affecting the classification. Thus items supported by Colonial Development and Welfare Funds appear in the Development Estimates. This matter is discussed in Chapter 3.

Colony (current) expenditures rose appreciably in 1960/61 (by 10 percent). The composition of expenditures has changed markedly from

1956/57 to 1960/61.[1] The first years included heavy expenditure on internal security during the emergency. More recently, most of the cost of Kenya's own military forces has been borne by the United Kingdom and since 1960 has not appeared in the estimates.

Table 2 shows the great increase in some principal items of *gross* expenditure in recent years. Expenditure on agriculture, under the Swynnerton Plan, and on African education has expanded greatly. In 1961/62 civil service salaries were raised in accordance with the terms of the Flemming award.

TABLE 2: Principal Items of Gross Expenditure

(£ million)

	1957/58			1960/61			1961/62 (Estimates)		
	Colony	Development	Total	Colony	Development	Total	Colony	Development	Total
Agriculture, forestry and fishing	3.1	1.4	4.5	4.8	2.0	6.8	4.7	4.4	9.1
Education	5.2	0.7	5.9	7.3	0.7	8.0	8.1	0.8	8.9
Health	2.5	0.3	2.7	3.1	0.3	3.4	3.0	0.2	3.2
Roads	1.4	0.6	2.0	1.7	1.1	2.8	1.8	1.1	2.9
Funds for local authorities	0.9	0.1	1.0	0.9	0.5	1.4	1.0	1.0	2.0
Law and order	5.9	0.3	6.2	7.7	0.8	8.5	7.1	0.5	7.6
Defense	1.6	0.2	1.8	0.3	0.1	0.4	0.4	—	0.4
Administration	3.0	0.1	3.1	4.1	0.4	4.5	4.2	0.3	4.5
Debt service (public debt)	2.5	—	2.5	3.4	—	3.4	4.3	—	4.3
Contribution to emergency fund	4.3	—	4.3	—	—	—	—	—	—
Others	8.1	2.3	10.5	9.4	1.8	11.1	8.7	1.1	9.8
Total	38.5	6.0	44.5	42.7	7.7	50.3	43.3	9.4	52.7

SOURCE: Economics and Statistics Division, Kenya Treasury.

Government expenditure in Kenya is high compared to that of the other East African states. In 1960/61 it amounted to £7.2 per head of population, which was nearly double that of Uganda, and two-and-a-half times that of Tanganyika. Kenya is also paying much more for government services than Tanganyika or Uganda. In the same year tax

[1] Some items have also been reclassified between Colony and Development Estimates during the period.

revenues in Kenya, which amounted to about 13 percent of Gross Domestic Product at market prices, were correspondingly higher per head of population than in Uganda and Tanganyika.

Taxation in Kenya faces the problems of the general low level of incomes (averaging £31 a person in 1960, measured at a Gross Domestic Product, factor cost, level), and the large proportion of income that is derived from subsistence (estimated at 22 percent in 1960). The first makes the collection of direct taxes expensive in personnel and in money; and the second limits the amounts of both direct and indirect taxes that can be raised. The distribution of incomes largely on a racial basis creates special problems in raising taxation. So far reliance has been placed on Asians and Europeans for the bulk of receipts. This accounts for the relatively high proportion of tax revenue, for a low income country, that is derived from direct taxation (see Table 3).

TABLE 3: Kenya Government Revenue from Principal Taxes (as a percentage of total tax revenue)

	1957/58	1958/59	1959/60	1960/61	1961/62[a]
Direct Taxes					
Income tax	40	39	35	34	32
Graduated personal tax	8	7	7	6	6
Estate duties	1	1	—	—	—
Total direct taxes	49	47	42	41	38
Indirect Taxes					
Customs duties	29	32	36	34	37
Excise duties	11	11	11	12	13
Other[b]	11	10	11	13	12
Total indirect taxes	51	53	58	59	62
Total of direct and indirect taxes	100	100	100	100	100

[a] Estimates.
[b] Stamp duties, entertainment tax, petrol tax, sugar tax, traffic licenses, trade licenses, other licenses.
SOURCE: Economics and Statistics Division, Kenya Treasury.

The principal direct taxes levied by the Kenya Government are personal and company income tax[2] which are collected by the East African Commissioner of Taxes, and the graduated personal tax which is collected by the Kenya Government. Revenue from income tax and the graduated personal tax amounted to £10.6 million and £1.8 million re-

[2] A corporations tax was introduced in the 1962 Budget.

spectively in 1960/61. Customs and excise duties which are collected by the East African Commissioner of Customs and Excise yielded £11.4 million and £3.9 million respectively in the same year. Table 3 shows the main direct and indirect taxes as percentages of the total of such taxes since 1957/58.

Recently, as is shown in Table 3, the proportion of total tax revenues provided from indirect taxes has risen from about one-half to nearly two-thirds and taxation changes introduced in the 1962 Budget reinforce this tendency for the relative importance of indirect taxes to rise. Increases in petrol and diesel duties and the higher levies on beer, spirits, cigarettes and tires and tubes are expected to raise customs and excise revenue by nearly 13 percent. The introduction of a new corporations tax of 10 percent on company incomes is an important move in the opposite direction, but in 1960, the last year for which information is available, clubs, trusts and companies only accounted for 46 percent of the total amount of income tax payable. The relative decline of direct taxes will also be accentuated by the removal of the lowest bracket of the graduated personal tax, the other important taxation measure in the 1962 Budget. Consequently the Revenue Estimates for 1962/63 assume an increase in receipts from direct taxes of only 3 percent. The tendency for income tax obligations to fall sharply in a time of business recession also decreases the yield of direct taxes. But the net effect in the near future is still blurred by the long time-lag between receipt of incomes to individuals and businesses and the date when the income tax is payable to the Government.

Since 1957, taxes have provided the Kenya Government with somewhat less than two-thirds of its annual revenue. The remainder has come from development revenues, principally loans and external grants, emergency receipts from the United Kingdom, payments on loans and income from property and the provision of goods and services. The decline in emergency receipts from 7 percent of total revenue in 1957/58 to nil in 1960/61 has been offset by an increase in development revenues from 13 percent to 20 percent of total revenue.

Until 1960, when political uncertainty began to have a major effect on economic activity, loans raised in Nairobi, where a market for East African securities had developed, were an important source of development revenues. In the three years 1957/58–1959/60 nearly £8 million or more than one-third of development revenue was obtained in this way. Kenya was also able to borrow on the London market, and in 1961 loans raised there still accounted for nearly one-half of the public debt (see Table 4). However, since 1959 external loan funds have been obtained almost entirely from governments and international bodies. The princi-

TABLE 4: Composition of Kenya Public Debt (as of June 30, 1961)

(£ million)

Loans raised in London Market	32.5	
United Kingdom Exchequer, Emergency and CDC loans	16.2	
Other United Kingdom loans	1.7	
IBRD loans	0.4	
Total external debt		50.8
Loans raised on East African Market	16.8	
Other East African loans	1.5	
Total loans raised in East Africa		18.3
Grand Total		69.2

Note: Sinking funds at current prices amounted to £4.8 million.
SOURCE: Economics and Statistics Division, Kenya Treasury.

pal source of loan finance has become Exchequer loans provided by the United Kingdom Government. The Commonwealth Development Corporation has been a frequent lender and two loans have recently been obtained from the IBRD for agricultural development. In the years 1957/58–1959/60, nearly two-thirds of total development revenue came from loans. Kenya's public debt, which does not include commitments under contractor finance arrangements, has been rising rapidly and at the middle of 1961 it amounted to £69.2 million which was approximately twice the 1954 figure.

Grants from Colonial Development and Welfare (CDW) funds and, to a lesser extent, from agencies of the United States Government have been the other major element in development finance. Over the years 1957/58–1959/60, CDW grants accounted for nearly one-fifth of receipts for development.

In the last few years, as local resources have declined, the Kenya Government has come to rely increasingly on grants and loans from the United Kingdom Government to finance its development expenditure. But the full extent of financial dependence on the United Kingdom Government in the last few years has been much greater. It includes the cost of Kenya's full-time military forces, overseas aid scheme contributions to the emoluments of civil servants, flood and famine relief and grants-in-aid to cover deficits in the recurrent budget. In 1960/61 and 1961/62 United Kingdom aid to Kenya, other than for development purposes, amounted to £6.2 million and £6.6 million respectively.

The Burden of Total Taxes by Income Levels

The general pattern of both direct and indirect taxes, as a percentage of income, appears to vary at different income levels. No firm assessment of the incidence of taxation by income levels is possible, but rough estimates for the year 1961/62 show a relatively light burden on the middle-income groups.

The lowest income group in the estimates, £75 a year, shows a proportion of taxation to income of 7.3 percent, but this is illusory since much of the direct tax in this bracket was not paid. Thereafter, the general pattern is that of a flat percentage burden of taxes through the middle and upper ranges of income, until the upper tail of income is reached— that is, income receivers from £150 to £600 pay about the same percentage of income in taxes, around 6.4 percent to 7.0 percent. Since real income from shambas is often omitted or allowed for only partially in the assessment of income taxes, the real burden of taxes is probably lower in the middle and upper-income levels, than at low-income levels. From £600 to £1,200 the percentage of total taxes to income rises from 7 percent to 12 percent. To the extent Europeans emigrate, there will be fewer people in these income levels. As agricultural development will bring more and more people into the middle-income levels, the low tax burden there is a problem which will require attention.

THE BUDGETARY PROBLEM

Since the early years of the Emergency, Kenya's current budget has been assisted by the United Kingdom Government. In the last half of the 1950's, as the Emergency waned and output rose, current budget help in the form of emergency grants and loans shrank and finally ceased after 1959/60.

But, since 1960, budget difficulties of another origin have resulted from dwindling business confidence and the rate of economic growth, sluggish for several years, came to a halt in 1961. Revenue figures have also been affected by the introduction of the Raisman formula in 1961/62, which diverted £1.2 million to the EACSO and by changes in taxation. The United Kingdom covered, by grant-in-aid, deficits in the recurrent budget of £2.8 million in 1960/61, and an estimated £3.4 million (of which £1.4 million went for famine and flood relief) in 1961/62. In addition, the United Kingdom is meeting the cost of Kenya's regular military forces (KAR), now £1.9 million a year, and payments for overseas civil servants in excess of local salaries, now £1.5 million net a year.

Net current expenditure was £33.5 million in 1960/61. Revised estimates show a total expenditure of £34.8 million in 1961/62, and budget estimates a total of £36.5 million in 1962/63. Thereafter, first forecasts for the next two years show that expenditure may rise steeply if major

TABLE 5: Current Budget Situation and Forecast

(£ million)

	1960/61 Actual	1961/62 Estimate	1962/63 Budget Estimate	1963/64 Forecast	1964/65 Forecast
Expenditure[a]	33.5	34.8	36.5	42.8	44.5
Revenue[b]	29.4	31.4	33.9	34.3	34.5
Surplus brought forward	1.3	—	—	—	—
Grant-in-aid, etc., assistance from U.K. Government	2.8	3.4	n.a.	n.a.	n.a.
Revenue plus U.K. aid	32.2	34.8	—	—	—
Remaining deficit	—	—	2.6[c]	8.5	10.0

[a] "Appropriation Account" data. Compensation of civil servants is excluded from the expenditures forecast for 1963/64 and 1964/65. These forecasts were made partly by the Kenya Treasury and partly by the mission.

[b] 1962/63 tax rates, real domestic income and prices are assumed in the forecast.

[c] £1.2 million covered by United Kingdom finance for expenditure on flood and famine relief.

changes in policies are not made and the budget deficit would rise to £10 million (see Table 5).

The main features of this present and prospective situation are that revenue at constant rates of taxation has in recent years ceased to expand, but prospective budget deficits are rising rapidly. Kenya has no reserves and has recently been depending on United Kingdom assistance for up to 10 percent of current outlays (excluding the KAR and the Overseas Aid Scheme).

In Table 5, we have included the following costs of independence: the KAR, independence celebrations, external representation, costs of passage of officers leaving, and £1.5 million a year for costs of some recurrent services at present included in development estimates and financed by Colonial Development and Welfare grants. The total of these accounts for £4.2 million in 1963/64 and 1964/65 of the increase shown in the table. But an independent Kenya may wish to incur other obligations, and we have made no provision for the portion of the cost of compensating expatriate civil servants to be borne by the Kenya Government.

The prospective deficit rises, as a percent of revenues, to 29 percent in 1964/65. The size of the prospective deficit results in part from assuming, on the receipts side, 1962/63 tax rates, and current real domestic product, and prices. A rise in production or prices will increase receipts, but to some degree boost outlay also. A drop in production or a considerable emigration of expatriate residents of Kenya will reduce income tax receipts and, to some extent, indirect taxes. The causes underlying this alarming trend are:

a. Expansion of services. Between 1961/62 and 1964/65, the forecast anticipates that the chief increases will total some £9.1 million and will comprise the following main items (additional amounts in £ million with percentage increases in parentheses):

Costs of independence, and reclassification from development estimates	2.3	
Defense outlay, including cost of the KAR	2.2	(35)
Education	2.7	(39)
Ministry of Works	0.9	(82)
Local government contributions	0.7	(47)
Health	0.3	(14)

Many of these increased services will bring in higher receipts to the Treasury eventually, but not much within the next few years. Generally, governments contemplating an increase in current expenditure of the extent forecast are assuming substantial economic growth and so naturally expanding revenues. Kenya's forecast of expansion in expenditure is partly the consequence of previous decisions to expand services and partly the result of political change. It is not attributable to the government services demanded and supported by an expanding economy.

b. Debt service charges. According to estimates made earlier in 1962, these charges will rise from £4.3 million in 1961/62 to an estimated £6.5 million in 1964/65, or by 51 percent. Less than half of the increase is self-servicing. The figures do not include payments to be made for contractor financed road projects which amount to £0.9 million in 1964/65 (see Chapters 3 and 7).

c. The dominant economic forces were spectacularly adverse in 1960–62, and no prompt and wide improvement is likely.

i. The Lancaster House Conference left, from the beginning of 1960 on, a cloud of economic uncertainty over the future of Kenya; and, in consequence, investment and enterprise in agriculture and business have fallen. Gross investment is now probably at the lowest level in eight years. A marked revival is unlikely until confidence is rebuilt after independence.

ii. Drought in 1960 and 1961, followed by unprecedented floods in late 1961, have depressed production and Treasury receipts and pushed up expenditure. A return to "average weather" in the future should have some favorable influence on production and the budget.

    iii. The terms of trade in the past several years have been poorer than at the beginning of the 1950's. An early major improvement seems unlikely.

d. Fiscal policy in recent years and in prospect. Successive Ministers of Finance have not had to finance all current outlays from local resources, since the United Kingdom has been willing to support a part. Economy campaigns have been waged by the Treasury, and outlays to be financed by an increased grant-in-aid have required specific approval in London; but the grants have in fact been received. We understand that Kenya has obtained an indication of continued grant-in-aid for 1962/63. A policy of depending on outside support will work only as long as that support continues.

Looking to the future, no major external financial help to the current budget, after independence, is in sight other than that from the United Kingdom under the Overseas Aid Scheme. If other outside support should appear, then the size of the budget problem would be reduced. But prospective deficits far exceed the amount of outside support that is likely.

In Chapter 3, the mission outlines its suggested development program for the years 1963/64–1966/67. Some of the projects we propose would lead to further expenditure on matters included in the recurrent budget. Thus, for example, the building of more schools will call for greater expenditure on teachers to staff them. In broad terms, we think that our proposals would add £0.6 million to the expenditure forecast above for 1963/64 and £0.9 million to that for 1964/65, bringing the prospective deficit in those years to £9.1 million and £10.9 million respectively.

Kenya Government outlays in the past have been influenced by the demands of the immigrant populations for government services. In the future, some decline in demand for services from these people may be offset, or more than offset, by rising demand for services from the African population. As we have seen, outlays for independence costs, defense, education, works and local government may rise substantially in the next few years. In addition, there will be substantial increases for public debt and pensions payments.

Production for the market by farms in the scheduled areas, and of other undertakings whose ownership is concentrated in the hands of Europeans and Asians, has made it possible to obtain relatively large receipts from both income taxes and indirect taxes. Since government revenue is in large measure derived from the Asians and Europeans, a fall in their numbers will cut receipts. Africans will in time take the place of immigrant people, in agriculture and in many business and government posts. But their incomes are likely generally to be lower at first, and because the individual income tax burdens lower incomes at lower percentage rates, income tax receipts will fall off disproportionately. Some businesses will close, because they were set up to supply European and Asian demand or because they have lost their entrepreneurs or chief skilled employees. Hence company income tax receipts will fall. If total production and income fall, indirect tax receipts will fall also.

MEASURES TO MEET THE BUDGETARY PROBLEM

A prompt and radical improvement in the budgetary situation, and continuing policies of financial prudence are essential to the progress of the economy. They are required to provide a foundation for successful development and to avoid a drastic and arbitrary cut in government services at a later date. They are among the necessary conditions for:

a. encouraging local Asians and Europeans to invest their savings in Kenya and to repatriate the large sums transferred abroad during the recent period of uncertainty;
b. encouraging these people to stay in Kenya and to contribute their critically needed skills to Kenya's growth;
c. attracting from foreign sources public and private funds for expanding production.

We think that the prospective budget deficit rising to more than £10 million is too large to be met by a single course of action. Economizing alone is unlikely to remove the gap. Increases in taxation to raise revenue by one-third can hardly be contemplated. Outside support of this magnitude for the current budget cannot be envisaged. A combined course of action to reduce expenditure, to raise taxation and to seek external assistance for the provision of specific services is required.

The level of services at present provided by the Kenya Government exceeds what can be supported at the increased 1962 rate of taxation, save possibly in unusual times when the economy is flourishing exuberantly, but further increases in expenditure are sought.

To continue and expand some recurrent services may be of greater potential benefit to the economy than to undertake some capital works. External finance for the latter may be available; but in the light of present policies for the provision of external aid, we doubt if any major and continuing support for recurrent services can be expected. To solve the budgetary problem, emphasis should therefore be placed on measures to raise revenue and to reduce expenditure. We would expect the greater contribution to be made by reducing expenditure.

Constitutional changes leading to independence in themselves provide the need for a reconsideration of government expenditure. Policies that were appropriate to colonial conditions, with the economy dominated by the expatriate communities and supported by the United Kingdom, may be unsuitable for an independent Kenya in which the African people will come progressively to assume a more important role in economic life. But the situation calls for a much larger reduction in expenditure than would be contemplated in easier times.

A thorough reappraisal of government outlays is needed, with the aim of cutting out low-priority items, including those not effectively furthering economic growth. Such a review should include the size of the civil service establishment, the grading of posts, levels of salaries, and the possible merging of services. A commission to review government expenditure was appointed in June 1962.

On March 30, 1962, we wrote a memorandum to the Minister of Finance about Kenya's budgetary problems. We recommended that a careful review of government expenditure should be undertaken forthwith and that the possibility of obtaining external support for individual current services should be explored. The effect of decisions to economize was regarded as unlikely to be immediate or sufficient to meet the situation. We therefore submitted our views on possible changes and increases in taxation.

In considering possible tax changes, we took into account the present economic situation and the changing nature of the economy. Many of the alterations to taxation that we proposed coincided with the views of the Minister of Finance and were introduced in his 1962 budget. He expected the increases that he made in taxation to yield £2.7 million gross in 1962/63. We estimated that the proposals we put forward would yield about £5.6 million gross in a full year, but did not recommend introducing all of them, or other tax measures immediately.

Part of the mission's tax suggestions mainly affected the incomes and undertakings of Europeans and Asians. Most of them placed significant burdens on all races. Inevitably, as expatriates become a less important part of the economy, the other 96 percent of the population must, even though their incomes are relatively low, increasingly shoulder the support of their government.

We have been concerned with the problems of administration and collection of taxes. Much progress has already been made in the substitution of local for expatriate staff in the assessment of income tax on personal incomes, but, during the next several years, the tax offices will still have the problem of training local people, integrating them into the staff and giving them increasing responsibility. The more rapidly the expatriate staff leaves and so needs to be replaced, the greater the problem will be.

Administrative difficulties have particularly conditioned some of our conclusions. We have examined the possibility of introducing a general, substantial sales or turnover tax, which has the advantage of spreading part of the burden of government widely over the population that enjoys the services of government. But we have concluded that for the next several years, difficulties of collecting such a tax, conjoined with the alternative, comparative ease of collecting customs levies and excises, make its introduction impracticable.

We are not able to forecast the rate of substitution of local for expatriate staff, or the effects of such changes on ability to administer the present tax laws. Quality and quantity of staff will be sufficiently serious problems so that during the next several years simplification of procedures should be a continuing aim of policy. The burden of administering company taxation has been recognized and measures to ease this burden are recommended below.

Direct Taxes on Individuals

We shall consider the prospects for increasing revenues from each of the major taxes in turn. Three direct taxes on individuals are now levied: the individual income tax, the graduated personal tax and the head tax.

The *head tax* is a flat rate local tax on Africans, levied by African District Councils in nonscheduled areas. According to the 1961 Estimates, it provides about £1.1 million—one-fifth of the local revenues of ADC's, or 3 percent of the total tax receipts of all Kenya government units. (In addition, a small head tax levy is imposed by location councils.) The typical charge now runs in the neighborhood of Sh.42 a year. This tax does not bear on central government revenues so we make no recommendations.

The *graduated personal tax* is levied by the Kenya Government on all races. It brought in £1.6 million in 1961/62—about 5 percent of the ordinary revenue of the central government, or a little less than 4 percent of the total tax receipts of all government units. It started at Sh.15 on incomes of under £120, and rose by steps to £10 on incomes of £400 and above.

In the 1962 Budget, the Minister of Finance abandoned the graduated personal tax on incomes below £120. Nonpayers had been sent to jail. Imprisonment was expensive, and so were repeated visits to those who eventually paid. The gross revenue (about £600,000) should not be entirely lost to government purposes, since local authorities will presumably increase their head tax rate.

We suggest that the receipts, and eventually the administration, of the graduated personal tax be turned over to local governments, to be offset by an approximately equal drop in grants to them from the central government. In the African District Councils, which this change would mainly affect, collection should be integrated with that of the head tax; with, initially, the central government collectors working along with local government collectors; and later, as it becomes feasible, relinquishing the collection altogether to the local people.

This change is intended to extend the financial responsibilities of local governments. It means that about £1.1 million of local resources would replace an equal amount of grants. Grants are now running much higher than £1.1 million, so that there is no question of over-financing the local units. Without this change the financing of rapidly rising local government expenditures will compel a still higher proportion of central government grants in local budgets. But these grants, now running in the neighborhood of 38 percent of local government gross outlays, should fall, not rise.

We suggest further that consideration be given to introducing into the brackets of the graduated personal tax one or two more levels above the present ceiling bracket of £400—say, at £600 and £800. The aim is to increase revenues by filling out a continuously progressive pattern of direct taxes, from the lowest level of the graduated personal tax to the highest bracket of the individual income tax.

The *individual income tax* is collected by the East African Income Tax Department from all races. Receipts in 1960/61 were about £5.4 million—a little more than one-sixth of the tax receipts of the central government. It starts at 10 percent (Sh. 2) and rises to 75 percent (Sh. 15) on chargeable incomes of over £9,000. The allowance (exemption) for single persons is £225, for married persons without children £700. There are further allowances for children, insurance and old age.

We have mentioned that estimates indicate that the burden of the main taxes is proportionately lighter on the middle-income groups than on others. Such a low rate in the middle ranges is inequitable, and will be an increasingly important fault of the tax structure as incomes from small farms rise, and as more Africans move into government work and other salaried occupations. The difficulty is to devise practicable taxes for this income range, since incomes in kind of farmers are hard to ascertain and are very difficult to tax even if their money equivalent is known. Our suggestions below (see section on customs and excise duties) meet the problem only partially and we think that a general consumption or turnover tax should in a few years be reconsidered, to decide whether it is then practicable to administer.

We have referred to difficulties in maintaining adequate staff to collect taxes. It was mentioned to us that if allowances under the individual income tax were raised further, more experienced staff would be available to assess company incomes. But the assessment of low personal incomes could, in the next several years, serve as useful training work for the junior staff. We recommend below simplifications in taxing business profits, where the chief administrative problems lie.

There is another persuasive reason why allowances should not be raised: a major goal, with respect to the over-all pattern of direct plus indirect taxes, is to move toward a continuously progressive structure, to include the increasing numbers of middle-income Africans. Raising allowances worsens the present tax burden pattern, permitting more of the middle-income groups to escape lightly. Some simplification in the collection of income tax might, however, be achieved by making the child allowance a fixed amount, irrespective of the age of the child. We understand that the number of children for whom allowances can be claimed is limited, and think this is desirable.

Our attention has been mainly directed toward the rates at which the individual income tax is levied. We have considered whether the highest rates should be lowered. We grant that they are high. But in view of the pressure on the budget, and of our judgment that it is not tax rates so much as political uncertainty and apprehension of possible confiscation that sap enterprise and investment, we suggest that they should be retained for the next few years.

To increase receipts and improve equity, a pay-as-you-earn (PAYE) system should be introduced, as soon as administratively and otherwise feasible. When a PAYE system is introduced, some portion of past tax liability is usually forgiven, to avoid doubling tax payments. The system is more equitable, in that people pay in accord with current incomes, and not as at present over a year later, when their current incomes may be greater or smaller than those on which they are assessed. A special problem of equity would arise if PAYE is introduced during a period when many taxpayers may be emigrating. The Government will not want to excuse these people from a portion of their tax obligations.

Taxes on Company Profits

Receipts from taxes on company profits, excluding contributions to the EACSO Distributable Pool Fund, mentioned at the beginning of this chapter, are estimated to have been £3.8 million in 1961/62. Company profits have been taxed at the rate of Sh.5.50 in the pound, or 27.5 percent. Dividend receivers have their share of their company's tax payments credited to their personal income tax liability. Closely held companies are subject to an additional penalty, tax of Sh.9.50 in the pound (47.5 percent) on excessive undistributed earnings, as defined in the statute. Usually they distribute enough of their earnings so that they escape the penalty tax.

We were told that the company profits tax had been kept low relative to that of many other countries of Africa in order to encourage investment. In our judgment, within a wide range of tax rates, potential investors will be influenced much less by the tax rate than by their estimates of probable gross profits, and by the prospects of political stability and the possibility of confiscation. Investors know that current rates of taxation need not last. Moderate, or even moderately high, taxes may discourage them less than conspicuously low taxes that will attract political attention and evoke antagonism to business, and that might later be raised to uncertain heights, and perhaps be joined by other measures against private business.

The company tax rate was also low compared with the rates on higher individual incomes, and we considered that a marked rise in company taxation was desirable. We therefore welcome the decision of the Minister of Finance to introduce a new corporations tax of Sh.2 in the pound, against which no credit will be allowed in the assessment of liability to individual income tax.

We also think that there would be merit in reducing, or in time eliminating completely, the credit given in individual income tax charges equal to the company taxes paid on dividends received by the individual. This change would move in the direction of encouraging investment. To the extent that stockholders in a public company are governed by their long-term interest, they would encourage their companies to withhold earnings from distribution in dividends, which would allow them to invest them instead. On capital gains they would, by the present rules, pay no taxes. The change should also reduce the incentive to create companies in order to save taxes. Consequently it should help to simplify the administration of company taxation, a critically important goal. It would also facilitate the calculation of effects of changes in company tax rates.

On the other hand, to drop suddenly the credit against individual income tax completely would be a hard blow to people with small incomes mostly derived from company dividends, and would drastically depress stock market quotations. We therefore recommend that, as a start, Sh.1.50 of the present company profits tax be no longer credited against individual income tax liabilities.

In 1961 the rate for insurance companies was Sh.5, and for companies mining specified minerals Sh.4. We suggest that the need for discriminatory rates of tax should be reviewed.

Depreciation Allowances

There is advantage in generous and easily understood depreciation allowances, since investment should thereby be encouraged. Action was taken by the Minister of Finance in the 1962 Budget to simplify and make more attractive the income tax relief given on capital expenditure. The capital depreciation schedule was very complicated to apply. We welcome the changes now introduced, including a 10 percent allowance in the year in which the expenditure is made on certain industrial plants and buildings. Over the life of these assets 110 percent of cost will be allowed for income tax purposes.

Tax Relief for Pioneer Industries

We do not support proposals to exempt the profits of new industries from taxation during their first years. Kenya needs existing enterprises to continue and to expand, as well as new ones to be established. Because of administrative difficulties, pioneer industry tax relief usually subsidizes only the latter. Furthermore, a common practice is to select certain new industries for support, and to reject others, and this introduces a further discriminatory aspect into the tax structure.

Pioneer industry tax-relief laws generally give the most subsidy to the firm that needs it least (the one that makes large profits quickly), and give little or no support to the struggling firm that needs it most. Its subsidy to the preferred new undertakings is at the expense of existing firms and other earners, who must be taxed more heavily because others are not taxed at all. A tax holiday law must, in any case, be carefully drawn to avoid conferring the tax advantage on already existing capital, withdrawn from an old enterprise and—perhaps by an indirect route—reinvested in a new enterprise.

We judge the evidence against the schemes is still persuasive, even if other countries give relief of this kind. Special tax concessions will, within a wide range, do much less to encourage investment and enterprise than a stable and continuing government policy of friendliness toward businesses carried on by whatever nationalities, so that businessmen can with reasonable confidence plan for the long-run future.

Customs and Excise Duties

The Budget raised customs and excise duties on the luxuries which are always popular with ministers of finance (beer, spirits and cigarettes), and on sugar, and on fuel and tires and tubes for road vehicles. Increases were made in duties on another group of luxuries: gramophones and records, perfumery, cosmetics and toilet preparations. These changes were expected to increase revenue by £1.8 million in 1962/63. (For a discussion of the present structure of customs and excise tariffs, see Chapter 5.)

Customs and excise duties are generally criticized on the grounds that they are regressive, bearing more heavily on low incomes than on high. No complete statistics are available but the general pattern of distribution of income is clear: most Africans earn less than £200; most Asians earn between £200 and £1,000 but some enter the highest groups; and Europeans mostly earn more than £500. These three broad racial groups also have their own distinctive consumption patterns which are due to custom as well as differences in income. Thus very few Africans will be directly affected by the increased duties on spirits, perfumes and petrol.

The effect of customs and excise duties on consumption is most important in the case of conventional necessities. Sugar is a commodity with a widespread demand (average consumption is about one pound per head per month). The 1962 increase in duties was expected to raise the price to the consumer by 3 cents per pound. The effect of this increase on urban families at the bottom of the income scale will be much greater than on those with higher incomes, but they no longer pay personal tax. Duties on essential commodities should continue to be handled with care with the consequences of changes on the poorest (and on minimum wages related to cost of living indices) in mind.

We have said earlier that in the future the African people must be expected to make a greater relative contribution to support government services. A general sales tax has been ruled out at this stage for administrative reasons, but in examining the possibility of taxing individual products we found it difficult to identify goods commonly purchased that are not subject to high rates of tax at present. Apart from basic items, such as maize, bread, meat, tea, sugar and perhaps milk, beer and mineral waters, the food consumption patterns of African workers do not yet seem to be settled. Textiles, consumption of which may be closely correlated with income and are subject to high protective duties (which at present yield large revenues), and bicycles, on which a minimum duty of Sh.36 is charged, are durable items for which demand is widespread.

Customs and excise duties are easily collected. We suggest that in addition to examining the possibility of raising duties on individual items, not excluding those subject to increases in the 1962 Budget, measures to increase revenue in the future might include a general rise—for example, 10 percent—in customs duties on all commodities taxed on importation except those that have been singled out for special treatment. This would be intended as a simple general tax on the whole community. It would, of course, also increase the protection given to local industries (see Chapter 5).

At present, rebates of both customs and consumption taxes on diesel fuel are granted to farmers and some other non-road users. The cost to the Treasury is about £500,000 a year. The effect is a lighter tax burden than would otherwise exist on all non-road users of internal combustion engines, which means, especially, large-scale farmers. Thereby, the use of tractors and other power equipment is made relatively more advantageous than it would otherwise be. We doubt whether in a country such as Kenya, with a large number of unskilled people who seek employment and who can gain agricultural skills in farming through employment on the larger farms, that the substitution of powered equipment for labor should be encouraged by tax measures. As African farmers work larger acreages and obtain powered equipment, these rebates will grow more difficult to administer: the productivity of the petroleum taxes could be undermined. We prefer assistance to farming that would be beneficial whether or not internal combustion engines are used. We suggest that the rebates should be withdrawn and in Chapter 4 recommend subsidies for the use of specified fertilizers.

Other Taxes

The tax changes affecting transport, made in the 1962 Budget, apply only to road transport. *Passenger journeys by rail and air* may also be taxed. Railway and domestic air services (other than charter flights) are provided by two undertakings, both responsible to the Common Services Organization. Passenger tickets issued by these undertakings for journeys in East Africa might be subject to an ad valorem tax of, say, 10 percent. Such a tax would be easy to collect. It would not be a large producer of revenue; but it would cause the traveler by air and rail as well as by road to make a contribution to the cost of government.

Trade License Charges have changed little since 1937. They are levied on sizes of stocks and vary from a minimum of Sh.45 a year to a maximum of Sh.375 on stocks of over £300 value. The present tax is inequitable in three respects:

a. The level of the tax has fallen behind the rise in the level of prices and the expansion in size of trading enterprises—a large proportion of stores pay in the highest bracket, and are undercharged relative to the small stores.
b. Turnover varies widely from one type of store to another: stores with slow turnover pay more compared to yearly sales than stores with fast turnover.
c. Services escape tax altogether.

We recommend that the whole system of charging for trade licenses be revised, with a view to instituting a more up-to-date and appropriate system of charges, based on the estimated value of annual sales classed in, say, five groups. Even the smallest store should pay some fixed charge.

Estate Duty was discontinued a few years ago with the aim of encouraging immigration and settlement in the country of people of property. As a measure to yield some revenue, and promote less inequality of income and wealth, we recommend that the estate duty be reimposed. The old pattern of rates, which ran from a minimum of 2 percent (above an exemption of £5,000) to a maximum of 25 percent on the largest estates, may be acceptable.

We have considered the possibility of introducing other taxes not currently used in Kenya. Among them are capital gains and wealth taxes. Market values in Kenya are now depressed for real and "confidence" causes so that we recommend against introduction of these taxes at present. We have also given some thought to taxes on production, but we are reluctant to propose measures that would burden and so discourage production. Our general aim, in a country that so urgently needs increased production, has been to tax mainly consumption in ways that will discourage production as little as possible.

One variety of tax on production, however, merits further consideration—*export taxes*—though we are reluctant to propose measures that would penalize production for export. Taxes on some of the principal exports could be easily administered and could become substantial revenue producers. They might also be used through a sliding scale of rates —low when world prices are at a low level, higher when world prices rise—to stabilize incomes in the export industries. If applied to produce of the scheduled areas, receipts from income tax paid by farmers would decline. African producers also pay cesses to their local authorities and, in the case of tea, to the Special Crops Development Authority. Consideration of export taxes would therefore need to include an assessment of payments made by producers at present in relation to the profitability of production. Measures to limit coffee production may be necessary as Kenya participates in a long-term international coffee agreement, and export taxes should be considered in conjunction with restrictions on planting (see Chapter 4).

Concluding Remarks

In East Africa, the problem of divergent tax rates among the three countries can be important. We have suggested changes in company taxation, in individual income taxes, and in customs and excise duties. All these taxes are administered by departments of the East African Common Services Organization. Uniform tax rates and procedures, with only moderate exceptions, have been set in all three countries.

Uniformity is especially important with respect to changes in customs and excise duties—where the preservation of the customs union is a special issue. Uniformity is also desirable in taxing incomes of companies and individuals, so that decisions on investment and enterprise are made on the solid basis of resource and other costs—which furthers economic efficiency and so is to the general advantage—rather than on the artificial basis of tax advantage or disadvantage. If one country—say, Kenya—should increase a tax rate considerably beyond the rates levied by the others, the consequence may be too much evasion and avoidance, and their concomitants, loss of revenue and deterioration of taxpayer morale.

We do not want to encourage an increasing divergence of tax levels and procedures. We expect that, in the future as in the past, the three Ministers of Finance will meet to discuss the tax proposals for their own territories. We hope that they will keep the critical tax rates and procedures reasonably in line.

The effect of the tax increases in the 1962 Budget, together with further measures of the kind we have suggested, is likely to be severe. Their total burden, financial and psychological, is likely to be greater than would be judged by summing up the effect of each of the proposals separately. The economic and fiscal effect of the recent changes should be tested and the state of the economy and the needs of the Treasury reassessed before proceeding further. The suggested tax changes which we outlined in our memorandum of March 1962 to the Minister of Finance were expected to increase the annual yield from taxation under current conditions by about £5.5 million. By adding this amount to existing revenues, to the net receipts of East African Common Services from taxation allocated from Kenya, and to local tax revenues, excluding services, we arrived at a figure of about 16 percent of the Gross Domestic Product at market prices in 1960. For the money economy only the proportion is about 21 percent. Taking into account the part played by government services, especially in the production of agricultural commodities, we would not consider proportions of this order of magnitude to be undesirably high.

We cannot overemphasize the great importance we attach to prompt and adequate measures to avoid the present budget deficit reaching alarming proportions. Increased tax revenues from all the proposals we have made will not alone solve the budgetary problem. In fact, we believe that a greater contribution needs to be made by the reduction of expenditure.

LOCAL GOVERNMENT

Local government in Kenya is well developed compared to that of many other countries at similar levels of average income. Relationship between the central government and local governments is the responsibility of the Minister of Local Government. In financial matters the Ministry is concerned with the provision of grant and loan assistance to local authorities. The Government also assists local authorities by recruiting officers experienced in local government treasury work and making them available as financial advisers to African District Councils. The development of African District Councils has been fostered by the local representatives of the central administration. Although many African District Councils are now elected, some senior officers may still be nominated by the central government and District Commissioners are often Council Chairmen. Many urban authorities have for long been largely autonomous. Financial stringency, however, has recently made them much more dependent on decisions of the central government.

Income and Expenditure of Local Authorities

The total gross expenditure of local authorities in 1960 is estimated as £11.3 million—£8.2 million revenue expenditure and £3.1 million capital expenditure. The outlays of local authorities have been rising much more rapidly than national income and central government expenditure, but still amount to only about one-quarter of total central government expenditures.[3] The rising trend reflects the development of local

---

[3] Ministry of Local Government, and Economics and Statistics Division, Kenya Treasury.

government authorities and their assumption of enlarged responsibilities. About nine-tenths of the expenditure is by municipalities and the African District Councils.

Revenues collected by local authorities are derived chiefly from poll taxes, land taxes, crop cesses and payments for services. Local government expenditure is heavily supported by grants and loans from the central government. The share of support of local government spending provided by Kenya Government transfers has been rising in recent years —from 34 percent in 1955 to 38 percent in 1960.

Central government grants for current expenditures by local authorities are made partly on the basis of contributing fixed proportions to local expenditure on specific services (see Chapter 8). They also take the form of grants in respect of other services which may be related to local taxes collected, and payments in lieu of rates on government property. Loans are provided by the Central Housing Board (see Chapter 8) and by the Local Government Loans Authority.

The most important of all the local government units, from the point of view of population and of finances, are the 33 *African District Councils,* one or more in each of six provinces. Their current budget incomes and outlays are now about half the total for all local government bodies; and their budgets have in recent years been growing the most rapidly of any major government unit. Their growth in finances, and in independence and responsibility, will (we understand at the time of this writing) be recognized in the near future by their being designated County Councils, and racial distinction among the local government bodies will be removed.

Estimates for 1961 envisaged a total expenditure on general fund (current) account of all ADC's of £5 million. Of this, 44 percent was to be spent on primary education, 14 percent on public health, 10 percent on roads and 8 percent devoted to location councils (there are a number of location councils in each district).

More than 40 percent of the revenue was expected from government grants, of which the two-thirds grant for education was the most important. There are also public health grants and grants related to the collection of local taxes. Forty percent of locally raised receipts were expected from the local poll tax and the remainder principally from cesses on produce and payments for services provided (dispensaries, housing rents, beer halls, markets, slaughter houses, etc.).

Capital expenditure was only expected to amount to £700,000 to be spent on water supplies, roads, dispensaries, markets and other buildings. Some £400,000 was expected to be provided by the central government in loans and grants, and the remainder by contributions by the ADC's from revenue and reserves.

The current budgets of the six *municipal authorities*—Nairobi, Mombasa, Eldoret, Nakuru, Kisumu and Kitale—have been growing nearly as rapidly as those of the ADC's. Nairobi spends about three-fifths of the total of all municipalities. About 25 percent of their revenues comes from rates on land (site value), and in 1957, the last year for which full information is available, most of the remainder was derived from a wide variety of services for which charges are made. Only 13 percent came from the central government and this was mostly in the form of payments in lieu of rates on central government property. Outlays, in turn, go back to these services: public health, public works, housing, markets and slaughter houses, etc.

On capital account, the municipalities spent £1.6 million in 1957. To the financing of this the central government contributed 23 percent by loans and 12 percent by grants. The remainder came from municipal revenue accounts (26 percent of the total), internal reserves and allocations of stock (25 percent) and from other loans and capital receipts (14 percent).

County and District Councils function in each of the seven counties and districts in the region of European rural settlement. Within each of the seven areas are one or more subordinate councils—urban district councils or rural district councils—numbering 26 in all. The seven Councils have recently had current budgets of only about £400,000, or 8 percent of the total budgets of the municipalities. Government grants provided three-quarters of their revenue in 1957, the remainder coming from rates and payments for services. Most of their expenditure was on roads, public health and their welfare services and administration. Capital expenditure amounted to less than £200,000, financed almost equally from central government and local resources.

The expenditure of *County District Councils*, which includes some urban councils, amounted to more than £200,000. Income arose mainly from trading service rates and government grants. Outlays were chiefly for public works, administration, sanitary services and trading services. Capital account income and outlay were each in the neighborhood of £.3 million. About 90 percent of income was from government loans and grants. Outlay was mainly for housing, sewerage, drainage and water supply.

Financial Assistance from the Kenya Government

Earlier in this section, we summarized various types of grants which are made to local authorities. Some of them vary directly with the expenditure of the local authority from its own resources on specified services. Others are related to the amount of revenue raised locally. In

addition the Ministry of Local Government provides other grants on no
set formula. We also mentioned that loan funds were supplied by the
Central Housing Board and the Local Government Loans Authority.

The Local Government Loans Authority is a statutory body,[4] consisting of government officials and nonofficial members with the Minister
for Local Government as Chairman. It is empowered to make loans to
local authorities for purposes for which they are authorized by law to
borrow and operates through a revolving fund—the Local Government
Loans Fund.

Its resources are obtained from an initial grant from the Government,
loans voted to it in the Development Appropriations, deposits by local
authorities, loan repayments and its annual surplus of income on revenue account. At the end of 1959 amounts provided from these sources
were as follows:

	£ million
Initial Grant	1.8
Loans from Development Funds	2.4
Deposits by Local Authorities	.7
Repayments	.5
Transfer from Revenue	.5
Total	5.9

Loans from the central government are mostly repayable over 30 years
at a rate of interest prescribed when the loan is taken up. Deposits by
local authorities are made for a maximum of one year. Interest is payable at various rates. To leave money on deposit with the Authority is a
convenient way for the local authorities to hold short-term cash surpluses.

The Authority has discretion to decide on loans, but in view of the
general shortage of capital, priority has been given to basic services. Up
to the end of 1959, £5.2 million had been advanced, of which £2.7 million was for sewerage, drainage, water supplies and roads and £1 million specifically for the Nairobi City Council. In the past Nairobi has
been able to borrow on its own account, both in London and Kenya,
but difficulties in borrowing on the market both in London and in East
Africa have brought Nairobi City Council works programs to the Authority.

Financial Relationships Between Central and Local Governments

Local governments have been increasing in importance, both abso-
lutely and relative to central government. Current outlays rose between

[4] Established under the Local Government Loans Ordinance (No. 9 of 1953).

1954 and 1960 at a rate averaging 17 percent a year; and capital outlays between 1954 and 1958 (the last year for which we have data) at 8 percent a year.[5] Arguments in favor of the relative expansion of local government, assuming it is based on local financial resources, are the sharper knowledge of local people of what they want, and their ability to weigh local benefits against local costs, and the better morale in taxing when tax receipts are obviously going to meet local needs. Africans have shown an especially strong desire to support education effectively.

A central government, however, can obtain experts and other civil servants of high quality more easily, and hence there is probably less efficiency and more financial irregularity in local governments. A central government has also greater financial capacity, especially in its ability to obtain revenues from income and customs and excise taxes. A central government would also be concerned with the need to effect some equalization of resources between richer and poorer districts in the state.

The development of local government in Kenya has followed no single pattern. In the nonscheduled areas it has been built up from the system of local administration established by the central colonial government. African District Councils have assumed responsibilities previously exercised by the local representatives of the central government, but the change is by no means complete or uniform. District Commissioners play a larger part in the work of some councils than in others. Experience in local government is limited. In the scheduled areas, local government institutions have been developed largely by the settler communities along lines familiar to them in the United Kingdom.

In Kenya levels of income in some areas are much higher than in others. These differences occur between town and country but also between areas well favored for agriculture and those suitable only for low-density cattle rearing. All these factors affect consideration of the transfer of responsibilities from the central government to local authorities.

We think that on balance the expansion of local government responsibilities and finances should continue. As local efficiency and resources make it possible, an increasing proportion of receipts should come from local revenues rather than from the central government. As a long-run pattern, local governments are now too much dependent on the central government; though for some years to come, the present financial relationship may be necessary.

Central technical advice and accounting assistance and checks should continue to be provided for local governments. The excellent Financial

---

[5] 1960 current outlay estimated from data provided to us by the Ministry of Local Government and Lands.

Adviser system should continue, and be expanded as desired by the ADC's or their successor government bodies. The Local Government Loans Authority adds a useful element of flexibility to the finances of local government projects. But a greater degree of equalization of resources seems to be required in the grant-and-loans system provided by central government. The long-term aim, we think, should be to provide a minimum level of education, health and transportation facilities for even the poorest districts.

To secure increasing revenues for local authorities is a difficult problem. We have already suggested that the graduated personal tax might, with supervision and assistance, be turned over to the local governments to administer and collect. This would add some £1 million gross to their receipts, and could increase efficiency of collection, as the local poll tax and the graduated personal tax would then always be collected as a unit, at the same time, and by the same people. The local governments should consider administering the below £120 impost, removed in the 1962 Budget, as a local tax.

Rising production of agricultural goods for local consumption implied in the mission recommendations for agriculture may be more of an advantage to local governments than to central government, as the real output is not so much subject to the financial uncertainties of world markets and price levels. Cesses now account for 6 percent of ADC receipts on current account, or £.3 million. Receipts from these levies should rise greatly during the next few years as production expands. Cesses on export products are a factor which could affect the consideration of proposals for export taxes.

For urban areas, the reform recommended above of the trade licenses tax, and its expansion toward heavier imposts on given turnover, could help against rising outlay claims. In these areas the shops themselves are larger, more readily subject to accounting checks, and closer together—and hence the administrative problem should be simpler. We have considered the trade licenses tax as a central government tax, but it seems suitable for adoption by local authorities as part of any policy adopted to decrease the financial dependence of local authorities on the central government. Municipalities are, however, likely to be confronted with a major problem. Much of their present income comes from rates on fixed property (predominantly European and Asian owned). Changes in the market value of this property[6] and of the increasing relative importance of property owned by the local authority (especially of housing) to privately owned land and buildings may

---

[6] Rates are actually assessed on the unimproved site value of the land.

require a major reconsideration of sources of revenue for urban local authorities.

Until more taxing powers are transferred to the local authorities they will continue to rely on central government grants to finance part of their current services and indefinitely on central government loans for capital works. We suggest that over the next four years 1963/64–1966/67, £1.5 million be allocated for loans to the Central Housing Board and £2 million for loans to the Local Government Loans Authority. Preoccupation with rising local demands should not, however, be allowed to divert the attention of local authorities as well as the central government from the equally desirable need for economy and increased efficiency.[7]

[7] As constitutional discussions were not completed, we have not been able to consider the role of regional authorities provided for in the framework of the Kenya Constitution. "Appendix II," *Report of the Kenya Constitutional Conference,* 1962, Cmd. 1700.

SUMMARY OF MAIN CONCLUSIONS AND RECOMMENDATIONS BY SECTORS

The following is essentially a list in compact form of most of our major recommendations and conclusions contained in Chapters 4 to 10. A fuller understanding of our proposals would of course require a reading of the complete text.

Basic Agricultural Policy

1. The country's rate of growth and improvement in the levels of living will continue to depend to a great extent on development in the agricultural sector. It must, therefore, be accorded the highest priority in the allocation of resources, both financial and technical, in the over-all program of development.

2. Within the agricultural development program, the most favorable economic results will be forthcoming from continued development along the lines set out under the Swynnerton Plan. Accordingly, we recommend a program devoted mainly to land consolidation, enclosure, and the development of cash production in the nonscheduled areas. Nevertheless, many circumstances have changed since the Plan was drawn up and some changes are now necessary. Details of changes proposed by the mission are dealt with more fully under the programs for development for particular crops and products. However, an important basic principle of the Swynnerton Plan might be restated in relation to future development: "whenever possible schemes should become self-supporting."

3. Prime consideration must be given to measures aimed at retaining Kenya's present professional and technical staff, at attracting more, and above all at greatly increasing the flow of personnel into and out of training institutions.

4. We see a real danger that a combination of pressure for land settlement in the scheduled areas and uncertainty about the future among non-African farmers will lead to a decline in production and export earnings in the years immediately ahead. This loss could seriously retard the progress of the country as a whole. We hope that the introduction of the high-density settlement scheme will help to restore confidence, but in any case there is an urgent need for measures specifically designed to

revive investment in the agricultural sector. The formulation of a firm attitude on the role of non-African farms, ranches and plantations in the new Kenya should be an early task of the Government.

5. Emphasis in the high-density scheme seems to be placed on the numbers to be settled rather than on the suitability of the size of the holding for efficient production. It is just as important for African farmers to be able to farm on a reasonable scale as it is for the highly mechanized commercial farmer.

Water for Agriculture

1. A comparatively high priority should be given to the development of irrigation settlement opportunities. The mission advises a cautious attitude toward the proposed second extension at Mwea-Tebere for the present; supports the proposal to establish a pilot irrigation project on the Kano Plain; and supports plans for a pre-investment technical and economic survey of the irrigation potentialities of the Lower Tana.

2. The mission recognizes the great importance of the development of reticulated water supplies. Revenues from users of new supplies in pastoral areas should be raised by charging water rates or grazing fees per head of stock.

Policies for Agricultural Production and Marketing

1. The most logical policy for Kenya to pursue would be to strengthen her trade drive in all accessible markets. We recommend the appointment of two commercially experienced market and trade development specialists to promote the export of meat and dairy products.

2. Secondly, we recommend a major emphasis in agricultural planning be placed on import saving where there are clear-cut advantages.

3. There now appears to be a stronger case than ever for very close East African collaboration in trade with as near an approach to a common trading policy as can be achieved, to include the extension of organized marketing arrangements for key commodities, the strengthening of measures to protect the important developing agricultural industries in all three countries against the impact of subsidized imports of competitive primary products. Agreed prices should not be so high as to protect inefficient production at the expense of consumers.

4. Some system of organized marketing is essential. Although modifications to the present arrangements may be necessary, Kenya should continue to exert control over the production and distribution of major foodstuffs.

5. The mission recommends the introduction of a comprehensive fertilizer policy for Kenya designed to encourage farmers—and in particular the smallholder—to use fertilizer in the right way; that there be a direct subsidy on the use of phosphate fertilizer, provided it is applied in accordance with recommendations of the Department of Agriculture; and that an Executive Committee be set up to ensure the fulfillment of the comprehensive policy.

6. The world supply situation for *coffee* calls for a reconsideration of the role of coffee in the future agricultural development of Kenya. As with other commodities, cooperation on an East African basis is desirable in regard to coffee. There is a strong demand for particular grades of Kenya's arabica coffee, and there may be scope for arrangements between the East African countries designed to ensure that exports limited under international agreement include as much high-grade coffee as possible.

7. There is scope for further expansion of the country's *tea* production and Kenya should make an effort to encourage new investment in tea plantations. The mission favors the SCDA plan which would increase new plantings of smallholders by 12,300 acres over the current plan.

8. There is also scope for the expansion of the *sisal* industry in East Africa. We endorse the proposal to set up a working party to investigate the prospects for the development of the industry among Africans. The functions of the SCDA might be expanded to cover this crop and to implement a plan of development. At the same time, the Government should endeavor to create the conditions for increased investment in the development of sisal estates.

9. The mission recommends that the Pyrethrum Board should continue its policy of controlling *pyrethrum* growing in accordance with estimated demand while intensifying research and its market development and promotion campaign.

10. There is potential for efficient production of *sugar* cane in Kenya. Having regard to the import saving possibility and the market outlook in East Africa, we feel Kenya should set early plans for an expansion of 50,000 tons. The mission recommends that plans be prepared for the expansion of the industry with production shared between factory-owned plantations and smallholdings.

11. Because of the surplus disposals situation and all its complications, we cannot recommend a policy of *maize* production in Kenya other than of self-sufficiency. The mission's view is that some form of organized marketing for maize is essential. The mission recommends that the principle of a guaranteed price to producers be retained, but the basis on which it has been established should be independently reviewed.

12. The guaranteed minimum return for *wheat* should be replaced by some form of crop insurance as soon as this is found practicable.

13. The Kenya Government should continue its policy of regulating the expansion of *rice* production in accordance with local demand. We recommend that the Kenya Government should continue to negotiate for a common policy in East Africa regarding rice, giving reasonable protection from external competition within the general framework of an import-saving policy.

14. Kenya should aim toward a far greater degree of self-sufficiency in *vegetable oil* production. Production of copra, cottonseed oil, and peanut oil can and should be expanded. The mission recommends that a small working party be set up to draw up plans for the development of castor oil. The mission considers that efforts to develop geranium oil in Kenya should be intensified.

15. The necessary finance to implement the comprehensive plan for development and diversification of the *dairy* industry submitted by the KCC should be sought.

16. The long-term outlook for *livestock* production is reasonably good. The expansion program of the KMC is justified and the mission suggests that the necessary financing should be sought.

Organization for Agricultural Development

1. There is a need for a reorganization of statutory and administrative arrangements for agricultural production and marketing.

2. Support prices should be related to farm costs at a level of desired efficiency taking into account prices or trends in international markets where transactions are on a strictly commercial basis. There is need for an independent technical body to analyze all the facts that need to be taken into consideration in price determination, including both farm costs and market trends.

3. On the marketing side, there seems to be a very real need for some streamlining of the Boards, their functions, and their consultative obligations. It would be advantageous for a single corporation to be responsible for the processing and marketing of all meats, both internally and for export. The mission feels there would be many advantages in having one strong, well-organized marketing corporation to handle both maize and wheat. In regard to the marketing and processing of horticultural and fruit products, a thorough investigation appears necessary.

4. In the development of cooperatives, the Government should make a continuing effort to encourage better management within the coopera-

tives, and encourage small organizations handling the same product to amalgamate into larger, more efficient unions.

5. We recommend that an agricultural census plan be adopted.

Agricultural Staff

1. The present rate of staffing in nonconsolidated areas needs to be increased. The wise course would be to retain a large number of expatriates of Agricultural Officer status for several years until adequately qualified Africans are available to replace them.

2. The location for postgraduate training should be decided by an experienced committee which would supervise overseas fellowships.

3. The permanent retention of both training colleges on a diploma basis may not be warranted. At an appropriate time, the diploma course at Siriba should be replaced by a two-year certificate course which would qualify students for appointment as Agricultural Instructor.

4. Additional buildings should be provided without delay at Embu to make possible the doubling of annual admissions to training courses for Agricultural Instructors.

5. Dormitories and classrooms should be provided at Farmers Training Centers, so that courses of instruction for Assistant Agricultural instructors may be initiated.

Research in Agriculture

1. A broader research program for pyrethrum is required to embrace plant breeding for high pyrethin content and the study of the biochemistry and physiology of the plant. The mission is of the opinion that Kenya should provide its own sugar cane breeding station. The mission endorses Kenya's policy of seeking technical assistance in legume research from overseas. More work is required to produce, by selection and plant breeding, grasses and clovers to suit conditions in each of the regions.

Animal Husbandry

1. There should be specialization of extension work in the livestock field using the established techniques of extension appropriately adapted to African conditions, and there should be some re-assignment of the field staff accordingly. The mission would suggest that veterinarians should be relieved of as many nonveterinary duties as possible.

2. Wherever practicable, training in animal husbandry and veterinary practices should be integrated with general agriculture.

3. All aspects of the *cattle* breed improvement program should be reviewed. Performance testing should have a place in the animal husbandry research and extension program, but for the present should be limited to the selection of sires for the artificial insemination stud. Pending the wider adoption of artificial insemination there is a good argument for increasing the number of "bull centers" which hold good quality sires for the use of surrounding farmers.

4. More portable abattoirs are needed. Additional rural collection centers will be required as the smallholder's dairy production increases.

Mining and Manufacturing

1. A positive policy toward the mineral sector would include the maintenance of the staff of the Mines Department at a high level of technical competence and the encouragement of genuine prospectors.

2. Expectations for the expansion of manufacturing industry depend mostly on private initiative, but more effective government assistance, including finance, is required. Generally, we do not think that an extension of the role of Government in production is required and we doubt whether it would be beneficial during the next few years.

3. The expansion of manufacturing depends partly on the establishment of a favorable climate for investment. Conditions likely to promote the maintenance and further development of production in private hands include a clear statement of policy toward private investment, reassurances about interference by the state with private undertakings, freedom to transfer earnings and repatriate original capital abroad.

4. Specific governmental assistance is also especially required to encourage the growth of industries which could be well located in East Africa to displace imports.

5. Customs drawbacks should be regarded as an extension of general customs tariff policy. The aim has been to rate raw materials duty-free in the tariff and not to load costs of production with import duties. In general this policy is appropriate for Kenya. Assistance should be selective in character. Protective duties should be imposed for a term of years, after which the need for them should be re-appraised. In the case of new industry, such protection should be contingent on agreement to establish production. It is important that the Triumvirate of the Common Services Organization for Commercial and Industrial Coordination should review industrial policy, including the criteria which the Tariff Protection Committee of officials uses in examining applications for protection.

6. We recommend that no further classes of product be subject to industrial licensing and that products subject to licensing be de-restricted as rapidly as commitments allow.

7. We suggest that the opportunity should be taken to reorganize the Industrial Development Corporation and to make more capital funds available to worthwhile industrial projects.

Tourism and Wildlife

1. While the development of the tourist industry in Kenya will require government support and encouragement, the greater part of the cost should be met through the investment of commercial funds.

2. There is a need for early measures for additional protection for wildlife if that important asset is to be of continuing value.

Power

1. Capacity is at present sufficient to meet the demand for electricity. When the need for additional power for the Nairobi area is foreseen, supplies should first be obtained from the Owen Falls station in Uganda. In consequence, the Seven Forks project in Kenya would not be justified in the next few years.

Roads

1. The Road Authority program should be reviewed to eliminate, curtail or postpone all but the most urgent items. Priority should be given to improvement of drainage works and bridges inadequate to carry the flow from heavy rains, followed by construction of roads required to assist in agricultural production and processing.

2. The mission recommends that contractor finance should not be resorted to for further road construction.

3. Funds for road maintenance should be decided annually by the Government rather than by allocating receipts from specific taxes.

Railways and Harbors

1. The mission believes that the tentative program of railway works prepared by EARH for the years 1963–67 is too large. A complete review of all new works, and of assumptions as to useful life of equipment and structures which the program plans to replace, is suggested. Any expansion of the system should reflect clear expectations of increased traffic above present capacity.

2. The replacement of expatriate administrative and technical staff needed for management and operation of transport and communications by local people should be gradual, and replacements in the more responsible positions should be made only through the appointment of capable and well-trained individuals.

3. At present, the railway rating structure is designed especially to stimulate agriculture by offering favorable rates. In turn, road haulage on parallel routes is restricted. We feel that this system may have little to recommend it in the long run. However, in the light of all the administrative and financial problems confronting Kenya, we do not suggest early changes.

4. Capital expenditure on harbors should be limited for the next few years to that required for safe operation, to complete projects already carried to a point where failure to complete would cause serious loss of funds already spent, or to prevent excessive delays in traffic under normal conditions.

Posts and Telecommunications

1. A new survey of demand should form the basis for revising programs for telephones, new post offices, etc.

Manpower

1. Programs of training should be accelerated. But there will nevertheless be a continuing need for expatriates, especially in specialized posts for the next few years.

2. There will inevitably be competition for the limited supply of trained manpower as localization progresses. The mission would regard it as undesirable for the Government to attempt to claim a disproportionately large share of the training facilities or of the output of students.

3. Since there will be a great financial need to simplify the administration, localization should be the occasion to reorganize the civil service with the objective of reducing the total complement below present establishment.

4. We think that under present conditions the economic arguments against temporary unemployment relief measures are serious ones. A more fruitful way of relieving unemployment could be brought about by promoting economic growth.

5. The Government should pursue a policy of raising statutory minimum wages toward a family standard as rapidly as conditions permit.

Education

1. The shortage of well educated and trained Africans needs to be overcome if the future development of the economy is not to be impaired. The mission believes that in the period immediately ahead special emphasis will have to be placed on the secondary level of education, and our suggested program particularly concentrates on establishing more secondary schools, increasing teaching staff and so enrolling more pupils.

2. The expansion of secondary education proposed by the mission will depend largely on an expansion in the numbers of expatriate teachers. The minimum task for Kenya will be to maintain a local supply of nongraduate teachers at least equal to their present ratio to secondary pupils.

3. In the mission's opinion, it would not make good economic sense to invest scarce resources in pursuing a primary school goal of "seven years of schooling for all" during a period when there is a critical need for a good share of these scarce resources at the post-primary level.

4. Recurrent costs of primary education should be shifted progressively to local school districts. Operating grants may, however, continue to be needed in some sparsely peopled districts.

5. Under Kenyan conditions, further general education is required beyond the primary level before embarking on specialized training. The mission therefore would not support proposals to establish a network of technical secondary schools. However, all secondary schools should have a strong science program.

6. The major part of vocational training at this level should be provided under the programs of the ministries, combined with those of private firms.

7. There is, however, a need for additional training at the technician level and we therefore support the proposals for an expansion of the Polytechnic.

8. Further expansion of university education should not have an exceptionally high priority at this time. As far as can reasonably be done, higher education should be put on a comparative cost basis: as a general principle, new courses of study would be started only when the cost per student would be less than the cost of sending students to overseas universities.

Health

1. There is an urgent need to meet particular deficiencies, but we do not believe a general expansion of hospital facilities can be undertaken.

2. To the extent that expansion does take place, it will depend on the availability of adequate staff. Expenditures to support programs for the training of staff to meet future personnel needs have thus been accorded priority.

3. The needs of extending both preventive and curative medicine into the rural areas are best met by assisting local authorities in the construction of health centers.

Housing

1. A country-wide housing survey should be undertaken to assess the relative needs in different areas, and to provide a basis for implementing government housing policy, in particular in relation to rent structures and the type of housing required.

2. The Central Housing Board has an important role as the principal instrument of the central government for promoting the construction of houses by local authorities. Accordingly, financial provision should be made for the Board to continue its activities, although the scale of known housing needs is so large that the size of financial allocations will have to be limited so as not to divert scarce public resources from other fields of investment with a higher priority.

3. Construction of houses by "self-help" methods should be encouraged. A greater part of the investment required for the buildings themselves would be found by their occupants. Substantial government action will be required to create conditions to encourage private construction.

4. The mission doubts the wisdom of attempting to meet general low-income housing needs by means of subsidies. There may still be a role, however, for the selective use of subsidies where important external economies are to be gained.

5. The mission approves the expressed policy of the Government to play a more restricted role as a supplier of housing for its employees.

Money and Banking

1. While we see no immediate need for a central bank and consider that decisions on future political cooperation in East Africa should come first, the operations of the East African Currency Board could nevertheless be developed step by step toward the eventual establishment of a central bank.

2. We recommend the appointment of a financial adviser to advise the three Ministers of Finance on currency and banking matters.

3. We recommend the establishment of an Agricultural Credit Corpora-

tion to add to the facilities provided by the commercial banks and to integrate the activities of the various governmental undertakings operating in that field at the moment.

Public Finance

1. A prompt and radical improvement in the budgetary situation and continuing policies of financial prudence are essential to the growth of the economy. A combined course of action to reduce expenditure, to raise taxation and to seek external assistance for the provision of specific services is required.

2. A thorough re-appraisal of government outlays is needed, with the aim of cutting out non-essential items and those not supporting economic growth. All proposed additions to expenditure should be examined according to need and priority.

3. We examined the possibility of introducing a general, turnover tax, but concluded that for the next several years, difficulties of collecting such a tax, make its introduction impracticable.

4. A major goal, with respect to the over-all pattern of direct plus indirect taxes is to move toward a continuously progressive structure. We suggest that consideration be given to introducing into the brackets of the graduated personal tax one or two more levels above the present ceiling bracket of £400.

5. Allowances under the individual income tax should not be raised. To increase receipts and improve equity, a pay-as-you-earn system should be introduced as soon as administratively and otherwise feasible.

6. There would be merit in reducing, or in time eliminating completely, the credit given in individual income tax charges equal to the company taxes paid on dividends received by the individual.

7. We do not support proposals to exempt the profits of new industries from taxation during their first years.

8. We suggest that in addition to examining the possibility of raising customs and excise duties on individual items, not excluding those subject to increases in the 1962 Budget, measures to increase revenue in the future might include a general rise in customs duties.

9. The whole system of charging for trade licenses should be reviewed and a more up-to-date and appropriate system of charges, based on the estimated values of annual sales, instituted.

10. Export taxes merit further consideration though we are reluctant to propose measures that would penalize production for export.

11. The expansion of local government responsibilities and finances should continue. As local efficiency and resources make it possible, an

increasing proportion of receipts should come from local revenues rather than from the central government. A greater degree of equalization of resources seems to be required in the grant-and-loans system pro vided by the central government.

ANNEXES

ANNEX A *PLANNING ARRANGEMENTS*

Development programing, one of the principal tasks of government, is at present the responsibility of the Minister of Economic Planning who is Chairman of the Development Committee which consists largely of ministers with economic portfolios. This committee should be an effective body for the collective consideration of development planning matters, prior to decision by the full Cabinet. The appropriate composition for such a committee would depend on the distribution of portfolios. We suggest, however, that it should consist of all those ministers who have a responsibility for major development expenditure.

We do not support proposals for the establishment of a planning commission to include members drawn from outside government. The administration itself should be more adequately placed to undertake the work of preparing public development programs than private individuals in Kenya, no matter how highly experienced they may be in their own particular spheres of activity. Moreover, development programs affect many aspects of economic and financial policy and it is doubtful whether private individuals could be given access to all the information required for the purpose. They are also unlikely to be able to devote sufficient time to the work without affecting their normal activities.

Having concluded that development planning is a function to be undertaken by government, with individuals and organizations in the private sector being consulted where advantageous, we considered the organization of this work. In some countries development planning is one of the Prime Minister's functions, in some it is a responsibility of the Minister of Finance, and in others it is the principal task of a Minister of Development Planning or Economic Affairs.

Generally, we think that development planning should be the responsibility of a minister with a central or coordinating role in the Government. Work in development planning requires the full cooperation of other ministers, and in formulating priorities and preparing programs which are within the country's capacity, choices will need to be made which will not always reflect the wishes of all ministers.

As development planning is generally one of the principal tasks of government, it is frequently a responsibility of the Prime Minister himself. The cabinet office has responsibilities for ensuring coordination generally within the Government, and under the cabinet system of government the position of standing of the Prime Minister among his colleagues gives the planning organization the necessary authority. The Minister of Finance is also in a central position in the government and development planning can be regarded as a natural extension of his role in fiscal matters. In some governments the Minister of Finance has wide responsibilities in the field of general economic policy and, in these circumstances, there are obvious advantages if he is also responsible for development planning. It is most important for the planning staff to be fully aware of financial difficulties and possibilities. This is most easily achieved if planning is included in the Ministry of Finance. If planning is divorced from the Ministry of Finance, programs may be prepared which, though suitable in other ways, do not give sufficient attention to fiscal prospects to be capable of adoption. On the other hand, the Ministry of Finance will be closely concerned with the day-to-day problems of financial administration. The work of preparing development programs for long-run economic growth in low-income countries involves different considerations from the preparation of the annual budget. Wherever the planning organization is located, however, it is most important that it should maintain constant and close contact with departments of the Ministry of Finance responsible for revenue, budgetary expenditure and the public debt.

In the past the Minister of Finance in Kenya has also been the Minister of Development, and development planning at the official level has been undertaken by the Development and Planning Division in the Treasury. The official in charge has also been responsible for external financial and technical assistance matters and public borrowing. While it may be satisfactory to combine these functions, the planning work undertaken by the Division has been confined almost entirely to financial budgeting. In July 1961, the Economic and Statistics Division was established in the Treasury, with responsibilities which were previously held by the East African Statistical Department. The Director of this Division should participate in the work of planning, particularly in relation to broad matters such as determination of the size and direction of each program and the likely growth of the private sector and its call for public services. The mission is also convinced that the Development and Planning Division is understaffed at present and that it should be expanded by the addition of a small number of officers able to contribute effectively both to this work itself and to the subject of external assistance, which the mission feels will need more attention if adequate programs in the public sector are to be possible. Arrangements for the preparation of programs within each ministry and for coordination with the central organization should also be reviewed. In this connection we would draw attention to our discussion in Chapter 4 of the role of the Division of Economics and Statistics of the Ministry of Agriculture.

We think that there should also be more consultation and coordination in planning between the Kenya Government and the units of the East African Common Services Organization. The present constitutional arrangements expressed in the Common Services Organization in themselves represent a substantial degree of cooperation in economic matters. Although ministers of the three territories will be jointly considering the development of the Common Services, there is at present no formal procedure for them to integrate their role in these matters with their individual responsibilities for those services which are solely a territorial responsibility. The mission feels that if the common services and territorial services are to be expanded where desirable to meet the needs of the territories in the light of their limited resources, more comprehensive arrangements for coordination of planning are required. If political conditions were propitious this might in time lead to coordination in development planning on an East African basis.

The mission has studied the programing arrangements of the East African Railways and Harbours, for example, and feels that the appropriate agencies of the territorial governments have an important role to play in assessing the future growth of total and specific traffics which form the basis of any capital program for a railway and harbors undertaking. It is suggested that the programs of the transport and communications services should be considered in relation to the traffic demands of the territories and the financial requirements of these services assessed in relation to those of the territorial governments, so that plans which are likely to be financially supportable emerge. The mission recommends that railway and port planning committees at the official level be set up, consisting of appropriate officers of the EARH and of relevant ministries of Uganda and Kenya, on the one hand, and of Tanganyika, on the other. These committees would enable a joint approach to development problems to be made at the official level. Such a pattern of two committees conforms to the geographical routing of the major services of the East African Railways and Harbours, but the mission would favor the establishment of a single committee embracing the whole of the system if that were found practicable in East Africa.

The present differences between the financial years of the governments and some of the common services cause complications for planning. We would hope that uniformity in this respect could be soon achieved.

In the more highly developed countries, where lands have been accurately surveyed and relatively systematically laid out, the problems of census taking can readily be overcome. Total enumeration is usually practicable, based on questionnaires and with no more than a single visit by the enumerator. In Kenya, the problem of census taking is not too formidable in the consolidated enclosed and planned African farming areas. However, in the farming and pastoral areas where there is no enclosure, the task is a truly formidable one, necessitating the development of suitable techniques of acreage measurement, of crop sampling, harvesting and yield assessment. The enumerator has to have the necessary training to perform the actual measurements himself. In most cases, more than one visit to the farm will be necessary during the year. As there are some 950,000 peasant farms in the nonscheduled areas, total enumeration is quite impracticable and effective sampling techniques need to be applied which will enable the necessary degree of accuracy to be obtained with the minimum number of farms in the sample. Otherwise, the costs and staffing requirements would be too great.

Agriculture in Kenya has been divided broadly into four divisions:

a. farms in the scheduled areas;
b. agriculture carried on by resident laborers in the forest and on farms in the scheduled areas;
c. peasant farms in the nonscheduled areas;
d. the pastoral zone (nonscheduled areas).

In the scheduled areas a full annual census of the 3,000 or so holdings has been undertaken through a postal inquiry for eight years, covering land utilization, crop acreages, livestock numbers, livestock production, labor employed, annual capital expenditures, and the like.

The resident laborers' agriculture in forests was covered as part of the 1960 sample survey. While these farmers, approximately 7,500 in number, might not appear numerically important, nevertheless they are important in respect of certain products, such as potatoes and vegetables.

In regard to the peasant farms in the nonscheduled areas, the only published statistics before 1961 covered merely the amount of the major cash crops that passed through central marketing organizations and statistics compiled from district agricultural records maintained in district offices. In 1960/61 a limited, partial agricultural census was attempted as

318

part of the 1960 World Census of Agriculture. This was conducted in a number of the peasant agricultural areas to assess land utilization, crop acreages, food crop production and livestock numbers. The areas contained covered some 735,000 farms. However, only 70 percent of the sample farms were measured on a holding basis, the remainder being roughly estimated by the use of transect or line survey methods which did not permit information on the structure of the individual holding to be obtained.

In the pastoral areas, the only statistics available are stated to be rough guesses of livestock numbers made by veterinary officers.

The original Kenya Unit of the East African Statistical Department, which became in 1961 the Economics and Statistics Division of the Kenya Treasury, has so far performed an excellent task within the limits of staff and finance available.

The Economics and Statistics Division is well aware of the inadequacy of present statistics for planning purposes. It is recognized, too, that the accuracy of the assessment of the Gross Domestic Product can be, and needs to be, improved. This would follow from a more precise recording of production within the nonmonetary sector which would result from a complete agricultural census. However, there is at present no provision for a complete agricultural census, although a limited scheme has been proposed for a small number of field enumerators to estimate the annual production of food crops covered by the 1960/61 survey, using crop harvesting techniques within randomly selected sample plots.

A Plan for Improvement

The requirements for the completion of a comprehensive, accurate agricultural census have been investigated. The idea would be for the recruitment and training of a large enough team to carry out a complete, comprehensive census in the one year. The costs of doing this would, in our view, be too high. A more practical scheme has now been worked out by the Economics and Statistics Division, to recruit a cadre of field enumerators, and to provide an intensive training course in census taking, with particular reference to peasant agriculture. This would include teaching the principles and hazards of sampling, and detailed training in the field techniques to be used. The team would be large enough to enumerate annually the number of farms required for, say, a 2 percent sample inside an area containing approximately one-fifth of the total number of farms. A five-year rotation of work would be maintained and, thus, changes could be assessed every five years on an area basis.

This team might well complete the areas not yet adequately covered in the 1960/61 Census and, in addition to the annual detailed census of around 4,000 farms, it would attempt annual assessments of production by sample cutting or harvesting of crops throughout the area. This data would, however, be useful only insofar as the assumption of no annual change in acreage is valid, a matter which would eventually need to be tested.

The existing staff of the Economics and Statistics Division is quite capable of undertaking the detailed planning and programing of the work and the analysis of the data.

The task requires measurements, especially in African farming areas, that involve a considerable degree of technical knowledge and skill. If the whole agricultural technical field force could be drawn into the operation for a complete production year or season, it might be possible to design a complete census operation which would be sufficiently accurate for national planning purposes. Such a diversion is not considered practicable.

It may be that, within a decade, with the experience and knowledge gained, and perhaps with budget difficulties not so acute, it may be possible to design a not too costly comprehensive census, based on a sufficiently narrow period of time, to enable nation-wide and accurate estimates of change to be made.

The scheme adopted should include the new settlement farms. It does not seem necessary to continue a complete enumeration annually of the farms presently established in the scheduled areas. This could be placed immediately on a three-year basis, and at the end of six years might well be put on the same basis as the more numerous African farms, i.e., a six-yearly one with annual sampling for crop yields and livestock production.

Kenya at present has the highly competent and locally knowledgeable statisticians to efficiently design a census-taking program, to train the necessary field staff, and to take full advantage of any advances in techniques that may have been achieved in this field by international specialists.

Name of Board	Date of Establishment	Legislative Authority	Statutory Powers and Duties	Other Functions	Composition
A. Development Boards					
A.1. Board of Agriculture (scheduled areas)	1955	Agriculture Ordinance, 1955 (No. 8 of 1955) Agriculture (Amendment) Ordinance, 1960 (No. 47 of 1960)	(a) To exercise the powers conferred upon it and to perform the duties imposed under the Agriculture Ordinance or any other written law; (b) To advise the Minister on all matters relating to its powers or performance of duties; (c) To carry out any other functions as may be allotted to it by the Minister; (d) Generally, to further the objects of the Agriculture Ordinance within the scheduled areas.	(a) To approve land development and conservation schemes; (b) To approve loans in respect of land conservation and development; (c) To administer G.M.R.	(a) Chairman appointed by the Minister; (b) The D.A. and the D.V.S.; (c) Respective Chairmen of Agricultural Committees; (d) One person appointed by the Board (non-scheduled areas); (e) Asst. Director of Agriculture (R.V.P.); (f) Two persons appointed by the Minister; (g) Subject to the provisions of Section 38 (2) of the Ordinance, associated members nominated under that Section.
A.2. Board of Agriculture (nonscheduled areas)	1955 (The Board evolved from the Land Settlement Board originally established in 1945)	Agriculture Ordinance, 1955 (No. 8 of 1955) Agriculture (Amendment) Ordinance, 1960 (No. 47 of 1960)	To advise the Minister regarding: (a) plans, recommendations and advice submitted by the Provincial Agricultural Committee, and generally on the formulation of plans in respect of the conservation and betterment of land in the N.S.A.; (b) the expenditure of funds; (c) the rules which the Minister may make in exercise of his powers under		(a) Chairman appointed by the Minister; (b) The D.A. and the D.V.S.; (c) A person appointed by the Board (scheduled areas); (d) 2 persons appointed by and from each Provincial Agricultural Committee; (e) 2 persons appointed by the Minister; (f) Subject to the provision of Section 137 (2)

Name of Board	Date of Establishment	Legislative Authority	Statutory Powers and Duties	Other Functions	Composition
			part X of the Ordinance; (d) the making of loans under part X of the Ordinance; (e) the establishment of local Land Development Boards; (f) the policy in respect of production in N.S.A.; (g) matters relating to the Annual Price Review.		of the Ordinance, associate members nominated under that Section.
B. Commodity Boards B.1. Coffee Board	1933	The Coffee Ordinance, 1960 (No. 26 of 1960)	(a) To convene an annual conference of delegates to elect members to the Board; (b) Issue and, after consultation with the Director, cancel or suspend planters' licenses; (c) Issue, suspend or cancel pulping station licenses; (d) Register coffee millers and distinguishing marks; (e) Account for export levies and maintain the Coffee Levy Fund; (f) Control, through the medium of rules, the cultivation and processing of coffee.		(a) Director of Agriculture; (b) 2 members appointed by the Minister; (c) 1 member appointed by the Coffee Marketing Board; (d) 7 producer members from Eastern growing area; (e) 4 producer members from Western growing area.
B.2. Coffee Marketing Board	1946	The Coffee Ordinance, 1960 (No. 26 of 1960)	(a) Either separately or in conjunction with the Coffee Board to convene a conference annually to elect members to the Board; (b) License all marketing	To advise the Minister on making of rules necessary for the proper carrying out of its duties.	(a) 2 members appointed by the Minister; (b) 1 member appointed by Coffee Board; (c) 9 producers elected at Annual Coffee Conference.

transactions of coffee—that is to say buying, selling, exporting, milling, warehousing or any other business (with the exception of retailing, purchases for own consumption, and the E.A.R. & H. warehouses);
(c) To hold and maintain the fund known as the Coffee Pool.

N.B. No mention has been made of (a) the Coffee Licensing Advisory Committee (established under Section 9 of the Coffee Ordinance), (b) the (Coffee) Standing Joint Committee (established under Section 10), and (c) the (Coffee) Advisory Panel (established under Section 11). All three Committees have certain statutory duties to advise the Coffee Board or the Coffee Marketing Board.

			Functions	Composition
B.3. Tea Board	1951	The Tea Ordinance, 1960 (No. 61 of 1960) and Tea (Appointments to the Board) Rules, 1961 (L.M. 276/61)	(a) To do all those things necessary, proper or for the benefit of both growers and the industry and in particular to license growers and factories; (b) To regulate, control and improve the cultivation and processing of tea; (c) To control pests and diseases; (d) The control, export and investigation of and research into all matters relating to the industry.	(a) The Director of Agriculture; (b) 7 persons representing licensees (S.A.), appointed by the Kenya Tea Growers Association; (c) 3 persons representing licensees (N.S.A.), selected by M.A. from the 4 growers of the Special Crops Development Authority; (d) A representative of the E.A. Tea Traders Association; (e) A representative of the S.C.D.A.
B.4. Cotton Lint and Seed Marketing Board	1954	Cotton Lint and Seed Marketing Ordinance (No. 50 of 1954)	(a) To make arrangements for the purchase from ginners of all cotton lint and seed and the sale or disposal of all lint and seed; (b) To recommend prices to M.A.; (c) To control and manage	(a) The Director of Agriculture (Chairman); (b) The Permanent Secretary, Commerce and Industry; (c) The P.C.'s Nyanza and Coast; (d) Not less than 7 members (actually 10)

Name of Board	Date of Establishment	Legislative Authority	Statutory Powers and Duties	Other Functions	Composition
			the Cotton Price Assistance Fund. (The Board may use the services of the Uganda Board.)		appointed by Governor according to prescribed formula, i.e.: 3 Nyanza–African 1 Coast–Arab 1 Coast–African 1 Other Producer (P.A.O. Southern R.) 1 Commercial 3 Ginners.

N.B. Provincial Cotton Committees for Nyanza and Coast Provinces have been established under Section 19 of Ordinance No. 50 of 1954 to advise the Board especially on financial matters. Composition of each Committee is P.C., P.A.O., 5 members (not less than 3 of whom shall be African or Arab).

Name of Board	Date of Establishment	Legislative Authority	Statutory Powers and Duties	Other Functions	Composition
B.5. Sisal Board	1946	Sisal Industry Ordinance, 1946 (Cap. 196/111)	(a) To promote the advancement and welfare of the sisal industry by advising upon measures to be taken, and on the undertaking of technical and scientific research; (b) To provide standard conditions of sale; (c) At the request of the Sisal Growers Association and with the consent of the Governor to take part in or promote any scheme for regulating production, treatment, planting, cultivation, storage, movement, transport, distribution, sale, price fixing, purchase, use or consumption of sisal or sisal fiber.	(a) Maintain liaison with the Kenya and Tanganyika Sisal Board; (b) Levy an annual cess on sisal fibre and tow produced; (c) Administer monies placed at its disposal for such purpose as research, etc.	(a) The Director of Agriculture; (b) 1 member nominated by the Minister; (c) The Chairman of the Kenya Sisal Growers Association Ltd.; (d) 8 members appointed by the Sisal Growers Association Ltd.; (e) 2 members of the Tanganyika Sisal Board.
B.6. Pyrethrum Board	1938	Pyrethrum Ordinance, 1956 (No. 9 of 1956)	(a) To do all possible to promote the industry; (b) To license growers;		(a) The Director of Agriculture; (b) 1 member from each

	Year	Ordinance	Functions	Composition
(continued from previous board)			(c) To purchase, store, grade, examine, prepare, process, sell, export and market pyrethrum products; (d) To investigate and conduct research; (e) To negotiate sales and contracts.	...elected area (of which there are 5); (c) 1 member for the "appointment" areas who shall come from N.S.A. (appointed by the Minister); (d) 2 members appointed by the Minister, skilled in commerce; (e) Up to 3 other members appointed by the Minister after consultation with the Board. *N.B.* New Bill will alter composition considerably.
B.7. Cereal Producers (S.A.)	1956	The Cereal Producers (scheduled areas) Ordinance, 1956	(a) To advise Minister on producer prices and cost structures; (b) To represent interests of Cereal Producers; (c) To further research; (d) To levy cesses.	(a) 10 elected producers; (b) 2 K.F.A. Directors.
B.8. The Wheat Board	1952	Wheat Industry Ordinance (No. 24 of 1952)	(a) To advise the Minister on the production, price, storage, marketing and distribution of wheat, flour and wheat feed; (b) To advise the Minister on matters relating to the import and export of wheat, flour and wheat feed; (c) To advise the Minister on the licensing of flour mills, the cost of marketing, etc.	(a) 4 wheat growers nominated by the Minister from the panels of names submitted by the Board of Agric. (S.A.) and the K.N.F.U.; (b) 2 members appointed by the Chambers of Commerce & Industry; (c) Managing Director of K.F.A. (co-opted).
B.9. Maize Marketing Board	1959	Maize Marketing Ordinance, 1959	(a) To act as the sole authority for the regulating, controlling and com-	(a) 3 producer representatives from a panel of names put forward by

Name of Board	Date of Establishment	Legislative Authority	Statutory Powers and Duties	Other Functions	Composition
			mercial distribution, etc. of maize and maize products; (b) To advise the Minister on prices; (c) To advise the Minister on: (i) proper relation of maize production to the needs of Kenya; (ii) the control over importation and exportation of maize.		the Cereal Producers Board; (b) 3 representatives selected from panels submitted by the Provincial Marketing Boards; (c) 4 members nominated by the Minister for their experience of commercial and urban conditions.
B.10. Provincial Marketing Boards (a) Nyanza Province Marketing Board (b) Central Province Marketing Board	1956 1959	Marketing of African Produce Ordinance, 1936 as amended by Ordinance No. 39 of 1955	(a) To organize the marketing of scheduled African produce; (b) To direct producers of scheduled produce on the cultivation, movement, storage and processing of scheduled produce.	(a) Act as agents of: (i) Maize Marketing Board for maize (ii) K.F.A. for wheat (iii) Government for rice; (b) Render storage service at railheads; (c) Distribute seed at cost.	Each Board consists of: (a) Chairman appointed by the Minister; (b) 6 to 9 other members of whom not less than half are appointed by the Minister, the remainder being appointed to represent producers.
B.11. Kenya Dairy Board	1958	Dairy Industry Ordinance, 1958 (No. 34 of 1958)	(a) To organize, regulate and develop the production, marketing, etc., of dairy produce; (b) To improve the quality of dairy produce; (c) To secure reasonable	To advise the Ministry on general matters concerning the dairy industry.	(a) Chairman; (b) 5 members appointed by the Minister from a panel of names submitted by Board of Agriculture (S.A.); (c) 3 members selected by

Name	Year	Functions	Powers	Composition
		prices for dairy produce; (d) To promote research; (e) To encourage the greatest possible degree of private enterprise in the industry.		the Board of Agriculture (N.S.A.); (d) 2 members appointed by the Minister to represent any organizations which in the opinion of the Minister should be represented; (e) 1 member representing the Association of Municipalities of East Africa. *N.B.* The new Bill will alter composition considerably.
B.12. Kenya Meat Commission	1950	Kenya Meat Commission Ordinance, 1950 (No. 13 of 1950)	To exercise exclusive rights to operate abattoirs, export meat and purchase or sell slaughter stock.	(a) A Chairman; (b) 4 members to represent stockowner of K.N.F.U. (a) and (b) to be appointed by Governor in Council; (c) 1 African representing African stockowners; (d) 2 members selected by the Minister for their business ability and experience; (e) 1 member representing the Minister for Finance; (f) 2 co-opted African members. *N.B.* New Bill will considerably alter composition of Commission.
		(a) To purchase stock; (b) To acquire, establish and operate abattoirs, storage concerns, refrigerator works, etc. for the purpose of slaughtering livestock, processing by-products, prepare hides, and chilling, canning and storing meat.		
B.13. African Livestock Marketing Organization (A.L.M.O.)	1952	Subsidiary to K.M.C. in the nonscheduled areas		(a) The D.V.S.—Chairman; (b) All the Provincial Commissioners; (c) The Chairman, K.M.C.; (d) Representative of the
		(a) Purchase slaughter stock in the nonscheduled areas under license for the K.M.C.; (b) To encourage and foster		

Name of Board	Date of Establishment	Legislative Authority	Statutory Powers and Duties	Other Functions	Composition
			livestock marketing by African traders.		Chief Commissioner; (e) The Principal Livestock Marketing Officer, Veterinary Department; (f) 7 members appointed by the Minister.
B.14. Central Artificial Insemination Station Board	1946	Nonstatutory Set up by the Minister	To control, guide and manage the Central Insemination Station.		Staff of the Veterinary Department.
B.15. Veterinary Board	1951	Veterinary Surgeons Ordinance, 1951 (No. 51 of 1951)	(a) To register Veterinary Surgeons; (b) To license persons to practice as Veterinary Surgeons in Kenya; (c) To control the practice of Veterinary Surgeons; (d) To be a disciplinary body in respect of the veterinary profession in Kenya.		(a) The D.V.S.—Chairman; (b) The Dean of Makerere Veterinary School; (c) 3 registered Veterinary Surgeons appointed by the Minister; (d) 2 persons appointed by the Minister of whom 1 must be a licensed Surgeon.
B.16. Pig Industry Board	1945	Pig Industry Ordinance (Cap. 210)	(a) To further the advancement and control of the pig industry; (b) To control the purchase, sale supply and export of pigs and pig products; (c) To license producers.	To fix prices and quality standards for pig producers.	(a) Director of Veterinary Services; (b) Director of Agriculture; (c) Commissioner for Co-operative Development; (d) 8 producers to be elected in such manner and from such electoral areas as M.A. shall prescribe after consultation with the Board. N.B. This composition was created by the recent amendment to the Ordinance.
B.17. Uplands Bacon Factory Board	1946	Cap. 211	To administer the factory as a limited liability company.		9 Directors.

B.18. Horticultural Products Committee	1959	Nonstatutory	To advise the Minister on horticultural development and marketing.	(a) Deputy Director of Agriculture; (b) One member representing each of the following: (i) K.N.F.U. (ii) Canning industry (iii) Nairobi wholesalers (iv) Horticultural Co-operative Union; (c) (i) Senior Horticultural Officer (ii) Market Research Officer (S.Pr.) (iii) Representative of C.C.D.
B.19. Canning Crops Board	1957	The Canning Crops Ordinance (No. 27 of 1957)	(a) To control the production and processing of crops grown for canning purposes; (b) To license growers of scheduled crops (at present only pineapples); and canning factories; (c) To fix growers' prices.	(a) The Director of Agriculture; (b) Permanent Secretary Min. of Com. & Ind.; (c) 4 representatives of the growers; (d) 1 representative of canning manufacturers; (e) 3 representatives of the canning industry.
B.20. Special Crops Development Authority	1961	L.N. 3÷2/61 (the Authority is established under Sections 190–191 of the Agriculture Ordinance)	To promote and foster the development of tea in the nonscheduled areas in the Nyanza, Central and Rift Valley Provinces excepting any parts set aside and leased under the Trust Land Ordinance (Cap. 100) to registered companies for the development or processing of tea.	(a) Chairman appointed by the Minister; (b) Permanent Secretary or representatives (c) Director of Agric.; (d) Chairman, Tea Board; (e) Gen. Manager, S.C.D.A.; (f) 1 member appointed by C.D.C.; (g) 4 African growers appointed by Minister.

Name of Board	Date of Establishment	Legislative Authority	Statutory Powers and Duties	Other Functions	Composition
C. Educational Board C.1. Egerton Agricultural College Governing Body	1955	Egerton Agricultural College Ordinance, (No. 21 of 1955)	To govern, control and administer the College.		(a) Chairman appointed by the Minister; (b) The Director of Agriculture; (c) The Director of Veterinary Services; (d) The Director of Education; (e) 8 members of whom 4 are appointed by the Minister, 1 by the Board of Agriculture (scheduled areas), 1 by R.A.S.K., 1 by K.N.F.U. and 1 by the Board of Agriculture (non-scheduled areas).

Source: Prepared by the Ministry of Agriculture and Animal Husbandry.

ANNEX D *THE NAIROBI–MOMBASA ROAD*

The cost of the project to build a modern road between Nairobi and Mombasa, with adequate width, good surface, proper drainage and water protection facilities, and easily negotiable grades and curves, should be weighed in both amount and timing against many other factors. The distance of Nairobi from the sea and the location of a large proportion of Kenya's population, agriculture, and productive economy in and west of the Nairobi area, with little between Nairobi and Mombasa, make the Nairobi-Mombasa road important in some ways but detract heavily from its immediate value in others.

The position of the road as a connecting link between the highlands and the sea gives it some strategic importance both commercially and militarily, as a supplement to the carrying capacity of the railway, and as a substitute for the railway in case of need. On the other hand, the carrying capacity of the railways is at present adequate, air transport would be used as an emergency supplementary carrier and, even in its present poor condition, the road can carry considerable traffic. All these factors indicate that the merits of reconstructing this road must be weighed carefully against the benefits and costs of other important road projects in establishing priorities within the road program for the allocation of funds for development. In the same way and for the same reasons, the entire road program and all major projects within it must be weighed against programs in other fields which seek inclusion in the development program.

The distance from Nairobi to Mombasa by the present road is 307 miles. Work to bituminize the portions of the road between Nairobi and the Machakos turn off (30 miles) and from Mombasa to Mackinnon road (55 miles) was completed in 1962. Between these points, there remains 222 miles of unpaved road, difficult to maintain and generally unsatisfactory to motorists in dry weather because of dust, and in wet weather because of mud. Other deficiencies in the road as now located and constructed stem from the inferior quality of the natural soils along the route, the poor alignment of the Ulu and Kibwesi sections, and the effects of low surface elevations and bad gradients in many sections which cause submergence under water during heavy rains.

The latest recorded traffic figures give 1961 averages as from 120 to 175 vehicles of all types in daylight traffic between Machakos and Mackinnon Road; with night traffic, these figures become 180 to 250.

Approximately one-third consists of commercial vehicles. Car traffic during holiday peak periods increases to three or four times normal average. There is no doubt that its poor condition deters motorists and commercial haulers from using the road. If the road were re-aligned and given a hard smooth surface, an appreciable increase in motor traffic both private and commercial could be expected. A significant factor in traffic volume is that local traffic is small. The area between Nairobi and the coast is sparsely settled and the volume of through traffic, plus some tourist traffic to game parks, will for some time be the only significant consideration in the usage of the road.

A first consideration in the establishment of its priority in any program is its essentiality at the present time in view of the current existence of other means of transport throughout the route of the road. The railways are today the primary means of moving goods between Nairobi and Mombasa and still serve usefully for the transport of passengers. Their rolling stock and equipment is in good operating condition. They have the ability at this time to carry all goods and all passengers presented for transport, though steps will be needed to improve their capacity if goods traffic increases rapidly over the next few years. They provide a wide range of rolling stock to meet the requirements of various types of cargo. East African Airways is providing reliable and fast air transport for both passengers and goods between Nairobi and coastal points and is in process of providing larger and more modern airplanes for the purpose. Airfields at both ends of the line are able to serve the new airplanes. Finally, looking at the Nairobi-Mombasa road itself as an existing carrier of traffic we find that it carries goods traffic and provides access for such local communities along its route as would likewise be served by an improved road. It could carry more traffic in an emergency than it carries at present.

In the sections of this report devoted to transport and communication, and in the chapter on agriculture, we have pointed out the need to concentrate road construction to meet the needs of the economy, and have indicated that the movement of tea to factories and of agricultural products of other types to processing plants or to collecting points for onward shipment are in our opinion more urgent than other road programs.

Two technically feasible solutions for the improvement of the Nairobi-Mombasa road have been suggested by proponents of the project. One is a complete re-alignment with easier gradients to produce a modern road; the cost of this would probably be in excess of £15,000 per mile, or a total of about £3.5 million for the currently unpaved section. A second solution offering a considerable initial saving over the first plan would be to pave the road on the present inferior alignment and with present grades. Retention of existing steep gradients and sharp curves, however, would slow traffic and add to the dangers of travel. A subsequent re-alignment to higher standards would add considerably to the total cost since a proportion of the expenditures for earthworks, paving and drainage in this cheaper plan would then be completely lost. Also as happened in 1961, the road, even if it had a good surface, is likely to be under water for a part of the rainy season with consequent possible damage and interruption of traffic. It is estimated that for the lesser standard of construction the minimum cost would be around £2.5 million as compared with the estimated minimum cost of £3.5 million for the road with better alignment and better grades.

The reconstruction of the road from Nairobi to Mombasa may eventually be justified. In view of its high cost and doubtful return, and the urgent need for other projects, the mission considers that this work should be postponed until more essential projects have been undertaken, including those in other fields of development.

ANNEX E *THE CAPACITY OF THE MOMBASA-NAIROBI-NAKURU RAILWAY LINES*

The assessment of the capacity of the line in relation to general increase in traffic is particularly concerned with traffic in the up direction from Mombasa to Nairobi and Nairobi to Nakuru. It is so concerned for two main reasons: first, because the heavier gradient is in the up direction (1.5 percent as against 1.18 percent in the down direction) and second, because movements up from the coast are substantially greater than those in the reverse direction (largely because of oil traffic). Thus, if there is enough capacity in the up direction, there will be enough capacity in the down, other things being equal, and although these two tonnages are tending to equate, up traffic is still predominantly the critical tonnage.

With steam traction, the train paths on the Mombasa-Nairobi section provide for a maximum of 12 through goods trains per day, two passenger trains, one stopping goods or through pick-up and one limestone train from Sultan Hamud to Athi River, plus engineering and other service trains and short distance pick-ups operating under control arrangements. With a maximum gross train load of 1,200 tons, the daily gross trailing tonnage lift cannot exceed 14,400 tons with steam traction, maximum movement to date has been below 8,000 tons. The limit with diesel-electric traction is estimated at 18,200 gross trailing tons per day, and with electric traction at 21,000 gross trailing tons per day.

Diesel locomotives have been introduced on the Nairobi-Nakuru section. The possible daily up-lift with diesel-electric traction over this section is estimated at rather more than 16,500 gross trailing tons, as compared with the maximum tonnage so far of less than 6,000.

It would not be possible to ease future problems on the Mombasa-Nairobi section by diverting diesel-electric locomotives, since the steam locomotives which would thereby be released are, to all intents and purposes, prohibited over any other section of the system because of damage which they cause to lighter weight rails. The Mombasa-Nairobi section is alone laid in 95 lb per yard/rail, the heaviest weight on any other section being 80 lb per yard. The problem of capacity on the Mombasa-Nairobi section may thus be dealt with in isolation.

Between 1949 and 1956 the increase in tonnages of commodities railed from the coast was 4.6 percent cumulative a year. To provide for peaks, primarily caused by ships bunching, for loss of goods capacity caused by

334

the necessity to run boat specials and to allow a margin to avoid bottlenecks in the port as a result of inadequate capacity on the railway, forecasts of capacity demands have been based on a total cumulative increase of 5 percent a year.

The cumulative increase from 1959 through to 1961, in deadweight tonnages of import cargo received at Mombasa, is over 5 percent a year. For planning purposes, therefore, the EARH is still working on this rate of growth in tonnages offering in the up direction from Mombasa to Nairobi. On this basis the limit for steam traction would not be reached until 1971.

Projections of growth over the next few years can only be very speculative, but actual performance since 1959 has fallen well below the rate of 5 percent per annum used by the EARH. Even when the limit for steam traction is eventually approached, other possibilities besides the introduction of electric traction, such as the building of a pipeline to carry oil products from Mombasa to Nairobi, should be considered.

STATISTICAL APPENDIX

TABLE S.1: Civil Population Estimates[a]

thousands

	1948	1950	1955	1956	1957	1958	1959	1960	1961[b]
European	30.8	36.2	52.4	57.7	62.7	64.7	66.4	67.7	66.0
Indo-Pakistani and Goan	100.0	144.4	144.1	151.9	161.7	165.0	169.9	174.3	178.0
Arab	24.4	26.1	31.6	33.0	34.3	35.5	37.1	38.6	39.0
Other	3.4	3.9	5.1	5.3	5.5	5.7	5.9	6.1	6.0
Subtotal	158.6	180.6	233.2	247.9	264.2	270.9	279.3	286.7	289.0
African	5,240.0	5,478.0	6,123.0	6,261.0	6,402.0	6,546.0	6,693.0	6,844.0	6,998.0
Total	5,399.0	5,659.0	6,356.0	6,509.0	6,666.0	6,817.0	6,972.0	7,131.0	7,287.0

[a] Pending the findings of the census to be held in Kenya in 1962, these estimates are based on a revised extrapolation of the 1948 census figures. It has now been assumed that the African population has increased by 2.25 percent per annum since 1948 rather than by 1.5 percent as had been done previously, following the recent census in Tanganyika and Uganda which indicated that similar earlier assumptions of population growth had been too low.

[b] 1961 figures are corrected to the nearest whole number and are calculated from mid-year estimates prepared by the Economics and Statistics Division of the Treasury and given as they appear in Trade and Supplies Bulletin, April 1962.

SOURCES: Kenya, Statistical Abstract, 1961; Trade and Supplies Bulletins.

TABLE S.2: Migration

	1950	1955	1956	1957	1958	1959	1960	1961	1962 (1st half)
Immigration:[a]									
European	3,503	5,715	6,685	5,541	5,102	4,681	3,628	3,204	1,887
Asian and Arab	4,111	5,873	6,089	5,058	4,066	4,054	2,801	2,282	1,036
African	76	96	174	172	116	134	124	124	81
Total	7,690	11,684	12,948	10,771	9,284	8,869	6,553	5,610	3,004
Emigration:[b]									
European	963	3,090	2,709	2,808	3,305	3,394	3,813	6,052	4,625
Asian and Arab	206	1,046	995	1,247	1,953	2,196	2,130	2,529	1,164
African	13	76	43	52	105	103	89	190	99
Total	1,182	4,212	3,747	4,107	5,361	5,693	6,032	8,771	5,888

[a] Includes visitors becoming new permanent immigrants.

[b] Excludes temporary emigrants becoming permanent emigrants.

SOURCE: Kenya, Economics and Statistics Division.

TABLE S.3: Total Reported Employment

(thousands)

	1946	1950	1951	1952	1953	1954	1955	1956	1957	1958	1959	1960	1961
In Agriculture:													
European	1.0	⎱1.6	1.4	⎱1.8	1.5	1.7	1.8	1.7	1.8	1.8	1.8	1.9	1.6
Asian	0.5	⎰	0.5	⎰	0.3	0.6	0.4	0.4	0.5	0.5	0.6	0.8	0.6
African	197.0	201.9	203.2	202.7	211.3	220.8	245.7	233.1	251.1	247.2	249.0	269.1	249.8
In Private Industry													
and Commerce:													
European	4.1	⎱23.7	7.3	⎱25.3	8.4	9.2	10.6	10.5	11.4	11.6	12.0	12.3	11.7
Asian	10.4	⎰	17.1	⎰	18.6	21.1	23.6	24.7	25.8	24.8	25.1	25.6	25.0
African	101.0	123.8	115.8	130.3	123.7	141.6	157.4	158.3	156.8	149.6	148.0	151.1	134.1
In Public Service:													
European	3.6	4.8	5.3	5.6	7.0	7.9	10.0	8.9	9.2	9.2	9.0	8.9	8.9
Asian	7.3	8.2	8.1	8.4	9.5	10.0	10.6	10.4	10.9	10.6	11.1	11.8	12.2
African	78.8	96.5	93.4	101.6	118.0	130.5	155.0	148.7	146.9	137.9	140.0	140.7	145.5
All Employees:													
European	8.7	12.8	14.0	14.8	16.9	18.8	22.4	21.1	22.4	22.6	22.8	23.0	22.2
Asian	18.2	25.5	25.7	26.3	28.4	32.7	34.6	35.5	37.2	35.9	36.7	38.3	37.8
African	376.8	422.2	412.4	434.6	453.0	492.9	558.1	540.1	554.8	534.7	537.4	560.9	529.4
Total	403.7	460.5	452.1	475.7	498.3	544.4	615.1	596.7	614.4	593.2	596.9	622.2	589.4

SOURCES: Kenya, *Statistical Abstracts; Trade and Supplies Bulletin;* East African Statistical Department, *Reported Employment Wages in Kenya, 1948–1960.*

TABLE S.4: Reported Unemployment[a] (Number of Adult Males as of June 30)

	1955	1956	1957	1958	1959	1960	1961	1962
Europeans	51	67	130	146	109	80	88	62
Asians:								
Industrial	38	178	206	181	252	283	236	35
Nonindustrial	12	11	116	118	143	121	117	12
Subtotal	50	189	322	299	395	404	353	47
Africans:								
Industrial	1,137	1,661	1,991	3,896	2,696	4,699	5,095	4,241
Nonindustrial	541	978	1,608	2,128	688	1,024	911	1,885
Domestic and other	776	824	1,450	1,768	1,151	1,827	1,743	2,133
Subtotal	2,454	3,463	5,049	7,792	4,535	7,550	7,749	8,259
Grand Total	2,555	3,719	5,501	8,237	5,039	8,034	8,190	8,368

[a] The figures relate only to adult male work-seekers on the books of the various Public Employment Offices in Kenya who had not been placed on the last day of June of each year shown except 1962, whose figures relate to April. The figures do not indicate the absolute level of unemployment at any one time especially for Asians and Africans.
SOURCES: Kenya, *Trade and Supplies Bulletins; Statistical Abstract;* East African Statistical Department, *Quarterly Economic and Statistical Bulletin.*

TABLE S.5: Gross Domestic Product by Industrial Origin

(£ million at factor cost)

	1954	1955	1956	1957	1958	1959	1960	1961[a]
Outside Recorded Monetary Economy:								
Agriculture	33.43	33.56	34.94	37.33	37.67	37.71	35.01	33.12
Livestock Products	10.13	10.51	10.63	11.72	11.80	11.66	10.99	10.43
Forestry	1.73	1.98	2.38	2.43	2.57	2.70	2.94	3.08
Fishing and Hunting	0.28	0.27	0.28	0.21	0.20	0.20	0.16	0.16
Total	45.57	46.32	48.23	51.69	52.24	52.27	49.10	46.79
Recorded Monetary Economy:								
Agriculture	19.82	19.98	24.90	23.78	24.75	25.32	29.44	28.71
Livestock	6.37	6.92	7.72	8.06	8.27	8.57	9.22	8.91
Forestry	0.55	0.77	0.81	0.68	0.68	0.79	0.81	0.90
Fishing and Hunting	1.65	1.47	1.62	1.02	0.90	0.89	0.53	0.52
Total	28.39	29.14	35.05	33.54	34.60	35.58	40.00	39.04
Mining and Quarrying	0.89	1.28	1.36	1.26	1.23	1.12	1.09	0.85
Manufacturing	14.14	17.44	18.18	19.80	20.52	20.23	21.62	22.73
Construction	6.31	8.04	9.34	9.63	8.38	7.94	7.86	7.83
Electricity and Water	1.24	1.45	1.75	2.09	2.36	2.56	2.79	2.90
Transport and Communication	11.84	15.18	15.78	18.64	17.69	19.03	20.34	21.14
Wholesale and Retail Trade	21.59	25.34	25.83	27.48	26.39	27.68	28.96	29.56
Banking, Insurance and Real Estate	1.38	2.22	2.52	2.83	3.26	3.46	3.54	3.88
Rents (including ownership)	4.83	5.26	5.80	6.65	7.51	8.05	8.70	9.30
General Government:								
Administration	6.68	10.03	9.20	9.72	9.89	9.91	10.64	11.61
Agriculture and Related Services	1.31	1.51	1.58	1.88	1.78	1.77	1.85	2.24
Local Authorities	1.61	2.26	2.29	2.53	2.89	3.15	3.35	3.48
Public Health and Education	2.52	2.74	3.15	3.88	4.73	5.19	5.84	7.68
Defense	1.78	2.68	2.54	2.12	1.11	1.43	1.37	1.50
Overseas Government	0.04	0.08	0.05	0.06	0.06	0.10	0.12	0.14
Total	13.94	19.30	18.81	20.19	20.46	21.53	23.17	26.65
Services	7.90	10.09	10.73	12.11	13.11	14.58	15.50	14.14
Government Officers Salaries Revision	—	—	—	—	—	—	1.75	—
TOTAL	158.02	181.06	193.38	205.91	207.75	214.03	224.42	224.80

[a] Provisional.
SOURCES: Kenya, *Statistical Abstracts;* Economics and Statistics Division.

TABLE S.6: Gross Domestic Product by Industrial Origin

(percentage)

	1954	1955	1956	1957	1958	1959	1960	1961[a]
Outside Recorded Monetary Economy:								
Agriculture	21.2	18.5	18.1	18.1	18.1	17.6	15.6	14.7
Livestock Products	6.4	5.8	5.5	5.7	5.7	5.4	4.9	4.6
Forestry	1.1	1.1	1.2	1.2	1.2	1.3	1.3	1.4
Fishing and Hunting	0.2	0.2	0.1	0.1	0.1	0.1	0.1	0.1
Total	28.8	25.6	24.9	25.1	25.1	24.4	21.9	20.8
Recorded Monetary Economy:								
Agriculture	12.5	11.0	12.9	11.5	11.9	11.8	13.1	12.8
Livestock	4.0	3.8	4.0	3.9	4.0	4.0	4.2	4.4
Forestry	0.3	0.4	0.4	0.3	0.3	0.4	0.4	0.4
Fishing and Hunting	1.0	0.8	0.8	0.5	0.4	0.4	0.2	0.2
Total	18.0	16.1	18.1	16.3	16.7	16.6	17.8	17.4
Mining and Quarrying	0.6	0.7	0.7	0.6	0.6	0.5	0.5	0.4
Manufacturing	8.9	9.6	9.4	9.6	9.9	9.5	9.6	10.1
Construction	4.0	4.4	4.8	4.7	4.0	3.7	3.5	3.5
Electricity and Water	0.8	0.8	0.9	1.0	1.1	1.2	1.2	1.3
Transport and Communication	7.5	8.4	8.2	9.1	8.5	8.9	9.0	9.4
Wholesale and Retail Trade	13.7	14.0	13.4	13.3	12.7	12.9	12.9	13.1
Banking, Insurance and Real Estate	0.9	1.2	1.3	1.4	1.6	1.6	1.6	1.7
Rents (including ownership)	3.0	2.9	3.0	3.2	3.6	3.8	3.9	4.1
General Government:								
Administration	4.2	5.6	4.8	4.7	4.8	4.6	4.7	5.2
Agriculture and Related Services	0.8	0.8	0.8	0.9	0.9	0.8	0.8	1.0
Local Authorities	1.0	1.3	1.2	1.3	1.4	1.5	1.5	1.6
Public Health and Education	1.6	1.5	1.6	1.9	2.2	2.4	2.6	3.4
Defense	1.1	1.5	1.3	1.0	0.5	0.7	0.6	0.7
Overseas Government	—	—	—	—	—	—	0.1	0.1
Total	8.8	10.7	9.7	9.8	9.8	10.1	10.3	11.9
Services	5.0	5.6	5.5	5.9	6.3	6.8	7.0	6.3
Government Officers Salaries Revision	—	—	—	—	—	—	0.8	—
TOTAL	100.0	100.0	100.0	100.0	100.0	100.0	100.0	100.0

[a] Provisional. SOURCES: Kenya, *Statistical Abstracts;* Economics and Statistics Division.

TABLE S.7: Composition of Gross Domestic Product by Type of Factor Income

(£ million at factor cost)

Factor Income	1954	1955	1956	1957	1958	1959	1960	1961[a]
Recorded Monetary Economy:								
Paid Employment	58.88	75.24	77.97	85.75	85.50	88.37	96.17	98.58
Operating Surplus	48.74	54.24	61.38	61.82	62.50	65.35	70.46	70.12
Rental Surplus	4.83	5.26	5.80	6.65	7.51	8.05	8.70	9.30
Subtotal	112.45	134.74	145.15	154.22	155.50	161.76	175.33	178.00
Imputed Product outside the Recorded Monetary Economy	45.57	46.32	48.23	51.69	52.24	52.27	49.10	46.80
Total (Gross Domestic Product)	158.02	181.06	193.38	205.91	207.75	214.03	224.42	224.80

[a] Provisional. SOURCES: Kenya, *Statistical Abstracts;* Economics and Statistics Division.

TABLE S.8: Gross Capital Formation[a]

(£ million)

Asset & Sector	1954	1956	1957	1958	1959	1960	1961[b]
Residential Buildings:							
Government	1.72	1.23	1.37	1.46	1.69	2.58	n.a.
EACS	0.76	0.90	0.38	0.16	0.20	0.08	0.12
Non-African Agric.	0.83	0.93	0.98	0.89	0.83	0.77	0.65
Private, other	2.60	6.82	5.28	4.61	4.52	3.38	0.73
Total	5.90	9.88	8.01	7.11	7.23	6.81	n.a.
Non-Residential Buildings:							
Government	1.68	2.87	2.89	2.33	2.30	2.44	n.a.
EACS	0.36	0.57	0.72	0.32	0.21	0.23	0.16
Non-African Agric.	0.57	0.64	0.65	0.56	0.58	0.52	0.40
Private, other	2.48	4.22	3.59	3.85	3.97	3.23	2.00
Total	5.09	8.29	7.85	7.05	7.07	6.42	n.a.
Construction & Works:							
Government	4.08	4.72	5.19	4.21	4.96	5.84	n.a.
EACS	4.02	0.92	3.38	2.70	2.08	0.97	1.16
Non-African Agric.	0.96	1.20	1.91	2.39	2.39	2.34	2.26
Private, other	0.70	0.90	0.99	0.85	0.80	0.75	0.70
Total	9.75	7.74	11.47	10.15	10.22	9.90	n.a.
Transport & Equipment:							
Government	0.42	0.54	0.41	0.44	0.48	0.61	n.a.
EACS	2.31	1.01	0.26	0.15	0.34	0.48	0.33
Non-African Agric.	0.85	0.85	0.83	0.83	0.83	0.79	0.75
Private, other	4.84	7.00	7.63	7.11	6.73	8.84	5.10
Total	8.42	9.40	9.12	8.52	8.38	10.72	n.a.
Machinery & Other Equipment:							
Government	0.68	0.91	1.09	1.18	1.05	0.86	n.a.
EACS	0.71	1.26	0.77	0.41	0.34	0.32	0.30
Non-African Agric.	1.19	1.23	1.14	1.05	1.08	1.01	0.94
Private, other	3.54	6.97	6.18	4.55	4.95	5.37	5.72
Total	6.11	10.37	9.18	7.18	7.41	7.56	n.a.
All Assets:							
Government	8.57	10.27	10.94	9.61	10.47	12.33	13.10
EACS	8.16	4.66	5.50	3.73	3.17	2.08	2.07
Non-African Agric.	4.39	4.84	5.51	5.71	5.71	5.43	5.00
Private, other	14.14	25.91	23.67	20.97	20.97	21.57	14.25
Total	35.27	45.68	45.62	40.02	40.33	41.41	34.42

[a] The data refer to expenditure on fixed capital assets only. They omit the African agricultural sector.

[b] Provisional.

SOURCES: East African Statistical Department, *Capital Formations in Kenya, 1954–1960;* Kenya, Economics and Statistics Division.

TABLE S.9: Land Areas as at December 31, 1961

(sq. miles)

A. Special Areas (Trust Land):		
Trust Land (Trust Land Ordinance)		49,867
The above figure includes:		
i. Forest Reserves	998	
ii. Townships and Trading Centers	47	
iii. Agricultural, Veterinary, Outspans, Railways and other Government Reserves	17	
iv. Alienated Land	37	
v. Open Water	86	
B. Special Reserves (Crown Land):		
Special Reserves (Crown Lands Ordinance)		858
Temporary Special Reserves		494
Special Leasehold Areas		1,012
Commercial Reserves and Special Areas		528
C. Nonspecial Areas:		
Forest Reserves		5,077
Municipalities, Townships and Trading Centers		562
Agricultural, Veterinary, Outspans, Railways and other Government Reserves		415
Alienated Crown Land		11,986
Royal National Park		8,524
D. Unalienated Crown Land part of which is suitable for Alienation:		
All other area including Northern Frontier and Turkana (but includes Swamps, Riparian and National Reserves)		17,856
Northern Frontier and Turkana		120,744
Crown Land earmarked for Africans		898
Open Water (other special area)		5,085
Private Land		1,043
Crown Land additional to Trust Land		11
Total Area		224,960

SOURCE: Kenya Lands Department, *Annual Reports.*

TABLE S.10: Production of Major Crops for Sale[a]

(thousand tons)

	1946	1955	1956	1957	1958	1959	1960	1961	1962[b]
Coffee[a]									
African	n.a.	1.0	0.8	1.5	2.3	3.6	4.6	7.9	8.1
Non-African	9.0	11.6	23.1	17.0	18.5	19.6	18.8	25.2	19.3
Total	9.0	12.6	23.9	18.5	20.8	23.2	23.4	33.1	27.4
Tea									
African	—	—	—	—	—	0.1	0.1	0.2	n.a.
Non-African	5.5	8.5	9.5	9.8	11.2	12.3	13.5	12.2	n.a.
Total	5.5	8.5	9.5	9.8	11.2	12.4	13.6	12.4	n.a.
Sisal									
African	—	0.3	0.8	0.1	—	1.5	3.0	6.3	n.a.
Non-African	27.0	37.6	38.8	41.0	46.0	53.7	59.6	56.0	n.a.
Total	27.0	37.9	39.6	41.1	46.0	55.2	62.6	62.3	n.a.
Maize[a]									
African	n.a.	116.0	58.1	57.0	69.6	79.7	73.2	62.7	62.5
Non-African	n.a.	89.3	96.5	80.0	87.5	76.5	70.4	76.4	73.7
Total	146.8	205.3	154.6	137.0	157.1	156.2	143.6	139.1	136.2
Pyrethrum									
African	n.a.	0.3	0.3	0.4	0.4	0.6	1.8	2.8	n.a.
Non-African	6.7	2.4	2.8	3.0	3.4	4.2	6.7	7.5	n.a.
Total	6.7	2.7	3.1	3.4	3.8	4.8	8.5	10.2	n.a.
Wattle									
African	n.a.	46.9	38.2	25.8	25.4	18.1	19.0	16.8	n.a.
Non-African	n.a.	20.2	23.8	23.6	36.1	28.3	31.0	37.1	n.a.
Total	n.a.	67.1	62.0	49.4	61.5	46.4	50.0	53.9	n.a.
Wheat[a]									
African	—	—	—	—	—	—	0.7	0.2	5.0
Non-African	73.0	132.6	120.9	125.1	102.1	96.2	126.7	99.5	68.3
Total	73.0	132.6	120.9	125.1	102.1	96.2	127.4	99.7	73.3

[a] Production in crop years applied to calendar years in which crop year ends, except for 1946 which indicates 1946/47 production.   [b] Preliminary.
SOURCES: Kenya, *Statistical Abstracts*; Economics and Statistics Division.

TABLE S.11: Estimated Acreages of Principal Crops in the Nonscheduled Areas, 1960/61[a]

(thousand acres)

Maize	2,891
Other cereals	1,165
Root crops	686
Temporary industrial crops[b]	334
Pulses and other temporary food crops	1,725
Permanent industrial crops[c]	217
Fruit	199
Total	7,216

[a] Adding together long and short rains plantings and counting twice areas planted with two crops simultaneously (e.g., maize and beans together).
[b] Including cotton, sugar, oilseeds and pyrethrum.
[c] Including coffee, tea, sisal, wattle and coconuts.
SOURCE: Kenya, *Economic Survey*, 1962.

TABLE S.12: Prices to Producers for Selected Agricultural Products

	1946/47	1950/51	1951/52	1952/53	1953/54	1954/55	1955/56	1956/57	1957/58	1958/59	1959/60	1960/61	1961/62
Wheat (Sh. per bag[a])	27.85	39.80	46.33	52.06	52.50	52.00	51.00	52.66	51.68	52.33	48.62	46.62	46.93
Maize (Sh. per bag[b])	17.50	28.80	35.00	38.25	38.72	35.15	35.15	37.98	34.98	27.00	32.00	35.50	n.a.
Coffee (£ per ton[c])	112.00	374.24	416.30	436.47	509.34	426.67	437.15	521.41	438.40	393.31	389.13	320.00	(348.00)

[a] Guaranteed price for 200 pounds of Grade I wheat naked, minus cesses.
[b] Guaranteed price for 200 pounds of Grade II maize naked, minus cess plus bonus.
[c] Total appropriation to producers divided by total production.
SOURCES: Kenya, *Statistical Abstracts*; Economics and Statistics Division.

TABLE S.13: Prices to Producers for Agricultural Products

	1946	1950	1951	1952	1953	1954	1955	1956	1957	1958	1959	1960	1961
Sisal (£ per ton)	35.51	116.03	183.96	133.64	72.15	64.64	59.14	59.86	53.30	53.32	67.79	81.34	72.89
Pyrethrum (Sh. per cwt)	140.0	239.5	275.6	289.8	275.6	276.1	293.2	292.1	288.0	285.1	302.6	313.63	n.a.
Cattle (Sh. per lb.)	0.50	0.73	0.85	0.99	1.10	1.10	1.10	1.18	1.20	1.20	1.20	1.25	1.28
Baconers (Sh. per lb.)	0.80	1.05	1.20	1.60	1.66	1.66	1.68	1.75	1.75	1.75	1.50	1.60	(1.74)
Butter Fat (Sh. per lb.)	1.50	2.46	2.54	2.89	3.00	3.33	3.21	3.15	3.07	2.38	2.75	2.76	(2.85)

SOURCE: Kenya, *Statistical Abstracts*.

TABLE S.14: Mineral and Industrial Production—Numbers of Establishments (Comparative Analysis by 1954 Industrial Groupings)

	1954	1956	1957
Mining	34	32	32
Quarrying	68	110	107
Meat, Dairy and Canned Products	32[a]	32	34
Grain Mill Production	54	46	53
Bakery and Confectionery	44	57	55
Miscellaneous Foods including Sugar	14[a]	14	19
Beverages and Tobacco	37	36	37
Textile Products	74	97	85
Footwear, including Repairs	72	65	47
Wood Products	87	101	108
Furniture	118	131	107
Paper Products and Printing	57	65	66
Chemical Products	48	46	50
Clay and Grass Products	26	34	39
Metal Products	49	67	71
Machinery	51	43	42
Transport Equipment	147	179	178
Miscellaneous Manufacture	31	35	36
Building and Construction	311	456	437
Electrical Contracting	37	48	43
Total 1954 Industrial Groups	1,391[a]	1,694	1,646
Industries not covered by 1954 Survey:			
Municipal Brewers		9	8
Public Shipbuilding and			
Rolling Stock Repairs		3	3
Public Construction		28	29
Electricity		10	10
Total 1956 and 1957 Industrial Groups		1,744	1,696

[a] Revised 1954 figures.

SOURCE: East African Statistical Department, *Kenya Survey of Industrial Production,* 1957.

TABLE S.15: Mineral and Industrial Production—Numbers Employed
(Comparative Analysis by 1954 Industrial Groupings)

	1954	1956	1957
Mining	2,228	2,787	2,269
Quarrying	4,742	6,088	5,595
Meat, Dairy and Canned Products	2,298	2,901	3,102
Grain Mill Production	2,543	2,332	2,505
Bakery and Confectionery	1,326	1,529	1,401
Miscellaneous Foods including Sugar	2,572	2,047	2,809
Beverages and Tobacco	2,209	3,934	3,993
Textile Products	2,477	3,048	3,039
Footwear, including Repairs	997	1,075	933
Wood Products	10,194	8,613	8,878
Furniture	1,388	1,611	1,463
Paper Products and Printing	1,899	2,390	2,493
Chemical Products	3,970	3,685	3,544
Clay and Grass Products	3,376	2,794	3,571
Metal Products	1,337	2,240	2,395
Machinery	1,684	1,751	1,525
Transport Equipment	4,024	5,303	5,345
Miscellaneous Manufacture	556	738	811
Building and Construction	20,412	25,429	22,029
Electrical Contracting	3,623	3,023	3,133
Total 1954 Industrial Groups	73,858[a]	83,318	80,833
Industries not covered by 1954 Survey:			
Municipal Brewers		83	121
Public Shipbuilding and Rolling Stock Repairs		3,533	5,875
Public Construction		30,730	31,023
Electricity		2,313	2,382
Total 1956 and 1957 Industrial Groups		119,977	120,234

[a] Revised 1954 figures.

SOURCE: East African Statistical Department, *Kenya Survey of Industrial Production,* 1957.

TABLE S.16: Mineral and Industrial Gross Production
(Comparative Analysis by 1954 Industrial Groupings)

(£ thousand)

	1954	1956	1957
Mining	316	481	492
Quarrying	720	1,309	1,163
Meat, Dairy and Canned Products	5,185[a]	5,844	5,848
Grain Mill Production	6,588[b]	6,737	7,107
Bakery and Confectionery	1,161	1,628	1,699
Miscellaneous Foods including Sugar	1,356[b]	1,789	2,322
Beverages and Tobacco	4,329	7,923	11,545
Textile Products	1,244	1,928	2,169
Footwear, including Repairs	720	905	884
Wood Products	1,778	2,275	1,938
Furniture	802	985	874
Paper Products and Printing	1,667	2,350	2,843
Chemical Products	4,603	5,230	4,816
Clay and Grass Products	2,256	2,717	3,497
Metal Products	937	2,706	2,820
Machinery	969	1,326	1,132
Transport Equipment	1,448	3,537	3,762
Miscellaneous Manufacture	740	972	1,038
Building and Construction	9,894	13,809	14,309
Electrical Contracting	1,568	4,045	4,011
Total 1954 Industrial Groups	48,281	68,496	74,268
Industries not covered by 1954 Survey:			
Municipal Brewers		42	82
Public Shipbuilding and Rolling Stock Repairs		1,326	2,193
Public Construction		14,037	17,853
Electricity		2,651	3,067
Total 1956 and 1957 Industrial Groups		86,551	97,463

[a] The production of fish has been transferred from group 3 to group 6 to accord 1956 classification.
[b] Revised 1954 figures.
SOURCE: East African Statistical Department, *Kenya Survey of Industrial Production*, 1957.

TABLE S.17: Electricity Generation and Distribution

	1946	1950	1955	1956	1957	1958	1959	1960	1961
Installed Capacity (thousand kw)									
Thermal	9.3	19.5	40.8	55.4	59.1	56.3	55.1	56.4	56.4
Hydro	6.7	7.0	25.5	25.9	25.9	25.9	25.9	25.9	25.9
Total	16.0	26.5	66.3	81.3	85.1	82.3	81.1	82.3	82.3
Generated and Imported (million kwh)									
Generated	44.9	89.0	208.9	245.6	267.9	213.7	212.2	221.3	215.2
Imported	—	6.8	22.3	23.1	23.4	114.1	151.1	181.3	211.0
Total	44.9	95.8	231.2	268.7	291.3	327.8	363.3	402.6	426.2
Power Station Use and Transmission Losses (million kwh)	10.4	20.0	36.6	45.6	48.5	61.2	62.2	66.8	69.2
Sales (million kwh)	34.5	75.8	194.6	223.1	242.8	266.6	301.1	335.8	356.9

SOURCES: Kenya, *Statistical Abstracts; Trade and Supplies Bulletin.*

TABLE S.18: Posts and Telecommunications Operating Statistics

	1947	1950	1955	1956	1957	1958	1959	1960	1961
Post Offices in Operation	155[a]	180	203	213	217	226	228	228	230
Postal Services: letters, cards and second class mail (million)	31.2	42.0	73.8	68.7	76.7	66.7	72.5	74.2	73.1
Parcels (thousand)	553	557	1,014	826	755	680	668	647	597[b]
International: telegrams handled (thousand)	315	440	535	549	508	531	521	499	481
Telephones in use (thousand)	8.2	12.7	27.1	29.4	32.5	36.3	39.7	42.7	45.0

[a] Figure for 1946.   [b] Provisional.
SOURCES: Kenya, *Statistical Abstracts*; East African Statistical Department, *Quarterly Economic and Statistical Bulletin*.

TABLE S.19: Motor Vehicles—Licensed and Newly Registered

	1947	1950	1955	1956	1957	1958	1959	1960	1961
Licensed Vehicles:									
Motor Cars	9,301	17,080	25,901	28,717	31,177	33,672	36,028	40,002	42,300
Commercial Vehicles	9,144	15,315	35,493	28,037	29,326	31,073	32,304	37,704	31,568
Other[a]	1,770	3,013	5,467	6,872	7,167	8,613	9,337	11,799	10,672
Total	20,215	35,408	56,861	63,626	67,670	73,358	77,669	89,505	84,540
Newly Registered Vehicles:									
Motor Cars	1,588	2,897	5,088	5,388	4,786	5,302	5,692	6,347	4,754
Commercial Vehicles	2,111	2,870	5,605	4,877	4,312	4,628	4,652	5,138	4,199
Other[a]	411	867	1,076	1,476	1,494	1,592	1,963	2,132	1,332
Total	4,110	6,634	11,769	11,741	10,592	11,522	12,307	13,617	10,285

[a] Includes motor cycles of all types, tractors, graders, rollers, cranes, three-wheelers, caravans and ambulances, etc.
SOURCES: East African Statistical Department, *Quarterly Economic and Statistical Bulletin*; Kenya, *Statistical Abstracts*; Economics and Statistics Division.

TABLE S.20: Public Health—Number of Beds and Patients

	1947	1950	1955	1956	1957	1958	1959	1960	1961
Hospital Beds	n.a.	n.a.	7,847	7,811	7,764	9,171	9,717	10,419	10,968
In-Patients ('000)	160	174	147	173	172	155	155	157	149
Out-Patients ('000)	811	955	1,216	1,313	1,034	932	1,030	1,167	1,176
Total ('000)	971	1,129	1,364	1,486	1,206	1,087	1,186	1,324	1,325

SOURCE: Economics and Statistics Division.

TABLE S.21: Nairobi City Water Sales

(millions of imperial gallons)

	1955	1956	1957	1958	1959	1960	1961	1962[a]
Quantity Leaving Treatment Works	n.a.	n.a.	2,604	2,878	3,313	3,528	3,591	1,842
Quantity of Water Consumed	1,703	1,867	2,154	2,347	2,716	2,995	n.a.	n.a.

[a] Six months only.
SOURCES: Kenya, Economic and Statistics Division; City Council of Nairobi.

TABLE S.22: Currency in Circulation—Coins and Total Currency[a]

(£ million)

	1950	1955	1956	1957	1958	1959	1960	1961
Total currency	29.6	60.4	60.7	60.7	58.7	57.3	60.4	59.2
of which coins:	8.9	11.3	11.2	10.6	9.9	9.5	9.4	8.7

[a] Currency in circulation in the East African currency area.
SOURCES: Kenya, *Statistical Abstract;* East African Currency Board.

TABLE S.23: Liquidity of Commercial Banks

(£ million)

Dec. 31	Deposits[a]				Loans Advances and Bills Discounted	Liquid Assets			
	Demand	Time	Savings	Total		Cash	Balances Abroad & E. Africa	Total	Liquidity Ratio[b]
1938	3.2	1.7	0.3	5.2	2.9	1.3	1.8	3.1	60
1946	20.5	2.2	1.1	23.8	2.8	3.3	15.9	19.2	81
1950	30.1	2.5	1.0	33.6	11.4	1.8	17.6	19.4	58
1953	37.6	2.8	1.6	41.9	20.3	2.3	17.1	19.4	46
1955	51.9	2.8	3.2	57.9	41.3	2.0	11.6	13.6	23
1956	43.4	4.1	3.9	51.4	35.7	2.2	10.5	12.7	25
1957	42.9	5.0	5.1	53.0	39.2	2.5	8.0	10.5	20
1958	39.9	6.1	6.2	52.2	34.3	3.0	10.4	13.4	26
1959	44.0	5.9	7.1	56.9	37.5	2.3	11.6	13.9	24
1960	40.3	4.4	5.5	50.2	42.2	3.0	−0.2	2.8	6
1961	41.2	4.1	7.1	52.5	39.0	3.1	5.6	8.7	17

[a] The different categories of deposits are defined as:
   Demand: subject to transfer or cashing by check at sight.
   Time: usually not subject to transfer by and lodged for a definite period subject to notice of withdrawal.
   Savings: lodged for no fixed period of time, and not subject to transfer by check.
[b] Total liquid assets as a percentage of total deposits.
SOURCES: East African Statistical Department, *Quarterly Economic and Statistical Bulletin;* Kenya, *Trade and Supplies Bulletin.*

TABLE S.24: Post Office Savings Bank

(£ thousand)

	1946	1951	1955	1957	1958	1959	1960	1961
Deposits	2,765	2,930	3,873	3,064	3,086	3,211	3,446	3,363
Withdrawals	2,182	2,566	3,161	4,130	3,590	3,421	5,346	4,000
Balances[a]	4,882	7,428	10,310	8,997	8,697	8,691	6,974	6,489

[a] Balances at December 31, including interest credited to depositors' accounts.
SOURCES: Kenya, *Statistical Abstract;* East African Statistical Department, *Economic and Statistical Review.*

TABLE S.25: Kenya Government Public Debt

(£ thousand)

Outstanding at June 30	Long-Term Loans raised in London[a]	Unfunded Debt from outside East Africa	Total Public Debt[a]
1954	28,306	234	33,065
1955	28,306	4,148	39,048
1956	32,531	5,449	47,104
1957	32,531	6,096	50,247
1958	32,531	8,111	54,506
1959	32,531	7,280	57,420
1960	32,531	11,939	62,896
1961	32,531	19,210[b]	69,171

[a] Includes £6,696,100 raised for the East African Railways and Harbours Administration.
[b] Including the following loans outstanding at June 30, 1961:

Colonial Development Corporation	£ 1,920,000
Barclays Overseas Development Corp. Ltd.	420,000
Scepture Trust Ltd.	374,912
Special Road Program Contractors	1,779,180
U.K. Exchequer	8,272,851
IBRD	395,505
	£13,162,448

SOURCE: Kenya, *Statistical Abstracts.*

TABLE S.26: Kenya Government Revenue[a]

(£ million)

	1951	1954/55	1957/58	1958/59	1959/60	1960/61	1961/62 Estimates[b]
Direct Taxation:							
Income tax	3.99	8.12	11.29	11.33	10.41	9.97	9.90
Graduated personal tax	1.02	1.70	2.22	2.17	1.94	1.82	1.81
Estate duty	0.13	0.16	0.26	0.25	0.09	—	—
Export duty	—	0.97	—	—	—	—	—
Indirect Taxation:							
Import duty	} 7.06	7.51	8.11	9.54	10.66	10.00	11.44
Excise		2.10	2.94	3.16	3.25	3.59	3.93
Stamp duties	0.38	0.46	0.60	0.58	0.66	0.54	0.45
Petrol tax	0.40	0.43	0.51	0.50	0.57	0.93	1.05
Other	0.52	0.97	1.40	1.40	1.46	1.43	1.50
TOTAL TAXES	13.50	22.37	27.34	28.93	29.03	28.28	30.08
Fines and Forfeitures	0.10	0.19	0.32	0.41	0.35	0.37	0.34
Income from Property	1.00	1.39	1.69	1.73	1.80	2.51	1.76[c]
Payment for Goods and Services	1.05	1.70	2.60	3.05	3.39	3.97	3.91
Reimbursements	1.78	1.54	1.68	1.66	1.45	1.12	2.13
Grants from Abroad:							
Emergency grant	—	9.00	1.50	0.75	0.80	—	—
CDW	0.78	1.03	1.74	1.06	0.84	1.59	} 2.35
Other	—	—	0.85	0.12	0.20	0.07	
Loans:							
U.K. (Emergency and Exchequer)	} 4.87	} 0.48	1.50	0.75	3.80	5.33	4.50
Local and other East African			2.21	3.67	2.17	0.40	} 1.89
Other			0.25	0.57	0.37	0.79	
TOTAL GRANTS AND LOANS	5.65	10.51	8.05	6.92	8.18	12.48	8.74
Miscellaneous[d]	0.28	0.89	1.82	1.71	1.92	1.81	1.60
GRAND TOTAL	23.36	38.55	43.50	44.39	46.12	46.24	48.56

[a] Gross of appropriations in aid; excludes short-term and grant-in-aid funds to finance deficit.

[b] Revenues have not been reallocated in line with Raisman Commission.

[c] Excludes Kenya's share of the Currency Board surplus.

[d] Includes extra-exchequer receipts, project earnings, withdrawals from renewals and other funds, etc.

SOURCES: Kenya, *Statistical Abstracts; Economic Survey,* 1962.

TABLE S.27: Kenya Government Expenditures[a]

(£ million)

	1957/58	1958/59	1959/60	1960/61	1961/62 Estimates[b]
General Services:					
Administration	3.08	3.56	3.75	4.50	4.50
Justice, Police, Prisons	7.82	7.14	6.91	8.53	7.59
Revenue Collection, etc.	1.03	1.05	1.07	1.23	1.18
Defense	1.80	1.71	1.59	0.42	0.37
Subtotal	13.73	13.46	13.32	14.68	13.64
Financial Obligations:					
Public Debt	2.47	2.71	2.86	3.43	4.28
Pensions and Passages	2.06	2.15	2.06	2.11	2.32
Transfers to Local Authorities	1.00	0.94	1.83	1.39	1.98
Subtotal	5.53	5.79	6.76	6.92	8.58
Economic and Community Services:					
Agriculture, Forestry, Game	5.39	6.21	6.20	6.94	9.17
Transport	3.18	2.70	3.09	3.37	3.28
Other, including Water	1.73	1.54	1.57	1.86	1.77
Subtotal	10.29	10.45	10.85	12.17	14.22
Social Services:					
Education	5.90	6.30	7.04	8.02	8.91
Health	2.76	2.75	2.95	3.39	3.27
Other	0.81	1.35	1.14	1.14	0.79
Sub-total	9.48	10.40	11.12	12.55	12.97
Unallocable	3.59	3.42	3.79	4.02	3.35
Emergency Expenditure, n.e.s.	1.83	0.43	0.54	—	—
Grand Total	44.45	43.94	46.39	50.35	52.75

[a] Total of current and development expenditures, gross of appropriations in aid.
[b] Functional classification only approximately comparable with other years.
SOURCES: Kenya, *Statistical Abstracts; Economic Survey*, 1962.

TABLE S.28: Total Reported Annual Wage Bill

(£ thousand)

	1946[a]	1955	1956	1957	1958	1959	1960	1961
Agricultural:								
European	500	1,527	1,633	1,960	1,971	1,934	2,058	2,087
Asian	100	206	196	247	242	283	412	363
African	2,400	7,475	7,459	8,440	8,633	8,617	10,033	9,824
Private Industry and Commerce:								
European	2,200	10,764	10,975	12,613	13,300	13,830	14,486	14,809
Asian	2,200	9,784	10,706	11,509	11,185	11,407	11,758	11,476
African	2,200	10,732	11,733	12,526	12,391	12,794	13,898	13,912
Public Service:								
European	2,000	10,400	9,742	11,005	11,320	11,306	11,322	13,357
Asian	1,600	5,128	5,261	6,050	5,951	6,180	6,562	7,381
African	1,700	11,063	11,074	12,534	12,539	13,223	14,371	16,463
All Employees:								
European	4,800	22,691	22,350	25,578	26,591	27,070	27,866	30,253
Asian	3,800	15,118	16,163	17,806	17,373	17,870	18,732	19,220
African	6,300	29,270	30,266	33,500	33,563	34,634	38,302	40,199
Total	14,900	67,079	68,779	76,884	77,527	79,574	84,900	89,672

[a] Figures rounded to the nearest £100,000.
SOURCES: East African Statistical Department, *Quarterly Economic and Statistical Bulletin; Reported Employment and Wages in Kenya,* 1948–60.

TABLE S.29: Statutory Minimum Wages[a]

(Sh. per month at January 1)

	1954[b]	1955	1956	1957	1958	1959	1960	1961	1962
Minimum Wage:									
Nairobi									
Under 21	62.50	71.50	75.00	75.00	75.00	75.00	73.00	74.00	74.00
Over 21			82.50	85.00	85.00	85.00	95.00	102.00	107.00
Kisumu									
Under 21	57.00	65.00	69.00	69.00	72.50	72.50	71.00	71.00	71.00
Over 21			76.00	78.50	82.50	87.50	94.00	98.00	103.00
Housing Allowance:									
Nairobi									
Under 21	11.00	13.00	13.00	13.00	13.00	13.00	13.00	13.00	13.00
Over 21			17.50	20.00	22.50	22.50	24.50	26.00	26.00
Kisumu									
Under 21	9.00	9.00	9.00	9.00	9.00	9.00	10.00	10.00	11.00
Over 21			12.00	14.50	17.00	17.00	18.50	20.00	22.00

[a] Minimum wages are operative in 13 towns in Kenya.
[b] April 1.
SOURCE: Kenya, Labour Department.

TABLE S.30: Cost of Living and Consumer's Price Indices[a]

	1947	1951	1957	1958	1959	1960	1961	June 1962
A. Nairobi Cost of Living Index (excluding rent) (Base: August 1939 = 100)								
Food, Drink and Tobacco	175	229	300	292	296	296	303	318
Clothing and Footwear	240	283	272	274	270	272	274	277
Household	169	226	265	262	263	263	265	268
Domestic Servants' Wages	180	240	415	432	431	447	472	486
Transport	138	193	222	223	223	222	228	236
Pharmaceutical Products	125	135	153	158	161	161	166	169
Amusements	135	147	171	174	186	186	189	190
Papers and Periodicals	127	158	158	188	188	188	188	206
Miscellaneous	192	226	264	267	275	273	273	273
All Groups	175	225	288	288	290	292	299	309
B. Nairobi Wage Earners' Index of Consumer Prices (Base: October–December 1958 = 100)								
Food					100	101	104	105
Beverages and Tobacco					103	103	104	112
Clothing and Footwear					100	102	103	102
Fuel and Light					93	93	99	99
Household Operation					98	101	99	95
Personal Care and Health					168	168	168	168
Recreation and Entertainment					102	102	102	102
Transport					100	117	117	117
Miscellaneous					100	125	162	162
All Groups					101	103	105	107

[a] On December 31.
SOURCES: Kenya, *Statistical Abstract; Trade and Supplies Bulletin.*

TABLE S.31: External and Interterritorial Trade

(£ million)

	1950	1951	1952	1953	1954	1955	1956	1957	1958	1959	1960	1961
External Trade												
Imports[a]	34.1	53.9	59.3	51.7	60.3	71.5	69.8	72.0	60.9	61.5	70.1	68.9
Re-exports	3.5	3.3	3.9	3.4	2.5	2.4	4.1	4.9	3.9	5.1	5.0	6.4
Retained imports	30.5	50.6	55.4	48.3	57.8	69.2	65.8	67.1	56.9	56.4	65.1	62.5
Exports	17.2	24.1	25.8	19.5	20.3	25.7	29.0	26.4	29.3	33.3	35.2	35.3
Balance	−13.4	−26.5	−29.6	−28.8	−37.5	−43.5	−36.8	−40.7	−27.7	−23.1	−29.9	−27.2
Interterritorial Trade[b]												
Imports from:	3.4	3.6	4.3	4.8	5.3	6.0	4.0	4.5	4.9	5.5	7.0	7.0
Tanganyika	0.7	0.9	0.7	0.8	0.8	1.2	1.5	1.5	1.5	1.8	1.9	1.8
Uganda	2.7	2.7	3.6	4.0	4.5	4.8	2.5	3.0	3.4	3.6	5.1	5.2
Exports to:	3.6	3.7	4.4	5.3	5.8	6.0	9.0	11.4	10.7	12.3	13.8	15.9
Tanganyika	2.4	2.0	2.3	2.5	2.8	2.5	4.4	5.4	5.6	6.5	7.6	8.9
Uganda	1.2	1.7	2.0	2.8	3.0	3.5	4.6	6.0	5.1	5.8	6.2	7.0
Balance	+0.2	+0.1	+0.1	+0.5	+0.5	—	+4.9	+6.9	+5.9	+6.8	+6.8	+9.0
TOTAL TRADE BALANCE	−13.2	−26.4	−29.5	−28.3	−37.0	−43.5	−31.9	−33.8	−21.8	−16.3	−23.1	−18.2

[a] Imports received direct from countries outside of East Africa, *net* of interterritorial transfers of imported goods.
[b] Relates to the exchange of locally produced and locally manufactured goods. Values shown for 1957 and previous years *include* excise duty on excisable commodities and customs duty charged on imported raw materials used in locally manufactured goods, and are therefore *not* comparable with subsequent years.

SOURCES: East African Statistical Department, *Quarterly Economic and Statistical Bulletin*; Kenya, *Trade and Supplies Bulletin*.

TABLE S.32: Domestic Exports—Main Commodities by Value

Principal Commodities	1950 Value (million)	1950 %	1951 Value (million)	1951 %	1952 Value (million)	1952 %	1953 Value (million)	1953 %	1954 Value (million)	1954 %	1955 Value (million)	1955 %	1956 Value (million)	1956 %	1957 Value (million)	1957 %	1958 Value (million)	1958 %	1959 Value (million)	1959 %	1960 Value (million)	1960 %	1961 Value (million)	1961 %
Coffee, not roasted	3.5	21	4.1	17	7.1	28	6.7	34	5.7	28	8.9	35	13.7	47	10.8	41	10.4	36	10.6	32	10.3	29	10.6	30
Sisal fiber and tow	4.1	24	6.9	29	4.5	17	2.5	13	2.0	10	2.0	8	2.1	7	2.1	8	2.3	8	3.5	10	4.6	13	4.2	12
Tea	1.3	8	1.4	6	1.3	5	0.9	5	2.1	10	2.8	11	2.6	9	2.9	11	3.2	11	3.6	11	4.4	13	4.0	11
Hides, skins and fur skins, undressed	1.9	11	2.2	9	1.1	4	1.6	8	1.4	7	1.3	5	1.2	4	1.5	6	1.0	4	1.6	5	1.8	5	1.6	4
Pyrethrum: flowers and extract[a]	0.6	3	0.6	2	0.7	3	0.6	3	0.9	4	1.2	5	1.2	4	1.1	4	1.8	6	2.2	7	3.0	9	3.1	9
Wattle bark extract	1.0	6	1.3	5	1.7	7	1.5	8	1.7	8	2.3	9	1.5	5	1.5	6	1.0	4	1.0	3	0.7	2	0.8	2
Maize, unmilled	0.7	4	0.7	3	2.4	9	0.3	2	1.0	5	1.7	7	0.1	—	0.5	2	1.9	6	1.1	3	0.2	1	—	—
Sodium carbonate	0.9	5	1.2	5	1.2	5	0.8	4	1.1	6	1.3	5	1.5	5	1.4	5	1.2	4	1.7	5	1.3	4	1.6	4
Meat and meat preparations	0.2	1	0.3	1	0.3	1	0.3	2	0.3	2	0.2	1	0.2	1	0.4	1	1.2	4	2.0	6	1.8	5	2.3	6
Cotton, raw	0.2	1	1.0	4	1.1	4	0.5	3	0.8	4	0.7	3	0.9	3	0.4	1	0.5	2	0.7	2	0.8	2	0.6	2
Butter (excluding ghee)	0.2	1	0.2	1	0.4	2	0.2	1	0.5	2	0.5	2	0.6	2	0.5	2	0.9	3	0.7	2	0.7	2	0.6	2
Preserved fruits	—	—	0.1	—	0.1	—	0.2	1	0.3	2	0.5	2	0.8	3	0.6	2	0.6	2	0.5	2	0.4	1	0.5	1
Oil seeds, oil nuts and oil kernels	0.1	1	0.3	1	0.6	2	0.5	3	0.3	2	0.3	1	0.4	2	0.5	2	0.5	2	0.6	2	0.6	2	0.4	1
Wool, raw	0.2	1	0.4	2	0.2	1	0.3	1	0.2	1	0.3	1	0.3	1	0.3	1	0.3	1	0.4	1	0.4	1	0.4	1
Copper, unwrought	—	—	—	—	—	—	—	—	—	—	—	—	—	—	0.4	2	0.4	1	0.4	1	0.5	1	0.5	1
Other	2.3	13	3.4	15	3.1	12	2.6	12	2.0	9	1.7	5	1.9	7	1.5	6	2.1	6	2.7	8	3.7	10	4.1	14
Total	17.2	100	24.1	100	25.8	100	19.5	100	20.3	100	25.7	100	29.0	100	26.4	100	29.3	100	33.3	100	35.2	100	35.3	100

[a] For the years 1950 to 1953 the annual values have been revised to include the value of Pyrethrum Extract which is not shown in the Annual Trade Reports.
SOURCES: East African Customs and Excise Department, Annual Trade Reports; East African Statistical Department; Kenya, Statistical Abstracts.

TABLE S.33: Quantity of Domestic Exports

(unit of quantity in '000)[a]

		1950	1951	1952	1953	1954	1955	1956	1957	1958	1959	1960	1961
Coffee, not roasted	Tons	10.3	9.9	16.9	14.8	10.8	19.4	26.7	22.3	25.0	25.8	27.8	32.2
Sisal fiber and tow	Tons	36	39	35	35.3	32.2	33.5	35.2	39.6	42.1	51.0	57.0	57.5
Tea	Tons	4.1	4.1	4.3	3.0	4.8	5.8	7.0	7.2	8.1	9.4	10.7	9.8
Hides, skins and fur skins, undressed	Tons	5.9	4.7	3.7	5.2	4.4	5.0	4.6	5.6	4.3	5.4	6.6	7.2
Pyrethrum flowers	Cwt	23	26	38	26	23	19	26	35	36	21	63	51
Pyrethrum extract	Centals	0.9	0.7	0.6	0.7	1.7	2.7	2.3	1.7	3.8	5.5	5.8	6.6
Wattle bark extract	Tons	24.1	22.2	24.0	22.1	24.2	33.2	21.8	26.3	19.0	19.3	14.3	17.0
Maize, unmilled	Tons	30.9	20.3	68.3	10.8	45.9	77.2	4.2	22.6	97.8	54.3	9.2	0.2
Sodium carbonate	Tons	101	124	112	74	102	117	137	116	104	148	115	143
Meat and meat preparations	Tons	1.2	1.7	1.7	1.5	2.0	1.0	0.8	1.6	6.0	8.4	7.1	7.3
Cotton, raw	Centals	29	39	61	42	61	52	69	31	49	71	78	55
Butter (excluding ghee)	Tons	0.6	0.6	1.2	0.6	1.3	1.5	1.9	1.5	3.2	2.4	2.3	1.9
Preserved fruits	Tons	0.1	0.4	0.8	2.0	2.4	4.1	6.2	5.2	5.2	4.9	4.5	4.5
Oil seeds, oil nuts and oil kernels	Tons	3.6	4.6	9.9	8.3	8.9	7.6	8.8	8.2	10.7	12.3	11.0	7.6
Wool, raw	Centals	11.9	14.7	12.0	14.5	12.3	13.8	16.7	16.2	16.7	22.4	21.2	25.6
Copper, unwrought	Tons	—	—	—	—	—	—	—	2.5	3.3	3.2	3.1	3.7

[a] 1 ton = 20 cwt. (long ton); 1 cwt. = 112 lbs.; 1 cental = 100 lbs.
SOURCES: East African Customs and Excise Department, Annual Trade Reports.

TABLE S.34: Classification by Stage of Production and Use of Retained Imports[a]

	1950	1951	1952	1953	1954	1955	1956	1957	1958	1959	1960	1961
	£ million											
Food, drink and tobacco	2.1	3.2	4.0	5.2	5.1	4.0	5.1	6.0	4.8	5.6	4.3	7.4
Producer's materials	11.0	19.7	19.4	16.2	19.4	22.7	23.0	23.4	21.6	20.1	24.1	22.5
Producer's capital goods	8.2	9.8	12.5	12.4	13.8	19.6	16.4	15.2	10.6	10.3	12.8	12.1
Spares and accessories		2.0	3.1	2.2	1.7	2.8	2.5	2.3	2.2	2.9	3.6	3.4
Consumers' goods	7.3	15.2	13.8	8.2	12.8	13.7	13.4	15.7	13.6	14.3	16.9	13.5
Miscellaneous	0.5	0.8	2.6	4.1	5.0	6.4	5.4	4.5	4.2	3.3	3.3	3.5
Total	29.2	50.6	55.4	48.3	57.8	69.2	65.8	67.1	56.9	56.4	65.1	62.5
	Percentage of total value											
Food, drink and tobacco	7	6	7	11	9	6	8	9	8	10	7	12
Producer's materials	38	39	35	33	33	33	35	35	38	36	37	36
Producer's capital goods	28	19	22	26	24	28	25	23	19	18	20	19
Spares and accessories		4	6	5	3	4	4	3	4	5	5	5
Consumers' goods	25	30	25	17	22	20	20	23	24	25	26	22
Miscellaneous	2	2	5	8	9	9	8	7	7	6	5	6
Total	100	100	100	100	100	100	100	100	100	100	100	100

[a] Net imports, minus re-exports (Cf. Table S.31, line 3).
SOURCES: East African Statistical Department, *Quarterly Economic and Statistical Bulletin*; Kenya, *Statistical Abstracts*.

TABLE S.35: Imports by Country of Origin

	1950	1951	1952	1953	1954	1955	1956	1957	1958	1959	1960	1961
						£ million						
Direct Imports[a]	—	—	—	—	—	—	84.6	88.0	77.0	78.8	90.0	88.7
Net Imports[a]	34.1	53.9	59.3	51.7	60.3	71.5	(69.8)	(72.0)	(60.9)	(61.5)	(70.1)	(68.9)
Unallocated, Parcel Post, etc.[a]	—	—	2.2	3.9	5.2	6.5	6.0	5.1	4.7	3.7	3.9	4.2
Total[a]	34.1	53.9	57.1	47.8	55.1	65.1	78.7	82.9	72.3	75.1	86.1	84.4
						Percentage of total value						
Country or Area:												
United Kingdom	58	42	48	56	49	49	45	40	38	39	36	36
India	8	8	6	5	7	5	6	7	6	5	4	5
Other Sterling Area	13	13	15	13	14	14	15	12	13	15	11	14
Total Sterling Area	77	63	69	74	70	68	66	59	57	59	51	55
West Germany	1	4	3	3	6	6	6	7	7	6	7	5
Italy	2	5	2	3	4	3	3	3	3	3	3	3
Other EEC	4	9	8	7	9	10	7	7	7	7	8	8
Total EEC	7	18	13	13	19	19	16	17	17	17	18	15
EFTA (excluding U.K.)	2	3	2	2	3	3	3	4	4	3	3	3
United States	5	3	7	6	3	4	4	3	4	4	6	6
Canada	1	—	1	—	—	—	—	1	1	1	—	—
Total Dollar Area	6	3	7	6	3	4	4	4	4	4	6	6
Japan	1	4	3	—	1	2	3	4	6	6	10	10
Iran	5	2	—	—	—	3	6	8	9	8	8	7
Other Countries	2	7	6	5	4	1	2	4	3	3	4	4
Total	100	100	100	100	100	100	100	100	100	100	100	100

[a] The aggregate for imports used here varies as the classification by countries in the Annual Trade Reports has changed. "Direct Imports" equal all goods entering the country (including those subsequently re-exported). "Net Imports" equal direct imports minus transfers of goods to Tanganyika and Uganda. Parcel Post has been subtracted for 1952 and subsequent years since they are not allocated by country of origin.

SOURCES: East African Customs and Excise, *Annual Trade Reports*.

TABLE S.36: Destination of Domestic Exports by Country

	1950	1951	1952	1953	1954	1955	1956	1957	1958	1959	1960	1961
Total Value (£ million)	17.2	24.1	25.8	19.5	20.3	25.7	29.0	26.4	29.3	33.3	35.2	35.3
Percentage of total value												
Country or Area:												
United Kingdom	35	30	30	32	31	31	25	26	29	24	25	24
India	5	4	6	6	8	7	6	7	3	4	4	4
South Africa	5	5	4	4	4	4	4	4	4	4	4	3
Other Sterling Area	10	10	8	9	10	6	7	7	8	8	10	10
Total Sterling Area	55	49	48	51	53	48	42	44	44	42	43	41
West Germany	10	10	15	21	16	18	19	23	21	24	18	17
Italy	1	2	3	2	2	4	3	2	2	4	4	3
Netherlands	5	6	6	3	3	5	5	4	4	4	3	4
Other EEC	2	5	4	2	3	3	2	3	3	3	3	2
Total EEC	17	23	28	28	24	30	29	32	30	35	28	26
EFTA (excluding U.K.)	1	2	2	2	3	3	2	3	2	2	3	3
U.S.	13	11	10	7	8	11	16	10	11	8	11	14
Other Dollar Area	4	6	3	2	3	2	4	2	2	2	2	3
Total Dollar Area	17	17	13	9	11	13	20	12	13	10	13	17
Japan	1	1	1	2	1	2	3	4	5	4	4	4
Other (includes ships' stores)	9	8	8	8	7	4	4	5	6	7	9	9
Total	100	100	100	100	100	100	100	100	100	100	100	100

SOURCES: East African Customs and Excise, *Annual Trade Reports*.

TABLE S.37: Kenya's Exports to Tanganyika and Uganda[a]

(£ thousands)

	To Tanganyika							To Uganda						
	1951	1953	1955	1957	1959	1960	1961	1951	1953	1955	1957	1959	1960	1961
Wheat flour	349	582	493	505	317	282	205	388	669	416	601	535	497	520
Beer, ales and stout	90	311	436	416	371	471	546	73	213	320	263	100	121	152
Dairy products, eggs & honey	146	138	43	41	52	66	81	98	239	342	635	635	582	694
Butter[b]	—	—	123	125	180	228	196							
Tea	134	168	57	369	436	330	491	49	78	10	119	131	114	71
Coffee, roasted	30	41	52	47	57	60	72	21	35	67	44	43	54	86
Meat & meat preparations	66	73	69	153	140	177	267	44	72	160	209	139	130	173
Cigarettes	—	41	95	1,734	895	975	1,102	—	75	65	1,603	751	788	633
Clothing	118	88	122	136	375	463	504	46	79	125	107	216	280	371
Footwear	167	98	189	203	333	375	400	108	89	267	242	246	263	313
Soap & soap preparations	—	—	37	49	209	223	441							
Insecticides	—	—	29	42	58	78	99							
Household aluminum utensils	75	63	70	88	133	176	125	77	45	82	64	102	120	81
Sisal bags, sacks & cordage	90	58	14	24	73	104	71	174	86	138	153	247	326	257
Paper, paper board and manufacture	27	26	43	60	77	129	222	51	50	102	155	203	236	273
Metal containers	7	135	74	56	139	184	113	6	49	115	27	93	59	84
Cement	—	3	33	302	682	729	681	58	121	61	80	95	70	59
Wood and timber	34	38	33	79	52	58	44	15	32	133	83	61	45	32
Steel doors & windows	—	—	16	69	85	144	180							
Salt								39	40	57	32	10	9	9
Coconut oil								—	82	47	66	44	38	83
Tobacco manufactured								—	—	—	492	195	179	167
Others	649	646	517	895	1,849	2,356	3,061	493	713	982	1,069	1,938	2,252	3,039
Total	1,982	2,505	2,545	5,393	6,513	7,608	8,901	1,740	2,767	3,489	6,044	5,784	6,163	7,047

[a] From 1959, the value of commodities traded excludes excise duty and customs duty on imported raw materials, so that the statistics are not strictly comparable with those for the previous years.

[b] Butter is included in Dairy Products in Uganda figures.

SOURCES: Kenya, Statistical Abstracts; East African Customs and Excise, Annual Trade Reports.

TABLE S.38: Kenya's Imports from Tanganyika and Uganda[a]

(£ thousand)

Commodity	1951	1953	1955	1957	1959	1960	1961
From Tanganyika:							
Wood and timber	125	66	156	152	69	41	37
Beans, peas and pulses	52	120	193	105	115	191	124
Coconut oil	114	70	42	89	150	103	64
Copra	30	40	29	88	49	63	49
Pyrethrum flowers	41	21	52	64	99	86	95
Cereals	114	23	18	43	107	144	101
Sugar	—	87	43	10	90	1	1
Tinned meat	22	57	37	16	48	30	30
Tobacco, unmanufactured	17	—	209	402	255	334	419
Electricity	—	—	73	68	64	62	57
Other	389	341	373	484	802	820	868
Total	904	825	1,225	1,521	1,848	1,875	1,844
From Uganda:							
Cigarettes	1,680	2,771	3,138	570	327	324	294
Tobacco, manufactured	71	66	78	2	1	—	—
Tobacco, unmanufactured	—	—	34	358	806	708	162
Maize, unmilled	6	131	—	—	—	—	22
Beans, peas and pulses	—	29	44	45	9	20	26
Cottonseed oil	166	264	317	344	682	821	761
Hydrogenated oils and fats	—	18	64	42	205	219	189
Cottonseed cake	44	122	24	37	26	41	28
Sugar, unrefined	386	353	813	871	469	1,452	1,582
Beer, ales and stout	5	—	14	50	16	4	7
Cotton fabrics (piece goods)	—	—	—	146	402	635	838
Other	315	214	286	527	697	896	1,243
Total	2,673	3,968	4,812	2,992	3,640	5,120	5,152

[a] From 1959, the value of commodities traded excludes excise duty and customs duty on imported raw materials, so that the statistics are not strictly comparable with those for the previous years.

SOURCES: Kenya, *Statistical Abstract;* East African Customs and Excise, *Annual Trade Reports.*

TABLE S.39: External Trade Indices[a] (1954 = 100)

	1950	1951	1952	1953	1954	1955	1956	1957	1958	1959	1960	1961
Domestic Exports:												
Quantity	98	104	122	99	*100*	123	150	141	170	185	195	204
Unit Value	87	116	106	96	*100*	103	95	92	85	88	88	84
Value	85	121	129	95	*100*	127	143	130	145	163	172	172
Net Imports:												
Kenya												
Quantity	—	—	—	—	*100*	115	107	108	95	95	105	114
Unit Value	—	—	—	—	*100*	103	108	110	106	107	110	100
Value	—	—	—	—	*100*	119	116	119	101	102	116	114
East Africa												
Quantity	68	78	82	77	*100*	127	110	116	103	102	108	117
Unit Value	93	115	123	112	*100*	100	103	103	101	101	105	99
Value	63	90	101	86	*100*	127	113	120	104	103	114	114
Terms of Trade:[b]	107	99	116	117	*100*	100	114	120	125	122	125	119

[a] The indices for the years 1955–61 have been revised.

[b] The import price index as a percentage of the export price index. Prior to 1954 the East African import price index is used.

SOURCES: East African Statistical Department, *Quarterly Economic and Statistical Bulletin; Economic and Statistical Review.*

TABLE S.40: Reported Completion of New Private Buildings—Main Towns[a]

	1950	1956	1957	1958	1959	1960	1961	First Half of 1962[b]
Number of New Buildings:								
Residential	516	830	773	636	676	559	122	23
Nonresidential	300	292	276	205	200	154	92	35
Total	816	1,122	1,049	841	876	713	214	58
Floor Area ('000 sq. ft.):								
Residential	1,368	3,021	2,920	2,070	2,335	2,089	483	94
Nonresidential	1,380	2,293	1,807	1,489	2,014	1,120	855	79
Total	1,748	5,314	4,727	3,559	4,350	3,209	1,338	173
Estimated Cost (£'000):								
Residential	4,116	5,182	4,861	3,539	3,797	3,277	794	142
Nonresidential	48	3,595	3,246	2,558	3,868	2,347	1,613	204
Total	4,164	8,777	8,107	6,097	7,665	5,625	2,408	347

[a] Figures cover Nairobi, Mombasa, Kisumu, Nakuru, Eldoret and Kitale. The statistics refer to new buildings only; extensions and alterations to existing buildings are excluded.

[b] Preliminary.

SOURCE: Kenya, Economics and Statistics Division.

INDEX

Aberdare Mountains, 170
Aden, 33, 104, 197, 257, 262
African District Councils (ADC), 12, 74,
    76, 99–100, 140, 174, 182–86, 188, 224,
    286; income and expenditure,
    294–95, 298–99
African Land Development Board
    (ALDEV), 265, 267
African Livestock Marketing Organiza-
    tion (ALMO), 102, 111, 129, 327
African Settlement Board, 76
Agricultural Credit Corporation (pro-
    posed), 111, 265–68, 272
Agriculture:
    cash crops, 70–72, 105, 116
    census, 108, 318–20
    credit, 74, 110, 259, 263–68, 272
    crop distribution, 65, table S.11, 345
    education, 14, 86, 89–92
    exports, 2, 18, 21–22, 25, 34–35, 63, 103,
        107, 121–23, 126, 128–30, 132–33,
        137–39, 155
    extension, 85–88
    government expenditure, 51–55, table
        4, 62, 88, 92, 108, tables 5, 6, 143–45,
        table 2, 275
    imports, 93, 103, 130–32, 134–38, 140,
        154–55
    income, 16, 70, 72
    investment in, 41–42, 69–70
    irrigation, 5, table 4, 62, 69, 77–81,
        136, 302
    labor force, 63, 70, 85, 121, 124, 210–11,
        table S.3, 340
    land, 66–67
    marketing, marketing boards, 31, 96,
        104–18, 121, 137, 321–30
    production, 2, 16, 21, 34, 41, 44–45,
        51–52, 63–64, 72, 86, 104–16, table
        S.10, 345, tables S.12, S.13, 346
    research, 86, 94–97
    road program, 184
    scheduled, nonscheduled areas defined,
        63

Special Crops Development Authority
    (SCDA), 53, 55, 122–23, 125, 143, 266,
    292, 329
subsistence farming, 63, 71
summary of conclusions and recom-
    mendations, 301–6
technical staff, 88–89
see also Cooperatives, Disease Control,
    Fisheries, Forests, Land, Livestock,
    Localization, Veterinary, and indi-
    vidual commodities
Agriculture, Board of (nonscheduled
    areas), 74, 77, 108, 321–30; (scheduled
    areas), 108–12, 135, 264, 321–30
Agriculture, Department of, 67–68, 86,
    91–92, 94–96, 100, 117, 154
Agriculture, Minister of, 44, 87, 105,
    109, 116
Agriculture, Ministry of, 42, 65, 81, 88,
    107–9, 111, 135, 138, 142–45, 317
Agriculture, World Census of (1960), 319
Ahero, 184
Albert, Lake, 188
Angola, 125
Arabs, 5, 6, 8, 13
Archer's Post, 102, 129
Arusha, 189, 197
Asian:
    craftsmen, 157
    employees, 211
    enterprise, 16, 51, 56
    farms, 34
    housing for, 252
    land tenure, 65–67
    migration, table S.2, 339
    personnel in civil service, 13
    personnel in transport and communi-
        cations, 180, 197–98, 206
    savings, 268, 283
    students, 226, 230–32, 234
    taxation, 276, 284
Athi River, 77–78, 334
Australia, 97, 130
Aviation, see Transport

Bahrein, 104
Balance of payments, 28–29, 40, 47, 57, 104, 259, 263
Baluhya, 5
Bank of England, 257
Banking, central, 33, 258–61, 271, 310
Banks:
    commercial, 20, 23, 29, 38–39, 110, 257, 259–65, 270, table 1, 262, table S.23, 353
    Land and Agricultural Bank, 84, 110, 167, 264, 267
    savings, 272
    The Land Bank, 55, 261
Bantu, 5
Barclays Overseas Development Corporation Ltd., 265
Baringo Abattoir, 102, 129
Barley, 18, 64, 68, 135
Bee hives, 103–4
Beecher Committee, 224
Beer, 155–56
Beryl, 149
Beverage industry, 155–56
Brazil, 125
Brick industry, 149, 158
British Overseas Airways Corporation (BOAC), 197
British Overseas Civil Service, 12–13, 213
British Petroleum Company, 148
B-P Shell Petroleum Development Company of Kenya, Ltd., 148
British Post Office, 206
Budget:
    colony estimates, 56, tables 1, 2, 274–75
    development estimates, 55, 56, 61, 175, 274
    1962, 277, 284–85, 289, 299
Building societies, 269–70, table 2, 270
Bukura, 149
Butere, 189

Calico Printers Association, 164
Canning Crops Board, 329
Canning industry, 128, 155
Capital outflow, 23, 263
Carbon dioxide, 149
Carpenter Committee, *Report of the Committee on African Wages,* 218

Cashew nuts, 65, 139–40
Cattle, 82, 98–101, 126, 128
Cement, 20, 28, 149, 158, 194–95
Central African Airways, 197
Central Housing Board, 252–54, 295, 297, 299–300
Central Province, 6–7, 10, 19, 81, 127, 135–36, 139
Central Province Marketing Board, 113, 326
Ceramics industry, 149
Cereal Producers Board (scheduled areas), 111, 325
Cereals, 114
Cereals and Sugar Finance Corp., 261
Ceylon, 122
Cherangani Hills, 102
Chromite, 150
Cigarettes, 28, 156
Civil Service, Kenya, 12–13, 37–38, 43, 212–15, 284
Coastal Provinces, 64, 96, 137, 139
Coconuts, 65, 155
Coffee:
    exports, 16, 18, 21, 25–27, 64, 105, 116, 120–21
    production and marketing, 41–42, 65, 67–68, 71–72, 111, tables 2, 3, 114–21, 155, 293, tables S.10, S.11, S.12, 345–46
    prospects, 35, 70, 116–21
    summary of conclusions and recommendations, 303
Coffee Board of Kenya, 116, 322
Coffee Marketing Board, 117–18, 322
Colonial Development Corporation (CDC), 122, 128, 146, 253, 270, 272
Colonial Development and Welfare (CDW), 45, 56, 63, 74–75, 95–97, 274, 278, 280
Comet aircraft, 28
Commonwealth Development Corporation, 278
Commonwealth Sugar Agreement, 131–32
Congo Basin Treaty, 27, 159
Constitution (April 1962), 10, 273
Construction industry, 22, 42, 157, 216, table S.40, 368
Contractor-financing, 57, 182–83, 256, 278
Cooperatives, 53, 111–14, 116–18, 265, 267

Copper, 146
Cost of Living Index, Nairobi, 21, 219, table S.30, 359
Cotton, 26, 28, 65, 68, 137–38, 162, 165
Cotton Lint and Seed Marketing Board, 137, 323
Council of Ministers, 9, 11, 14
Craib, Dr. Ian (Craib "B" Plan), 140–41
Crown Land Ordinance of 1902, 8
Currency, 33, 39, 257–63, 267, 271, table S.22, 353
Customs Department, 160
Customs, 30, 154, 156–58, 203, 273, 276–77, 290–91
    drawback, table 2, 160–64
    protective, 155–56, 159, 162–65
    rates, 159–60
Customs union, see East African customs union

Da Gama, Vasco, 8
Dairying, 64, 111, 113–14, 126–28, 155
Dalgleish, A. G., A Survey of Unemployment, 36, 216
Dar es Salaam, 155, 188, 190, 193, 195–97, 200, 202
Dar es Salaam College, 13, 236
Debt, public, 39, 57, table 4, 278, table S.25, 354
    service, 39, 58, 275, table 2, 281
Defense expenditures, table 2, 275, 281
Dekker, K. Douwes, 131
Development Committee, 14, 315
Development Fund, 253
Development Plan, Ten Year (1946–55), 76
Development and Planning Division (Treasury), 316
Devonshire White Paper of 1923, 9
Diatomite, 149
Disease control, 68, 75, 94, 97–99, 130, 142, 190
    see also Health, Tsetse fly
Dodoma, 190

East Africa High Commission (now EACSO), viii, 9, 29–30, 32, 141, 211

East Africa, University of, 13–14, 54, 236–37
East African Agriculture and Forestry Research Organization, 95
East African Airways Corporation (EAAC), 28, table 3, 59, 196–200, 273, 332
East African Cereals Pool, 132
East African Commissioner of Customs and Excise, 276–77
East African Common Services Organization (EACSO), vii, 20, 30, 32–33, 45, 57, 59–61, 113, 131, 135, 180–81, 188, 190–91, 193, 197–98, 215, 257, 273–74, 279, 291, 293
    development programs, table 3, 59
    Directorate of Civil Aviation, 198, 200, 202
    Distributable Pool, 32, 273, 288
    Meteorological Department, 202
    planning arrangements, 317
    see also EAAC, EAPT, EARH
East African Currency Board, 33, 39, 257–59, 261, 263, 267, 271
East African customs union, 28–33, 104–6, 121, 154, 163–64
East African Economic and Fiscal Commission, 29
East African federation, 11, 30, 260
East African Income Tax Department, 286
East African Industrial Council, 164
East African Industrial Management Board, 167
East African Industrial Research Organization (EAIRO), 166
East African Posts and Telecommunications Department (EAPT), 32, table 3, 59–61, 203–6, 214–15, 268, 273
    expenditure (proposed), table 7, 205
East African Power and Lighting Company, Ltd. (EAPL), 147, 176–79
East African Railways and Harbours (EARH), 19, 32, 48, 59–60, 188–96, 209, 211, 335
    capital expenditures (forecast), table 3, 191–92, table 5, 196
    development program, table 3, 59–60
    planning arrangements, 317
East African School of Cooperation, 116

East African Statistical Department, 107, 316, 319

East African Tourist Travel Association, 171

East African Veterinary Research Organization, 97

Ecuador, 126

Education:
adult, 237
agricultural, 14, 36, 86, 89–92
bursaries and fees, 235–36
Cambridge School Certificate, 91
Department of, 90
government expenditure, 49–50, table 1, 53–54, table 4, 62, table 4, 237, table 5, 238, 281
higher, 213
overseas study, 88, 141, 188, 213–15, 237, 243, 245–47, 250
primary, 13, 221–30
science-technical, 233–34
secondary, 213, 221–24, 230–34, table 3, 231
summary of conclusions and recommendations, 309
teachers, 223–24, 227–30, 233, 235–37
television, 208
trade and vocational, 187–88, 201, 206, 234–35

Education, Institute of (proposed), 237

Education, Ministry of, 226–27, 229, 233–35

Egerton Agricultural College, 90–91, 141, 330

Eldoret, 154, 178, 181, 183–84, 216

Elgon Nyanza, 92

Embu, 91–92, 184, 187

Emigration, 23, 279–80, table S.2, 339

Empire Cotton Growing Corporation, 95, 137

Entebbe, 197, 200

Ethiopia, 4

European:
employees, 211
enterprise, 16, 51, 56
housing for, 252
land tenure, 65–67
personnel in civil service, 13
personnel in transport and communications, 180, 197–98, 206

savings, 268, 283
students, 226, 230–32
taxation, 276, 283–84

European Economic Community (EEC), 27, 105, 120–21, 129

European Settlement Board, 82–83

Ewaso Ngiro, 77, 81

Exports:
cargo handled (Mombasa), table 4, 194
commodities by value, table S.32, 361
destination by country, table S.36, 365
earnings, 18, 23, 25–26, 28–29, 35, 57, 63–64, 86, 104, 139
external and interterritorial, table S.31, 360, table S.37, 366
hides and game animals, 114, 128, 157, table 1, 173
miscellaneous, 158
prices, 22, 26
quantity of, table S.33, 362
tariffs and taxes, 121, 163, 292–93, 299
see also Agriculture, Coffee, Tanganyika, Uganda (trade with)

Farmers' Institute, 91–92

Farmers' Training Centers, 92

Fertilizer, 82, 92–95, 190

Finance, Minister of, 43–44, 261, 284–85, 288–89, 293, 316

Finance, Ministry of, 316

Fisheries, 141–42, 167

Flemming Award, 275

Flour, 28, 135

Food and Agriculture Organization (FAO), 35, 130, 141, 158, 240

Food industry, 154–55

Foreign exchange reserves, 33, 39, 259

Foreign trade, 105
see also Exports, Imports, Trade

Forestry, table 1, 53, table 4, 62, 140–41, 157

France, 4

Frazer, Professor A. C., Report of the Commission on . . . Research on an East African Basis, 166

Frobisher, Ltd., 148

Fruits, 114, 155

Furniture manufacture, 157

Galana River, 5
Galole, 77, 79
Game Department, 75
General Agreement on Trade and
    Tariffs (GATT), 26
Germany, 8, 27, 83, 116, 120, 122
Gichuru, J. S., viii
Gilgil, 178
Glass, 150
Goats, 98–100, 103
Gold, 25, 146–47
Goldthorpe, J. E., *The African Popula-
    tion of East Africa,* 15
Government and public administration:
    development planning, 14, 212, 315–17
    expenditures for, 12, table 2, 275,
        294–300, table S.27, 356
    local government, 11–12, table 2, 56,
        167, 294–300
    organization, 11–15
    see also ADC, Treasury
Government expenditure:
    budget: current and forecast, table 5,
        280–85; deficit and measures to
        meet, 279–81, 283–94; past, 95, 215,
        247, table 2, 275, 279
    capital proposed: agriculture, 73, 75,
        77, 141–45; education, 225, 228, table
        4, 237; health, table 6, 248–49; irri-
        gation, 78–79, 81; transport, table
        6, 199
    commission to review, 43, 284
    current: agriculture, 108, 141, 282;
        education, 225–26, table 5, 238;
        health, table 7, 248–49; localization,
        215; road maintenance, 185
    developmental recurrent: 47–49, 51–55,
        table 1, 53, table 4, 62, 88, 92, table
        6, 144–45, 175, 256
    gross: table 2, 275, table S.27, 356
    resources for: table 2, 56
    see also EACSO, EAPT, EARH
Government Printer, 158
Government revenues: 160, 186, table 3,
    276, 277, table 4, 278, table S.26, 355
Governor of Kenya, 11
Governor's Conference, 9
Grain milling, 154–55
Graphite, 149
Greeks, 8

Gross domestic product (GDP), 20,
    150–51, 168–69, 211, 247, 274,
    276, 294, 319
    by factor income, table S.7, 342
    by industrial origin, tables S.5, S.6,
        341–42
    by sectors, Chart 1, 17
    per capita, 18, 21, 38
Guardian Assurance Company, Ltd., 128
Gypsum, 149

Haddon-Cave, C. P., "Real Growth of
    the East African Territories," 20, 31
Haiti, 125
Health, 14, 238–51, 309, table S.20, 352
    expenditures for, table 1, 53, table 4,
        62, 247, tables 6, 7, 249, 281
Health, Ministry of, 240, 243–44, 247–48,
    251–52
Hides and skins, 26, 87, 92, 114, 128, 157
Homa Mountains, 149
Horn of Africa, 4
Horticultural and Canning Crops Board,
    112, 329
Horticultural Products Committee, 329
Hospital Funds, 248
Hospitals, 240–41, 245–46, 248, 250,
    table S.20, 352
Hotels, 167, 171
Housing, 251–56, 310
    government expenditure for, table 1,
        53, 55, table 4, 62

Imperial British East Africa Company, 8
Imperial Chemical Industries, 150
Imports:
    cargo handled (Mombasa), table 4, 194
    composition of, table 34, 363
    controls, 44
    customs duty drawback on, 160–64,
        table 2, 161
    electricity, table 1, 77, 176–79
    interterritorial, table S.31, 360
    licensing, 105
    miscellaneous, 44, 156–58, 194
    quotas, 163
    savings, 29, 104–5, 128, 131–32, 134,
        136, 153–54

sources of, table 35, 364
value of, 23, 25, 262–63, table 31, 360
see also Agriculture, Tanganyika,
    Uganda (trade with)
Income:
    and GDP, 22
    national, 20–22, 31, 210–11
    per capita, 21, 154, 221, 290
Independence, 1, 10, 11, 33, 45, 51, 56,
    62, 88, 109, 179, 212–13, 259
    costs of, 281
India, 8, 9, 122, 140, 197, 246, 261
Indian Ocean, 4, 154
Indonesia, 125
Industrial Council, East African, 164
Industrial Development Corporation
    (IDC), 54, 152, 166–67, 169
Industrial Development Ordinance of
    1954, 167
Industrial land, 166–67
Industrial licensing, 164
Industrial Research Council (proposed),
    166
Industry:
    credit, 263
    government expenditure for (pro-
        posed), table 1, 54, table 4, 62
    growth of, 20
    investment in, 34–35, 38–39, 150–51
    labor force, 150–53, table 1, 152, table
        S.3, 340, table S.15, 348
    manufacturing, 150–69, 306–7
    production, 42, 151, table 1, 152, tables
        S.14, S.15, S.16, 347–49
    tax relief for, 289
Industry, Department of Commerce
    and, 160
Institute of Administration, 213, 215
Insurance and insurance companies, 38,
    110, 128, 261, 270, 289
Internal security, 43, 51, table 1, 53, 55,
    table 4, 62
International Bank for Reconstruction
    and Development (IBRD), vii–viii,
    63, 74–75, 182, 259, 265, 272, table
    4, 278
International Civil Aviation Organiza-
    tion (ICAO), 202
International Coffee Agreement (1962),
    119–21

International Confederation of Free
    Trade Unions, 219
International Monetary Fund, 259
International Telex, 204
Investment:
    capital formation, 18, 22–23, 46, table
        S.8, 343
    depreciation allowance, 289
    disinvestment, 69, 86, 281
    foreign, 38–39, 150–51
    in industry, 34–35, 38–39, 150–51, 165,
        167–68
    private, 22, 42, 44, 172–74, 288–89
    public, 21–22, 42
    tax and concessions, 288–89
Iran, 27
Iraq, 104
Iron ore, 149
Irrigation, 5, table 4, 62, 69, 77–81, 136,
    302
Ismaili community, 252
Italy, 8, 120

Japan, 27, 126
Jinja, 197
Joint Sisal Board, 124
Juba River, 8

KAR, 279–81
Kabete Veterinary Institute, 97–98, 100
Kabianga, 92
Kagwe, 149
Kajiado, 102
Kamba tribe, 18
Kampala, 13, 19
Kano Plain Pilot Project, 80
Kaolin, 149
Karatina, 250
Karuri, 247
Kavirondo, Gulf of, 98
Kenya Broadcasting Corporation, 207–8
Kenya Calling, 84
Kenya Coffee Board, 116, 118
Kenya Constitutional Conference, vii
Kenya Cooperative Creameries, Ltd.
    (KCC), 53, 110, 126–27, 129, 155
Kenya Dairy Board, 112, 126, 326

Kenya Development Program (1960–63), 45–46
Kenya Farmers Association (KFA), 114, 265
Kenya Federation of Employers (KFE), 219
Kenya Land Order in Council, 66
Kenya Meat Commission, 52, 111, 128–29, 155, 235, 327
Kenya Medical Services, 245
Kenya, Mount, 4, 170
Kenya Polytechnic, 234, 237
Kenya Power Company, Ltd. (KPC), 176–79
Kenya Regional Forecast Office, 202
Kenya Road Authority, 182, 184–88
Kenya Savings Bonds, 269
Kericho, 178, 181, 183
Kiambu, 75, 168
Kibwesi, 331
Kikuyu, 5, 66, 79–80
Kilindini, 193, table 4, 194, 195
King George VI Hospital, 245–46
Kioga, Lake, 188
Kipevu, 178
Kipsigis, 6
Kisii, 5, 92, 184
Kisumu, 5, 7, 19, 167, 178, 181, 183–84, 189, 193, 195, 197, 199, 202, 207, 296
Kitale, 84–85, 149, 178, 181, 189, 197, 199, 296
Kitui, 243
Kuwait, 104

Labor force, 37, 47, 210–21, table 1, 218, 308–9, tables S.3, S.4, 340–41
Annual Enumeration of Employees, 211, 216
unemployment, 23, 36, 49, 215–17
see also Agriculture, Industry, Localization
Labor organizations, 219, 221
Labour, Department of, 219
Labour, Minister of, 44, 211, 214, 216
Labour, Ministry of, 219
Lamu, 148
Lancaster House Constitutional Conference, 10, 262, 280

Land:
areas, table S.9, 344
availability, 67–68
classification (nonscheduled areas), 70–72, table 1, 71
consolidation and enclosure, 34, 66–67, 70, 72–73
industrial, 166–67
policy, 8, 10
settlement, 50–52, table 1, 53, table 2, 56, 57, table 4, 62, 76–77, 87, 264–66
tenure, 65–67, 80
use, 34, 64–65
Land and Agricultural Bank, 84, 110, 167, 264, 267
Land Bank, the, 55, 261
Land Development and Settlement Board, 264–66
Land Registration Ordinance, 66
Landing and Shipping Company, 194
Lands Department, 167
Legislative Council, 9
Legumes, 81, 97
Leseru, 184
Licensing:
aircraft and air personnel, 200
coffee planting, 116, 118
flour mills, 135
imports, 105
industrial, 31, 159, 164–66
motor vehicles, table S.19, 351
oil prospecting, 147–49
power companies, 177
radio and television, 207
road haulage operators, 191
tea planting, 68
textile manufacture, 156
trade license charges, 291–92
Likoni, 178
Lindi, 188
Livestock, 18, 42, 64, 68, 70–71, 74, 87, 92, 97–102, 129, 190, 198
African Livestock Marketing Organization, 87, 102, 111, 129, 327
Central Artificial Insemination Station Board, 328
Pig Industry Board, 111, 328
see also, Disease Control, Veterinary
Loans, external, 39–40, 55, table 2, 56, 57–58, 193, 207, table 4, 278

see also U.K., U.S., IBRD
Local Government Loans Authority,
    295, 297, 299–300
Localization, 212–15
    government expenditure for, table 1,
        53, table 4, 62
    of agricultural staff, 88–90
    of civil service, 13, 37–38
    of forestry staff, 141
    of transport and communications staff,
        180, 187, 193, 198, 206, 209
Location Councils, 12
Lodwar, 200
London, 89, 197, 257, 273
Lumi Basin, 77–78
Luo tribe, 80

Macalder-Nyanza Mine, 146
MacGillivray, Laurie and White, Report
    of the Committee on the Organiza-
    tion of Agriculture, 107, 110, 112–13
Machakos, 92, 239–40, 331
MacKenzie, K. W. S., viii
MacKinnon Road, 147, 331
Madagascar, 195
Magadi, 4, 150, 158, 189
Maize, 18, 64, 68, 93–94, 96, 103, 110–12,
    114, 132–34, 154–55, 261, 325, tables
    S.10, S.11, S.12, 345–46
Makere College, 89–90, 236, 245–46
Malawa, 78
Malindi, 8, 178, 197, 199
Manufacturing, see Industry
Mariakani, 92, 113
Marigar, 102
Marimba, 92
Marketing boards, see Agriculture
Marsabit National Game Reserve, 170
Masai, 6, 18, 242
Masai-Amboseli Game Reserve, 170, 174
Masai-Mara Game Reserve, 170, 174
Maseno, 91–92
Match manufacture, 157
Mau Mau Emergency, 7, 10, 13, 20, 38,
    77, 212, table 2, 275, 279
Mau Summit, 183
Mauritius, 158, 195
Mbagathi, 206
Mbeya, 200

Meat, 26, 41, 64, 155
Mehta Oil Company, 148
Menneer, S. S., 43
Meru, 149, 170, 174, 187
Meteorological services, 201–3
Middle East, 103
Military bases, 217
Milk, 20, 113–14, 127
Minerals and mining, 94, 146–50, 306–7,
    tables S.14, S.15, S.16, 347–49
Mines and Geology, Department of,
    146–47
Miwani, 131, 178
Molasses, 155
Mombasa, 5, 7, 8, 19, 31, 37, 50, 60, 147,
    150–51, 154–55, 158, 167, 170, 178,
    181, 184–85, 188–90, 192, 197, 199,
    202, 207–9, 240, 247, 250, 296, 331–33
Moshi, 193, 197
Mozambique, 125
Mtito-Andei, 149
Mtwara, 188
Muguga, 97
Muslim, 6
Musoma, 197
Mwanza, 181, 193, 195, 197
Mwea, 77–78, 136, 302

Nairobi, 6–7, 11–12, 19–21, 50, 90, 95, 123,
    151, 154–55, 158, 167, 170, 176–79,
    181–85, 189, 192, 197–200, 202–4,
    207–8, 251, 257, 261, 277, 295, 331–33
Nairobi City Council, 256, 297
Nairobi Cost of Living Index, 21, 219
Nairobi National Park, 170
Nairobi Polytechnic, 54
Nairobi Wage Earners' Index, 218
Naivasha, 97, 147
Nakuru, 7, 84–88, 129, 154, 167, 178, 189,
    190, 240, 296, 334
Nandi, 6, 178
Nanyuki, 19, 149, 178, 184, 189
National and Grindlays Finance and
    Development Corporation, 265
National income, 20–22, 31, 210–11, see
    also GDP
National Institute of Agricultural
    Engineering, 139
Native Lands Trust Ordinance, 66

Native Tenure Rules (1956), 66
Ndomba, 92
Netherlands, 120
New Guinea, 148
Newlyn, W. T., " 'Take-Off' Considered in an African Setting," 20
Ngong, 92, 170
Nickel and chrome ore, 149
Nile, 5, 77, 80, 188
Nilo-Hamitic, 5
Nilotic Juluo tribe, 5
Niobium, 150
Njoro, 178
Northern Frontier Province, 81
Northern Province, 4, 6, 64, 142, 186, 326
Nyando River, 80
Nyanza, 4–7, 25, 96, 116–17, 127, 136, 138, 142, 146, 147, 149, 155
Nyanza Province, 112, 131
Nyeri, 6, 122, 176, 178, 181, 183–84
Nytil Textiles, 164

Oil crops, 72, 138, 155
Owen Falls, 19, 176–79, 209

Paper, 150, 157–58
Pemba Island, 148
Perkerra, 77
Petroleum, 27, 146–49, 194–95, 291, 334–35
    oil refinery, 60, 158, 185, 194, 196
Phosphate, 94
Pig Industry Board, 111, 328
Pineapples, 71, 155
Planning, Minister of Economic, 315
Planning Organization, 212
Population, 5–7, 15–16, 21, 23, tables S.1, S.2, 339
Port Reitz, 194
Portuguese, 8
Posho, 133
Post Office Savings Bank, 39, 261, 268–69, 272, table S.24, 354
Post offices, 203–6, 308, table S.18, 351
Postmaster General, 203
Potatoes, 64
Poultry, 114
Power, 153, 176–79, 307

electric, 19–20, table 1, 177, table 2, 178, 208–9, table S.17, 350
geothermal steam, 147
Power Securities, Ltd., 176
Price indices, 20, 26, table S.30, 359
Printing industry, 158
Pulses, 64
Pyrethrum, 18, 26, 64–65, 68, 71–72, 91, 93, 97, 114, 125–26, 166, 324, tables S.10, S.11, S.13, 345–46

Radio and television, 200–1, 206–8
Railways, see Transport
Rainfall, 4–5, 34, 64, 202
Raisman Commission, 30–32, 279
Ramisi, 131
Rentals, housing, 252; industrial land, 167
Research:
    agricultural, 95–97, 135–36
    industrial, 159, 166
    market, 139
    medical, 251
Rice, 18, 64, 68, 77, 80, 95–96, 136–37
Rift Valley, 4–5, 81, 113–14, 149, 170
Riwa, 101
Roads, see Transport
Rockefeller Foundation, 95, 101, 247
Royal Air Force, 202
Royal College, 14, 90, 213, 215, 234, 236–37
Rudolf, Lake, 4–5, 142

Sagana, 184
Salt, 150
Samburu, 102, 170
Sangalo Livestock Improvement Center, 92
Savings, private, 38, 269; see also Banks
Savings and Loan Society, Ltd., 167
Sawmills, 57
Serengeti Park, 170
Seven Forks, 179, 209
Seychelles, 195
Sheep, 82, 98–100, 102, 128, 130
Shell Oil, 148
Sherwood, Holmet, The Fertilizer Requirements of the Kenya Highlands, 93

Shipping, *see* Transport
Shoes, 157
Silver, 146
Siriba Training College, 90–91
Sisal, 16, 18, 21, 26, 41, 64–65, 68–69, 72, 76, 114, 124, 156–57, 195, 324, tables S.10, S.11, S.13, 345–46
Soap, 150, 158, 167
Soda ash, 146, 150, 158
Soda, caustic, 166
Sodium carbonate, 26
Soil, 93
    conservation, erosion, 65, 71, 81, 100
Solai, 189
Somalia, 4, 10
Sondu, 184
South Africa, 197
South African Airways, 197
Southern Line, Ltd., 195
Southern Provinces, 64, 113–14
Special Crops Development Authority, *see* Agriculture
Standard Bank Finance and Development Corporation, Ltd., 128, 265
Statistics, 108
Stock exchange, 261
Subsidies:
    ALMO, 129
    broadcasting, 207
    common services, 32
    education, 228
    fertilizer, 93–95, 291
    housing, 253
    industry, 162–63
    rice consumption, 136
Subsistence economy, 12, 20–21, 35, 63, 71
Sudan, 4
Sugar, sugar cane, 28, 64, 68, 71, 80, 130–32, 155, 162, 261, 290
Sultan Hamud, 334
Swahili, 6
Swine, 103, 128
Swynnerton, R. J. M., *A Plan to Intensify the Development of African Agriculture in Kenya*, 2, 14–15, 41, 51, 63, 66, 69–73, 83, 87, 106, 124, 127, 275, 301

Tabora, 200

Taita Hills, 149
Tana River, 5, 69, 77–81, 177
Tanga, 188–89
Tanganyika:
    currency, 33
    customs union, 29, 30–33
    disease control, 98
    education, 116, 235–36
    electric power imports from, table 1, 177
    export prices, 26
    GDP, 19, 151
    growth rate, 31
    IBRD report on, 165
    industrial research, 166
    labor disputes, 189
    money and banking, 257, 261, 268
    public finance, 273, 275–76
    pyrethrum, 126
    roads to, 181, 184, 188
    sisal, 123–24
    trade with, 9, 23, 27–31, 106–7, 128, 132, 134, 137, 154–56, 158, table S.31, 360, table S.37, 366, table S.38, 367
    see also East African listings
Tanganyika, Lake, 188
Tanganyika Railways and Port Service, 193
Tanneries, 92
Tariff Protection Committee, 164
Tariffs, 9, 26, 45, 189–91, 290–91; *see also* Customs
Taxation, 44, 276, 311–12
    and budgetary forecast, 282–83
Taxes:
    administration and collection, 32, 284–86, 291–92
    direct on individuals, 285–89
    embarkation (proposed), 199–200
    estate duty, 292
    export, 121, 292–93, 299
    government revenue from, table 3, 276–79
    income, 32, 273, 278–79, 285–86, 288–89, 299
    increases, 44, 284–85, 293–94
    land, 38
    local, 184, 294–95
    PAYE system (proposed), 287
    rebates, 291

relief for new industries, 289–90
sales, 285, 287, 290
trade licenses, 291–92, 299
transport, 291
Tea:
exports, 16, 18, 26, 64
marketing and production, 41, 53, 55,
69–71, 97, 111, table 4, 122, 181, 184,
tables S.10, S.11, 345
prospects, 121–23
summary of recommendations, 303
Tea Board, 323
Tea Research Institute, 97
Tebere, 78, 136, 302
Telecommunications, 200–6, 209, 308,
table S.18, 351
Television, 206–8
Textiles, 28, 105, 154, 156, 165, 291
Thika, 167
Thomson's Falls, 178, 189
Tile, 158
Tobacco, 28, 156
Topography, 4, 64
Tororo, 94, 177–78
Tourism and wildlife, 20, 170–75, 307
government expenditure for, table 1,
53, table 4, 62, 170, 174–75
Ministry of, 171
Trade:
balance of, 28, 104, 263
external, 260, table S.31, 360, table
S.39, 368
indices, table S.39, 368
interterritorial, table S.31, 360
terms of, 21, 26, table S.39, 368
see also Exports, Imports, Tanganyika,
Uganda (trade with)
Transport:
air, 19, 28, table 1, 53, table 4, 62,
196–203, 209
harbors and shipping, 19, 60, 193–96
inland waterways, 188, 195
railways, 12, 19, 60, 181, 188–93, 209,
334–35
Road Fund, 186
roads, 19, 50, table 1, 53, 57, table 4,
62, 172, 175, 181–88, 209, 281, 291, 331
summary of conclusions and recommendations, 307–8
Treasury, 14

Development and Planning Division,
316
Economics and Statistics Division,
107–8, 316–17, 319–20
Trinidad, 88
Troup, L. G., *Report Inquiry into the
1951 Maize and Wheat Prices*, etc.,
112
Tsavo National Park, 170
Tsetse fly, 53, 87, 98–99, 101, 238
Turbo, 184
Turkana, 5, 6, 239

Uaso Nyiro National Park, 170
Uganda:
currency, 33
customs union, 29, 30–33
disease control, 98
education, 227, 235–36
electric power imports from, 176–79
exports, 26, 150
GDP, 19, 151
growth rate, 31
IBRD report on, 165
industrial research, 166
money and banking, 257, 263, 268
public finance, 273, 275–76
railway, 8–9, 195
roads to, 181, 184, 188
textile plant, 156
trade with, 9, 23, 27–31, 106–7, 128,
132, 134, 154–56, table S.31, 360,
table S.37, 366, table S.38, 367
see also East African listings
Uganda Development Corporation, 164
Uganda Railways and Harbours Organization, 193
Ulu, 331
Umba River, 8
United Kingdom:
and land settlement, 83–84
and local industry, 156
British Foreign Office, 9
civil service allowance, 37
Colonial office, 9, 11, 14
financial aid to EACSO, 181, 274
financial aid to Kenya, 43, 45, 47–48,
202, 275, 277–80, 282
insurance firms, 270

medical students to, 246
military bases, 217
Overseas Aid Scheme, 13, 213, 280–81
Protectorate, 8
teacher supply from, 233
teleprinter link with, 201
trade with, 26–27, 155, table S.35, 364, table S.36, 365
Treasury bills, 258
see also Banks, commercial
UNICEF, 240, 243
United Nations Special Fund, 79
United States:
aid, 168, 213, 278
cotton competition, 137
teacher supply from, 233
Uplands Bacon Factory, 111, 155, 328

Vasey Formula, 226
Vegetables, 114
Veterinary Board, 328
Veterinary Department, 91–92, 99–101
Veterinary Research Organization, East African, 97
Veterinary Services, 113
Victoria, Lake, 4–6, 8, 19, 64, 77, 80, 98, 142, 147, 181, 188, 193, 195
Viton and Pignalosa, Trends and Prospects of World Sugar Consumption 1960 (FAO), 131
Voi, 148

Wages, annual bill, table S.28, 357
Wages, statutory minimum, table 1, 217–21, table S.29, 358

Walker, A. J., "A Health Center Policy for Kenya," 242
Wanjii hydroelectric plant, 177
Water, table 1, 53, table 1, 62, 74–75, 108, 239, table S.21, 352
see also Irrigation
Water Resources Authority, 75
Wattle, 26, 64, 114, 139, 158, tables S.10, S.11, 345
Wellcome Institute, 97
West Africa, 104
West Chylulu National Reserve, 170
West Suk, 101, 149, 242
Wheat, 18, 20, 64–65, 68, 81, 90, 93, 96, 111, 134–37, 154–55, 261, 325, table S.10, 345, table S.12, 346
Williams, M. H., Report to Kenya Government on Agricultural Credit in Kenya, 266
Wool, 102–3, 129–30
Works, Ministry of, 157, 166, 182, 185, 187, 197–98, 202, 234, 281
World Bank, see IBRD
World Health Organization (WHO), 240, 247
World Meteorological Organization (WMO), 202
World War I, 9
World War II, 166

Yala, 184

Zanzibar, 8, 11, 33, 257, 262
Zinc, 146